International Ethics

International Ethics

Concepts, Theories, and Cases in Global Politics

SECOND EDITION

Mark R. Amstutz

ROWMAN & LITTLEFIELD PUBLISHERS, INC.

Lanham • Boulder • New York • Toronto • Oxford

ROWMAN & LITTLEFIELD PUBLISHERS, INC.

Published in the United States of America
by Rowman & Littlefield Publishers, Inc.
A wholly owned subsidiary of The Rowman & Littlefield Publishing Group, Inc.
4501 Forbes Boulevard, Suite 200, Lanham, MD 20706
www.rowmanlittlefield.com

P.O. Box 317, Oxford OX2 9RU, UK

British Library Cataloguing in Publication Information Available

Library of Congress Cataloging-in-Publication Data
Amstutz, Mark R.
  International ethics : concepts, theories, and cases in global politics / Mark R. Amstutz.
—2nd ed.
    p. cm.
  Includes bibliographical references and index.
  ISBN 0-7425-3582-7 (cloth : alk. paper) — ISBN 0-7425-3583-5 (pbk. : alk. paper)
  1. International relations—Moral and ethical aspects. I. Title.
  JZ1306.A48 2004
  172'.4—dc22

                                                                      2004012466

Printed in the United States of America

♾ The paper used in this publication meets the minimum requirements of American National Standard for Information Sciences—Permanence of Paper for Printed Library Materials, ANSI/NISO Z39.48-1992.

Brief Contents

Contents

Cases

Tables and Figures

Introduction

A FUNDAMENTAL AIM of this study is to demonstrate, through arguments and illustrations, that moral values are an essential element of international relations and that international ethics are foundational to global politics. Although international relations scholars have increasingly recognized the importance of moral values and ethical reasoning in international affairs, political realism continues to serve as the dominant paradigm in international relations. Even though realism does not deny international ethics, it allows little room for moral reasoning, focusing instead on the quest for national security and the promotion of economic and social well-being.

In this book, I argue that the realist notion that international politics is fundamentally a quest for political power and economic interests is false and untenable. Instead, I suggest that international politics is rooted in ethics and that states and other nonstate actors share a basic moral vocabulary that influences the individual and collective choices of states. To be sure, the ethical analysis of foreign policies and global structures is fraught with significant epistemological and methodological challenges. However, the difficulty of applying moral principles to concrete issues and problems does not invalidate the possibility of or the responsibility for morally assessing political actions and institutional structures.

Realists assert that international society is a realm of power and necessity, not morality and choice. Because no common authority exists in the international system to protect states and to resolve disputes, some political thinkers have suggested that states' overriding interests are national security and material well-being. These interests, it is suggested, automatically displace morality. George Kennan, for example, argues that because a statesman's primary duty is to secure the vital interests of states, foreign affairs are essentially amoral. He writes,

> Government is an agent, not a principal. Its primary obligation is to the interests of the national society it represents . . . its military security, the integrity of its political life and the well-being of its people. These needs have no moral quality. They are the unavoidable necessities of national existence and therefore are subject to classification neither as "good" or "bad."[1]

Kennan thinks that because interests such as security, political independence, and national well-being are essential to the survival and economic viability of states, they have no moral quality. But why should vital interests be amoral? Are not human interests rooted partly in morality? And does not the pursuit of foreign policy goals involve

1

moral judgment? As Arnold Wolfers has wisely observed, international relations are not beyond the scope of morality but are themselves based on moral norms.[2]

A brief perusal of contemporary international developments illustrates the pervasive and significant role of moral values and ethical judgments. Consider the following events, each of them involving important moral norms:

1. In the aftermath of the post–Cold War disintegration of Yugoslavia, a major war broke out among Muslim, Serb, and Croat peoples, focusing mainly on the multinational state of Bosnia-Herzegovina. Prior to the October 1995 cease-fire, which provided the basis for the subsequent Dayton Peace Accord, the war had claimed more than a half million casualties, including 250,000 deaths, and had resulted in more than one million refugees.[3] One of the most evil aspects of the Bosnian war was the gross violation of human rights, the most grotesque of which was "ethnic cleansing," that is, the detention, forced removal, or killing of persons because of their ethnicity and religion. Although all three warring parties were guilty of these atrocities, the main offenders were the Bosnian Serbs, who forced the evacuation of tens of thousands of Muslims from their towns and villages. When the media published photos of emaciated Muslim men in overcrowded, inhumane detention camps, there was universal moral condemnation for this evil behavior. In light of this senseless war, should Western powers have intervened to halt the killing and the human rights abuses? Are major European powers partly responsible for failing to prevent ethnic genocide? Should the United States have used its superior military power to punish the Serbs, thereby deterring future aggression?

2. In 1994, Hutu militia in Rwanda carried out a killing rampage against the Tutsi minority that resulted in more than 800,000 deaths and more than two million refugees. More people were killed in this 100-day extermination campaign than in any other previous genocide in a comparable period of time. The genocide ended only when the Tutsi rebel force, the Rwandan Patriotic Front (RFP), defeated the Hutu military and paramilitary forces. In 1993, a peace accord had been signed between the Hutu and Tutsi leaders that called for a ceasefire, power-sharing, and supervised elections. To help ensure implementation of the agreement, the UN deployed a 2,500-member peacekeeping force. When the genocide commenced in April 1994, the UN peacekeepers sought to provide some safety to leaders, but were unsuccessful. After 10 Belgian peacekeepers were killed, the Security Council ordered the peacekeeping forces reduced to 500 troops. No Western power offered to intervene militarily to halt the genocide. Only when the killing had subsided did France send a military force to establish a protective zone to curb further killing and to facilitate humanitarian relief. In view of the scope of the genocide, should Western powers have intervened militarily to halt the killing?

3. In September 1991, Haitian president Jean-Bertrand Aristide was overthrown in a military coup. To pressure Haiti's military to reinstate Aristide, economic sanctions were imposed. When these measures failed to alter the Haitian military government, the United States, backed by Security Council authority, prepared for military intervention. Although the crisis eased in 1994 when military rulers gave up power and allowed Aristide to resume office, the restoration of democracy did little to improve the economic, social, and political quality of life. Indeed, nearly ten years after the

restoration of Aristide, Haiti remained a corrupt, unstable, and unproductive country. Political conditions began to deteriorate in 2000 after political opposition groups charged that the 2000 parliamentary elections had been rigged. By early 2004, Aristide had lost significant popular support, and after rebel groups had taken control of significant portions of the countryside, Aristide and his family fled the country in March 2004. To fill the vacuum of authority, the Security Council authorized a U.S.-led peacekeeping mission. In light of the failure to improve the human rights in Haiti, was the first U.S. intervention to reinstate Aristide morally justified?

4. In a 1994 state referendum, voters in California overwhelmingly approved Proposition 187, which called for an end to state health, social, economic, and educational benefits for all illegal residents. Although courts have declared this action unconstitutional, the issue of legal and illegal immigration raises profound moral concerns for the United States and other Western industrial countries. How restrictive should immigration policies be? Which peoples should be given priority? Should countries provide equal treatment to legal and illegal immigrants? Is it morally legitimate to halt "boat people" (migrants fleeing their homeland by sea) and return them to their country of origin?

5. In light of egregious international economic inequalities, how much foreign economic assistance should developed countries give to poor states? Are developed nations morally obligated to assist the economic development of low-income states? If developed countries are morally responsible for alleviating Third World poverty, to whom should the aid be given: to governments themselves for infrastructure development and welfare programs or to nongovernmental humanitarian organizations?

6. In May 1998, India carried out five nuclear tests, thereby demonstrating its nuclear capabilities to the international community. Shortly thereafter, Pakistan, India's neighbor and enemy, also carried out five nuclear tests, thereby also signaling its nuclear capabilities. Because these tests violated both the nonproliferation regime as well as the Comprehensive Test Ban Treaty, President Bill Clinton, as required by U.S. foreign policy statutes on nuclear nonproliferation, immediately imposed economic sanctions on both states.[4] The mutual nuclear testing by both India and Pakistan is clearly a dangerous international development because it creates a potential arms race between the two countries and increases regional instability and insecurity. From a moral perspective, the nuclear tests raise numerous issues. For example, is the existing nonproliferation regime—a regime that allows nuclear powers to keep their weapons of mass destruction while disallowing other states from gaining them—morally legitimate? Is the expansion of the nuclear "club" beneficial or harmful to world order? Given the poverty of both Pakistan and India, are their weapons development programs morally justified?

7. Finally, Muslim fanatics commandeered four large passenger airplanes on September 11, 2001, and flew two of them into the World Trade Center in New York City and another into the Pentagon in Washington, D.C.[5] Because the jets were full of fuel, they caused massive fires, resulting in the collapse of the World Trade Center's twin towers and major destruction to a section of the Pentagon. This terrorist attack, which caused the death of more than 3,000 persons, was the single most destructive act of aggression against the territory of the United States, eclipsing the destruction

caused by the Japanese attack on Pearl Harbor in 1941. Given the unprecedented harm caused by the 9/11 attacks, the United States government responded with a comprehensive antiterror campaign.

Although President George W. Bush referred to this conflict as a "war on terror," it is radically different from a conventional war since the enemy is not a state but a fanatical movement or nonstate actor that carries out destruction against civilians in a covert manner. After administration officials defined the war on terror as a campaign against terrorists and those who habor them, the U.S. armed forces embarked on a war against Afghanistan. It did so because the Taliban, Afghanistan's ruling authorities, had refused to turn over Osama bin Laden and other Al Qaeda operatives that were partly responsible for the 9/11 terrorist attack. Although the U.S. forces were able to achieve regime change quickly, they were not successful in capturing bin Laden and many of his fighters. In view of the enormous danger posed by contemporary terrorism, was the U.S. military action against Afghanistan justified? Is war against states harboring terrorist organizations morally legitimate, even if they are not directly responsible for terror?

As these multilateral issues suggest, contemporary international relations involve fundamental moral choices. Although not all international relations issues involve moral values, most foreign policy decisions are based in part on ethical judgment. Moreover, the development of the international community's rules, procedures, and structures will similarly depend on values and norms that are partly moral.

This study explores two distinct dimensions of international political morality: the role of moral values in foreign policy and the ethical foundation of the rules and structures of global society. Some scholars and decision-makers have suggested that moral values have no place in foreign policy because each sovereign state is entitled to its own moral norms. Additionally, some theorists have argued that in view of the international community's cultural diversity, there is, and can be, no common international political morality. This conclusion, however, is untenable for two reasons. First, although cultural diversity is a feature of global society, state and nonstate actors share a common moral vocabulary that influences international relations. These shared basic norms provide the basis for moral claims on issues such as self-determination, human rights, the use of force, and humanitarian relief. Second, and more significant, despite the reality of cultural pluralism, there is no necessary or logical connection between the empirical fact of cultural pluralism and the normative belief that there is no morality in global society. The normative belief in moral relativism does not and cannot follow necessarily and logically from the fact of cultural diversity. Morality, after all, is based not on consensus but on perceived moral obligations.

This is a study in applied international political ethics. Although I address important philosophic issues, such as the epistemological and substantive challenges posed by cultural pluralism, the major aim of this book is to describe and assess the nature, role, and impact of international political morality on the individual and collective conduct of foreign relations. This task is undertaken by examining the nature and legitimacy of moral values and the role of ethical strategies and traditions in applying moral values to specific issues such as human rights, war, and foreign intervention.

This study also examines the ethical nature of the rules, structures, and informal patterns of the international system itself. Whereas the morality of foreign policy focuses on the role of moral norms in international relations, international ethics is concerned with the justice of global society, including the moral legitimacy of the nation-state and the structures and dominant patterns of the international community. For example, are territorial boundaries morally significant? Is the norm of nonintervention a principal ethical rule of international society? If it is, can the norm be violated to protect other moral norms, such as basic human rights? Is humanitarian intervention morally defensible? Are the egregious economic and political disparities among states morally acceptable? Do high-income states have a moral obligation to admit a large number of refugees?

This book comprises two distinct dimensions. The first part, chapters 1 through 3, analyzes conceptual and theoretical issues. Chapter 1 defines the nature of morality and ethics and the role of political morality in foreign policy, illuminating the limits and possibilities of a moral foreign policy. Chapter 2 examines different methodologies for applying moral reasoning to political action, focusing on rule-based analysis (often defined as deontological, or Kantian, ethics) and ends-based analysis (often defined as consequentialism). Chapter 3 describes the nature of ethical traditions and their role in structuring moral analysis. Although many different ethical traditions are utilized in international ethics, this study focuses on the two traditions that have had greatest influence in the United States in the postwar era: realism and idealism. The remainder of the book—chapters 4 through 10—focuses on seven important ethical issues in global politics: political reconciliation, human rights, military force, foreign intervention, covert operations, economic sanctions, and global political justice.

Throughout this study, I use case studies to illuminate and apply moral norms to specific international relations issues and problems. To encourage ethical analysis, each case study concludes with a brief discussion of relevant moral questions and concerns raised by a particular conflict or problem. Because the test of political morality is whether it contributes to a more just global society, the challenge in international ethics is not simply to identify appropriate moral values but to apply them to transnational issues and global problems. The aim of this book is thus to encourage ethical reflection that contributes to political judgments resulting in a more just, humane world.

This book involves several major changes from the first edition. To begin with, two new chapters have been added—one (chapter 4) dealing with the ethics of political reconciliation and the other (chapter 8) examining the ethics of unconventional military operations. The first topic is increasingly significant as political communities seek to overcome the bitter legacy of war and political oppression involving human rights abuses, political fragmentation, and distrust. The second theme is important because of the growing threat of international terrorism, especially in the aftermath of the destruction of New York City's World Trade Center in 2001. Since nonstate actors generally are the primary agents of terrorism, traditional military strategies designed for interstate conflict are unlikely to be effective in deterring and defeating terrorists. Chapter 8 thus explores some of the ethical challenges in using covert force.

A second major change is the addition of five new case studies. These include the NATO intervention in Kosovo in 1999 (chapter 1), the promotion of political reconciliation in South Africa after the fall of the apartheid regime (chapter 4), the 2003 preventive war against Iraq (chapter 6), the 2001 war against the Taliban in Afghanistan (chapter 8), and economic sanctions against Cuba (chapter 9). In addition, I explore and assess a number of new topics relating to chapter themes. For example, I analyze the nature and role of preemptive and preventive force (chapter 6) as well as the problematic nature of torture and targeted assassination in carrying out counterinsurgency or counterterror operations (chapter 8). Moreover, I have expanded the analysis of foreign intervention by contrasting three types of action—political, strategic, and humanitarian (chapter 7).

Finally, I have updated the analysis and the case studies to reflect insights from the growing and evolving scholarship on international political ethics as well as to incorporate important developments regarding the cases. For example, since the debate on global warming has shifted significantly in recent years, my analysis seeks to incorporate the important changes in global politics regarding the stalemate over the Kyoto Protocol. Similarly, a significant literature has developed on humanitarian intervention and in particular over the Rwanda genocide. Chapter 5 incorporates some of the significant scholarship that has emerged in recent years on this topic.

In preparing this study, I have benefited from the assistance and encouragement of numerous persons. As with the first edition, I again thank my parents, Mahlon and Ruth Amstutz, for teaching me as a young boy the value of personal integrity and the importance of moral reflection. I also thank my students—especially those in my Ethics and Foreign Policy course—for encouraging and challenging my thinking on many of the issues examined in this book. I also gratefully acknowledge the financial assistance of Wheaton College and in particular the Aldeen Development Fund for giving me a grant to get the original study underway. Finally, I thank Jennifer Reynolds and Rebecca Miller, my teaching assistants, for providing invaluable research and editorial support.

Chapter One

Morality and Foreign Policy

The "necessities" in international politics, and for that matter in all spheres of life, do not push decision and action beyond the realm of moral judgment; they rest on moral choice themselves.[1]

—ARNOLD WOLFERS

Man's moral sense is not a strong beacon light, radiating outward to illuminate in sharp outline all that it touches. It is, rather, a small candle flame, casting vague and multiple shadows, flickering and sputtering in the strong winds of power and passion, greed and ideology. But brought close to the heart and cupped in one's hands, it dispels the darkness and warms the soul.[2]

—JAMES Q. WILSON

There does not exist such a thing as international morality.[3]

—SIR HAROLD NICOLSON

What passes for ethical standards for governmental policies in foreign affairs is a collection of moralisms, maxims, and slogans, which neither help nor guide, but only confuse, decision.[4]

—DEAN ACHESON

THIS CHAPTER examines the nature and role of moral values and ethical reasoning in international relations. It begins by identifying distinctive features of the terms *morality* and *ethics* and then explores the nature and bases of international political morality, addressing the challenge posed by cultural pluralism to the conceptualization and application of such morality in global society. It then examines the role of moral norms in foreign policy, giving special emphasis to the goals, methods, and problems of applying international morality. The chapter illustrates the role of international political morality with a case study on the 1999 NATO intervention in Kosovo.

MORALITY AND ETHICS

The word *morality* derives from the Latin *mores*, meaning custom, habit, and way of life. It typically describes what is good, right, or proper. These concepts, in turn, are often associated with such notions as virtue, integrity, goodness, righteousness, and justice. The term *ethics* is rooted in the Greek *ethos*, meaning custom or common practice. Because its root meaning is similar to that of *morality*, the two concepts are often used interchangeably. Strictly speaking, however, the two terms represent distinct elements of normative analysis: *morality* referring to values and beliefs about what is right and wrong, good and bad, just and unjust and *ethics* referring to the examination, justification, and critical analysis of morality. Because of the significance of these elements in international ethics, I explore each of them more fully below.

The Nature of Morality

Moral values have at least three important distinguishing features: they command universal allegiance, they demand impartiality, and they are largely self-enforcing. The claims of universality mean that moral norms are binding on all peoples. Immanuel Kant articulated this requirement in his famous *categorical imperative*, which calls on persons to treat others as having intrinsic value and to act in accordance with principles that are valid for others.[5] As one scholar has explained, universalization means that if "I ought to do X, then I am committed to maintaining that morally anyone else ought to do X unless there are relevant differences between the other person and myself and/or between his situation and mine."[6]

The second dimension of morality—the impartiality of norms—helps to ensure that morality is not simply a means to clothe and advance self-interest. Because of the propensity for human selfishness, philosophers have emphasized the need for dispassion and disinterest. As a result, they have argued that morality must be defined and applied in terms of the perspectives and interests other than those of the actor. For example, in his classic work *A Theory of Justice*, John Rawls argues that moral principles should be based on impartiality by requiring that they be selected through a "veil of ignorance," that is, defining and selecting norms without knowledge of who will benefit from them.[7]

A third important feature of morality is its self-enforcing quality. Unlike law, which is enforced by government, morality is applied mainly through the voluntary actions of persons. The decision to abide by moral obligations is rooted in the beliefs and values that people hold. In a short article titled "Law and Manners," which was published in 1924 in *The Atlantic Monthly*, English jurist John Fletcher Moulton defined the moral domain as "obedience to the unenforceable." According to Moulton, human affairs involve actions in three different realms: legal, moral, and voluntary. In the domain of the law, persons fulfill the legal norms because of government's capacity to enforce its norms. In the third domain, the realm of free choice, persons are free to do as they wish. Between these two realms is the area of morality, or what Moulton termed "manners," by which people behave in accord with "consciousness of duty" rather than the coercive rules of public authority. Moulton describes this domain as follows: "It is the domain of obedience to the unenforceable. That obedience is the obedience of a man to that which he cannot be forced to obey. He is the enforcer of the law himself."[8] Morality, whether private or public, individual or collective, involves a duty to obey moral precepts that are accepted as inherently binding because of their claims to rightness or justice.

Although morality is pervasive in human life, it is concerned mainly with a particular dimension of human affairs, namely, individual and collective judgments involving moral values. It is not concerned with choices and actions in the nonmoral realm.[9] Because government policies have a society-wide impact, most political affairs, whether domestic or international, involve some level of moral judgment. For some decisions, such as military intervention to halt genocide or the development of a weapon of mass destruction, moral considerations are primary; for others, such as selecting the UN secretary-general or determining the level of foreign economic assistance to a particular country, the role of moral norms will be limited. However, regardless of the issues, foreign policy will generally involve moral values.

The Nature of Ethics

Fundamentally, ethics involves choosing or doing what is right and good and refraining from choosing or doing what is bad or evil. From an ethical perspective, the good is realized by the application of appropriate moral norms to private and public affairs. This is no easy task, especially in domestic and international politics, in which government decisions do not lend themselves to simple moral verdicts. This difficulty is partly due to the complexity of public affairs as well as to overlapping and even competing moral values that are often involved in specific political issues and policy dilemmas. As a result, decision makers must select the most desirable action from a number of available alternatives, each involving moral limitations. Thus, if political decisions are to be developed and implemented on the basis of morality, *ethical reasoning* will be required. At a minimum, this process will entail identifying the moral dimensions of issues (a process sometimes called moral imagination), selecting relevant moral norms, critically assessing the issue or problem in the light of morality, applying morality to the potential alternatives, and then implementing the preferred action. Thus, ethical reasoning in international relations will involve the identification, illumination, and application of relevant moral norms to the conduct of states' foreign relations.

Another important dimension of international ethics involves the assessment of rules, practices, and institutions of global society in light of relevant moral norms. In effect, international ethics is concerned with the moral architecture of the international system, that is, the moral legitimacy of the patterns and structures of global society. For example, international ethics addresses such issues as the fairness of the existing international economic order, the justice of global institutions, and the justice of international regimes (rules and semi-institutionalized patterns of decision making in specific issue areas) in such areas of common concern as refugees, energy, biodiversity, and waste disposal. The aim of such moral reflection is to assess the justice of the existing world system. In addition, international ethics is concerned with the implementation of the rules and structures of global society. Are the rules applied fairly and impartially? For example, are the international rules governing fishing and pollution applied equitably? Are the judgments of the International Court of Justice fair and consistent?

In this chapter and the next, I examine two dimensions of political morality in world politics. Here I examine the nature and sources of international political morality and then analyze the relationship of moral norms to the development and implementation of foreign policy. In doing so, I specifically assess some of the major aims, methods, and problems involved in explicitly integrating moral norms with the foreign policies of states. In chapter 2, I examine alternative strategies for applying international political ethics. That is, I identify and assess three different methodologies for carrying out ethical decision making.

THE NATURE AND BASES OF POLITICAL MORALITY

Personal morality is frequently identified with political morality. Although the two are related, they are not identical. Individual morality consists of moral values and norms (i.e., principles, rules, prohibitions, and duties) that are applicable to the conduct of persons in their personal or private relations. The Ten Commandments, the admonition to "love your neighbor as yourself," and obligation to truth telling are examples of personal morality. Political morality, by contrast, consists of moral values and norms that are applicable to the political life of communities, including neighborhoods, cities, states, and the international community itself. Examples of political morality include such norms as the equality of persons, freedom of conscience, equal treatment under the law, the right of self-defense, and nonintervention. Although political morality is rooted in personal morality, the former differs from the latter both in the nature of its norms and in the sphere in which moral norms are applied. Whereas individual morality governs the actions of individuals, political morality applies to the public decisions of political or government officials acting on behalf of public institutions.

Fundamentally, a political community is one in which a government exists with the authority to make society-wide decisions. It is a society based on a hierarchical distribution of power, with rulers and subjects having different levels of authority and thus different types of political responsibilities. It is a mistake to assume that the responsibilities of citizens and rulers are identical; individual and political moralities are not symmetrical. Although citizens and government officials share similar moral obligations as human beings, their different roles in political society place different moral obligations on them. As Lea Brilmayer observes, "The prohibitions found in interpersonal morality cannot be mechanically transplanted into a code of conduct for public officials."[10] Political morality may allow some actions that are prohibited by personal morality. For example, a soldier may kill in wartime, or a state may carry out capital punishment, but such actions are not synonymous with murder. Similarly, a state may tax its citizens, but an individual may not steal or extort resources from another person. Political morality thus provides norms for the just and effective use of legitimate power in political society. Although it is beyond the scope of this study to describe the nature and bases of legitimate political authority, it is significant, for our purposes, that political morality not only helps justify government authority but also provides norms for judging political action.[11]

Domestic and international politics are qualitatively different. Although scholars differ in their explanations of these differences, one widely accepted comparison characterizes domestic politics as a hierarchical system in which sovereign authority exists to make society-wide decisions and international politics as a nonhierarchical system without common authority to make and enforce decisions. Domestic society is the realm of authority, whereas international society is the realm of anarchy (i.e., no authority to impose order). In view of the structural differences in domestic and international politics, some scholars argue that the political moralities of domestic and international communities are also qualitatively different.

Some realists, for example, argue that in domestic society moral judgments are possible because typically cultural and moral values are widely shared, whereas in global politics, in which cultural and moral pluralism is prevalent, few moral judgments are possible. According to this perspective, whereas domestic society provides a rich and substantive political morality, international society provides a limited moral menu. Indeed, for some realists the only morality is that which promotes and protects the territorial security and economic well-being of a state. However, other scholars argue that differences between domestic and international politics have been greatly exaggerated and that moral values are far more significant in global society than realists suggest.

This group is represented by two types of thinkers: communitarians, who believe that states are significant moral actors in global society, and cosmopolitans, who regard the individual, not the state, as the major moral actor. Michael Walzer, a communitarian, gives a prominent place to international political morality by deriving states' international obligations from the "domestic analogy," that is, by arguing that states have rights and duties in global society analogous to the rights and duties of individuals in domestic political society. [12] For Walzer, international political morality entails such norms as the prohibition against aggression, the right of political sovereignty and the corollary right of self-defense, the duty of nonintervention in other states' domestic affairs, the protection of human rights, and the duty to settle disputes peacefully. By contrast, Charles Beitz, a cosmopolitanist, develops a global morality based on the rights and well-being of persons, challenging the morality of the existing Westphalian political order of sovereign states.[13] Because territorial boundaries are not morally significant in his cosmopolitan ethic, the autonomy of states can be qualified by the moral claims of individuals. In effect, since the rights of states ultimately depend on the rights of persons, human rights must take precedence over state sovereignty.

In assessing the role of political morality in foreign policy, scholars have periodically made two errors. First, some have simply denied the relevance of morality to international affairs. For them, although moral norms might be relevant to interpersonal relations or even to domestic political affairs, they have little to do with interstate political affairs. Global politics is the realm of necessity, and there can be no right and wrong when the survival of the state is at stake. However, as Arnold

Wolfers noted at the outset of this chapter, the fundamental choices of statesmen are rooted in moral values. Thus, international politics is not divorced from ethical judgment but rests on morality.

The second error, frequently related to the first, is the tendency to deny the existence of political morality altogether. Here, morality consists solely of norms governing individual private behavior. George Kennan illustrates both of these errors in the following passage:

> Moral principles have their place in the heart of the individual and in the shaping of his own conduct, whether as a citizen or as a government official. . . . But when the individual's behavior passes through the machinery of political organization and merges with that of millions of other individuals to find its expression in the actions of a government, then it undergoes a general transmutation, and the same moral concepts are no longer relevant to it. A government is an agent, not a principal; and no more than any other agent may it attempt to be the conscience of its principal. In particular, it may not subject itself to those supreme laws of renunciation and self-sacrifice that represent the culmination of individual moral growth.[14]

Although Kennan is correct in his claim that personal morality should not govern the behavior of diplomats, his failure to recognize that political morality is an essential element of all normative decision making in global politics is a serious error. To be sure, the political morality applicable to interstate relations is not the same as personal morality. Thus, the challenge in bringing moral norms to bear on global political relations is to first identify and then apply relevant norms of international political morality.

Before exploring the role of morality in foreign affairs, it will be helpful to briefly address the validity of political morality. Because of the growing influence of postmodern subjectivism, there has been a growing skepticism in the contemporary world about the legitimacy of moral claims in public life. This has been the case especially for political morality in global society, in which cultural pluralism is much more pronounced than in domestic society.

Sources of Political Morality

Because philosophers hold a number of theories about the source of moral values, political theorists have offered a variety of justifications for political morality. Three of the most important theories include foundationalism, constructivism, and consensualism. The foundationalist approach assumes that international morality is rooted in universal, unchanging first principles that are apprehended by reason. The constructivist approach, by contrast, derives moral values from general conceptions of justice (or the common good) through deductive arguments based on hypothetical cases. Finally, the consensual approach derives political morality from existing agreements among member states.

The foundationalist perspective assumes that transcendent moral norms exist and that such universal standards can be apprehended by rational reflection. Foundationalist thinkers such as Thomas Aquinas, John Locke, and Kant believed that morality was valid and true not because it made the world better or more humane (pragmatism) or because it increased the happiness and well-being of persons (utilitarianism) but because it was divinely ordained by a transcendent Creator. An example of international morality from a foundationalist perspective is the belief that universal human rights exist and that they are rooted in a transcendent moral law (natural law) that is universal and unchanging. Another illustration is the just-war doctrine, which provides moral principles for defining when and how force can be utilized in pursuing just international relations. Foundationalists recognize that the international community is comprised of a large number of nations, each with its own cultural norms and social patterns; and, although such cultural and social diversity results in different value systems, there is nonetheless substantial consensus among moral value systems at a foundational level.

The constructivist thesis assumes that moral values are derived from hypothetical arguments. Whereas foundationalists assert that the basis of morality consists of transcendent norms whose truth and validity are inherent in the created order, constructivists ground morality in instrumental, deductive reasoning. For example, constructivists might deduce moral values from political and normative premises (e.g., political liberalism, justice as fairness, or some related normative proposition) through hypothetical arguments guided by logic and impartiality. Rawls illustrates this moral theory in an important essay titled "The Law of Peoples," in which he seeks to extend his domestic theory of justice to international society.[15] Rawls imagines an "original position," in which representatives from different societies gather to impartially develop norms of international justice. He argues that a just "law of peoples" can be developed only if the societies themselves have achieved a minimal level of justice. Rawls specifies three minimal conditions for well-ordered societies, whether liberal or not: They must be peaceful, they must be perceived as legitimate by their own people, and they must honor basic human rights. Rawls assumes that when representatives from liberal and nonliberal societies meet to develop a just "law of peoples," they will be able to define minimal norms that will advance justice within international society. Some of these rights and duties of "peoples" include a right to freedom and independence, the equality of peoples, the right of self-defense, the duty of nonintervention, the obligation to fulfill treaties, and the responsibility to honor human rights.[16]

A third view of political morality is consensual theory, sometimes called ethical positivism.[17] According to this approach, political morality is rooted in binding norms expressed by the formal and informal rules of domestic society, whereas international political morality is rooted in the shared norms embodied in the conventions, informal agreements, and declarations that states accept as obligatory in their international relations. These shared norms are obligatory because they are part of international law and morally obligatory because they specify norms conducive to order, justice, or the perceived common good. Some thinkers have argued that, because it is impossible to derive "ought" from "is," it is similarly impossible to derive international ethical obligations from existing interstate legal conventions. However, scholars such as Terry Nardin have convincingly demonstrated that to the extent that law establishes binding obligations on individuals, groups, and states, it fulfills the criteria of an ethical framework.[18] In her seminal study on twentieth-century international legal and political ethics, Dorothy Jones has illuminated how international law has produced an authoritative and widely accepted framework, or "code," of international peace. This framework, she argues, is a normative system because it prescribes behavior that is conducive to global order and international harmony. Jones's study thus reinforces the claim that international morality can be based on consensual norms and multilateral declarations.[19]

It is significant that international law has established a category of law that is binding apart from the consent of states, thereby recognizing the limitations of consent as a basis of political morality. This type of international law—known as the *jus cogens*—refers to peremptory norms that are authoritative because the norms are inherently valid. Such norms, rooted in the values and practices of civilized society, include prohibitions against piracy, slavery, terrorism, and genocide. To some extent, the Tokyo and Nurem-burg tribunals that prosecuted Japanese and German military officials for crimes against peace and humanity were based in part on this tradition of international law.

Although moral intuition, rational construction, and consent can each contribute to the development and articulation of international political morality, political morality must ultimately be grounded in norms that transcend human experience. Thus, this study proceeds from the belief that political morality, however it is justified, is based on normative principles of right and wrong, justice and injustice.

The Challenge of Cultural Pluralism

One of the significant challenges in defending international political morality is the absence of a shared, universal morality. Because the international system is comprised of many different nation-states, each with its own social patterns and values, cultural pluralism is a prevalent feature of the international community. Moreover, not only do peoples from different cultures hold different political moralities, but their moral systems have also evolved over time. Because of the evident variability and pluralism of global morality, some thinkers have concluded that there is no universal morality applicable to the international community. In their view, the only morals in international society are the subjective, relativistic values associated with each society. This perspective, known as the doctrine of *cultural relativism*, holds that because notions of right and wrong, justice and injustice, are rooted in each society's cultural mores, there is no universal moral code.

Although competing and conflicting moralities can inhibit the development of moral consensus and call into question the role of moral values in international politics, they do not necessarily substantiate the cynic's conviction that morality is nothing more than the subjective preferences of the powerful. To begin with, morality is concerned with what "ought" to be, not with what "is." Because the diversity of cultural norms and social practices is a manifestation of what "is," the existence of cultural pluralism does not threaten the notion of moral obligation. Moreover, it is important to emphasize that cultural and social pluralism is generally concerned with secondary norms, not basic principles. Although peoples from different cultures do not normally share particular beliefs about women's rights, government structures, and policies of distributive justice, there is generally widespread commitment to such notions as truth and justice as well as agreement about such fundamental norms as the dignity of human persons, freedom from torture, impartial application of the law, and freedom of conscience. Walzer calls this shared morality "minimal" to differentiate it from the particular, more developed "maximal" moralities found in each society.[20] Moral minimalism is a "thin" morality not because it is unimportant or makes few claims on human beings but because its claims are general and diffuse. Because of this shared minimal morality, Walzer claims that human beings from different societies "can acknowledge each other's different ways, respond to each other's cries for help, learn from each other and march (sometimes) in each other's parades."[21]

In light of the distinction between minimal and maximal moralities, the claim that all morality is subjective and relative is not empirically sustainable. Although maximal norms vary significantly from culture to culture, there is also a high level of global consensus about thin morality, namely, those norms that are essential to social and political life. Thus, although humans often disagree about many issues and social and economic values, there is also significant agreement about the necessity of such foundational principles as truth telling, beneficence, promise keeping, courage, self-control, and justice.[22] A. J. M. Milne has argued that moral diversity in global society cannot be total because some moral values are necessary to sustain social life. According to him, the international community's common morality includes such norms as: respect for human life, pursuit of justice, fellowship, social responsibility, freedom from arbitrary interference, honorable treatment, and civility.[23]

One way of illustrating the existence of common morality is to imagine the likely response to the arbitrary denial of property in different cultures. For example, if a number of persons were to visit various remote regions of the world and, on arriving in these distant, isolated areas, were to walk up to strangers and take some of their possessions, how would these strangers respond? What would mothers do if the visitors were to take their children from their arms? In all likelihood, they would oppose the arbitrary deprivation of their property and, most assuredly, resist the removal of their children. In addition, they would do so because of the universality of social values regarding friendship, family bonding, self-control, and property.

The pervasiveness of political morality has been convincingly demonstrated by Walzer's study of the ethics of war, *Just and Unjust Wars*, in which he argues that throughout history human judgments and arguments in wartime demonstrate a consistency and continuity in moral reasoning. According to Walzer, the structure of moral reasoning is revealed not by the fact that soldiers and statesmen come to the same conclusions but by the fact that they acknowledge common difficulties, face similar problems, and talk the same language. "The clearest evidence for the stability of our values over time," writes Walzer, "is the unchanging character of the lies soldiers and statesmen tell. They lie in order to justify themselves, and so they describe for us the lineaments of justice."[24]

In the final analysis, cultural relativism is a wholly unacceptable ethical theory because it is impossible to live with the doctrine's severe consequences. If there are no standards, everything is possible, and if everything is possible, torture, forced expulsion, systematic violation of human rights, denial of freedom, and religious persecution are not wrong. Although moral values and cultural patterns vary across societies, there is significant agreement among primary norms. For example, most human beings have a basic moral intuition that gross violations against other human beings are wrong. Thus, it does not follow, as cultural relativists assert, that there are no universal norms. Despite the existence of moral and cultural pluralism among secondary and tertiary norms, most thinkers reject cultural relativism. They do so, as Thomas Donaldson has noted, not because of compelling evidence for moral absolutism (i.e., the notion that eternal, universal ethical norms exist and are applicable to human actions) but because relativism is itself intellectually indefensible.[25]

THE DEVELOPMENT OF A MORAL FOREIGN POLICY

What role do moral principles play in the conduct of foreign relations? First, morality helps define the goals and purposes of states and other actors. Moral norms do not provide policy directives, but they can offer a general vision and broad direction and provide the moral norms by which to illuminate and define a country's vital interests. As the late theologian John C. Bennett noted, moral values contribute to public policy debates on foreign policy goals by providing "ultimate perspectives, broad criteria, motives, inspirations, sensitivities, warnings, moral limits."[26] In effect, moral norms can establish the boundaries for policy deliberation and execution.

Moral norms also provide a basis for judgment. Without standards, evaluation is impossible. Moral norms thus provide an ethical foundation for assessing the foreign policies of states as well as for judging the rules and structures of international society. For example, the widely accepted norms of international human rights provided the basis for the widespread condemnation of Serb "ethnic cleansing" carried out against Muslims during the 1992–1995 Bosnian War. Moreover, the growing recognition of ecological interdependence has resulted in an increasing international acceptance of principles and practices that seek to protect the earth's environment. Thus, when Saddam Hussein deliberately sought to destroy Kuwait's environment during the Persian Gulf War (by dumping oil into the sea and setting hundreds of oil wells on fire), his destructive actions were condemned worldwide.

Finally, moral norms provide the inspiration and motivation for policy development and implementation. Morality, in effect, provides the "fuel" for the government "engine." For example, the U.S. government's decision to intervene in Somalia in December 1992 to permit humanitarian relief was inspired in great measure by the humane concerns of leaders to alleviate starvation and keep hundreds of thousands of people from dying. And the NATO decision to intervene in Kosovo in 1999, a case examined below, was similarly inspired by humanitarian norms. In his important study of foreign aid, David Lumsdaine shows that the principal motivation for Western countries' substantial postwar foreign economic assistance to poor nations was morality. Although many factors and motivations influenced the giving of economic aid, the major inspiration and motivation was donor countries' "sense of justice and compassion."[27] Lumsdaine argues that international political morality, or what he terms "moral vision," shapes international relations. Contrary to realist claims that global politics is simply a realm of necessity, he claims that international relations involve freedom of action based on moral choice. As a result, international politics is an environment in which "conceptions of fairness and compassion, human dignity and human sympathy, justice and mercy" can be applied to the reform of global society.[28]

As will be made clear in chapter 2, there is no simple, easy method of applying political morality to foreign policy. One reason that international political action is generally morally ambiguous is that foreign policy issues and problems typically involve multiple and frequently conflicting moral norms. Thus, the process of moral reasoning must identify and apply the relevant moral criteria and, where moral conflict occurs, make the necessary trade-offs among the relevant criteria. Moreover, developing a moral foreign policy is a challenging task because an ethical decision-making strategy requires that morality be applied to the goals, means, and results of political action. However, because moral norms rarely result in ethical action at all three levels, trade-offs among the goals, means, and potential outcomes are generally inevitable.

Methods

How are moral norms applied in global politics? Among the different ways that moral norms influence international relations, three instruments are especially noteworthy: 1) the conscience of decision makers, 2) the influence of domestic public opinion, and 3) the influence of international reputation.[29] William Wilberforce, the early-nineteenth-century British parliamentarian, illustrates the first approach. After becoming a Christian, Wilberforce concluded that slavery was immoral and contrary to the will of God. For nearly four decades he led the fight in the House of Commons against this inhuman practice, first seeking to abolish the slave trade and then attempting to abolish slavery altogether.[30] President Jimmy Carter also demonstrates the significant influence of a leader's moral values. As a result of his strong convictions about human rights, his administration pursued an activist human rights policy, leading U.S. officials to publicly condemn repression and the abuse of basic rights and to halt foreign assistance to repressive military regimes.

The role of domestic public opinion in foreign relations—the second method by which morality is applied to foreign policy—is applicable only in democratic societies, in which a government's continuing authority and influence depend on its perceived legitimacy. To be sure, public opinion is not an automatic by-product of the thinking and analysis of the masses. Rather, public opinion is developed, organized, and mobilized by elites, including the media, interest groups, professional associations, and political parties. The important role of public opinion in foreign affairs in democratic societies is illustrated by the inability of the government of the Netherlands to accept deployment of NATO nuclear missiles in the early 1980s. Although the Dutch government was committed to such a deployment, the mass opposition to such action delayed the Netherlands' acceptance of cruise missiles for several years. In the United States, the role of mobilized public opinion was especially influential in the imposition of economic sanctions against South Africa. As a result of mass mobilization against South Africa's apartheid policies, many corporations halted their operations in South Africa, and universities and local and state governments adopted policies requiring divestment of stock for companies continuing their South African operations. The growing public opposition to apartheid also resulted in government action. In

1985, Congressional debate forced the Reagan administration to adopt modest sanctions, and a year later Congress imposed, over presidential objections, much more substantial sanctions.

Finally, the application of international political morality is influenced by global public opinion. Because public opinion is comparatively weak in the international community, its impact on government decision making is limited. Still, dominant international perceptions of power and morality do affect the foreign policy behavior of states. Just as an individual's reputation is based on other people's perceptions, so too the reputation of states is derived largely from people's perception of international actions. For example, the growing perception in the United States and other industrial powers in 1997 and 1998 that the Swiss government failed to return financial assets to Jewish people at the end of World War II has significantly tarnished Switzerland's financial reputation.

Foreign policy behavior can contribute to a state's reputation as a reliable, credible, and moral actor, or it can damage such a reputation. Because a state's influence is rooted to a great extent in public perceptions, governments continuously assess the impact of their decisions on global public opinion. For example, during the Cuban missile crisis of 1962, U.S. officials considered numerous options in responding to the Soviet Union's installation of medium-range ballistic missiles. According to Robert Kennedy, the main reason that direct military intervention was deemed unacceptable is that it would have harmed the international reputation of the United States.[31] Moreover, although some military officials advocated the limited use of nuclear arms in the Vietnam War, this action was never seriously contemplated by government leaders, in part because of the loss of prestige and influence that the United States would have suffered from such action.

Problems

Scholars and statesmen have called attention to a number of important challenges to the effective integration of morality into the fabric of foreign relations. One of the most common criticisms of international ethics is the belief that the decentralized structure of global society allows little room for moral judgment. Although the decentralized, anarchic structure of global society places a premium on national security and the promotion of national well-being, the priority of national interest does not obliterate the moral claims of other actors in the international community. Politics, after all, is the means by which actors pursue the common good in light of competing and conflicting individual and group interests. If actors pursued only self-interest in domestic or international politics, there would be no place for moral action. However, international politics, like domestic politics, involves the quest for order and justice based on the cooperative actions of actors.

Scholars and statesmen have also questioned the role of morality in foreign affairs because moral norms have been repeatedly misused in global politics. Rather than guiding and judging policies, morality has been used to clothe and justify national interests, resulting in rigid, moralistic foreign policies. In addition, rather than contributing to the process of moral reflection, morality has been used as an ideological and moralistic instrument, fashioning a self-righteous and hypocritical policy that has contributed to cynicism rather than public justice. In effect, morality has not contributed to justice because of the absence of impartiality.

The dangers of moralism are clearly illustrated in American history, especially during the late nineteenth and early twentieth centuries, when political leaders sought to define and justify U.S. foreign policy through morality. For example, President William McKinley supposedly relied on divine guidance in using military force to end Spanish colonial rule in Cuba and the Philippines, and when President Woodrow Wilson intervened in Veracruz, Mexico, he did so on the basis of the moral conviction that such action would foster greater democracy in Mexico. More recently, the Carter administration used foreign aid to reward states that improved human rights and to punish those that violated basic human rights. Because the use of moral language in foreign policy has often led to moralism, fanaticism, inflexibility, and utopianism—qualities that are inimical to orderly international relations—some scholars, including historian Arthur Schlesinger, Jr., and diplomatic historian George F. Kennan, argue that foreign policy should be based on national interests, not morality. Schlesinger writes, "Saints can be pure, but statesmen must be responsible. As trustees for others, they must defend interests and compromise principles. In politics, practical and prudential judgment must have priority over moral verdicts."[32] Both Schlesinger and Kennan note that when moral values dictate foreign policy, foreign policy becomes inflexible, simplistic, utopian, and fanatical, perverting, if not eliminating, the process of prudential reasoning.

Although the misuse of morality can lead to cynicism and the denial of moral values, moral duplicity and hypocrisy do not justify the removal of moral values from international politics. Indeed, because human choices involve morality, domestic and international politics are inescapably moral enterprises. At the same time, it is essential to recognize that the integration of morality into the fabric of decision making and judgment poses dangers. For example, because political action is partly an exercise in self-interest, public officials frequently apply moral norms to the conduct of foreign relations with partiality, thereby encouraging an arrogant and moralistic foreign policy. Moreover, because most political conduct typically involves multiple moral norms, moral action will inevitably involve trade-offs among relevant competing norms. Because no public actions are ever completely right and just, the application of political morality should always be undertaken with humility and self-criticism. This is why Stanley Hoffmann has observed that an essential norm of the international system is the virtue of moderation, or what he calls "the morality of self-restraint."[33]

In the following section, I illustrate the important, though ambiguous, role of moral values in one case study—the 1999 NATO war against Serbia. This case is important because it shows the complex and at times contradictory role of political morality in the design and execution of foreign policy. As I argue below, while the use of force brought to an end the Serb abuse of human rights in Kosovo, the resort to war dramatically increased the immediate suffering of the victims for whom the war was being waged.

BACKGROUND

Kosovo, a poor, small province of Serbia, is a multiethnic community of two peoples. Of its two million citizens, the vast majority (about 80 percent) are Albanian Muslims, or Kosovars; the dominant minority (about 10 percent) are Orthodox Christian Serbs. Ever since the medieval era, political and religious animosity has existed among major ethnic groups throughout the Balkans, and especially within this small territory, where Kosovars and Serbs have historically competed for power. In 1912, as Turkey's influence in the Balkans was waning, Serbs conquered Kosovo. Since a majority of the province's population at that time was Albanian, the imposition of Serb control effectively imposed a colonial order on the territory.[34] Despite the cultural and political cleavages between these two ethnic groups, Joseph Tito, Yugoslavia's postwar dictator, managed to impose and sustain political order within Kosovo. He did so in part through a federal governmental structure that permitted ethnic and cultural diversity not only within the province but also throughout Yugoslavia. To recognize the significant Albanian presence in Kosovo, the ruling Communist regime granted the territory governmental autonomy within the Serb Republic. This action, which was formalized in the 1974 Federal Constitution of Yugoslavia, allowed the majority Albanians to develop and celebrate their distinctive cultural and national interests.

The unraveling of the multiethnic status quo can be attributed to several political events in the latter phase of the Cold War. First, the death of Tito, Yugloslavia's charismatic communist leader, marked the beginning of the end of the modern state of Yugoslavia. With his death in 1980, the authority of the federal government declined, leading to increased ethnic and political fragmentation among Yugoslavia's distinct republics.

Second, in 1988 the government of Serbia suspended Kosovo's political autonomy and imposed direct rule from Belgrade. This action by Serbian president Slobodan Milosevic was undertaken to foment Serb nationalism and to consolidate Serb power within Kosovo, presaging future Serb actions in other parts of Yugoslavia. While the lifting of Kosovo's autonomous status pleased the minority Serbs in Kosovo and fueled the nationalistic ambitions of Serbs elsewhere, Albanians responded with rage. Ethnic animosity toward Serbs greatly intensified in the early 1990s when they began replacing institutions and policies, such as the public financing of Albanian schools, that had been accorded Kosovar cultural legitimacy. Warren Zimmerman, the last U.S. ambassador to Yugoslavia before the country fell apart in the early 1990s, wrote that "under Milosevic, Kosovo took on all the attributes of a colony."[35] And Misha Glenny, one of the most astute observers of Balkan politics, noted that the reimposition of Serb rule "transformed Kosovo into a squalid outpost of putrefying colonialism."[36]

Finally, the collapse of Communist rule in the Soviet Union and Eastern Europe in 1989–1991 undermined the authority of the Yugoslavian government. With the loss of Communist Party authority, ethnopolitical tensions began to rise throughout Yugoslavia, eventually leading to the collapse of the federal state as various republics (Slovenia, Croatia, Bosnia & Hercegovina, and Macedonia) demanded political independence from the central government in Belgrade. As different republics pressed for political self-rule, the ethnic animosities within and among these political communities greatly intensified, fueling the tensions in autonomous provinces like Kosovo.

However important these events may have been in the growing ethnic tensions within the Balkans, by themselves they would have been insufficient to cause the Kosovo war. What ignited the conflict was the simultaneous demand by Serbs and Kosovars to press for political autonomy and sole political control of the same land. By imposing Serbian control over Kosovo, Serbs fueled Albanian nationalism and the quest for Kosovar self-rule. Given the overwhelming power of the Serbs, the original Albanian response was framed by the Democratic League of Kosovo (LDK), the major political party of Kosovars. The party, led by Ibrahim Rugova, a pacifist intellectual who was committed to nonviolent resistance, called on Albanians to meet Serbian oppression with noncooperation, withdrawal, and peaceful nonparticipation. Rugova's philosophy was guided by the hope that, as Tim Judah has noted, Kosovo would at some future time "simply drop into Albanian hands like ripe fruit."[37] Since Serbia monopolized all political decision-making and refused to let "elected" Kosovar legislators meet, Rugova's "shadow" government existed in theory only. Indeed, because all Kosovar political and governmental activities were considered illegal, Kosovars were forced to hold their "governmental" meetings in foreign countries.[38] While the strategy of noncooperation helped to maintain order temporarily, it did not lead to greater stability. Indeed, it ironically resulted in increased Kosovar nationalism as living conditions declined and human rights abuses increased.

One expression of this radicalization was the emergence of the Kosovo Liberation Army (KLA), a military group committed to the political independence of Kosovo. Whereas the LDK's "phantom" government was guided by principles of nonviolence and passive resistance, the KLA's major goals were to undermine Serb rule through violence and to press for political self-determination. Although the KLA was established in Western Europe in the early 1990s, it did not begin carrying out military operations until 1995. In the beginning the covert operations were small and limited in scope—in part because of the difficulty in training and equipping its guerrillas. But when Albania imploded in 1997,[39] the disintegration of the Albanian police and army created a ready supply of weapons for the KLA. In turn, this development resulted in more guerrilla operations within Kosovo. As KLA violence became more pervasive and lethal, Serb leader Slobodan Milosevic responded by increasing the Serb military and police forces

and imposing greater political repression, including widespread deportation and ethnic cleansing.[40] As Stanley Hoffmann has noted, however, Milosevic's goal was not to carry out police actions but to eliminate the KLA threat altogether: "What the Serbs are doing is not a police operation against political dissenters or ordinary criminals. It is the destruction of a movement of national liberation from extremely repressive rule, the crushing of a drive for self-determination."[41]

As a result of Serb repression, tens of thousands of Kosovars were forced from their homes and villages and many began fleeing the country. It is estimated that by late 1998 some 250,000 Kosovars had been displaced and were facing inhumane living conditions. To seek to ease the humanitarian crisis, the United States dispatched Richard Holbrooke, the U.S. negotiator who had brokered the Dayton Accords that ended the Bosnian war, to help restore peace. In his October 1998 negotiations, Holbrooke succeeded in arranging a Serb cease-fire and a promise from Milosevic to reduce Serb military forces in Kosovo to prewar levels. To ensure compliance with the negotiated settlement, a monitoring force (the Kosovo Verification Mission) of some 1,500 international observers was established to report on human rights violations. Once the cease-fire was in place, however, the KLA, which had not been a part of the October negotiations, used the peace to resupply their fighters and to prepare for the resumption of guerrilla operations and terror attacks. As a result, sporadic fighting resumed in early 1999, bringing to an end the Holbrooke cease-fire. And when Serbs carried out a massacre of 44 civilians in the village of Racak in January, Western authorities concluded that collective action needed to be undertaken if widespread human rights abuses were to be prevented.

Led by the United States, a consortium of leading powers (known as the Contact Group)[42] agreed to impose a settlement on the Serbs and Albanians in Kosovo. Meeting in a chateau in Rambouillet, France, in February, Western leaders presented the terms of a cease-fire to both Serbian and Kosovar delegates. Fundamentally, the Rambouillet accord promised to maintain Serb sovereignty over Kosovo, to restore the autonomous status of Kosovo, and to demand a cease-fire between KLA and Serb forces.[43] To facilitate compliance with the cease-fire, Serbs had to withdraw their army and reduce their police force to prewar levels (about 2,500 police), the KLA had to accept demilitarization, and Serbia had to allow a large (30,000) NATO peacekeeping force to ensure domestic order. As expected, Serb leaders refused the Rambouillet settlement, believing that the introduction of NATO troops in Kosovo was inconsistent with their claim of sovereignty. But to the surprise and chagrin of Western leaders, the Kosovar delegates, led by the KLA's Hashim Thaci, also refused to accept the Rambouillet accord. Since Albanians were fighting not only to end Serb repression but, more important, to assert the right of political independence, Rambouillet was regarded as a second best alternative. Only after repeated negotiations with other Kosovar leaders, coupled with the growing awareness that NATO would not protect Kosovars from further ethnic cleansing if they refused the Rambouillet settlement, did the Kosovars finally accept the terms of accord.

THE ETHICS OF SELF-DETERMINATION

In confronting group demands for political self-determination, one of the difficult ethical challenges of post–Cold War international politics is to determine which peoples have the right to claim political autonomy in the international community. For example, do the Kosovars have the right to secede from Serbia and establish their own political community? What about the Kurds in Iran, Iraq, and Turkey? If the Palestinians are entitled to statehood, can the Chechens demand this right as well? Fundamentally, the collective right of self-determination, as I will argue in chapter 7, depends largely upon political power—on the ability to make and sustain a claim to self-rule in the face of political actors who oppose such a development. Since no ethical framework exists by which a people's right to self-rule can be defined, the claim of self-determination depends less on morality than on the ability to defend the claim. As a result, the collective right of self-determination has been con-

sidered legitimate historically if a people can demonstrate the collective will and military capacity to claim and sustain political independence by exerting sole and ultimate control over a specified territory. In effect, the moral legitimacy of self-determination has depended in great measure on fulfilling two conditions: internal sovereignty, where ruling authorities demonstrate control over political life within a territory, and external sovereignty, where other states publicly acknowledge this fact.

Typically, when a people demand political autonomy and press this claim with violence, the result is often war. Rarely have states peacefully accepted the demands for self-rule by minority groups. And when groups have sought to secede from an existing state, the ruling regime has generally opposed such action with force. For example, when Confederate states sought to secede from the United States, Abraham Lincoln resorted to war to maintain the union. And when Chechens sought to secede from Russia in the early 1990s, the Russian government used brutal force to keep Chechnya within the Russian state. Even President Clinton expressed sympathy toward the Russian government as it faced increasing terrorist threats from Chechens, comparing Yeltsin's policies toward the Chechen war to those of President Lincoln during the Civil War.[44] Thus, when Albanian Muslims began demanding the right of political self-determination in the mid-1990s, Serbian authorities responded with violence. Like other governments that have faced similar demands for political autonomy from ethnic groups, the Serbs were so committed to keeping control of Kosovo that they were prepared to use political oppression, human rights violations, and war itself to counter the violence from the KLA. As Zimmerman notes, Milosevic saw the KLA as a "mortal threat. He could live with Rugova's noncooperation but not with the KLA's armed confrontation."[45]

Historically, Serbs have regarded Kosovo as the symbolic center of the Serb nation. Because this small territory holds many of Serbia's holiest Orthodox monasteries and churches and is the site of an epic medieval battle with Muslims, Serb nationalism is deeply associated with the region. Indeed, Serb political leaders view the territory as their nation's Jerusalem. Although the borders of Balkan political communities have historically been deeply contested, since the end of World War I and especially since the end of World War II the Serb claim to Kosovo has been internationally accepted. Since the 1974 Federal Constitution of Yugoslavia made Kosovo an autonomous province of Serbia, the dispute over the sovereignty and self-determination of the region is not constitutional but sociological, since Serbs have been a minority of the territory ever since they conquered it in 1912. The decline in the proportion of ethnic Serbs within Kosovo during the Cold War was the results of two trends—the continued population growth rate of Albanians and, second, the ongoing emigration of Serbs to other parts of Yugoslavia.[46] Julie Mertus defines the sociological reality as follows: "The fact remains that Kosovo has become increasingly populated by ethnic Albanians who refuse to give up their language and culture and that, despite Serbian hegemonic control over the region, Serbs keep leaving."[47]

To counter the rising Kosovar claim of self-rule and to satisfy the increasing Serb desire for direct control over the economic, cultural, and political life of Kosovo, Slobodan Milosevic revoked Kosovo's political autonomy in 1988. But rather than reducing ethnic tensions, the reimposition of Serb rule from Belgrade greatly intensified ethnic animosity between Serbs and Kosovars. More significantly, the imposition of Serb repression had the ironic effect of further increasing Albanian nationalism, which, in turn, further intensified the demands of political independence. To be sure, the "civilizational" animosity between Albanian Muslims and Serb Orthodox Christians fueled the growing conflict between these two peoples. But the dispute was not over religion or ethnicity per se but over political power and more particularly the quest for culturally homogenous communities. Serbs, no less than Kosovars, sought to create political regimes that were conducive to the cultural, religious, economic, and political interests of their own people.

It is important to stress that the humanitarian crisis in Kosovo was fundamentally a by-product of a political conflict between two peoples. Although ethnic conflict had been simmering for many years in the region, the increasing aggressive action of the KLA had greatly exacerbated human rights abuses. To help avert ethnic violence in Kosovo, the Bush administration sent an early warning to Milosevic during the Christmas holidays in 1992, shortly before President Clinton took power. Thus, long before the rise of the KLA, the United States had regarded Kosovo as a territory vulnerable to ethnic violence and had threatened military action if Serbia used force against Kosovars.[48] Once Clinton took office, however, the U.S. government focused virtually all efforts on the containment of the Bosnian war. Not until after the Bosnian war had been brought to a halt through a negotiated peace settlement in Dayton, Ohio, in November 1995 did attention begin to shift toward other potential conflicts in the Balkans.

Fundamentally, the conflict between Albanians and Serbs in Kosovo was over political control of land, not over human rights abuses, political repression, or unjust, discriminatory policies. To be sure, the conflict had aggravated human rights violations. But the fundamental tensions derived from a quest by two peoples to govern the region of Kosovo. Kosovars, to their credit, had managed to define the conflict largely in humanitarian terms. But while the KLA-Serb conflict had resulted in gross violations of human rights, secret killings, and ethnic cleansing, Serb violence was the result of a political contest, not simply the by-product of ethnic hatred of Albanians. As Judah notes, the Kosovo conflict was fundamentally a "struggle between two people for control of the same piece of land."[49] Thus, while the Rambouillet initiative was designed to halt the military conflict, the accord failed to address the future status of Kosovo. Thus, the Western initiative was not designed to resolve the political dispute but only to halt the humanitarian suffering that had resulted from the political conflict.

THE ETHICS OF WAR

In March 1999, Secretary of State Madeleine Albright sent U.S. emissary Richard Holbrooke to Belgrade to warn President Milosevic that if he did not accept the Rambouillet accord NATO would initiate war. Since China and Russia, veto-wielding members of the Security Council, were staunchly opposed to using force against Serbia, the Western Alliance had resolved to threaten military action outside of the normal United Nations peacekeeping framework. For China and Russia, foreign intervention was inappropriate because the conflict in Kosovo was fundamentally a domestic political issue. While foreign states might assist in resolving the conflict, the fundamental challenge was for the Serbs and Kosovars to resolve the dispute. Western states, however, regarded the widespread abuse of human rights in Kosovo as a threat to the peace and security of the Balkans. For them, the time had come to defend the primacy of human rights in the face of political oppression and ethnic cleansing by Serb military and paramilitary forces.

There can be little doubt that NATO's goal of halting gross human rights abuses, including ethnic cleansing, was morally legitimate. For President Clinton, ending the humanitarian crisis in Kosovo was "a moral imperative,"[50] while for Secretary of State Madeleine Albright, "Kosovo was not going to be this administration's Munich"[51]—that is, it was not going to accept appeasement as the British government had done in 1939 toward Germany. Czech president Vaclav Havel claimed that the Kosovo war was probably the first one ever waged for moral values rather than the pursuit of national interests. "If one can say of any war that it is ethical, or that it is being waged for ethical reasons," he wrote, "then it is true of this war."[52] For Havel, as for other Western leaders, the decision to use force against Milosevic was morally correct because "no decent person can stand by and watch the systematic, state-directed murder of other people."[53]

But if NATO's goals in Kosovo were morally legitimate, the means—an intense air war against Serbia and Kosovo—raised serious ethical concerns. Since foreign policy must be concerned not only with goals but also with the means and anticipated results, the challenge in devising an effective yet moral foreign policy must necessarily reconcile means and ends. The fact that widespread ethnic cleansing was morally repugnant did not obviate the need to devise a morally prudent strategy that achieved the desired goals. But for many foreign policy observers, including former secretary of state Henry Kissinger the decision to rely solely on bombing to halt Serb oppression and ethnic cleansing was not the most appropriate means.[54]

In particular, NATO's war strategy was challenged morally for a number of reasons. First, since NATO was seeking to halt ethnic cleansing in Kosovo, a credible military strategy should have involved the use, or at a minimum the threat of use, of both ground and air operations. Not only did the bombing campaign prove ineffective in achieving the desired humanitarian objectives but it had the paradoxical effect of compounding human suffering for the Serb victims. As soon as NATO bombers began attacking Kosovo and Serbia, Serbian military and paramilitary soldiers in Kosovo embarked on a systematic campaign of ethnic cleansing (known as Operation Horseshoe), forcing tens of thousands of Kosovars to flee west toward Montenegro and Albania and south toward Macedonia.[55] Indeed, within a week the ethnic cleansing campaign had forced more than 300,000 Kosovars to leave the country. And by the end of the war, the United Nations High Commissioner for Refugees (UNHCR) estimated that 848,100 Kosovars had fled Kosovo—444,600 to Albania, 244,500 to Macedonia, 69,900 to Montenegro, while 91,057 had been airlifted to other countries.[56] Rather than alleviating human suffering, the immediate effect of the war was to greatly aggravate the humanitarian crisis. This is why Leon Wieseltier argues that the Kosovo war was "a good fight badly fought."[57]

A second shortcoming of NATO's strategy was that the pursuit of a risk-free war compromised the moral objectives of the war. Because NATO sought to minimize military casualties, it carried out its air war from an altitude of 15,000 feet or higher—that is, high enough to avoid ground fire and missiles yet too high to carry out precision bombing and thereby minimize civilian casualties. The problem with such a riskless strategy was that it effectively undermined the norm of human equality, the core humanitarian principle for which the war was being waged. Since a risk-free air war communicated the message that NATO personnel were of greater value than the lives of those for whom the war was being waged, the risk-averse strategy was morally problematic. As Paul Kahn notes, risk-averse humanitarian warfare is contradictory because the morality of ends, which are universal, is incompatible with the morality of means, which privilege a particular group of people.[58] Noting the inconsistency between NATO's goals and means, Kissinger noted that "a strategy that vindicates its moral convictions only from altitudes above 15,000 feet deserves to be questioned on both political and moral grounds."[59]

A third limitation of the war strategy was the failure to devise a plan to force an early Serb capitulation. Western leaders had no doubt assumed that systematic bombing would result in the withdrawal of Serb military and paramilitary forces from Kosovo. But rather than undermining ethnic nationalism, the bombing had the paradoxical effect of reinforcing Serb nationalism and increasing their determination to maintain control over Kosovo. While NATO's ineffectiveness in achieving political objectives was no doubt due to its failure to accurately anticipate Serbian resolve, it was also due to the complex political nature of a multilateral war campaign—war by committee, as some critics termed it. Since the major decisions of the war required the consent of the NATO member states, the collective approach to decision-making led to a cautious and limited air campaign. But the failure to escalate rapidly the scope and intensity of the bombing no doubt contributed to the belief that Serbia could survive an air campaign. Had the scope and lethality of the bombing increased in the early phase of the war, the suffering within Kosovo and civilian casualties with Serbia may have been greatly reduced. Even after dropping more than 20,000 bombs that resulted in greater than $60 billion in economic destruction in Serbia and Kosovo, Milosevic was still unwilling to give up control of Kosovo. In-

deed, only when NATO began targeting the principal communications, electrical, and power infrastructure of Serbia did the air campaign begin to severely undermine Serb resolve. In fact, only when NATO began making preparations for a ground invasion and Russian president Boris Yeltsin signaled his unwillingness to support Serb intransigence did Milosevic finally capitulate to NATO.

In the final analysis, NATO achieved its goal of the withdrawal of all Serb military, paramilitary, and police forces from Kosovo. Even though a large NATO peacekeeping force was immediately introduced after Serbia gave up control of Kosovo, the transfer of authority to a multinational force led to the return of most of the 850,000 Kosovar refugees. But the return of the Kosovars to their destroyed villages was accompanied by widespread acts of revenge against Serbs. Despite the efforts of the 42,500-member NATO peacekeeping force (known as Kosovo Force or KFOR) to maintain political order, the return of Kosovars resulted in widespread ethnic cleansing of Kosovo Serbs. It is estimated that in the aftermath of the Kosovo war, more than 150,000 Serbs fled the province, leaving Pristina, Kosovo's capital, with only about 200 Serbs out of a population of 500,000. But the most daunting challenge that the UN interim governing authority (UNMIK) has had to confront in the absence of Serb authority is the maintenance of law and order in the face of widespread anarchy. Historian Timothy Garton Ash visited Kosovo in early 2000 and observed that while Albanian-Serb hatred continued to inflame political passions, the more daunting challenge was the pervasive lawlessness.[60] Rather than leading to human rights for Kosovars, the "Albanization" of Kosovo had, in his view, resulted in corrupt, anarchic rule by gangs that threatened the well-being of all Kosovars.

In sum, a war designed to promote human rights has itself resulted, at least in the short-term, in morally ambiguous outcomes. It may well be that Kosovo might eventually become a humane, prosperous community. But the immediate effects of the war have done little to eradicate ethnic animosity and have contributed to widespread criminality that threaten human rights and the renewal of economic development.

MORAL REFLECTIONS

This case study illuminates the complexity and ambiguity of pursuing moral objectives in foreign affairs. Contrary to the widespread realist assumption that foreign policy involves solely the pursuit of national interests, the Kosovo war illuminates the significant role of moral values in defining foreign policy goals as well as the ethical challenge of devising appropriate strategies in the pursuit of moral objectives. The following questions illustrate some of the important moral issues raised by this case:

- When the quest for self-determination involves violence leading to widespread human rights abuses, how should foreign governments respond? How much human suffering must occur before foreign states should consider military intervention to protect innocent civilians?
- Humanitarian intervention involves violence in the service of human rights. When confronting competing obligations of state sovereignty and human rights, which norm should take precedence? Vaclav Havel has observed that the Kosovo war gave precedence to human rights over the rights of the state.[61] Did the defense of human rights in Kosovo justify foreign military action?
- According to widely accepted moral principles of warfare, the use of force should be proportionate to the political ends being pursued—that is, the means should be commensurate with the ends. It has been estimated that around 5,000 Serb military

and paramilitary members were killed by its bombardment, while the economic destruction in Yugoslavia has been estimated at $60 to $100 billion. Moreover, the Serb campaign against Albanians is thought to have killed 10,000 civilians. Given the high human and material cost of the NATO war, was the resort to war morally justified? Was the violence justified by the outcomes? In other words, were the material and human losses of the war justified by the goal of ending a humanitarian crisis?

- The immediate effect of the NATO war was the forced deportation of nearly 900,000 Kosovars to neighboring countries and the internal displacement of nearly 500,000 others. After Serbia capitulated, most Kosovar refugees returned to their destroyed villages and towns. In view of the significant humanitarian crisis in the immediate aftermath of the war, was the short-term suffering justified by the long-term promise of greater stability in Kosovo?
- Assuming the Kosovo war was justified by the egregious human rights abuses carried out by the Serbs, was NATO's risk-free air strategy morally appropriate? Why or why not?
- Does the failure to secure United Nations sanctions undermine the moral efficacy of the Kosovo war? Must multilateral peacekeeping missions be approved by the international community in order for them to be morally legitimate?
- Finally, given NATO's humanitarian goals, did the risk-averse air strategy undermine the morality of the war? Should NATO have been prepared to increase military risk in order to limit civilian casualties?

SUMMARY

In this chapter I have argued that moral values and ethical reasoning are essential dimensions of foreign policy decision making. While the political challenges in the international community may differ from those commonly found in domestic society, the quest by states for territorial security, economic well-being, and the preservation of a stable, humane global order are rooted in moral values. As Arnold Wolfers's statement at the outset of this chapter suggests, foreign policy decision making is not beyond moral judgment but rests on moral choices. To be sure, personal morality cannot be applied directly to public policies, nor can widely shared moral norms be simplistically used in the conduct of foreign affairs. As I will argue in later chapters, the challenge in defining a prudent foreign policy is to identify interests and relevant moral norms and then to integrate them through ethical reasoning in defining the ends, means, and likely outcomes of political action. Frequently, moralists give priority to intentions, but focusing solely on goals is insufficient. Indeed, the great moral challenge in political life is to define just ends and then to devise morally appropriate strategies to achieve them. Thus, in developing a moral foreign policy, ethical reasoning must identify and rank order goals in light of shared moral norms and assess the moral legitimacy of alternative strategies in light of anticipated outcomes. As the Kosovo case illustrates, foreign policy making is often a daunting task involving competing and conflicting values and resulting in highly ambiguous outcomes. NATO's action to halt Serb ethnic cleansing was undoubtedly a just cause, yet the pursuit of humanitarianism proved to be a difficult and morally ambiguous enterprise.

Chapter Two

Strategies of Ethical Decision Making

When it comes to politics, we get no moral Brownie points for good intentions; we will be judged by the results.[1]
—PETER BERGER

What is wrong is not the impulse to give foreign policy a moral content, but the presumption that doing so is an uncomplicated business, one not requiring calculation and compromise but merely purity of intention. Cheap moralists are as dangerous as cheap hawks—indeed they are often the same people.[2]
—OWEN HARRIES

Moral Politics is an art of execution: principles unaccompanied by practical means or by an awareness of possible trade-offs remind one of Peguy's famous comment about Kant—his hands were pure, but he had no hands.[3]

—STANLEY HOFFMANN

IN THE PREVIOUS CHAPTER, ethics was defined as a moral reasoning process involving the identification, interpretation, and application of moral principles to specific issues or problems. In carrying out this task in the political sphere, statesmen and political thinkers rely on distinct strategies and traditions. *Ethical strategies* provide alternative decision-making methodologies based on different emphases being given to goals, means, and consequences. *Ethical traditions*, by contrast, provide substantive systems that structure moral reasoning and action. Unlike ethical strategies, which are mainly methodological tools, ethical traditions provide a normative structure of rules and principles that are regarded as authoritative. Both ethical strategies and ethical traditions are important in international ethics because they provide the tools and instruments by which moral values are applied to issues and problems of global society.

In this chapter, I examine the nature and role of two dominant strategies to ethical decision making: ends-based action and rule-based action. These two strategies are illustrated with case studies on nuclear deterrence and famine relief. In addition, I describe and assess a third approach, a tridimensional ethical model, that judges international political ethics by its comprehensive emphasis on goals, means, and results. This approach is illustrated with a case study on the Reagan administration's Strategic Defense Initiative (SDI), a program that explored the feasibility of developing a protective shield from strategic nuclear attack. In the next chapter, I examine the nature and role of ethical traditions in international affairs.

ENDS-BASED ACTION

This approach, generally defined by philosophers as *consequentialism* or *teleological ethics* (from the Greek *teleos*, meaning "end" or "issue"), assumes that the morality of an action must be ultimately judged by the good results that are realized. In contrast to rule-based action, which assumes that the morality of a decision should be judged by the faithfulness with which moral rules are applied, consequentialism believes that the most important moral criterion is the overall outcome. Political actions typically involve three distinct elements: goals or intentions, means, and results. Although all three elements are incorporated into ends-based thinking, the consequences of human choices are given priority. According to this view, the moral legitimacy of an action, as noted by Peter Berger at the outset of this chapter, ultimately depends on its consequences.

Thus, for the consequentialist, the goals and means of political actions must be morally justified by the results of such actions. Policies involving questionable intentions and means might be morally permissible if sufficient good is achieved by those policies. To illustrate, an ends-based analysis of nuclear deterrence might regard the possession and threat of nuclear weapons (generally considered to be evil) as a morally legitimate strategy in helping to prevent nuclear aggression and to promote world order (considered good). Although the failure of deterrence could result in a nuclear war (an evil), the probability of such a conflict occurring has been considered so small that nuclear deterrence, although itself partly evil, has been considered a conditionally moral policy. In short, most ends-based analyses of nuclear strategy have assumed that preventing nuclear aggression through limited, credible threats (deterrence) is a morally legitimate strategy.

One of the major philosophical expressions of ends-based thinking is *utilitarianism*, a doctrine that assumes that individual and collective actions should be judged mainly by their "utility" or results. As Jeremy Bentham (1748–1832), the founder of this movement argued, "Nature has placed mankind under the governance of two sovereign masters, pain and pleasure."[4] The task of government is thus to establish policies that maximize collective pleasure and minimize collective pain. He proposed that policy making should be judged by the principle of *utility*, which he defined as the "greatest good for the greatest number." Because Bentham was concerned with increasing the scientific basis of policy making, he developed a number of quantitative norms for measuring societal pleasure and pain. Subsequently, his disciple and friend, John Stuart Mill (1806–1873), sought to further refine utilitarianism by distinguishing between desirable and less desirable pleasures.

More recently, political philosophers have distinguished between two types of utilitarianism: [rule *utilitarianism* and *act utilitarianism*.] The former applies the principle of utility to rules and procedures, holding that such norms derive their ethical legitimacy from their "procedural utility," that is, their perceived fairness and expected contribution to the common good. In global politics, such utilitarianism applies to the norms and structures of the international community's political, economic, and legal systems, and the validity of such norms and structures depend on their overall effect on individual and global welfare. The moral legitimacy of a basic rule, such as nonintervention, is thus judged in terms of its contribution to global order and international peace as well as its impact on the welfare and security of individual countries. Rule utilitarianism, in short, judges the inherent "usefulness" of policies and structures in terms of their consequences.

Act utilitarianism, by contrast, applies the utility criterion to particular actions, holding that the moral legitimacy of decisions must be based on the extent to which overall good (i.e., utility) is maximized in each specific circumstance. Political actions based on act utilitarianism are thus judged in terms of their anticipated results. For example, the decision of whether the United States should assist a country or region facing a major financial crisis (as was the case with Mexico in December 1994 and with East Asia in 1997–1998) would be determined by the anticipated short-term and long-term consequences of such aid.

Ends-based thinking is an influential ethical strategy in domestic and international politics in great part because government decisions are judged generally in terms of results rather than intentions. As a result, political ethics, whether domestic or international, tend to be consequentialist. However, the widespread support for ends-based action in public life should not obscure the strategy's significant limitations. One of these is decision makers' inability to fully determine or predict policy outcomes. Because policy making is at best a probabilistic science in which outcomes depend on many factors over which decision makers have little or no control, government initiatives frequently fail to promote desired goals. For example, although economic sanctions are often imposed to foster behavioral reforms, economic penalties seldom lead to desired behavioral outcomes. Similarly, foreign aid is often given to promote democracy and economic prosperity even though such aid sometimes fails to advance desirable outcomes and can even undermine the goals being pursued. Given the indeterminacy of public policies the moral assessment of political action from an ends-based strategy is thus likely to involve significant uncertainties and ambiguities.

A second and more important limitation is the inability of ends-based thinking to provide an authoritative ethical standard by which to evaluate action. Bentham, who defined the principle of utility as the greatest good for the greatest number, provided a number of general norms by which to judge this principle. However, his conceptualization of outcomes, like that of other consequentialist political thinkers, provides no clear, unambiguous standard by which to define and judge results. Whether the end is defined as stability, pleasure, happiness, fairness, human rights, or economic and social well-being, there is no widely accepted framework by which to assess political outcomes. In short, although an ends-based perspective needs to be incorporated in political ethics, consequentialism alone does not provide a fully satisfactory ethical methodology for applying morality in international affairs.

Because politics is fundamentally about the art of the possible, political action is generally judged primarily by its results. As noted previously, ends-based analysis is the dominant ethical methodology in politics. The following case study illustrates the nature and role of this methodology in terms of the ethics of nuclear deterrence.

CASE 2-1: THE ETHICS OF NUCLEAR DETERRENCE

BACKGROUND

Historically, military force has been viewed as a morally legitimate means to protect and defend vital interests and to deter aggression. Theologians and strategists have developed an elaborate moral theory of military force, known as "just war," that specifies when a state may resort to war and how such a war should be conducted. After nuclear weapons were invented in 1945, it was clear that the new weapons could not easily be encompassed by existing conceptions of military force. In particular, traditional just-war norms designed to help determine whether, when, and how force should be used in settling global conflicts no longer applied to nuclear weapons because of their extraordinary destructive power. Typically, atomic (nuclear) bombs were many thousand times more powerful than conventional arms, and hydrogen (thermonuclear) bombs were many million times more powerful than conventional weapons. As a result, a war between two nuclear powers could threaten not only the mutual destruction of the two combatants but also, in the words of Jonathan Schell, "the extinction of the species." "To say that we and all future generations are threatened with extinction by the nuclear peril," Schell wrote in 1982 in *The Fate of the Earth*, his influential and popular account of the nuclear dilemma, "is to describe only half of our situation. The other half is that we are the authors of that extinction."[5]

The development of nuclear arms thus posed profound moral issues. Was it morally permissible to possess such weapons? If so, could a state threaten their use? In addition, if the threat failed to deter action, could nuclear arms be used? After atomic bombs were used in Hiroshima and Nagasaki, it became evident that nuclear arms could not be encompassed by conventional strategic thought. The power of these new weapons was so overwhelming that they could no longer be regarded as instruments of warfare. Nuclear and thermonuclear weapons provided a nation with military power but not with usable force to compel a foreign state to alter its behavior. One of the first thinkers to recognize the moral and strategic problem posed by the nuclear invention was Bernard Brodie, who in 1946 observed, "Thus far the chief purpose of our military establishment has been to win wars. From now on its chief purpose must be to avert them."[6] Subsequently, strategists continued to emphasize the strategic significance of nuclear arms while calling into question the military utility of such weapons. Henry Kissinger, for example, describes the radical challenge posed by nuclear arms to traditional strategic thought: "In the past the military establishment was asked to prepare for war. Its test was combat; its vindication, victory. In the nuclear age, however, victory has lost its traditional significance. The outbreak of war is increasingly considered the worst catastrophe. Henceforth, the adequacy of the military establishment will be tested by its ability to preserve peace."[7]

Fundamentally, nuclear weapons pose two major moral problems. First, because their destructive power is based not only on blast but also on heat and radiation, nuclear weapons can inflict greater and longer-term destruction, involving both immediate human suffering from severe burns and long-term genetic deformities. Second, because of their extraordinary power, nuclear weapons are indiscriminate instruments of mass destruction. As a result, they cannot be regarded as war-fighting instruments that give states another means of implementing policy. Because of the qualitative differences between nuclear and conventional arms, the former, unlike the latter, does not provide usable force to compel an enemy. "A weapon," writes George Kennan, "is something that is supposed to serve some rational end—a hideous end, as a rule, but one related to some serious objective of governmental policy, one supposed to promote the interests of society which employs it. The nuclear device seems to me not to respond to that description."[8] Although nuclear arms are not useful war-fighting instruments, they are a vital element of the national security of some states. Their usefulness, however, does not lie in their ability to compel through force but in their ability to prevent aggression. Indeed, because of their extraordinary power, nuclear arms are history's most formidable instruments of deterrence.

Given the significant qualitative differences between conventional and nuclear arms, the traditional prudential and moral analysis of war is not immediately applicable to nuclear power. Michael Walzer, for example, argues that nuclear weapons "are the first of mankind's technological innovations that are simply not encompassable within the familiar moral world."[9] Indeed, he suggests that they "explode" the theory of just war.

Because nuclear weapons are the most powerful weapons ever devised by human beings, a nuclear military capability can provide a state with a dramatic expansion in perceived national power. At the same time, because nuclear weapons are instruments of indiscriminate destruction, they do not provide a state with usable military force, especially if an enemy state also has such weapons. This is the situation that developed between the United States and the Soviet Union in the late 1940s after the latter became a nuclear power. Moreover, as both states expanded their nuclear arsenals in the 1950s, they became mutually vulnerable to each other's nuclear power. By the early 1960s, both superpowers had achieved arsenals sufficiently large and invulnerable that a condition of mutual assured destruction (MAD) emerged, a condition by which neither state could win a major war but both could lose. MAD was not a policy; rather, it was a condition reflecting a nuclear "balance of terror" by which each rival could destroy the other, even after being subjected to a nuclear surprise attack.

Because nuclear arms imposed mutual vulnerability on the superpowers, the American challenge in devising a moral strategic policy was to reconcile the demands for national security with the demands for global order without increasing the risks of nuclear war. Not surprisingly, nuclear deterrence, that is, prevention by threat, emerged as the principal American strategic doctrine. As articulated by U.S. strategists, nuclear deterrence would help keep peace by inhibiting aggression through the implicit threat of unacceptable nuclear retaliation. According to deterrence theory, as long as U.S. nuclear forces could carry out unacceptable punishment, no rational state would risk major aggression. Moreover, the credibility and stability of deterrence were assumed to rest on two essential conditions. First, societies needed to be vulnerable (there could be no effective strategic defense). Second, nuclear forces needed to be sufficiently invulnerable to carry out nuclear retaliation involving unacceptable damage. As a result, deterrence did not rest so much on the number, quality, or size of strategic weapons as on their invulnerability to attack. As long as a significant part of a state's nuclear arsenal could be used to retaliate following a major nuclear attack, deterrence would remain credible.

THE MORAL JUSTIFICATION OF DETERRENCE

War is evil. It is evil because it results in death and destruction. Despite its evil effects, war can be morally justified when certain moral conditions are fulfilled.[10] However, from an ends-based, or consequentialist, approach, which is the perspective I am seeking to illuminate here, war can be morally justified when the good outcomes of war outweigh the evil undertaken in war. Thus, when the anticipated results justify the means—when a war results, for example, in the restoration of a just peace without excessive destruction—a war can be morally justified by a consequentialist ethic.

However, if conventional war can be morally justified under some circumstances, this is not the case for nuclear war. Michael Mandelbaum, for example, writes, "In the sense that the term 'war' connotes some proportion between damage done and political goals sought, an all-out nuclear conflict would not be a war at all."[11] Similarly, the U.S. Catholic bishops, in their influential 1983 pastoral letter on nuclear strategy, argue that a nuclear war is morally unacceptable and that every effort must be taken to ensure that nuclear arms are never used in resolving international disputes. As a result, the bishops argue that the church should emphasize not the morality of war fighting but the avoidance of nuclear war altogether. The letter observes, "Traditionally, the church's moral teaching sought first to prevent war and then to limit its consequences if it occurred. Today the possibilities for placing political and moral limits on nuclear war are so minimal that the moral task . . . is prevention."[12] In sum, strategic thinkers and ethicists have generally agreed that nuclear war is morally wrong because the political goals could not legitimize the society-wide destruction resulting from a major nuclear conflict.

Like nuclear war, nuclear deterrence is evil. It is evil because it threatens to do what is morally impermissible, namely, to carry out mass destruction. Although threats and actions are not morally identical, nuclear deterrence bears some of the evil of nuclear war because the credibility of deterrence rests partly on the fact that nuclear weapons might be used. In assessing the morality of nuclear deterrence from an ends-based perspective, the issue comes to this: Can the implicit or explicit threat of nu-clear retaliation be morally justified by the policy's alleged contributions to peace and security? Because the answer will depend on the good that is achieved in light of the evil involved in the threat, I briefly examine various costs and benefits, evils and goods, involved in nuclear deterrence.

In assessing the evil involved in nuclear deterrence, numerous factors need to be considered. First, the aim of deterrence is not to inflict destruction but to prevent unwanted behavior through the promise of unacceptable punishment. Thus, deterrence does not intend evil; rather, it seeks to do good (e.g., prevent aggression or foster peace) by threatening evil (retaliation). Second, the extent of evil involved in explicit or implicit nuclear threats is difficult to ascertain, in great part because of the infinite number of degrees of intention involved, varying from a bluff (a threat without a commitment to fulfill it) to assured retaliation (certain punishment in response to aggression). Third, although scholars hold different views on the moral effect of intentions and actions, ethicists generally concur that intentions do not bear the same moral consequences as actions. As a result, because the threat of force is normally considered to involve less evil than the use of force itself, nuclear deterrence is likewise not considered to be morally commensurate with nuclear war. Finally, not all strategic policies are morally equivalent. Because a major aim of deterrence is to achieve political goals without resorting to nuclear war, strategies that maintain a robust "firebreak," or gap, between conventional and nuclear arms (thereby maintaining a low risk of nuclear conflict) will be judged more acceptable morally than those strategies that undermine the firebreak.[13] Thus, nuclear strategies that inhibit resort to war (e.g., counter-value strategies based on massive nuclear retaliation) will be deemed more morally preferable than those that encourage limited nuclear war-fighting strategies (e.g., counterforce strategies based on small, accurate, flexible threats).[14]

Despite the evil involved in relying on nuclear arms, such weapons contribute to the well-being of global society in a number of ways. First, nuclear deterrence can inhibit aggression. Because of the enormous power of nuclear arms, nuclear or conventional attack is virtually unthinkable. John Mearsheimer writes, "The more horrible the prospect of war, the less likely war is. Deterrence is more robust when conquest is more difficult. Potential aggressor states are given pause by the patent futility of attempts at expansion."[15] Second, nuclear deterrence can promote international stability and foster world peace. It does so because deterrence helps preserve the status quo. In international politics, nuclear deterrence fosters global stability because it prevents aggression and forcible changes in global cartography. A number of scholars have argued that despite significant conflict between the United States and the Soviet Union during the Cold War, the existence of a nuclear balance between them and their respective allies resulted in a "long peace," unprecedented in modern history. In writing about the postwar peace, strategist Thomas Schelling observes, "Those 40 years of living with nuclear weapons without warfare are not only evidence that war can be avoided but are themselves part of the reason why it can be."[16] Finally, nuclear weapons can provide security at a comparatively low cost, thereby conserving scarce national resources. For example, in extending the nuclear shield to Western Europe during the Cold War, the United States was able to deter potential aggression from the much larger conventional Warsaw Pact forces by maintaining a defense strategy of "flexible response" based in part on nuclear arms.

From a consequentialist, or ends-based, perspective, nuclear deterrence is considered morally legitimate when the strategy's beneficial outcomes (e.g., the prevention of aggression, the fostering of regional peace, and the maintenance of global order) outweigh its evils (e.g., the threat to carry out massive nuclear retaliation). This is the conclusion of many strategists and ethicists who have examined this extraordinarily complex moral problem. Walzer, for example, argues that in conditions of supreme emergency—when the existence of a state is threatened by potential aggression—nuclear deterrence can provide a morally defensible strat-

egy. In defending nuclear deterrence, he writes that "we threaten evil in order not to do it, and the doing of it would be so terrible that the threat seems in comparison to be morally defensible."[17] Following a similar consequentialist logic, the U.S. Catholic bishops conclude their pastoral letter on nuclear strategy by conditionally endorsing deterrence. Deterrence, they suggest, can be justified only temporarily while states seek to reduce political tensions and carry out arms control and disarmament. They conditionally defend such a strategy in light of geopolitical realities because that they believe that it contributes to "peace of a sort."[18]

From an ends-based perspective, nuclear deterrence is morally permissible only if deterrence succeeds in keeping peace and nuclear retaliation is unnecessary. However, how is strategic success to be ascertained? For example, numerous scholars have argued that the general global peace achieved during the Cold War was a result of the existence of nuclear weapons and the implicit strategy of nuclear deterrence. Historian John Lewis Gaddis has argued that the "long peace" of the second half of the twentieth century was due in part to the superpowers' nuclear arsenals, which made major war between them unthinkable.[19] Schelling also attributes the unprecedented Cold War order to nuclear weapons.[20] Others, however, have argued that nuclear weapons and the threats they pose have been largely irrelevant to global order.[21] Because the efficacy of deterrence can be proved ultimately only by its failure, it is impossible to either confirm or disprove the claim that nuclear weapons contributed to the Cold War's long peace. Still, there can be little doubt that the existence of major nuclear stockpiles contributed to fear of nuclear war, which in turn inhibited major military conflict between superpowers.

MORAL REFLECTIONS

This case study raises several important issues about the strategy of nuclear deterrence as well as the ends-based ethical reasoning used to justify it.

- Given the extraordinary destructiveness of nuclear armaments, are such weapons fundamentally immoral? Because nuclear arms "explode" the just-war doctrine, is it moral for states to possess and threaten to use them?
- Although it is evident that war and the threat of war are both evil, is the threat of war less evil than war itself? As suggested previously, is nuclear deterrence more moral than nuclear war?
- Because deterrence might fail, does the possibility of carrying out nuclear retaliation undermine the moral justification of deterrence? More particularly, is it immoral to declare a policy of deterrence if there is no intention of ever fulfilling the threat? In effect, is a policy of deceit morally permissible if it contributes to global order and inhibits aggression?
- Is the resort to nuclear war, however limited, ever morally permissible? If deterrence fails, is it morally permissible to carry out the promised nuclear punishment?
- Is the proliferation of nuclear weapons contrary to the order and well-being of the international system? In mid-1998, both India and Pakistan, sworn mutual enemies that have fought three wars in the postwar era, each carried out five nuclear tests. Western nations, especially the United States, strongly condemned these nuclear tests, implying that the attempt to acquire nuclear weapons was contrary not only to the nonproliferation norms but also to international morality. Is the development of nuclear capabilities by India and Pakistan contrary to international ethics?
- Is an ends-based ethic an adequate methodology for judging nuclear deterrence? Is it an adequate ethical strategy for assessing and implementing a moral foreign policy?

RULE-BASED ACTION

Rule-based analysis, known as *deontological thinking* (from the Greek word *deon*, meaning "duty" or "obligation"), denies what consequentialist analysis asserts, namely, that an action is good or bad, depending on the goodness or badness of its consequences. Deontologists assert that actions should be judged by their inherent rightness and validity, not by the goodness or badness of policy outcomes. Because deontological thinking places a premium on duty and right intention, rule-based analysis is agent-centered, emphasizing duties and obligations of actors, not the results of decisions. Thus, this approach or methodology appeals to the goodness of policies themselves, not to their effects. As a result, ethical decision making is determined mainly by the morality of goals and intentions. Decisions that disregard moral obligations or utilize morally questionable means are themselves immoral, even if desirable outcomes are achieved. For example, from a deontological perspective, the fire bombing of Dresden and Tokyo, carried out by the allies to defeat Germany and Japan, is regarded as immoral because civilians were part of the intended targets of those raids. Because reliance on evil means can never be condoned, even if it results in good outcomes, the use of evil means (intentionally killing civilians) cannot be justified by good intentions (defeating the Axis powers).

However, how can a statesman or political decision maker know what his or her ethical duties are? How are goals and methods to be determined to ensure ethical action? Immanuel Kant, the eighteenth-century German philosopher and father of rule-based analysis, argues that the rightness of a rule or action should be based on the *categorical imperative*. This principle has two key dimensions: First, persons should be treated as having value themselves (i.e., persons are always ends, never a means to an end). Second, individuals should act in accordance with principles or maxims that can be universalized.[22] Kant defines the universalization norm as follows: "Act only on the maxim through which you can at the same time will that it should become a universal law." In other words, ethical decision making should be judged on the basis of the extent to which a principle should be applied to others. It is important to emphasize that in Kantian ethics moral obligations should be fulfilled not because they are more effective in creating a better, more just world but because that is what moral action requires. "An action done from duty has its moral worth," Kant observed, "not in the purpose to be attained by it, but in the maxim in accordance with which it is to be decided upon." Finally, how can persons discover which moral principles should guide their behavior? According to Kant, reason is the faculty by which norms can be discovered and applied.

A deontological approach contributes important perspectives about the development of ethical behavior, especially its emphasis on good intentions and the inherent value of persons. A Kantian perspective is important because it guards against the relativism of consequentialism. However, critics of rule-based analysis have suggested that deontological ethics is overly rigid in requiring universal or absolutist morality. In view of the vagaries and contingencies of life, some critics argue that principles need to be adapted to the specific cultural environment and particular circumstances in which actions are carried out. Lying is wrong, but under some circumstances, so goes the argument, it might be morally permissible, such as to protect a child from a madman or to threaten massive destruction to prevent aggression. Moreover, critics argue that Kantianism is unduly optimistic in at least two respects. First, it assumes that human beings have the capacity to rationally identify appropriate moral rules. Second, it assumes that human beings will behave in accordance with known moral obligations.

Although political actions based solely on moral obligations are rare, rule-based action is nonetheless undertaken periodically in global society by states and other international nonstate actors in fulfillment of perceived moral duties. For example, throughout the Cold War era, Western democratic countries provided significant economic assistance to developing nations, in great part because of the conviction that economically prosperous states had a moral obligation to assist poor peoples. In his study of postwar foreign aid, David Lumsdaine found that the strongest source of support for assisting poor countries was "the sense of justice and compassion."[23] Similarly, countries have often responded to the great human suffering perpetrated by civil war by allowing refugees to temporarily settle within their borders, and government and nongovernment actors have frequently provided massive food aid to alleviate hunger and starvation. Additionally, beginning in 1997, the United States provided foodstuffs to North Korea, a communist enemy state, to relieve starvation in that land.

To illustrate rule-based action, I next examine the humanitarian assistance that the United States provided Soviet Russia in 1921–1923.

CASE 2-2: FAMINE RELIEF FOR SOVIET RUSSIA

BACKGROUND

In 1921, a massive famine developed in Soviet Russia, threatening the lives of some thirty million persons. Seven years of civil and international wars had devastated agricultural production, and when drought hit the Volga valley in the southwestern region of the Soviet Union, it resulted in a disastrous crop failure, leading to unprecedented mass starvation. Hundreds of thousands of Russian peasants fled their rural communities in search of food, flooding major cities and further aggravating famine-related epidemics, especially typhus and smallpox. The Bolshevik revolutionary rulers recognized that the famine threatened not only the lives of tens of millions of Russians but also the new Marxist regime itself. In light of Soviet Russia's famine, the Russian author Maxim Gorky was authorized to make a public appeal for humanitarian assistance.

At the time of the famine, U.S. foreign relations with the Soviet Union were bitterly strained. After communists had forcefully taken control of the Russian regime in 1918, President Woodrow Wilson refused to recognize the new regime or to establish diplomatic relations with it, preferring instead to isolate the Soviet government in the hope that it would be overthrown. In the aftermath of the Bolshevik Revolution, U.S.-Soviet trade came to a virtual halt, with the Wilson administration refusing to accept Russian gold for U.S. imports because it regarded such gold as "stolen." Three issues in particular had contributed to poor relations between the West and the new Soviet government. First, the revolutionary regime had resorted to propaganda to destabilize Western governments. Second, the Soviet government had repudiated prerevolutionary foreign debts. Third, the Soviet government had expropriated foreign holdings without providing compensation, as required by international law.[24] Although U.S. investment in Russia was comparatively small, the U.S. government regarded the Soviet communist policies as contrary to international law and a threat to peaceful global political relations. Not surprisingly, when Warren Harding became president in 1921, he reaffirmed the policies that his predecessor had instituted. The United States would not attempt to overthrow the Soviet regime but would seek to weaken it politically and commercially through isolation.

The Soviet appeal for famine relief presented U.S. policy makers with a moral dilemma. On the one hand, the famine offered an opportunity to further undermine the communist government. For some, the Russian famine of 1921 appeared to be "divine retribution for Bolshevist crimes,"[25] whereas others regarded the human suffering as another instrument by which to undermine the power of the new Soviet state. At the Tenth Party Congress in March 1921, V. I. Lenin, the Bolshevik head of government, had warned his communist comrades that a major crop failure would weaken his regime and could possibly lead to the toppling of the government and the end of Soviet communism. Thus, when the crop failure became even more severe than first anticipated, the famine appeared to provide a means to advance the very goals being officially pursued by the U.S. government.

On the other hand, the severe famine offered people of goodwill an opportunity to respond to human needs—to fulfill the "good Samaritan" principle of caring for human beings in need, regardless of their race, gender, or nationality. During the nineteenth century, international humanitarian relief had been increasingly accepted as a legitimate moral obligation of peoples and states, so that by the early twentieth century famine relief was a widely accepted moral norm within the international community. For example, in the aftermath of World War I, the American people had established the American Relief Association (ARA), a nongovernment humanitarian relief organization, to coordinate famine relief in war-torn Europe. Internationally, the League of Nations, the international government system established in the aftermath of World War I, had explicitly recognized humanitarianism. According to the League's charter (Article 25), member states were expected to provide humanitarian relief in times of crises. Other evidence of the further acceptance of global society's commitment to humanitarian relief was the establishment of the International Red Cross in 1921 to strengthen coordination of international humanitarian aid.

AMERICAN HUMANITARIAN ASSISTANCE

The American response to Gorky's appeal was initiated, developed, and implemented largely by Herbert Hoover, President Harding's secretary of commerce.[26] Hoover had played a key leadership role in developing and guiding the U.S. humanitarian relief effort in Central Europe in the aftermath of World War I; and, although he was a cabinet officer, Hoover continued as head of the ARA, the principal nongovernmental relief organization in the United States. Hoover's background and moral sensibilities made him especially well equipped to address the Russian appeal for famine relief.

Fundamentally, there were two alternative policies that Hoover and other leading U.S. officials could pursue: provide assistance and thereby help alleviate human suffering or disregard the appeal and thereby reinforce the isolationist strategy of U.S. diplomacy. Hoover, along with other government leaders, decided immediately that the first moral obligation of the American people was to alleviate human suffering. Hoover recommended to Secretary of State Charles Evans Hughes that the United States provide famine relief through the ARA, but only

if four preconditions were met. First, the Soviet government had to release all Americans confined in Russian prisons. Second, the Soviet government needed to officially declare a need for relief. Third, relief workers needed to have complete freedom of movement without Soviet interference. Fourth, the Soviet government needed to provide free transportation and housing for American personnel. The ARA, for its part, would provide relief impartially to all persons in need and would carry out its work in a nonpolitical manner.[27] After brief consultations, the Soviet government agreed to these terms.

Although the ARA served as the major organization for collecting and distributing relief supplies, the U.S. government provided substantial assistance in supporting and funding the effort. At President Harding's request, in December 1921 Congress approved a humanitarian relief request of $24 million ($20 million for grain purchases and $4 million for medical supplies), a sum that was about 1 percent of the total 1921 U.S. government budget. By early 1922, the ARA had established some 35,000 distribution centers in Russia and was regularly feeding more than 10 million persons at the height of the famine in mid-1922. By mid-1923, most regions in Soviet Russia had regained agricultural self-sufficiency, resulting in the termination of the American relief effort by the end of the year. It has been estimated that the American relief effort, which involved the transfer of some 540,000 tons of food, or about 90 percent of the total, was responsible for saving at least 10.5 million lives. As Benjamin Weissman notes, the major effect of the American relief mission was "the defeat" of the worst famine in the history of modern Europe.[28]

THE ETHICS OF U.S. FAMINE RELIEF

The U.S. government's decision to permit and then directly support humanitarian relief illustrates rule-based ethical analysis, as the dominant motive in undertaking the relief mission was to respond to humanitarian needs regardless of how such aid might impact the political system. Although the U.S. government was embarked on a campaign to isolate and weaken the

Communist government, and although famine provided a natural means by which to undermine the regime, American leaders and citizens believed that it was their moral duty to relieve starvation. American officials made the commitment to humanitarian relief rather than to realpolitik because they recognized that international morality "obliges nations with food surpluses to aid famine-stricken countries regardless of their political regime."[29]

From an ethical perspective, the American policy was moral in its goals and methods but morally problematic in its overall consequences. Famine relief saved the lives of millions of peasants, but it also unwittingly helped keep in power a despotic, revolutionary regime. Although scholars differ on the impact of the humanitarian relief program on the stability of the Soviet regime, some argue that the assistance helped stabilize and strengthen the communist regime. George Kennan, for example, argues that the Soviet government was "importantly aided, not just in its economic undertakings, but in its political prestige and capacity for survival" by the American humanitarian assistance.[30] Regardless of how much ARA's relief program contributed to the stabilization of the Soviet communist regime, it is evident that American benevolence directly contradicted its official policy of undermining the Bolshevik regime.

MORAL REFLECTIONS

This case study suggests a number of important moral issues about both famine relief and the ethical methodology employed in developing the aid policy.

- Since the U.S. decision to offer famine relief to Russia was influenced in part by the reliance on a rule-based ethical methodology, did U.S. policy succeed in fulfilling the humanitarian norm?
- If U.S. leaders had applied a consequentialist methodology, what might have been the response to Gorky's appeal for food?
- In view of the great human suffering and political oppression imposed domestically by the totalitarian communist regime in the decades following the famine—suffering that led to more than thirty million deaths and untold human rights abuses— would the denial of food aid have been a morally appropriate response? In other words, would efforts to undermine the existing communist regime through the denial of food aid have been a moral response?
- In view of the differences between rule-based and ends-based analysis, how should policy makers determine which ethical methodology is appropriate in making foreign policy? Is a rule-based strategy morally superior to an ends-based strategy, as most ethicists contend?

TRIDIMENSIONAL ETHICS

The two ethical strategies sketched previously emphasize different ways of applying moral norms to international relations. Moreover, the alternative methodologies apply moral values and judgments to different elements of ethical decision making. Ends-based analysis judges the morality of acts mainly on the basis of their consequences, whereas rule-based analysis judges the morality of acts mainly on the basis of goals and intentions. Philosophers typically identify with the latter approach, whereas decision makers typically rely on the former. Although both the consequentialist and the deontological viewpoints offer important perspectives in developing ethical decision making, neither approach is sufficient. Indeed, both are essential in developing morally prudent foreign policies and just global political relations. Stanley Hoffmann has written, "I repeat that morality is not merely a matter of ends or intentions, and that the likely consequences of acts must be taken into account . . . . [A] morality that relies exclusively on expected, calculated outcomes is not acceptable either: no statesman can be sure of all effects, and confident that he will be able to avoid perverse ones altogether. Neither pure conviction nor unbridled 'consequentialism' will do."[31]

As noted previously, ethical actions typically involve three distinct elements: motives, means, and results. Whereas political actions are commonly judged in terms of one or possibly two of these dimensions, a sound ethical strategy must assess action in terms of each of these dimensions. Political ethics, in effect, should be tridimensional. Table 2-1 identifies eight different decision-making scenarios based on this tridimensional framework. From the eight possible options, the most desirable policy is clearly scenario 1 and the least desirable is scenario 8. To the extent that good intentions are important in decision making, scenarios 5, 6, and 7 are morally problematic, although scenarios 5 and 7 have some legitimacy since good ends are realized despite the evil intentions. Moreover, it is clear that scenarios 5 and 7 are morally preferable to scenarios 2 and 4, both of which have bad outcomes.

Because few public policy issues are totally evil (scenario 8) or totally good (scenario 1), most issues and problems in global politics are likely to involve a mixture of justice and injustice. When confronted with choices among different decision-making issues, such as between scenarios 2 and 3, how should the statesman decide? One possible approach is to rely on a particular ethical strategy, choosing actions that are consistent with either an ends-based or a rule-based methodology. All that is required is to select a consequentialist or deontological methodology and to apply it as consistently as possible.

Another preferable approach is to make the necessary trade-offs between means and results, translating ethical intentions and purposes into actions that will maximize morally desirable outcomes. This approach is essentially the practice of *pru-*

Table 2-1 Three Dimensions of Moral Judgment

	Motives	*Means*	*Consequences*
Scenario 1	good	good	good
Scenario 2	good	good	bad
Scenario 3	good	evil	good
Scenario 4	good	bad	bad
Scenario 5	bad	bad	good
Scenario 6	bad	good	bad
Scenario 7	bad	good	good
Scenario 8	bad	bad	bad

SOURCE: Adapted from Joseph S. Nye, Jr., *Nuclear Ethics* (New York: Free Press, 1986), 22.

dence, or practical wisdom. From an ideal, tridimensional perspective, prudence is best implemented in public affairs by the pursuit of moral goals through morally legitimate means that result in good outcomes (scenario 1). Decision-makers pursue prudence when they seek to implement the common good by weighing different alternatives and then choosing the best one in light of relevant moral criteria.

According to Alberto Coll, the prudence tradition, as exemplified by Aristotle, Thomas Aquinas, and Edmund Burke, has two distinctive features. First, while acknowledging the evil of human affairs, prudence insists on the ultimate authority of morality over circumstances, of "ought" over "is." Second, prudence regards human virtue and personal character rather than religion, ideology, or worldview, as the major determinants of moral statecraft.[32] A well-developed moral philosophy, although important, is not sufficient to ensure moral action in the political world. Moral leadership thus depends not on technical competence but on character and personal integrity.

However, because prudential decision making provides no fixed norms to guide the process of trade-offs among relevant norms, decision making in foreign affairs can quickly succumb to consequentialism. To protect the tridimensional system from becoming simply a tool of ends-based thinking, decision-makers need to follow norms that contribute to moral accountability. One useful set of rules has been developed by Nye, who argues that ethical decision making is encouraged when it is guided by the following five norms: 1) clear, logical, and consistent standards; 2) impartiality (i.e., respect for others' interests); 3) a presumption in favor of rules: 4) procedures that protect impartiality: and 5) prudence in calculating results.[33] In short, a tridimensional ethical framework can contribute to moral action provided that decision makers rely on norms that protect the moral reasoning process from consequentialism.

To explore the nature and role of the tridimensional strategy, I next explore the morality of President Reagan's Strategic Defense Initiative (SDI).

CASE 2-3: THE ETHICS OF SDI

BACKGROUND

In the early 1980s, President Ronald Reagan called on the U.S. scientific community to investigate the possibility of developing a defensive system against ballistic nuclear missiles. In his famous "star wars" speech, delivered on March 23, 1983, the president suggested that because it was preferable "to save lives than to avenge them," the United States should explore the feasibility of shifting its nuclear strategy from offense to defense. Thus, he proposed that the U.S. scientific community explore the technologi-

cal feasibility of developing a comprehensive defense system against ballistic missiles. As perceived by President Reagan and some of his advisers, the short-term aim of the initiative was to provide limited protection from deliberate or accidental attack; the long-term aim would be to render strategic nuclear arms "impotent and obsolete."[34]

As envisioned by some scientists, the idea of SDI involved a multilayered defensive system. Because the trajectory of a ballistic missile typically involves several stages, strategic defense would attempt to destroy enemy missiles and warheads in each of them, but especially in the first (boost) and last (terminal) phases. Scientists acknowledged that the most important phase in which to destroy a missile was in its first phase, when the missile was flying more slowly and all its warheads were still together. Once the missile entered space and launched its warheads, tracking and destroying the nuclear warheads would be much more difficult. The other critical phase for SDI was the terminal stage, when warheads were reentering the atmosphere. According to SDI reasoning, if it were possible to destroy 50 percent of all enemy missiles and warheads in each of the four major missile phases, then only 6 or 7 warheads out of 100 launched would reach their targets. Although a success rate of 93 percent or 94 percent would still allow for mass destruction, SDI advocates argued that an increased defensive capability would greatly contribute to national security from deliberate or accidental attack.

From 1984 until 1990, the U.S. government devoted more than $20 billion to SDI research. When the program was launched, some defense analysts estimated that a modest strategic defense system would cost as much as $150 billion and that a comprehensive system might cost more than $1 trillion.[35] However, the most damaging criticism of SDI came from the scientific community, which argued that a comprehensive shield was technologically unfeasible in the near future. In an important article in 1985, four influential thinkers argued that there was no prospect that science and technology could in the near future "make nuclear weapons 'impotent and obsolete.'"[36]

The SDI also raised profound issues about shifting the national security paradigm from strategic offense to strategic defense. Would a shift from mutual assured destruction (MAD) toward mutual assured security (MAS) foster peace and world order? If military conflict among superpowers were to occur, would the existence of SDI reduce wartime destruction? In the final analysis, was SDI morally desirable? In exploring the morality of SDI here, I assess the proposed initiative using a tridimensional framework that emphasizes moral judgment based on intentions, means, and outcomes.

TRIDIMENSIONAL ASSESSMENT

The fundamental aim of SDI was to defend a country from ballistic missile attack. Because the initiative's basic goal was to develop and deploy a ballistic missile defense system that would protect society from nuclear aggression, the intentions of SDI were morally unassailable. Thus, at the level of *intentions,* SDI was wholly ethical.

At the level of *means*, SDI sought to develop a system of satellites, missiles, laser beams, and other instruments that would protect society from deliberate or accidental nuclear attack. Whereas the existing offensive nuclear policy also sought to protect society, SDI's method was radically different. Whereas MAD inhibited nuclear aggression by threatening unacceptable nuclear retaliation (deterrence), SDI aimed to protect society by destroying nuclear missiles. In promoting SDI, Reagan administration officials emphasized the moral superiority of SDI over MAD by noting that the former would destroy weapons only, whereas MAD would destroy cities. Of course, Reagan's comparison was disingenuous, as SDI was not an unambiguous defense system. As Leon Wieseltier observed at the time, "The notion that SDI is a purely defensive system is an insult to intelligence. If a laser beam can hit a missile that has been launched, it can hit a missile that has not been launched, too. Between offense and defense, these systems are essentially ambiguous."[37] Although SDI proponents viewed the space-based defense initiative as purely defensive, SDI critics argued that such a system could also be offensive, increasing a state's overall strategic nuclear capabilities. Thus, given SDI's uncertain role involving both defensive and offensive capabilities, the means of SDI were necessarily morally ambiguous.

At the level of *likely consequences* SDI presented even greater challenges. Using three widely accepted arms control goals (war avoidance, the minimization of destruction in war, and the reduction in weapons expenditures), strategic defense could be considered moral to the extent that it reduced the risk of war, decreased the potential for wartime destruction, and reduced the cost of military defense. In terms of the war-avoidance standard, however, SDI was unlikely to be as effective as MAD because the latter policy sought to keep the peace through the threat of nuclear retaliation, whereas SDI sought to protect society by destroying nuclear missiles and warheads. As noted earlier in this chapter (see Case 2-1), it is widely assumed that nuclear deterrence contributed to global order and stability during the Cold War. Given the record attributed to nuclear deterrence, most strategists doubted that a shift in strategy from nuclear offense to nuclear defense would strengthen international peace.

Minimizing the destruction and violence of war—the second standard—could of course be realized much more effectively by SDI than strategic offense. Because SDI sought to protect society from missile attack, SDI was clearly more effective than strategic offense in limiting wartime damage. Thus, SDI was morally superior to MAD in fulfilling this arms control norm.

Finally, although policy advocates differed greatly on the anticipated cost of developing and deploying a comprehensive strategic defense system, it was clear that deploying even a modest strategic defense system would be exceptionally expensive, costing as much as $500 billion. Although the replacement of MAD with a MAS system could potentially reduce long-term national security expenditures, the transition from strategic offense to strategic defense was expected to be difficult, unpredictable, and very costly. Clearly, from a short- and medium-term budgetary perspective, maintaining the existing strategic nuclear system was preferable to undertaking the expensive and uncertain transition to a MAS security.

Thus, although SDI was morally impeccable at the level of intentions, the program's means

and likely outcomes raised profound moral questions. To be sure, SDI was morally troubling because of its inordinate costs. However, SDI's more serious shortcomings were doctrinal. Because SDI tended to undermine deterrence, some SDI critics argued that the shift from MAD, a predictable and stable global order based on strategic offense, to MAS, an uncertain and elusive global order based on an unpredictable strategic defense, might lead to greater global instability.

MORAL REFLECTIONS

When President Reagan was seeking support for his initiative, he claimed that SDI was a more moral system than nuclear deterrence because the former was defensive, whereas the latter was offensive.

- Assuming that a comprehensive strategic defense system could have been developed, was President Reagan's judgment about the moral superiority of MAS over MAD justified? Was the evil involved in nuclear deterrence reduced by the adoption of an SDI strategy?
- In Case 2-3, it was suggested that from a tridimensional perspective SDI was morally ambiguous. Do you agree with this assessment? Why or why not?
- If decision-makers had assessed SDI on the basis of an ends-based strategy, how would the initiative have been assessed morally? What would have been the moral judgment of SDI from a rule-based strategy?

SUMMARY

International political action can be undertaken using a variety of ethical strategies. The three major types of decision-making strategies are ends-based analysis, rule-based analysis, and tridimensional analysis. Each of these approaches is distinguished by different emphases given to intentions, goals, and outcomes. Although each of these ethical methodologies can contribute to the moral basis of a sound foreign policy, I have suggested that a comprehensive, tridimensional strategy might offer the most effective approach to integrating morality with international political action.

Chapter Three

The Role of Ethical Traditions

There is a truth in realism that ought not to be lost sight of: In the hands of public officials, moral principle is too easily transformed into crusading doctrine, which invites misperception, rhetorical manipulation, and public hypocrisy.[1]
                                    —CHARLES BEITZ

A democratic definition of the national interest does not accept the distinction between a morality-based and an interest-based foreign policy. Moral values are simply intangible interests.[2]
                                    —JOSEPH S. NYE, JR.

It is the easiest thing in the world to proclaim a good. The hard part is to think through ways by which this good can be realized without exorbitant costs and without consequences that negate the good. That is why an ethic of responsibility must be cautious, calculating a perennially uncertain mass of means, costs and consequences.[3]
                                    —PETER BERGER

MOST HUMAN ACTIONS are based on moral presuppositions. Whether or not persons recognize such moral predispositions explicitly, human decision making will be based, of necessity, on moral assumptions. The moral assumptions that influence human choices are not random but tend to be a part of general ethical paradigms or traditions. Although these ethical perspectives vary greatly in terms of their nature and relevance in global politics, they play an influential role in the conduct of foreign relations, providing ethical road maps to decision-makers. Thus, when statesmen develop and implement foreign policies, they utilize particular ethical frameworks that establish the parameters within which issues are debated and decided.

For example, Otto von Bismarck, Germany's chancellor from 1870 to 1890, pursued domestic and international policies that were profoundly influenced by his realist Christian worldview—a dualistic Lutheran perspective emphasizing a radical distinction between the temporal and spiritual realms. As a devout believer, Bismarck pursued a life of personal piety, but as a statesman he believed that he was responsible for using political power to bring about political order, even if it entailed power politics and war. By contrast, William E. Gladstone, a British prime minister in the late nineteenth century, sought to carry out his political responsibilities as a Christian idealist—a believer who, unlike Bismarck, assumed that there was no radical discontinuity between personal and political morality, between individual obligations and government duties. In examining the leadership styles of these two prominent European statesmen, it is clear that different religious and ethical perspectives influenced the nature and style of their leadership.[4]

As noted earlier, when political leaders and government officials apply moral values to public policy decisions, they use ethical strategies that guide the process of ethical reasoning and moral judgment. In the previous chapter, I described two major ethical methodologies that linked good and bad, right and wrong, to substantive moral rules (rule-based action) and to consequences (ends-based action). In this chapter, I explore a related but different dimension of ethical decision making, namely, the nature and role of ethical traditions in the making, implementation, and interpretation of foreign policy. Whereas ethical strategies provide procedures and methodologies for applying moral norms to political decisions, ethical traditions provide the framework for structuring the process of moral decision making. Thus, whereas ethical strategies influence how moral values are applied in public life, ethical traditions provide the substantive norms and principles for judging political decisions and public policies.

This chapter begins by sketching the nature and role of ethical traditions in foreign affairs. It then examines realism and idealism, two of the most influential ethical traditions in twentieth-century American foreign relations, and illuminates their role with two case studies: one ancient (the Peloponnesian War) and the other modern (President Jimmy Carter's human rights policy).

THE NATURE AND ROLE OF ETHICAL TRADITIONS

Terry Nardin defines a tradition as "the thing handed down, the belief or custom transmitted from one generation to another."[5] As utilized here, an ethical tradition refers to a system of substantive moral rules and normative principles that have been passed along from generation to generation and that have been recognized as imposing binding obligations, achieving, as one scholar notes, authority that is something equivalent to "the force of law."[6] Although traditions are based on a variety of sources, including religion, political consent, law, and culture, widespread customary practice is essential in the development of a tradition. Indeed, a tradition's authority is a direct by-product of the extent to which its values, practices, and customs have been institutionalized.

A number of different ethical traditions influence the conduct of contemporary international relations. Indeed, in their study *Traditions of International Ethics*, Terry Nardin and David Mapel identify twelve major ethical traditions, including international law, realism, natural law, Judeo-Christianity, Marxism, Kantianism, utilitarianism, liberalism, and human rights.[7] Some of these traditions utilize ends-based analysis (e.g., realism, utilitarianism, and Marxism), whereas others rely on rule-based analysis (e.g., natural law, Kantianism, liberalism, and human rights). Although all these traditions have influenced modern international politics, the analysis here focuses on only two of these: *idealism* and *realism*. These two traditions are important because they have served, and continue to serve, as dominant U.S. foreign policy paradigms.

Before analyzing idealism and realism, it is important to call attention to one problem posed by competing ethical traditions. Although traditions provide the moral architecture to identify and apply morality to the conduct of foreign relations, the existence of competing and conflicting moral traditions poses a serious challenge to the universal demands of moral obligation. Because statesmen and political officials from a given country often rely on different traditions, the ethical deliberations that they undertake are likely to result in different emphases, if not different policy conclusions. Moreover, because statesmen from different countries are even more likely to apply different ethical traditions, the challenge in reconciling conflicting moral claims is even greater in international diplomacy. For example, Dutch political leaders applying Kantian, realist, and legal traditions are likely to draw different policy conclusions about genocide in Rwanda or about peacemaking within Bosnia. However, French, Indian, Russian, and Japanese diplomats, representing not only divergent ethical traditions but also divergent political cultures, are likely to draw policy conclusions even more disparate than officials from a single country.

David Welch observes that, because policy conclusions drawn from a particular tradition are likely to be accepted only by adherents to that tradition, the existence of a plurality of traditions poses a major challenge, namely, how to select the most desirable one.[8] However, if a tradition is to be adopted on moral grounds, ethical criteria extrinsic to any particular tradition will be required to select the most desirable one. Because such criteria do not exist, Welch concludes that there is no authoritative ethical method of selecting a preferable tradition. Thus, Welch suggests that, rather than relying on an ethical tradition, one should apply ethics based on moral consensus, or what he terms "conventionalism." According to such a system, right and wrong, justice and injustice are defined by consent among the relevant parties. Whatever they agree to regard as just or legitimate is just or legitimate.[9]

Although an ethical system rooted in agreement might be more palatable in confronting the problem of cultural pluralism noted in chapter 1, consensus does not provide a satisfactory basis for morality. As English philosopher David Hume observed long ago, consent provides no adequate basis for morality because it is impossible to develop a theory of moral obligation from existing facts, that is, to derive "ought" from "is."[10] To be sure, identifying shared moral norms among different societies can contribute to the development of authoritative moral regimes. For example, postwar efforts by the United Nations and its related agencies to define human rights have resulted in a more robust doctrine of rights. Notwithstanding significant differences in human rights conceptions, transnational discussion and deliberation have contributed to the internationalization of rights. However, the proliferation of global human rights discourse has not necessarily strengthened the ethical foundation of international rights claims. Indeed, as contemporary history has demonstrated, regimes not only have frequently pursued policies involving gross human rights violations but also have sought to justify such actions.

Despite the challenges posed by competing ethical traditions, there is no need to jettison them. Although a plurality of traditions can make authoritative ethical judgments more difficult, it need not paralyze ethical reasoning. Indeed, the existence of multiple traditions can provide alternative systems for judging moral action, thereby strengthening moral analysis.

REALISM

Realism, arguably the oldest ethical tradition relevant to international relations, dates from the origins of political thought in the ancient Greek civilization. The historian Thucydides, author of the classic *History of the Peloponnesian War*, is often regarded as the father of realism. Other ancient and modern political thinkers who contributed decisively to the development of this tradition include St. Augustine, Niccolò Machiavelli, and Thomas Hobbes. In the twentieth century, scholars such as Herbert Butterfield, E. H. Carr, Robert Gilpin, Hans Morgenthau, George Kennan, and Reinhold Niebuhr have contributed to the further development and application of realism in modern international relations.

Like most traditions, political realism is not easily defined, in part because it is a living, dynamic tradition that is continuously evolving and also because it is a pluralistic movement comprised of distinct strands. For example, the Christian realist strand emphasizes the role of human nature in the development and maintenance of political order, whereas classical realism emphasizes the nature, role, and distribution of power in the development of political order, whether domestic or international. Moreover, *structural realism*, sometimes called *neorealism*, focuses on the nature and implications of political structures of global society. Such an approach differs from classical realism in that it disregards human nature and political morality and focuses exclusively on structural patterns and behavioral norms that explain the political behavior of states in the anarchic international environment.

Characteristics

Despite significant disparities among its different schools, the ethical tradition of realism is a coherent and powerful political worldview, deeply influencing the nature of decision making in the international community. Some of the tradition's most important elements include a pessimistic view of human nature, the priority of power in developing and maintaining political order, the primacy of the state in global politics, the anarchic character of international society, and the priority of consequences in making ethical judgments. I now briefly examine each of these norms.

First, realists assume that human nature is motivated mainly by self-interest. Because individuals and groups tend to seek their own interests first, often in disregard for or at the expense of the interests of others, the establishment of a peaceful and just order is a difficult and never-ending task. In developing political order, realists believe that political action should always be guided by how human beings are likely to behave rather than on how they ought to behave. Although realists hold a pessimistic view of human nature, they believe that the development of order and justice in the anarchic global community can be advanced through policies based on power. Because realists assume that peace is a by-product of an international balance of power, they believe that the management of power is a central requirement in pursuing a moral foreign policy. Only by balancing and counterbalancing the power of other states can a state contribute to global order and thereby help establish the precondition for international justice.

Second, realism emphasizes power. In fact, Hans Morgenthau, arguably the most influential postwar international relations realist, views politics, whether domestic or international, as essentially a struggle for power.[11] This struggle is more pronounced in global society because there is no central authority to moderate and resolve interstate disputes. Not surprisingly, Morgenthau views statesmen as officials who "think and act in terms of interest defined as power."[12] Moreover, because there is no central authority to ensure the existence of nation-states and the promotion of their national interests, Morgenthau argues that if statesmen disregard power, they will become the victims of those who have learned to acquire and use it.

Third, realism is characterized by its state-centric approach. It assumes that, although many actors participate in global politics (e.g., international organizations, nongovernmental organizations, multinational corporations, religious movements, and individuals), the main actor is the nation-state. The dominance of nation-states is rooted in the fact that they are sovereign, that is, independent, self-governing political communities not subject to any higher authority. Because power is the principal determinant of a state's capacity to act independently in the world community, the degree of a state's self-government will depend greatly on its own political, military, and economic resources. However, a state's capabilities will also be due in great measure to the capabilities of other states, which can challenge other states' power. Nation-states are a relatively recent development, dating from the mid-seventeenth century, and although they might someday be replaced by other structures, such as a global federal government or regional political unions, realists assume that nation-states will remain the principal actors in global politics in the foreseeable future.

Fourth, realism assumes that the international community is a decentralized, anarchic environment—a self-help system. According to Kenneth Waltz, such a system is one "in which those who do not help themselves, or who do so less effectively than others, will fail to prosper, will lay themselves open to dangers, will suffer."[13] Because there is no common authority in the world, each state's survival and well-being ultimately depends on its own capabilities and resources. Moreover, because the survival of states is not ensured, the most fundamental national interest is assumed to be survival. Although there are a variety of means by which states can promote their interests in the international community, realists assume that military force is the most important. Because the protection of vital interests ultimately depends on the capacity to punish aggression, states continuously seek to deter aggression by expanding their military resources and establishing alliances.

Finally, realism is characterized by its reliance on consequential ethics. Realism is often critiqued as being an amoral approach to international politics because power is regarded as the main instrument of foreign policy and national security as its principal end. One scholar, for example, argues that realism's excessive concern with national security "dissolves moral duties";[14] another suggests that the realist tradition simply excludes morality altogether from foreign policy.[15] Perhaps the most extreme realist perspective about international ethics is taken by traditional theorists such as Machiavelli and Hobbes and modern scholars such as George F. Kennan, who argue that politics is essentially an amoral activity. Kennan writes, "Government is an agent, not a principal. Its primary obligation is to the interests of the national society it represents . . . its military security, the integrity of its political life and the well-being of its people. These needs have no moral quality. They are the unavoidable necessities of national existence and therefore are subject to classification neither as 'good' or 'bad.'"[16]

However, most realists do not deny morality. Indeed, they assume with Aristotle that politics is rooted in ethics. As Morgenthau has noted, "Realism is aware of the moral significance of political action."[17] Thus, realism, is distinguished not by its amorality or immorality but by a morality of a different sort, one that differentiates political ethics from personal ethics and judges action in terms of consequences. Because of the radically different nature of individual and political obligations, realists assume that individual morality, such as the Sermon on the Mount, is not directly applicable to political action. Moreover, they believe that basing policy decisions on abstract moral principles is harmful to the conduct of foreign relations because it undermines the national interest and makes compromise more difficult. Rather than relying on isolated, detached moral norms, realists believe that decision making should be guided by the virtue of *prudence*, that is, rational decision making that seeks the greatest good from among relevant, morally acceptable alternatives. The aim is not to ensure compliance with particular moral rules and norms but to ensure the most effective realization of goals. Fundamentally, then, realism is a consequentialist-based tradition.

To illuminate some of realism's norms, I next examine Thucydides' classic exposition of the Peloponnesian War.

CASE 3-1: THE PELOPONNESIAN WAR

BACKGROUND

During the fifth century B.C., Greece was comprised of numerous independent and largely self-sufficient city-states. Because each city-state was responsible for its own security and economic welfare, ancient Greece was similar to the contemporary international system—a decentralized, anarchic political system lacking a central governing authority. States promoted their economic and security interests through military alliances and commercial trade, with two city-states dominating the interstate relations of the region: Athens, a democratic, commercial, and outward-looking regime, and Sparta, an oligarchic, agricultural, and inward-looking regime.

Early in the fifth century, the Persians tried to

extend their empire into Greece but were successfully repulsed, in great measure because of the military collaboration between Athens and Sparta. After defeating the Persians, the Spartans retreated to the Greek peninsula south of Athens (the area known as Peloponnese), and throughout the remainder of the century confined their influence largely to this region. Although Sparta had a mighty army, it limited its influence largely to the Peloponnesian peninsula, fearing that its large helot slave population might rebel if the army were away conquering new territories. As a result, Sparta's military alliance system, known as the Peloponnesian League, was confined mainly to the surrounding region. The Athenians, by contrast, attempted to deter future Persian threats by increasing their naval power and extending their economic influence throughout the Aegean Sea. Moreover, Athens institutionalized its influence in the region by establishing the Delian League, a widespread defensive alliance system comprised of some 200 city-states.

In the mid-fifth century, relations between Athens and Sparta began to deteriorate, resulting in a war (sometimes called the First Peloponnesian War), lasting from 460 to 445 B.C. This conflict ended with a negotiated settlement based on Sparta's recognition of Athens' regional influence in exchange for Athens' surrender of land acquired during the war. Although the truce was supposed to last for thirty years, within ten years tensions between the two regional powers had resumed, eventually resulting in a second war: the Great Peloponnesian War (431-404 B.C.).

ORIGINS OF WAR

Three developments contributed to the origins of the Great Peloponnesian War. First, a conflict developed between Corinth, a Spartan-aligned city-state at the mouth of the Peloponnesian peninsula, and Athens. The dispute arose when a civil war broke out in Epidamnus, a former colony of Corcyra (modern-day Corfu) located on the northwestern coast of Greece. The democratic forces of Epidamnus, after appealing unsuccessfully to Corcyra for help, requested assistance from Corinth, which decided to help. However, this pledge of Corinthian assistance angered Corcyra, which then dispatched a naval force to regain control of its former colony. En route, the Corcyrans engaged and defeated Corinthian naval forces. Fearing a counterattack from Corinth, Corcyra asked Athens for help. After carefully deliberating the pros and cons of involving itself in this conflict, Athens decided to provide modest assistance to Corcyra. Its decision was based partly on its fear that failure to support Corcyra would result in the latter's becoming aligned with Sparta. Because Corcyra had the second-largest navy in the region, its alliance with Sparta would shift the regional balance of power toward Sparta. Such a development was unacceptable to Pericles, the main military and political strategist of Athens.

A second factor contributing to the outbreak of war was a revolt at Potidaea, a former Corinthian colony on the northern Aegean coast. Because Potidaea was part of the Delian League, Athens feared that Potidaea, in response to Corinthian prodding, might revolt against Athens. Thus, it demanded that Potidaea tear down its fortifications, send away its Corinthian magistrates, and free its hostages. These actions, Athens assumed, would place Potidaea at its mercy and thereby deter rebellion. The Athenian's suspicion about Potidaea turned out to be justified, as Potidaeans had sent envoys to Sparta to request help in their rebellion.

The third development precipitating war was Athens' imposition of a limited economic embargo on Megara, a Spartan-aligned city-state located just west of Athens. The Athenian decree barred Megarians from harbors of the Athenian Empire, thereby harming the commercial sectors of Megara. Because Megara had helped Corinth in its conflict with Corcyra, Athens issued the decree to punish Megara and thereby, it was hoped, to deter other city-states from assisting Corinth.

In his *History of the Peloponnesian War,* Thucydides argues that the roots of war were sown in the growing imbalance of power between Athens and Sparta. In his words: "What made the war inevitable was the growth of Athenian power and the fear that this caused in Sparta."[18] However, Donald Kagan argues that Athenian power was not growing in the aftermath of the Thirty Years' Peace. Indeed, the only growth in Athenian power resulted from the Corinthian initiative against Corcyra in 433, some twelve years after the end of the first war.[19] Thus, for Kagan, the origins of the war are rooted not in the bipolar (Athens-Sparta) hegemonic system, which had resulted in some regional stability, but in the crises in Corcyra, Potidaea, and Megara. Although none of these developments alone would have been decisive in starting a war, taken together they fostered growing distrust and insecurity, rooted in great part in the shifting perceptions in the balance of power. For example, after Athens became aligned with Corcyra, Corinth threatened to join the Athenian alliance if Sparta failed to support its claims. As a result, Sparta felt compelled to assist Corinth. Athens, too, felt constrained by potential shifts in the regional balance of power. For example, its decision to help Corcyra was driven by fear that Corcyra, with the second-largest naval fleet, might become aligned with the Spartan league if it did not provide military support. Because a Corcyra-Corinthian-Spartan alliance would have radically altered the regional balance of power, Athens felt compelled to aid Corcyra. In addition, once Athens imposed the Megarian Decree to deter other city-states from helping Corinth, it refused to alter or withdraw the order, believing that modifying the decree would only invite other demands.

THE WAR

The war itself lasted from 431 to 404 B.C. During the first ten years there was a stalemate between Athens and Sparta, but after a temporary truce of six years, military power began to shift in favor of Sparta, in great measure because of Athens' imperial overextension. In 416, Athens decided to invade Sicily, most of whose city-states were aligned with Sparta. Despite its superior naval forces, Athens was unsuccessful in gaining control of the island. Indeed, when its forces were defeated at Syracuse, Athenian morale broke, and its military and economic power never recovered. Although Athens continued fighting for another decade, its military and economic power continued to wane. By the beginning of the fifth century, the Athenian Empire had all but collapsed, and in 404 Sparta compelled Athens to level its city walls.

REALISM AND THE WAR

The contemporary interest in this ancient war between Sparta and Athens is due in great measure to Thucydides' masterful account of the war, a history that not only describes the nature and historical evolution of the war but, more important, illuminates profound insights about the human condition and political life. Written from a realist perspective, Thucydides' study not only reveals important norms of the tradition of political realism but also applies those norms to the

interpretation of events. In effect, Thucydides' history illuminates principles that can be conducive to order and security within a decentralized global community. One scholar has suggested that Thucydides' analysis of international relations is so insightful that there is little that is now known about global politics that was not revealed by Thucydides long ago.[20] I next briefly examine some of the most important norms illuminated by Thucydides' study.

The first realist principle illustrated by the Peloponnesian War is the importance of power in interstate relations. Because in ancient Greece, as in the modern world, there was no central authority to regulate interstate relations, the security and well-being of city-states was ultimately in the hands of each state. Thus, when Persia attempted to conquer Greece, the joint military cooperation of the two leading Greek city-states, Sparta and Athens, helped defeat Persian aggression.

Thucydides' realism also illustrates the importance of a balance of power in fostering stability in an anarchic, decentralized system. Realists believe that, in the absence of government, the only effective way of developing and maintaining global order is through the maintenance of a fundamental equilibrium of power. Such a balance can be established and maintained locally, regionally, and internationally through the parties themselves and through alliances with other states. Because the only effective deterrent against aggression is countervailing power, realists assume that states need to have sufficient power to inhibit aggression and, in the event of war, to defeat an enemy state militarily. Thus, when a state increases its military and economic power, the opposing state must seek to counterbalance such changes by increasing its own power. During the Peloponnesian conflict, Spartan and Athenian officials were especially sensitive to developments that might alter the fundamental balance of power that existed in the region. Indeed, Thucydides suggests that Sparta's decision to go to war was rooted in its belief that the Athenian Empire had become too powerful and that the failure to challenge the perceived imbalance would result in even greater future suffering.

A third realist principle illuminated by the war is the importance of alliances in interstate relations. Alliances are significant because they facilitate and institutionalize economic, political, and military cooperation among states. They provide, in effect, a means to increase power. For example, Athens's establishment of the Delian League, a political and economic alliance with some 200 other Aegean city-states, contributed immeasurably to its economic prosperity and military security. However, alliances can also result in entangling relationships that can initiate and exacerbate conflict. In fact, the outbreak of the Peloponnesian War can be directly attributed to allies of Athens and Sparta. As Thucydides' account suggests, alliances can contribute to a balance of power but they can also serve as instruments of entanglement, compelling major actors into conflicts in which they have no direct, vital interests. For example, in the Peloponnesian War Sparta had no direct interests in defending Corinth, except in maintaining a regional balance of power. Similarly, Athens had no direct, vital interests in the events in Corcyra. However, because the failure of either Sparta or Athens to respond to its allies might alter the regional balance of power, each hegemon felt compelled to get involved, thereby expanding the nature and scope of the conflict. Alliances, in short, can help keep peace through the equilibrium of power, but they can also expand the scope and intensity of conflict.

A final realist norm illuminated by Thucydides is a pessimistic view of the morality of individual and collective behavior. It is a pessimistic account because human nature is assumed to be motivated mainly by self-interest, power, and fear. For Thucydides, the natural human condition is not peace, prosperity, and justice but competition, conflict, uncertainty, fear, and injustice. In light of such assumptions about human nature, political behavior within domestic societies (city-states) is regarded as competitive, conflictual, and fearful; however, it is also influenced by "honor," which involves defending and advancing the interests of the political community to which citizens belong. Notwithstanding the limitations of human nature, Thucydides views the city as a moral community, because

the governing authorities have the potential of advancing justice through rational deliberation. However, this is not the case in the anarchic interstate system, in which relations among city-states are governed by rivalry, conflict, and fear; and, because there is no authoritative way to reconcile interests and to promote the common good, there can be little hope for justice. The best that can be hoped for is a stable, peaceful interstate environment resulting from a balanced constellation of power.

This pessimistic view of interstate political relations is most graphically illustrated in the famous debate preceding Athens's conquest of the island of Melos. In the famous Melian dialogue, the Athenians make clear that, given their status as a dominant power, they have a right to rule Melos. Thucydides describes the Athenian perspective as follows: "The standard of justice depends on the equality of power to compel and that in fact the strong do what they have the power to do and the weak accept what they have to accept."[21] Thus, the Melians can either accept Athenian rule on the basis of their dominant power or suffer defeat and annihilation. To the extent that a common good exists in the interstate system, it is to be determined and implemented by the powerful. The Melians reply that because they value political independence more highly than safety, they would prefer to fight than become Athenian slaves. After warning the Melians to surrender, the Athenians conquer the island, killing its soldiers and making slaves of women and children.

MORAL REFLECTIONS

Thucydides' account of the Peloponnesian War is part history and part political theory. By relying on a realist conception of politics, Thucydides describes and interprets events from a particular perspective, thereby illustrating the profound impact of ethical traditions on political analysis and political action.

■ Given the significant influence of the realist paradigm on Thucydides' writing, does the realist perspective distort history? Does the tradition impair the develop-

- ment of an objective account of the Athenian-Spartan war?
- The Peloponnesian War also raises several critical issues regarding the analysis of international relations. First, is power as important as realism alleges in ensuring the security of states and in fostering a stable world order?
- Is it true, as realism claims, that states are naturally inclined to counter hegemonic power by pursuing a balance of power?

- Is classical realism's pessimistic account of human nature valid, and does it explain the conflict and uncertainty in international political society?
- Does realism provide an adequate account of the role of morality in international affairs? Is it true that the anarchic international system is governed mainly by the quest for security, thereby allowing little freedom for moral action?

IDEALISM

Like realism, political idealism is a tradition rooted in ancient thought, although its application to politics, especially international relations, is comparatively recent. Two early thinkers who contributed to its early development were Thomas Aquinas, a thirteenth-century Catholic theologian, and Dante Alighieri, a fourteenth-century Italian scholar. Aquinas believed that reason could help define and establish a just political order. Despite human sinfulness, natural law could be apprehended by reason, thereby providing a basis for political justice. Dante, too, contributed to the development of the idealist tradition by emphasizing the vital role of international governmental institutions in promoting world order. In *Of Monarchy*, he argued that centralized political authority was essential for resolving interstate disputes. More particularly, he suggested that a world government ruled by a monarch was the most effective way of promoting global peace.

The most important elements of political idealism emerged in the eighteenth and nineteenth centuries with the contractarian theories of John Locke and Jean Jacques Rousseau and the liberal philosophies of thinkers such as Adam Smith, Jeremy Bentham, and John Stuart Mill. The former theories are significant because they emphasized consent as a basis of legitimate political authority, whereas the latter are important because they emphasize individual rights, especially freedom. Another significant strand of idealism emerged in the nineteenth century with the writings of the German philosopher Immanuel Kant. His analysis is important because it calls attention to the major role of domestic and international structures in promoting global order. In *On Perpetual Peace*, Kant argued that peace among nation-states is best maintained through an informal federation of republican regimes. Although Kant thought that some centralization of global power was necessary in global society, international structures alone were insufficient to ensure international peace. In addition, states themselves had to be governed responsibly, and this could occur only if regimes were based on limited, constitutional authority.

Twentieth-century statesmen and thinkers have also contributed to the further development of political idealism. For example, President Woodrow Wilson, generally considered the father of the League of Nations, developed and popularized the belief that global order could best be realized through international law and global institutions rather than realist power politics. Wilson had so much confidence in the human capacity to establish peaceful and just human communities that he espoused self-determination as a basis of world order. According to this notion, peoples sharing a common nationality and culture had a right to political self-rule. Although this claim contributed to the decolonization movement of the mid-twentieth century, it has also contributed to significant political turmoil in the post–Cold War era, as no common definition exists to determine which peoples are entitled to self-determination. President Jimmy Carter also contributed to the resurgence of political idealism in the late twentieth century with his optimistic conception of international relations and his Wilsonian confidence in law and human rights.

The idealist tradition has been expressed historically through three distinct strands: classical idealism, political liberalism, and internationalism.[22] *Classical idealism*, represented by thinkers such as Locke, Bentham, Mill, and Richard Cobden, is characterized by a belief that relations among individuals, groups, and states are fundamentally harmonious and by an emphasis on law and constitutionalism in promoting human dignity domestically and peace internationally. In the nineteenth century, idealists expressed their optimism about the cooperative and harmonious nature of human interrelationships by espousing "commercial pacifism," the belief that international trade was conducive to global peace.[23] Thus, classical idealism's distinctive feature was its optimism about the establishment and maintenance of community life, whether at the familial, local, national, or international level.

Political liberalism, the second type of idealism, is concerned with the establishment of government structures that best secure and protect human rights, especially individual liberty, the most fundamental right. Liberal theorists, such as Thomas Jefferson and James Madison, believed that because the major impediment historically to human freedom had been tyranny, the protection of individual rights required a limited, constitutional regime—one that was based on dispersed power and accountable to people through periodic elections. Although theorists have historically defined human freedom in a variety of ways, liberals have emphasized two types of liberties: basic and political-civil. Basic liberties, sometimes termed "negative freedoms," are concerned with the protection of individuals from arbitrary authority and include such rights as the freedom of conscience, the freedom of speech, the freedom of assembly, and the freedom from arbitrary imprisonment (habeas corpus) as well as the freedom to own property. Political and civil rights are those individual freedoms that are necessary to maintain a participatory, constitutional government. Political liberalism thus celebrates individual freedom and the imperative of limited, constitutional government.

The third expression of idealism is *internationalism*, an approach that emphasizes the important role of domestic structures in determining the nature of global relations. According to Kant, the father of this approach, the most effective way of promoting global peace was through the development of a "pacific federation" of liberal states. Although international institutions were important in facilitating conflict resolution and in promoting harmonious global relations, the essential precondition for world peace was the proliferation of "republics," that is, liberal regimes based on limited, constitutional authority.[24]

In the twentieth century, other practitioners and scholars have further developed internationalism. President Wilson, for example, was especially influential in propagating this approach with his call for a different type of global politics, one rooted in public opinion, open participation, and law. With the establishment of the United Nations and the growing number and influence of nongovernmental organizations in the mid-twentieth century, a more robust and formalized internationalism emerged. This approach, known as *liberal internationalism*, was based on several core assumptions. These include the following: 1) nonstate actors are increasingly important in global politics; 2) states are not unitary-rational actors; 3) national security is important, but it is not the sole or necessarily the most important state interest; 4) international institutions participate as independent actors in global society; and 5) significant international cooperation is possible both through direct initiatives of states and through international institutions.[25] Additionally, whereas classical idealism and political liberalism emphasize human nature and political morality, liberal institutionalism is mainly concerned with structural factors that contribute to global cooperation. Moreover, modern internationalism is concerned mainly with whether structures promote global cooperation, not with the effectiveness of law and institutions in global society.[26]

Characteristics

Notwithstanding the continuing evolution of political idealism and the development of differing doctrines, this tradition has remained grounded in several core assumptions. These include an optimistic view of human nature and community life, the primacy of morality over power politics, the priority of human rights and constitutional government, and the important role of law and international institutions in building political order.[27] I next examine each of these four core assumptions.

The first distinctive feature of political idealism is its optimistic view of political life, including the establishment and maintenance of a just international order. For most idealists, this optimistic view of international affairs is rooted in a benign view of human nature. Idealists have faith in the long-term beneficence and benevolence of human nature, believing, as Michael Smith has noted, that human nature "will eventually express its true interests in peace and a thoroughly reformed international system."[28] Because human beings are fundamentally good, the evil and injustice in the world is due largely to the unjust and imperfect political and economic structures of global society. Idealists also base their optimistic political assessment on the effectiveness of human reason in developing norms and facilitating international coordination and cooperation. For them, the ability to promote international peace and tranquillity is rooted in human enlightenment and rational communication and negotiation. Still other liberals view international peace and tranquillity as an automatic by-product of the utopian conviction that the vital interests of states are fundamentally complementary. This notion, which historian E. H. Carr defines as the "doctrine of harmony of interests,"[29] was expressed in a variety of ways in nineteenth-century international relations but especially in the belief that free trade encouraged international peace.

Although idealists, especially liberal institutionalists, deemphasize human nature and political morality, it is clear that idealists share an optimistic view of international political life. They believe that global harmony is possible and that states, although motivated to maximize national gains, can work cooperatively toward the common good. Although idealists might not attribute their optimistic assessment of global relations to political morality, it is clear that their assumptions about international relations are rooted in an optimistic view of individual and collective behavior.

A second distinctive feature of idealism is the important role assigned to moral values in defining foreign policy interests and strategies. Whereas realism's struggle for power leaves little room for moral judgment in foreign affairs, idealism emphasizes moral norms in developing and implementing foreign policy. Moreover, to the extent that realists make room for ethical judgment in international relations, they do so through a consequentialist strategy. Idealists, by contrast, emphasize rule-based ethics, seeking to ensure that the goals, intentions, and outcomes are consistent with common morality. However, it is important to emphasize that modern international relations scholarship has disregarded the impact of human nature on global politics while deemphasizing the role of political morality. As noted previously, liberal internationalism stresses structures and institutions, paying little attention to the role of ethics and moral values in structuring analysis of foreign policy and international politics. For example, for contemporary neoliberal scholars global social and economic cooperation is to be explained largely by structural conditions, rather than moral values. Despite the modern predilection to emphasize empirical analysis, the tradition of idealism is nonetheless grounded in political ethics.

The third distinctive feature of idealism is the priority given to human rights and to the constitutional structures essential to protecting these rights. This dimension of the idealist tradition is rooted in the doctrine of political liberalism, which developed during the seventeenth, eighteenth, and nineteenth centuries. Liberal political thinkers, such as Locke, Rousseau, Bentham, and Mill, developed theories that asserted the priority of individual rights and the responsibility of government in securing and protecting such rights. Because government oppression was thought to have been a major barrier historically to individual rights, liberal theorists argued that a primary task of government was to secure and protect such rights by establishing limited constitutional regimes. While liberal theorists devised a variety of procedures and institutions to this end, an essential feature of liberal thought was the need for periodic elections and shared government authority to ensure limited government and to inhibit tyranny.

Because the idealist tradition is rooted in liberalism, individual rights, human dignity, and political freedom are primary. Because the tradition is confident that procedures and institutions can be established to foster and protect basic rights, idealists are fundamentally optimistic about the expansion of human dignity and the promotion of communal justice. Moreover, the idealist tradition assumes that because interstate conflicts and wars are often the result of autocratic, illegitimate regimes, the spread of constitutional, democratic governments can help foster peace and global order. For example, President Wilson, who contributed significantly to the establishment of the League of Nations, believed that making governments and international diplomacy more responsive to public opinion would lead to a more stable, just international order. In fact, Wilson, along with other idealists of his era, had so much faith in the general public that he believed that secret diplomacy was counterproductive to global order. Indeed, this conviction became a rallying cry of the League of Nations' principle of "open covenants openly arrived at."

A final distinctive feature of idealism is the priority of international law and transnational organizations. Whereas realism emphasizes the balance of power in promoting international order, idealists believe that law and international structures—especially regimes and international governmental and nongovernmental organizations—contribute decisively to the development of global cooperation and world order. As noted earlier, the modern idealism expressed in the early part of the twentieth century gave special emphasis to international law and organization, whereas liberal institutionalism, the more recent expression of idealism, has emphasized state and nonstate actors that contribute to transnational cooperation and to the development of international regimes.

To illustrate the role and impact of the idealist tradition on foreign policy, I next explore President Jimmy Carter's human rights policy.

CASE 3-2: PRESIDENT CARTER'S HUMAN RIGHTS POLICY

BACKGROUND

During the 1977 presidential campaign, Democratic Party candidate Jimmy Carter emphasized repeatedly that if elected he would make the promotion of human rights a foreign policy priority. According to Zbigniew Brzezinski, his national security advisor, Carter's commitment to human rights reflected his own religious convictions as well as his political acumen. Brzezinski writes, "He deeply believed in human rights and that commitment remained constant during his Administration. At the same time, he sensed, I think, that the issue was an appealing one, for it drew a sharp contrast between himself and the policies of Nixon and Kissinger."[30]

The idea that human rights should be an integral element of U.S. foreign policy did not originate with Carter. Indeed, throughout the twentieth century, statesmen and leaders, beginning with Wilson, had periodically sought to promote human rights abroad. For Wilson and other idealists, the myth of American exceptionalism had convinced them that the world would be a better place if other countries were to adopt America's traditions of individual rights and implemented its institutions of representative government. Moreover, other recent administrations had emphasized human rights, albeit through quiet diplomacy. However, as R. J. Vincent has observed, what was different about Carter's human rights policy was the adoption of human rights both "as a standard by which to judge the conduct of others and as a set of principles that was to guide its own foreign policy."[31]

It needs to be emphasized, too, that before Carter assumed the presidency, a number of developments were underway within Congress that greatly reinforced Carter's human rights initiatives. Two of the most significant of these legislative actions were the hearings and legislative proposals of the House of Representatives Subcommittee on International Organizations and the passage of the 1975 Jackson-Vanik amendment, which linked most-favored-nation (MFN) status to compliance with human rights norms.

Beginning in 1973, Congressman Donald Fraser, chairman of the House Subcommittee on International Organizations (later renamed Human Rights and International Organizations), began holding hearings on human rights. After initial hearings, in 1974 the subcommittee issued a report calling on the U.S. government to more effectively defend human rights around the world. By the time the Fraser subcommittee ended its work in 1978, it had held some 150 hearings and was responsible for several important changes in U.S. foreign policy statutes. One of the most significant of these—the amending of Section 502B of the 1961 Foreign Assistance Act—required "that, except in extraordinary circumstances, the President shall substantially reduce or terminate security assistance to any government which engages in a consistent pattern of gross violations of internationally recognized human rights." Thus, when Carter began his presidency in 1977, Congress had already established a number of major human rights initiatives making foreign security assistance and MFN status conditional on human rights.[32]

It is important to emphasize that the principal inspiration for the development and implementation of human rights initiatives was the president himself. In fact, his idealistic worldview not only provided an optimistic outlook on international affairs but also contributed to the importance of human rights. In his inaugural address, Carter called attention to the priority of human rights and especially individual liberty. "Because we are free," Carter said, "we can never be indifferent to the fate of freedom elsewhere." Several months later, the president set forth his conception of human rights and political democracy in an important speech at the University of Notre Dame. In that address, Carter described his idealistic political worldview as follows:

Because we know that democracy works, we can reject the arguments of those rulers who deny human rights to their people. We are confident that democracy's example will be compelling. . . .We are confident that democratic methods are the most effective, and so we are not tempted to employ improper tactics here at home or abroad. . . . Being confident of our own future, we are now free of the inordinate fear of Communism which once led us to embrace any dictator who joined us in that fear. I am glad that that is being changed. . . . We can no longer separate the traditional issues of war and peace from the new global questions of justice, equity and human rights.[33]

After describing major elements of his worldview, Carter outlined several foreign policy initiatives that expressed his core convictions. Not surprisingly, his first policy initiative was human rights, not international peacekeeping, U.S.-Soviet relations, or nuclear arms control, as might have been the case under the previous Republican Party administrations.

CARTER'S HUMAN RIGHTS POLICY

After assuming office, President Carter faced the challenge of translating the human rights vision that he had articulated in the campaign into an operational policy. This was not easy, as his human rights ideas were deeply rooted in moral convictions but were not integrated into a public philosophy about international affairs. One former aide has noted that because Carter had a moral ideology but no political ideology, his human rights policy reflected "strong moral impulses tethered somewhat loosely to a set of political goals."[34] However, if U.S. foreign policy was to advance the cause of human rights, it was essential to establish realistic policies and priorities that would effectively advance such rights.

The Carter administration sought to promote human rights abroad in a variety of ways. First, it used public diplomacy—pronouncements, policy statements, declarations, and condemnations— to draw attention to the priority of rights and to regimes in which major abuses were occurring.

Second, it emphasized human rights initiatives within regional and international organizations, encouraging the further institutionalization of human rights norms. Third, it strengthened the U.S. institutional support for human rights by transforming the Department of State's Office of Human Rights into the Bureau of Human Rights, headed by an assistant secretary of state. A major task of the new bureau was to prepare an annual report on human rights abuses and violations in foreign countries.[35] Finally, the Carter administration used sanctions to promote human rights. For example, during Carter's term, the U.S. government cut its security assistance to at least eight countries and its economic aid to an even greater number of countries because of major human rights abuses.

As Carter administration officials began to express human rights concerns publicly and privately, profound tensions began to emerge not only between the United States and other governments but within the administration itself. For example, when a reporter asked an administration official in the new administration how the U.S. government viewed continuing Soviet threats against human rights activist Andrei Sakharov, the Department of State issued a statement expressing admiration for Sakharov's role as a champion of human rights within the Soviet Union. "Any attempts by the Soviet authorities to intimidate Mr. Sakharov," the statement went on to say, "will not silence legitimate criticisms in the Soviet Union and will conflict with accepted international standards in the field of human rights."[36] However, Soviet government officials did not appreciate this shift in U.S. foreign policy. In their view, no other state had a right to tell the Soviet government how to treat its citizens. As a result, Soviet Ambassador Anatoly Dobrynin immediately protested to Secretary of State Cyrus Vance, and shortly thereafter Tass, the Soviet news agency, denounced the U.S. statement as an "unsavory ploy." Given the Soviet Union's superpower status and the need to balance human rights concerns with other legitimate interests, such as arms control, nuclear proliferation, and global order, the United States immediately backed off from its public denuncia-

tion of Soviet human rights. However, this was not the case with lesser powers, especially Latin American authoritarian regimes with whom the U. S. strategic interests were minimal. As a result, the United States pursued a more vigorous human rights policy toward countries such as Argentina, Brazil, Guatemala, and Uruguay than toward Indonesia, the Philippines, and South Korea, where security interests were at stake.

However, as Carter officials discovered, pursuing human rights often necessitated trade-offs with other core interests. As one observer noted at the time, although self-determination, majority rule, minority rights, and international order are all desirable, most of the time we can enjoy only some of these good things in life, and then only at the expense of others. "Refusing to accept this fact of life is like refusing to grow up because adults lead such sordid lives."[37] To develop a more coherent human rights strategy, Carter signed a presidential directive on human rights (P.D. 30) to clarify goals and establish clear policy priorities. Among other things, the directive established priorities among major types of human rights, emphasized the role of positive sanctions, prohibited aid to regimes guilty of serious rights violations, and encouraged the use of international financial institutions in promoting human rights.[38] Despite these explicit guidelines, the tensions surrounding the administration's human rights initiatives persisted as the administration sought to balance human rights with other important foreign policy goals.

ASSESSING THE POLICY

Despite inconsistent policy implementation, some scholars and officials regard Carter's human rights policy as a major foreign policy success. Brzezinski, for example, identifies human rights among the foremost foreign policy achievements of the Carter administration. In his view, the human rights policy was important because it encouraged the identification of the United States with the ideals of justice, equity, majority rule, self-determination, and human dignity.[39] Others credit the reduction of human rights abuses in authoritarian regimes (e.g., Argentina, Indonesia, and Uruguay) to the international human rights campaign.

However, this policy was also strongly criticized by many. Some argued that it was hypocritical because of its selective and inconsistent application. Others, such as Joshua Muravchik, argued that the policy lacked balance because it focused attention on individual human rights abuses while overlooking system-wide violations by totalitarian regimes. As a result, the Carter administration emphasized the less serious human rights abuses of authoritarian regimes while neglecting the more egregious systematic suppression of freedom in totalitarian regimes.[40] In addition, Carter's human rights policy was criticized for its conceptual confusion about rights. Rather than clarifying and prioritizing rights, some critics suggested that Carter added to the conceptual muddle. For example, Jeane Kirkpatrick, who served as U.S. ambassador to the United Nations during the Reagan administration, argued that Carter increased conceptual confusion by the broadening of the definition of rights. As Kirkpatrick noted, "Human rights in the Carter version had no specific content, except a general demand that societies provide all the freedoms associated with constitutional democracy, all the economic security promised by socialism, and all of the self-fulfillment featured in Abraham Maslow's psychology."[41]

In short, the tradition of political idealism contributed decisively to the foreign policies of President Carter. The tradition not only provided a worldview by which international events and developments were assessed but also served as a source of inspiration and guidance in public affairs. As this case study suggests, the development and implementation of Carter's human rights policy were a direct by-product of the president's idealistic worldview.

MORAL REFLECTIONS

I have suggested that ethical traditions influence the conceptualization of issues and the development and execution of policies.

- In light of this case study, what are some distinctive policy features that are rooted in the tradition of political idealism?
- What policy strengths and weaknesses can be attributed to idealism? If President Carter had relied on political realism rather than idealism in defining and implementing human rights, how might the policy have differed?
- Would a human rights policy rooted in political realism have been more effective, or less effective in promoting international human rights? Why or why not?

SUMMARY

Ethical traditions play an indispensable role in international relations. In a world in which moral values are being increasingly neglected, undermined, or misused, traditions provide a structure for identifying and applying relevant moral norms to international relations. By illuminating widely shared moral values, ethical traditions help guide individual and collective political action, thereby contributing to the development of humane foreign policies and just international structures. Ethical traditions also provide the moral architecture necessary to critique and assess the foreign policy behavior of states and the international structures of global society. Ethical traditions are not self-validating. As a result, the plurality of traditions requires that the competing and conflicting claims of different traditions be examined with care and reconciled when possible.

Chapter Four

The Ethics of Political Reconciliation

The extension of forgiveness, repentance, and reconciliation to whole nations is one of the great innovations in statecraft of our time.[1]

—WALTER WINK

The deadly cycle of revenge must be replaced by the new-found liberty of forgiveness.[2]

—POPE JOHN PAUL II

A duty to prosecute all human rights violations committed under a previous regime is too blunt an instrument to help successor governments which must struggle with the subtle complexities of reestablishing democracy. . . . Rather than a duty to prosecute, we should think of a duty to safeguard human rights and to prevent future violations by state officers or other parties.[3]

—CARLOS SANTIAGO NINO

IN CONFRONTING the crimes and injustices of former regimes, emerging democratic governments have pursued a variety of strategies, ranging from denial to trials. The challenge of how best to reckon with regime atrocities—a process scholars have termed "transitional justice"[4]—will depend, of course, on the emerging regime's commitment to justice and human rights and on the political resources available to address the crimes and injustices of former governments. Some of the major goals pursued by transitional regimes include the restoration of the rule of law, the consolidation of democratic institutions, justice for human rights victims, and political reconciliation and national unity.

RECKONING WITH PAST REGIME OFFENSES

Fundamentally, these strategies have involved two distinct approaches—engagement or denial, accountability or avoidance. The engagement approach is based on the assumption that before nations can be healed and reconciled, regime wrongdoing must be disclosed, acknowledged, and redressed through appropriate strategies of accountability. Although it may be desirable to emphasize the immediate restoration of communal relationships and the consolidation of constitutional norms, this approach assumes that healing can take place only when past atrocities have been confronted directly. Coming to terms with past collective wrongdoing is important because the failure to do so may result in latent, festering problems that impair normal interpersonal and civic relationships. Just as the failure to excise a cancer from the human body can lead to serious illnesses or even death, so too can the failure to explicitly address collective offenses result in severe social and political pathologies.

The foundation of any strategy of accountability is the discovery, disclosure, and acknowledgment of truth. There can be no reckoning with past regime offenses if there is no knowledge of wrongdoing. In effect, if a community is to effectively come to terms with past regime offenses, the public must have knowledge of regime atrocities and crimes and which individuals, groups, or organizations are chiefly responsible for them. While investigations of limited offenses may be undertaken by private organizations, major human rights violations, especially those involving state organizations, need to be carried out by government-appointed commissions, such as South Africa's Truth and Reconciliation Commission (TRC) or Chile's National Commission on Truth and Reconciliation. Although disclosure and public acknowledgment of past human rights violations does not necessarily lead to justice or reconciliation, scholars regard truth as indispensable to an engagement approach and essential in political healing. José Zalaquett, an influential human rights scholar and a leading advisor to Chilean president Patricio Aylwin, for example, has observed that disclosure and acknowledgment of truth is an "inescapable imperative."[5]

The most widely used strategy of accountability in political communities is legal prosecution. In constitutional regimes, courts have the responsibility for determining criminal behavior and for punishing wrongdoing. Once evidence is obtained, an offender is prosecuted and then punished, if found guilty. Although punishment of legal offenses raises a number of moral, political, and legal challenges, especially when the wrongs inflicted in society are pervasive, some scholars argue that the restoration of the rule of law and the integrity of the constitutional order requires that wrongdoing be publicly prosecuted. Quite apart from the long-term effects of trials on victims and offenders, the immediate impact of such initiatives is the reinforcement of the supremacy of the law. The punishment of offenders can take a variety of actions, ranging from financial reparations and community service to incarceration. Courts and political authorities can, of course, mitigate sentences through compassionate acts of mercy or legal pardons. Although mercy and pardon have a similar effect in qualifying the punishment of an offender, mercy is an ethical action motivated by humanitarian considerations, whereas pardon is a legal act motivated by a political judgment about the common good for society.

Besides legal retribution, states also apply accountability through other strategies, such as official purges, restitution, reparations, public apologies, truth commissions, and even political forgiveness. Although these strategies are rooted in truth, each reckons with past wrongdoing in a different manner. Purges impose accountability by demanding that leaders, agents, and supporters of the discredited regime must be restricted from politics and even barred from government service. Restitution and reparations impose accountability by the transfer of tangible resources to victims and their families. Whereas restitution involves the return of stolen or confiscated property, reparations provides for financial resources as a symbol of a regime's culpability and as an aid to the restoration of communal relationships. Public apologies—the expression of remorse by government leaders for past regime offenses—can also foster political healing through truth-telling followed by public acknowledgment of, and contrition for, past collective offenses. The most significant innovations in the disclosure of past wrongdoing are official truth commissions, which are ordinarily established to uncover and disclose the nature and magnitude of past regime atrocities. Finally, political forgiveness—the lifting of debts or penalties for collective wrongdoing—is also a form of accountability because the mitigation of the deserved punishment is granted only after truth has been acknowledged and leaders have expressed remorse for the offenses.

The second major strategy for reckoning with past collective offenses is avoidance or denial. Governments that pursue this approach frequently do so for a number of reasons. First, since responsibility for regime wrongdoing is often pervasive throughout society, it is rarely beneficial to focus on the culpability of only a small number of perpetrators and decision-makers. Additionally, the prosecution and punishment of leaders and agents may further polarize society. As a result, some governments assume that the best approach is avoiding trials and scapegoating altogether.

Another reason why governments may try to avoid confronting past regime offenses is the belief that accountability may inhibit national reconciliation. Since the crimes, injustices, and structural evils of the past cannot be undone, some leaders assume that the best approach is to allow the balm of time to heal the social and political wounds of the past. Confronting the unjust, evil deeds of the past will only increase resentment, distort priorities, and inhibit political healing. Thus, the best way to address past offenses is to neglect and avoid past wrongdoing and focus instead on present social and political challenges and the promises and hopes of the future.

Finally, government officials pursue avoidance and denial in the belief that a forward-looking strategy is most likely to prevent human rights crimes and atrocities from reoccurring. To this end, they give priority to the building and consolidation of a humane political order over claims of retributive justice. Rather than seeking to settle legal claims about past collective offenses, this approach emphasizes the institutionalization of constitutional norms and structures and the renewal of political morality. The former is indispensable in fostering a humane political order that protects human rights, while the latter is essential in fostering reconciliation.

The two most common expressions of the avoidance approach are historical amnesia and amnesties. Amnesia is the deliberate effort to deny the past or to neglect memory. Amnesties, by contrast, are public acts that relieve offenders of their individual and collective responsibility. Whether through denial or amnesties, this approach focuses on the consolidation of new legal and political order by focusing on the restoration of peace and the pursuit of national reconciliation. Its goal is the institutionalization of a new constitutional political order by emphasizing the present and the future and by neglecting memory. In effect, it disregards the legacy of past offenses. Tadeusz Mazowiecki, Poland's first democratic prime minister, emphasized this approach when he called on his people to draw a "thick line" between the present and the past in order to focus exclusively on building a new democratic order.[6]

THE QUEST FOR POLITICAL RECONCILIATION

In common usage, the term "reconciliation" denotes the restoration of friendship or the reestablishment of communal solidarity. From a religious, especially biblical, perspective, reconciliation implies the renewal or restoration of broken relationships—between God and humans and among humans themselves. Historically, political thinkers and public officials have been reluctant to view reconciliation as a legitimate goal of politics. Because of the religious connotations of the term, they have generally regarded reconciliation as a spiritual process for restoring interpersonal relationships. As a result, theologians have tended to view reconciliation chiefly as a spiritual concept relevant to an individual's relationship to God and secondarily as a process between persons, thereby underestimating its social and political dimensions.[7]

What does political reconciliation mean? Fundamentally, reconciliation involves the rebuilding of understanding and harmonious relationships. To become reconciled is to overcome alienation, division, and enmity and restore peaceful, cooperative relationships based on a shared commitment to communal solidarity. Trudy Govier and Wilhelm Verwoerd have suggested that political reconciliation should be conceived as the building or rebuilding of trust. They define trust as an attitude of "confident expectation" where persons anticipate that other individuals or groups will act in a decent, competent, and acceptable manner. When people place their trust in others, they of course become vulnerable to others, but the risk of vulnerability is deemed acceptable precisely because of the relative certainty that no harm will result from such trusting attitudes and behaviors.[8]

In *Trust: The Social Virtues and the Creation of Prosperity*, Francis Fukuyama argues convincingly that social trust is indispensable to the development of orderly, creative, and prosperous societies. He shows that countries with a high level of social capital—that is, a high degree of commitment to shared values and voluntary cooperation through civic associations—enjoy greater economic growth than countries with limited social and economic solidarity.[9] Clearly, without trust, societies are incapable of developing the networks of voluntary cooperation indispensable to participatory, economically productive societies. As trust presupposes truth-telling, promise-keeping, and social solidarity, conceiving reconciliation in terms of trust provides a tangible way of defining political reconciliation.

A significant argument in favor of political reconciliation is the historical experience of modern domestic and international political life. Although conflict is inevitable in politics, deep, ongoing animosity is not inevitable. Peace is possible, hatred can be transformed into friendship, and distrust and enmity can evolve into harmonious, cooperative relationships. For example, the historic animosity between France and Germany, evident in both the First and the Second World Wars, has been replaced by growing cooperation based on shared economic interests and increasing understanding by their citizens. The creation of institutional structures of cooperation, such as the European Coal and Steel Community (ECSC) and the European Economic Community (EEC), have greatly facilitated this process. Similarly, the deep animosity between Germany and the United States during the Second World War has also given way to a peaceful, harmonious bilateral relationship based on Germany's institutionalization of democratic norms and institutions.

The process of national reconciliation is also illustrated by the numerous peace accords that have ended civil wars in countries such as El Salvador, Nicaragua, and Namibia. To be sure, the ending of domestic conflict does not imply reconciliation, but before antagonists can move toward cooperative, harmonious relationships, they must halt the fighting. The quest for political reconciliation is also evident in the successful pursuit of political accommodation among opposing groups in multilingual and multicultural nations, such as Belgium and Switzerland. More recently, the quest for reconciliation has been emphasized as a part of the transitional justice process of emerging democratic regimes. In the 1980s and 1990s, transitional regimes created truth commissions not simply to construct an official account of past regime offenses but also to promote national unity. The ostensible purpose of truth-telling was the belief that the discovery and public acknowledgment of past regime wrongdoing would contribute to political healing and foster national reconciliation. Although truth may not necessarily lead to national unity, it is unlikely that a cohesive, coherent, and productive society can emerge from historical amnesia or denial.

Even if reconciliation is regarded as a legitimate goal of political communities, there will likely be significant disagreement over the priority of such a goal relative to other political concerns. Should the nascent democracy pursue national unity and political reconciliation first, and then seek to consolidate democratic institutions and the rule of law—or should the emerging democratic order first pursue legal accountability and justice, and then seek to foster national reconciliation and domestic stability? The strategy pursued will depend in great part on how the task of political healing is conceived.

Michael Feher distinguishes between two different approaches to national reconciliation and the restoration of political community. According to him, "purists" are those who demand full legal accountability as a precondition for political healing. They assume that criminal behavior needs to be exposed, stigmatized, and punished in order to consolidate the rule of law, without which democratic government is likely to fail. Purists, who are typically represented by human rights activists and nongovernmental organizations, thus tend to believe that justice must be secured for victims before reconciliation can occur. By contrast, "pragmatists," represented chiefly by political leaders and governmental agencies, tend to view national reconciliation as a precondition for the consolidation of democracy and the rule of law. For them, amnesty and forgiveness are morally legitimate because they provide a means for overcoming deep political cleavages and promoting political reconciliation and national unity.[10]

In light of these two distinct approaches to political reconciliation, how should deeply divided communities pursue political healing and national unity? Should a regime follow the "Nuremberg trials" model and seek to identify and punish the major offenders and then pursue communal reconciliation through the slow process of building democratic institutions? Or should a regime consolidate national unity by minimizing differences between political antagonists and focusing instead on the shared goal of pursuing, in the words of Abraham Lincoln, "a just and lasting peace among ourselves and with all nations"?[11] As noted earlier, scholars' and decision-makers' skepticism about the pursuit of political reconciliation derives in great part from the widespread belief that the primary moral task of the state is justice. As a result, the prevailing worldview on transitional justice is that emerging democratic regimes should first identify and then prosecute offenders, and second pursue national unity through reconciliation. Indeed, the prevailing approach in most emerging democratic societies is guided by the principle "first justice, then peace."

Despite the importance of justice, the "first justice, then reconciliation" strategy itself is conceptually flawed and often unworkable. It is flawed because the approach assumes that the pursuit of justice and the quest for peace are in fundamental tension, and that the former must be fulfilled before the latter can be undertaken. And it is an unrealistic and unworkable strategy because the conditions of strict justice—that is, the demand that punishment must be commensurate with the nature of the offenses—can never be fully fulfilled. In effect, by making reconciliation conditional on the prior fulfillment of justice, this approach relegates community healing and the promotion of national unity to a subsidiary role.

The "first justice, then peace" approach is also problematic because reconciliation is not an automatic or even inevitable by-product of justice. It may be possible to rectify some past offenses and restore some moral equality between victims and victimizers, but justice per se does not necessarily foster the preconditions for community. While the prosecution and punishment of some offenders may help restore the credibility of criminal justice institutions and contribute to legal accountability, imposing some justice will not necessarily create community. Establishing a minimal order, defined as the absence of war, is not the same as creating a harmonious ordering of society—what George Weigel calls *tranquillitas ordinis*.[12] The latter can be created only by developing harmonious relationships based on a shared commitment to the common good based on human dignity. More particularly, restoring communion will occur only when antagonists demonstrate empathy and compassion toward each other and carry out mutual actions that help rebuild collective social and political ties. Thus, political healing is likely to occur only when antagonists confront and overcome past offenses and pursue actions based on shared moral values.

RETRIBUTIVE JUSTICE VERSUS RESTORATIVE JUSTICE

Retributive Justice

The prevailing method used by governments to confront criminal offenses is legal retribution. The retributive justice tradition, rooted in both deontological and utilitarian reasoning, demands that offenders be held accountable for their wrongdoing through prosecution and punishment. According to retributive justice theory, when perpetrators commit an offense against other persons, they destroy the fundamental moral and legal equality among human beings. To repair ruptured relationships between victims and victimizers and restore their moral equality, offenders must be diminished through public condemnation, and victims must regain their former moral status. Retribution is the process by which this fundamental equality is restored. The retributive justice paradigm is thus based on the belief that a humane political community can be sustained only if wrongdoing is prosecuted and punished, for only if offenders are held accountable can a community confidently pursue and advance its future collective well-being.

Diane Orentlicher, an international human rights scholar, argues that states have a legal and moral duty to prosecute egregious human rights crimes. Because the international legal order is based in part on international human rights law, states must prosecute individuals who are responsible for serious human rights violations. She argues that when states fail to fulfill this obligation, the international community should take action against them.[13] The distinguished legal scholar Carlos Nino, by contrast, argues that there is no duty to prosecute because such state action depends on the environmental constraints faced by the new regime. Indeed, Nino claims that criminal prosecution may risk provoking further violence and returning to undemocratic rule. As a result, rather than viewing prosecution as a duty, he argues (in the epigraph at the outset of the chapter) that the state's primary responsibility should be protecting human rights and preventing future abuses.

If prosecution of past wrongs is deemed essential to consolidating the emerging democratic regime, perhaps the best that can be achieved is the trial of senior government officials responsible for the decisions that resulted in crimes. But such a strategy poses enormous obstacles because the evidence for criminal culpability of government officials and senior military leaders is likely to be difficult to obtain. Not surprisingly, Germany found it easier to prosecute soldiers who killed citizens trying to flee East Berlin than the leaders who established the evil regime of totalitarian communism. And while Argentina was successful in prosecuting the junta leaders responsible for widespread killing and disappearances, the top leaders found guilty were subsequently pardoned because of the political instability caused by the trials. In pardoning the five senior leaders, Carlos Menem said that his action was designed to "create conditions that permit the definitive reconciliation among Argentineans."[14]

Restorative Justice

Given the limits of legal retribution, a growing number of scholars and public officials have relied on a restorative conception of justice—a perspective that emphasizes healing and restoration rather than punishment. Unlike retributive justice, which places a premium on individual rights and the prosecution and punishment of offenders, restorative justice emphasizes the restoration of communal bonds through social and political reconciliation. Its aim is not to right wrongs, but to restore a stable social and political order. Whereas retribution focuses chiefly on objective wrongdoing, restorative justice emphasizes the transformation of subjective factors that impair community, such as anger, resentment, and desire for vengeance.[15]

Some have suggested that restorative justice is simply a strategy of easy reconciliation— seeking to create a new beginning without coming to terms with the past. But restorative justice does not disregard past wrongdoing. Rather, it seeks to describe comprehensively and fully the truth about past offenses, recognizing that antagonists may have widely divergent perspectives about the nature, causes, and culpability for past offenses. To the extent that the parties can agree on the awful truth about past crimes and injustices, the restorative justice perspective encourages individuals, groups, and institutions to admit culpability, express repentance, and authenticate remorse through acts of reparation and restitution. At the same time, restorative justice deemphasizes the division of society into perpetrators and victims, preferring instead to view most or all of society as victims or survivors.

President Abraham Lincoln illustrates the restorative approach through his efforts to foster the political healing of the United States from the injustices of slavery and the bitter, destructive Civil War. Rather that seeking legal retribution against political and military leaders of the Confederacy, Lincoln's strategy called for reconciliation among all peoples.[16] Mahmood Mamdani similarly assumes that in the aftermath of deadly political violence, such as Rwanda's 1994 genocide, a restorative approach offers the most promising hope for healing and peacekeeping. He suggests that communal healing, what he terms "survivor's justice," must be based on changes in the underlying political institutions that have permitted ongoing political violence. Thus, rather than focusing on the culpability of individual perpetrators, Mamdani suggests that the fundamental blame for the genocide should be placed on the underlying rules and practices of the political regime.[17] Accordingly, he suggests that victims, but not offenders, should be identified and acknowledged because identifying perpetrators would lead to excessive focus on their culpability, thereby detracting from the needed cultural and political reforms necessary for promoting reconciliation.

It is important to stress that restorative justice is not an attempt to bypass the rule of law. Although the restorative approach does not demand adherence to strict legalism, it nevertheless demands truth-telling coupled with contrition as the way to heal individual and collective injuries. Offenses have resulted in a moral inequality between perpetrators and victims, so restorative justice seeks to restore the moral equality of citizens—not through the law but through the moral reformation of persons. This is achieved when offenders acknowledge their responsibility and victims refrain from vengeance and acknowledge empathy toward their former enemies. Although morally demanding, such behaviors have the effect of liberating victims from being captive to anger and resentment. In effect, such attitudinal and behavioral changes result in moral autonomy for both offenders and victims.

If the preconditions of restorative justice are fulfilled, individuals and communities may grant individual and collective forgiveness. Such forgiveness, which is likely to occur only after victims perceive the offenders' contrition as authentic, would be expressed by recognizing the offenders' humanity and modifying legitimate claims of restitution and retribution. Although individual forgiveness is essential to the moral rehabilitation of victims as well as the restoration of communal bonds, such forgiveness will not necessarily abrogate legal claims for punishment and reparations. Indeed, offenders should be prepared, as an expression of the authenticity of their remorse, to accept a state's legal punishment. In effect, political forgiveness may modify and reduce, but not abrogate, the claims of legal retribution. Most significantly, forgiveness increases the possibility of reconciliation. But whether the renewal and restoration of relationships results in reconciliation is up to the individuals and collectivities. Restorative justice creates the environmental context in which communal bonds can be restored, but whether or not such restoration occurs depends on the voluntary actions of individuals and political groups.

In the aftermath of significant collective atrocities, the only effective way of confronting systemic human rights abuses and preventing their repetition is through a comprehensive strategy of moral reconstruction and political renewal. Only through a multidimensional strategy that seeks to restore legal, social, cultural, political, and spiritual life are peace and justice likely to be realized. Legal retribution can, of course, contribute to regime accountability for egregious state crimes and injustices, but legalism alone cannot achieve the moral reconstruction necessary to restore a broken and divided society. Ernesto Sábato, the distinguished head of Argentina's truth commission, observed in his prologue to the commission's report *Nunca Más* ("never again") that the commissioners were not in search of "vindictiveness or vengeance," but "truth and justice." In his view, courts should pursue their "transcendent mission" based on a strategy of truth and justice because national reconciliation is possible only if the guilty repent and justice is based on truth.[18]

One of the most important efforts to apply the restorative justice paradigm to regime offenses is the South African experiment in truth-telling. This experiment was directed by the Truth and Reconciliation Commission (TRC), a body established by the South African parliament to investigate gross human rights violations of the apartheid era in the belief that the disclosure of past offenses would contribute to political reconciliation and national unity.

CASE 4-1: PROMOTING POLITICAL RECONCILIATION IN SOUTH AFRICA

THE APARTHEID REGIME

In 1948, the National Party (NP), the political party of the Afrikaner (Boer) people, gained control of parliament. For the next forty-four years they would govern the Republic of South Africa. Although racial discrimination and segregation had characterized South Africa since colonization in the mid-seventeenth century,[19] the Afrikaners established a far more comprehensive and pervasive system of racial segregation. Indeed, this program—known as apartheid, or separate development—imposed the most far-reaching racial engineering ever practiced in the modern world.[20] For example, the government imposed more stringent racial segregation by forcing the relocation of more than 3.5 million persons between 1960 and 1983. These forced removals further intensified the problem of overpopulation in the already crowded all-black Bantu homelands,

increasing the proportion of the total African population in the homelands from 40 percent in 1950 to 53 percent in 1980.

As a result of the growing social, economic, and political inequalities in South African society, black political opposition to the apartheid regime increased. At first, the political opposition was limited chiefly to the actions of labor groups and the two major African opposition groups—the African National Congress (ANC) and the Pan-African Congress (PAC). But in the 1970s, political opposition efforts intensified both domestically and internationally. In 1973, the United Nations General Assembly declared apartheid "a crime against humanity," and four years later the Security Council imposed trade sanctions (an arms embargo) on South Africa as a way to foment political reform. As domestic and international condemnation of apartheid increased, the South African regime began to carry out modest structural reforms in the early 1980s.[21] Rather than mollifying public opinion, reforms only intensified the opposition's political demands. In response to growing violence, the government imposed a state of emergency that gave security forces increased authority to detain political opponents and use force against those threatening public order. The intensification of the liberation campaign is demonstrated by the growth in political violence, rising from seven thousand deaths during the 1960–1989 period to more than fourteen thousand during the 1990–1994 period preceding the establishment of multiracial democracy in April 1994.[22]

ESTABLISHING MULTIRACIAL DEMOCRACY

In February 1990, President F. W. de Klerk set in motion a reform process that would culminate four years later in the election of Nelson Mandela as president of a new multiracial democratic regime. The transition began with lifting the ban on the ANC and other opposition political groups, releasing Nelson Mandela and other political prisoners, and the partial lifting of the state of emergency. Following two years of intense negotiations among the country's political elites, especially the governing NP and the ANC, delegates to the Convention for a Democratic South Africa (CODESA) signed an Interim Constitution in November 1993 that established the basis for a transitional government. According to the Interim Constitution, the transitional Government of National Unity was tasked with establishing a permanent constitution and creating the preconditions for national unity.

Fundamentally, South Africa could have pursued one of three strategies in confronting past crimes and injustices: amnesia, punishment, or truth-telling. The first strategy, based on forgetting and denial, would seek to draw a line between the present and the past, and concentrate all political and economic resources on the consolidation of constitutional democracy. The second strategy, legal retribution, would demand full legal accountability for past offenses, believing that the consolidation of democracy and the rule of law were impossible without the prosecution and punishment of offenders. The third

strategy, the one adopted by South Africa, represented an intermediary approach between the extremes of impunity and comprehensive trials, between denial and retribution. Following the psychoanalytic model of mental health, it assumed that acknowledging the truth about the past was indispensable to healing society and consolidating constitutional government. As a result, it placed retributive justice at the service of truth, and to maximize its discovery and disclosure, conditional amnesty was offered to offenders who fully confessed their culpability. Fundamentally, South Africa's "third way" strategy combined a backward-looking focus on truth-telling and accountability with a forward-looking emphasis on the moral restoration of society and the promotion of national unity.[23]

South African leaders selected the third strategy in great part because it reflected a political compromise among the major political forces in the country, but also because they believed that neither historical amnesia nor trials provided options conducive to national healing. Indeed, based on the experiences of previous truth commissions, they assumed that it was most likely to foster the consolidation of a democratic order, contribute to the restoration and healing of victims, and encourage national reconciliation. As viewed by leaders, traditional legal and political strategies rooted in retributive justice were unlikely to foster unity and national reconciliation. What was needed was an alternative strategy that gave priority to the healing of victims, the public acknowledgment of past crimes and injustices, and the restoration of communal bonds. Such an approach would provide a demanding multidimensional strategy that emphasized legal accountability yet called for political accommodation, social reconciliation, and the moral reconstruction of society. The 1993 Interim Constitution's postamble captured the spirit of this strategy when it declared "a need for understanding but not for vengeance, a need for reparation but not for retaliation, a need for *ubuntu*[24] but not for victimization."

In his book on the TRC, Archbishop Desmond Tutu, the commission's chairman, claims that it would have been unwise, indeed impossible, to impose retribution, or what he terms "the

Nuremberg trial paradigm,"[25] on South Africa. Due to South Africa's limited political and economic resources, it was imperative that it use them with care in the consolidation of new democratic structures by balancing different claims, including "justice, accountability, stability, peace, and reconciliation."[26] In Tutu's view, applying retributive justice would have placed an undue burden on the nation's courts and would have given little emphasis to the restoration of victims and the promotion of political reconciliation. Tutu instead advocated the strategy of restorative justice, believing that such an approach would best pursue political healing and justice. For him, restorative justice was the preferred strategy because it promoted communal solidarity and social harmony by seeking to restore broken relationships, heal victims, and rehabilitate perpetrators. Most importantly, for Tutu, restorative justice was consistent with the African social tradition of *ubuntu*, which placed a premium on harmony, friendliness, and community.[27]

THE TRC

In mid-1995, the South African parliament passed the Promotion of National Unity and Reconciliation Act, which called for the establishment of a truth commission. As conceived by this parliamentary act, the major purpose for creating the TRC was to uncover knowledge about past gross human rights violations in the belief that public acknowledgment of such truth would contribute to the consolidation of democratic society and promote national unity and reconciliation. Fundamentally, the goal of the TRC was to discover information about gross human rights abuses during the apartheid era.[28]

The seventeen-member commission—led by Archbishop Desmond Tutu, the 1994 recipient of the Nobel Peace Prize—was divided into three committees.[29] The truth committee focused on human rights violations, the amnesty committee was responsible for determining which applicants would receive amnesty, and the reparations committee was responsible for making recommendations on financial and other assistance to human rights victims as well as offering suggestions on how to foster national healing.

The human rights committee pursued factual truth by gathering evidence about gross human rights violations that were perpetrated during the apartheid era by state security officials as well as by members of the liberation movement. More than 22,000 victim-statements were completed and some 160 victims' hearings were held throughout the country, involving more than 1,200 victims and their families. These hearings were widely publicized by the media and left an indelible impact on South African society. Based on the evidence accumulated through investigations, victim statements and institutional hearings, the TRC published its findings and recommendations in a five-volume report, released in October 1998.[30]

One of the most significant, yet problematic, elements of the TRC process was the provision of conditional amnesty to offenders. The logic for the amnesty was set forth in the Interim Constitution's postamble, which declared that, "in order to advance such reconciliation and reconstruction [of society], amnesty should be granted in respect of acts, omissions and offences with political objectives and committed in the course of the conflicts of the past." Since truth was considered essential to individual and collective healing, political leaders believed the investigation and disclosure of past injustices and gross human rights was indispensable to the moral reconstruction of society. To encourage perpetrators' confession, the TRC promised amnesty to those who fully confessed politically motivated crimes.[31] Of the more than seven thousand persons who applied for amnesty, however, only about twelve hundred were granted amnesty.[32]

Compared with other truth commissions, the TRC is undoubtedly the most expansive and elaborate truth commission ever established. To begin with, it functioned much longer than most other commissions.[33] Second, because the commission was created by an act of parliament and not by a decision of the executive, the TRC had significant authority. For example, it could subpoena witnesses, compel disclosure of information from governmental agencies, requisition documents from organizations, and even disclose the names of alleged perpetrators.[34] Third, unlike most other commissions, which have carried out their investigation in secrecy, the TRC carried out its work openly, providing much media coverage of the human rights hearings. Finally, the TRC had the authority to grant amnesty to offenders who confessed their politically motivated crimes, provided their disclosure was complete.

THE ETHICS OF THE TRC

Scholars and activists have raised a number of concerns about the TRC model of transitional justice. For example, some TRC critics have questioned the legitimacy of the restorative justice paradigm, claiming that such a model undermines core societal norms (such as accountability, blame, and punishment) essential in building a stable, humane society. They claim that if societies fail to identify and condemn evil, the consolidation of human rights will be thwarted. Others claim that fidelity to the law requires not only prosecution of crimes of violence but also the condemnation of the immoral laws and unjust structures and the prosecution of leaders who were responsible for their enactment. John Dugard, for example, critiques the TRC for minimizing the "memory of apartheid" by failing to hold leaders accountable for the establishment of the immoral rules of apartheid.[35] Archbishop Tutu, however, claims that trials would have been expensive and would have diverted political attention from the pressing need to consolidate constitutionalism and foster job creation. In his view, the forward-looking restorative justice paradigm offered the advantage of diverting scarce resources to the consolidation of democratic institutions and the promotion of national unity by balancing the claims of justice, accountability, stability, peace, and reconciliation.[36]

Critics have also challenged the legitimacy of reconciliation as a public policy goal. As noted earlier, a number of scholars have called into question the need to deliberately promote national unity and political reconciliation. Rajeev Bhargava, for example, writes that rather than promoting reconciliation through public policies, societies should promote a limited public order—or what he terms "a minimally decent society." He claims that reconciliation is an exces-

sively demanding political goal.[37] Crocker similarly argues that reconciliation is a potentially dangerous and undemocratic doctrine because it could threaten individual rights. For Crocker, as well as for other scholars committed to political liberalism, the only legitimate way to reckon with past atrocities is through "democratic reciprocity."[38] But democratic procedures do not necessarily or automatically foster community. Indeed, electoral democracy may, as Fareed Zakaria has noted, exacerbate political tensions and weaken community.[39] As a result, rather than enhancing individual freedom, democratic procedures might in fact impede communal solidarity and thereby threaten human rights. Thus, since democratic decision making presupposes a stable, unified community,[40] the consolidation of democracy is likely to occur only if national unity is strengthened through the cultivation of shared values and the development of strong institutions.

TRC critics have also expressed concerns about the presumed healing properties of truth. Truth commissions are based on the premise that knowledge of the past, coupled with the acknowledgment of the truth, will contribute to the healing of victims, the promotion of peace, and the restoration of communal relationships. Building on the biblical admonition that if people know the truth, it will set them free (John 8:32), truth commissions have pursued investigations into regime wrongdoing in the hope that such knowledge would foster individual and collective healing. The TRC, for example, is based on the belief that truth and reconciliation are inextricably linked—that the disclosure of past wrongs contributes to personal healing and communal reconciliation. If truth is to foster reconciliation, both factual and interpretive knowledge will be needed. Indeed, knowledge of the past can contribute to political healing only when it is widely known and shared and, most importantly, when victims and offenders individually and collectively confront the painful past by "working through" the legacy of suffering, anger, and guilt.[41] Of course, while truth-telling may not be a sufficient condition for reconciliation, it most surely is a necessary element insofar as knowledge of the past permits individuals and collectives to confront their responsibility for past injustices.

Finally, TRC critics have alleged that the model failed to distinguish between the atrocities committed by the state and those committed by the liberation movement. Although the military conflict between the state security forces and the ANC guerrillas (*Umkhonto we Sizwe* or MK)[42] was a covert, unconventional war, the TRC believed that rules of war were nonetheless applicable to such a conflict. In particular, it viewed terror, civilian killings, abductions, and torture not only as gross human rights violations but also as violations of the laws of war.[43] Accordingly, it believed that it was morally obligated to investigate all major human rights abuses, regardless of who had perpetrated the crimes. As TRC vicechairperson Alex Boraine observed, "The goal of the TRC was to hold up a mirror to reflect the complete picture. In particular, its objective was to identify all victims in the conflict and to confront all perpetrators of gross human rights violations."[44]

ANC leaders took strong exception to the TRC approach of treating all political violence alike. Instead, they claimed that it was imperative to distinguish between the crimes and injustices of an evil, discriminatory system and the military operations of a liberation movement. Not only was the idea of moral equivalence morally problematic; it was also counterproductive to the healing and restoration of South Africa. Accordingly, ANC leaders tried to influence the TRC's findings and conclusions and when this failed, they unsuccessfully sought a court injunction to halt the publication of the TRC final report. According to deputy president Thabo Mbeki and other ANC leaders, the fundamental charge was that the TRC, by calling attention to the crimes and abuses of the MK, was attempting to criminalize the liberation struggle. According to Mbeki, the TRC's emphasis on the MK's crimes and abuses gave the impression that "the struggle for liberation was itself a gross violation of human rights."[45]

Another contentious element of the TRC theory was the offer of conditional amnesty to offenders who confessed. Since many victims' families were eager to bring to trial political leaders and security agents who were responsible for killings and abductions, the offer of conditional amnesty was deeply offensive to some human rights activists and victims. As a result, the amnesty provision (Section 20-7 of the TRC Act) was challenged before the country's Constitutional Court. The court, however, unanimously upheld the provision.[46] This meant that perpetrators who had committed politically motivated crimes during the apartheid era could be exempt from criminal or civil liability.

In sum, South Africa's truth and reconciliation experiment represents the most successful governmental initiative to promote peace and harmony through the discovery and acknowledgment of truth. Perhaps South Africa could have pursued the consolidation of multiracial democracy through amnesia and pardon or through trials of former regime leaders. But either strategy would have no doubt compromised essential goals—amnesia would have disregarded the past and retribution would have diverted scarce resources away from the quest for national unity and political reconciliation. Since the foundation for authentic reconciliation is truth-telling, the TRC's focus on the disclosure and acknowledgment of truth helped nurture a moral basis for pursuing the consolidation of communal solidarity. Of course, truth-telling could not ensure peace, but without it, long-term communal unity and peace would have been impossible. As one TRC official observed, "While truth may not always lead to reconciliation, there can be no genuine, lasting reconciliation without truth."[47] This point was reinforced by a *New York Times* editorial that lauded the commission's work as the most "comprehensive and unsparing examination of a nation's ugly past" that any truth commission has produced thus far. "No commission can transform a society as twisted as South Africa's was," the editorial goes on, "but the Truth Commission is the best effort the world has seen and South Africa is the better for it."[48]

The South African TRC process did not call for either individual or political forgiveness. Individuals could—and did—forgive perpetrators, but this act was entirely personal. Moreover, the TRC did not call on Afrikaner organizations to repent or on victims groups to forgive. Rather, the TRC established a process that focused on the disclosure of individual and collective offenses in the hope that such confession would create a psychologically and politically safe environment that might foster empathy, compassion, and reconciliation among antagonists. To be sure, whether or not individual victims chose to forgive was entirely a personal decision. The TRC, however, did offer conditional amnesty (limited institutional forgiveness) to perpetrators who confessed their wrongdoing. And while this partial forgiveness depended solely on truth-telling and not on repentance, it nonetheless helped foster a public dialog where healing, restoration, and reconciliation were emphasized.

In the final analysis, the significance of the South African experiment in transitional justice is not measured solely by the extent of truth, national unity, and political reconciliation achieved within the country. Rather, it also depends on the extent to which restorative justice is accepted as an effective strategy in confronting and overcoming past regime offenses. Judged by that standard, the TRC model provides one of the most promising innovations in moral politics in modern times.

MORAL REFLECTIONS

Despite South Africa's noteworthy peaceful consolidation of multiracial democracy, the country's strategy of reckoning with past politically inspired offenses raises a number of important issues about the nature and role of moral values in pursuing reconciliation in the aftermath of systemic injustices:

- Does the quest for truth morally justify amnesty for perpetrators? Does the quest for national unity through truth-telling justify overriding victims' demand for justice?
- What is the appropriate balance between backward-looking memory and forward-looking hope, between the discovery and disclosure of past offenses and the consolidation of constitutional government? How can the quest for accountability through a backward-looking quest for truth be reconciled with a forward-looking quest for political healing and reconciliation?
- Is the quest for political reconciliation a morally legitimate goal, especially when the search for communal healing is based on the disclosure and acknowledgment of truth rather than trials?
- Is restorative justice a morally legitimate strategy in confronting past regime offenses? Is this approach a valid alternative to the more widely accepted strategy of legal retribution? Does the restorative model provide adequate accountability and memory?

RECONCILIATION THROUGH POLITICAL FORGIVENESS

In the 1990s, a number of scholars began to explore the potential role of forgiveness in politics and, in particular, how such an idea might contribute to the healing of nations in the aftermath of widespread injustice and criminal wrongdoing. Hannah Arendt once observed that the only way to overcome past wrongs, or what she termed the "predicament of irreversibility," is through forgiveness, a doctrine she regarded as Jesus' greatest contribution to political thought.[49] Like justice, forgiveness entails accepting and admitting the wrongs of the past, but unlike justice, it seeks to overcome the legacy of past wrongs through repentance and reconciliation. Forgiveness does not solve the injustice of the past, but it does create the possibility for a new, more just, and more peaceful political order through the restoration of relationships. Because forgiveness offers the possibility of reconciliation among enemies, a growing number of scholars have called attention to its potentially significant role in international affairs. Patrick Glynn, for example, writes, "Nations may cling to the angry past or embrace the hopeful future. But the path to peace and prosperity for all nations today lies through the gate of forgiveness."[50]

Because forgiveness is seldom applied in domestic politics and even more rarely in international politics, it will be helpful to first explore its nature and role in interpersonal relations. In common usage, forgiveness implies, first, the cancellation of a debt or the pardoning of a past wrong and, second, the restoration of a relationship. Theologians commonly define the process of interpersonal reconciliation through confession and pardon as involving four distinct but interrelated elements. First, the offender confesses the evil committed, openly admitting responsibility for wrongdoing. Second, after acknowledging personal guilt, the wrongdoer apologizes for the injury committed, frequently demonstrating the authenticity of contrition through acts of restitution. Third, in response to the wrongdoer's contrition, the victim declines vengeance and instead pursues restoration through forgiveness. Finally, on the basis of the mutual interactions between the wrongdoer and the victim, the parties move toward reconciliation, creating a new relationship based on a restored moral foundation.

Repentance and forgiveness are often difficult to apply in personal life. This is so because unjust human actions frequently result in significant bitterness and anger, encouraging a desire for vengeance and restitution. Additionally, practicing forgiveness is difficult because the moral virtues on which it depends—such as the courage to confront the past, the humility to repent, the self-control to limit anger and oppose vengeance, and the magnanimity to pursue reconciliation—are rarely cultivated in society.

However, if forgiveness is challenging in interpersonal relations, it is much more difficult in public life.[51] This is true for two reasons: first, because political morality, as noted in chapter 1, is not identical with personal morality and, second, because responsibility for political action is frequently elusive and difficult to assign. For example, who is responsible for the Bosnian War? For South Africa's apartheid? For Rwanda's genocide? To be sure, although political leaders and government officials bear primary responsibility for devising and implementing policies that resulted in these crimes and injustices, they are not the only responsible actors. Indeed, all members of a political community also bear some responsibility through their actions or inactions.

Forgiveness in public life is similar to individual forgiveness. Following the interpersonal model sketched previously, we can conceive of international political forgiveness as entailing four elements. First, forgiveness requires complete truth-telling—a full accounting of past communal wrongs. This means that a past aggressive war or other international injustice requires that a state acknowledge its collective responsibility for wrongdoing. This truth-telling must be public so that knowledge of the past evil becomes part of the collective conscience of society. Second, leaders must acknowledge past wrongs and express public contrition for the injury committed. If the apology is to be genuine, the expiation needs to be specific, concrete, and public, often expressed through financial reparations or restitution. Third, forgiveness requires that the group or state that has been victimized acknowledge the contrition and repentance of the wrongdoers and not pursue vengeance or seek retribution. Rather than attempting to rectify past wrongs, the victims pursue the restoration of political relationships based on the renewal of trust and the cancellation of debts. Finally, the forgiveness process culminates with reconciliation—the restoration of just political relationships in which enemies learn to live and work with each other. Such a condition is possible only when trust is restored through the renewal of a society's moral order.

It is important to stress that forgiveness does not deny accountability through restitution, reparations, or even partial retribution. But whereas retributive justice demands full legal accountability through trials and punishment, forgiveness emphasizes the political healing and moral restoration of communal relationships. According to the forgiveness model, such healing is likely to occur when offenders acknowledge culpability, express remorse for their offense, and promise not to carry out the offense again, and when victims reduce or altogether cancel offenders' moral debts or deserved punishment. Although public apologies have become commonplace in domestic and international politics, the practice of authentic collective forgiveness is rare in contemporary political life. This is especially the case not because forgiveness lifts offenders' debts, but because of the demanding nature of this ethic, requiring that offenders voluntarily and openly confront their moral culpability.

As a result, the ethic of political forgiveness is rare in public life and, when applied in international affairs, it is usually evident in a partial or limited manner. In the South African case just examined, for example, although leaders did not seek reconciliation through political forgiveness, the TRC did pursue moral accountability through truth-telling and encouraged confession through the promise of amnesty. In effect, the TRC followed dimensions of the forgiveness ethic. In the case analyzed below—President Ronald Reagan's 1985 trip to West Germany to celebrate German–American political reconciliation—a different aspect of the forgiveness ethic is emphasized. Here the healing and restoration of collective relationships occurs through reforming German political culture and developing deep political ties between two peoples committed to constitutional democracy.

The German–American case is problematic, however, because it illuminates the difficulty in overcoming the lingering pain from war and, in particular, the lasting emotional scars resulting from genocide. In particular, the Reagan visit to the cemetery in Bitburg, Germany, raises difficult issues about the extent to which past gross human rights abuses can be overcome, even after governments have admitted culpability, provided substantial reparations, and sought reconciliation through the reformation of national attitudes, values, and institutional practices.

BACKGROUND

In January 1985, the White House announced that President Ronald Reagan would visit West Germany to commemorate the fortieth anniversary of the defeat of the Axis powers. Subsequently, the White House announced that President Reagan would lay a wreath at the German military cemetery at Bitburg as a gesture of German–American reconciliation and at the Bergen–Belsen concentration camp as a commemoration for the many Jews who died there and in other concentration camps. Soon after the planned visit to Bitburg was announced, it was discovered that forty-nine members of the Waffen SS, the Nazi movement's elite police force, were among the two thousand German soldiers' graves.

The decision to visit Bitburg precipitated much criticism from American Jewish groups, war veterans, and the media. Within one week of the announced visit, fifty-three senators signed a letter urging President Reagan to call off his Bitburg visit; subsequently, the U.S. Senate decisively passed a resolution recommending that President Reagan "reassess his planned itinerary." In addition, some 257 members of the House of Representatives wrote to West German chancellor Helmut Kohl urging that he release President Reagan from his Bitburg commitment. However, the most potent moral criticism of the planned trip was from Nobel Laureate Elie Wiesel, a survivor of the Holocaust. In a brief address at a White House ceremony honoring his selection for the Congressional Gold Medal of Achievement, Congress's highest award, Wiesel observed,

> I belong to a traumatized generation. And to us, as to you, symbols are important. And furthermore, following our ancient tradition—and we are speaking about Jewish heritage—our tradition commands us "to speak truth to power." . . . I am convinced, as you have told us earlier when we spoke that you were not aware of the presence of SS graves in the Bit-

burg cemetery. Of course, you didn't know. But now we all are aware. May I, Mr. President, if it's possible at all, implore you to do something else, to find another way, another site. That place, Mr. President is not your place. Your place is with the victims of the SS.[52]

After the discovery of the SS troops' graves and the ensuing political opposition to the planned trip, the Reagan administration faced a foreign policy dilemma. The dilemma was fundamentally rooted in morality, including the responsibilities involved in acknowledging, accepting, and overcoming the historic evil of the Holocaust. White House officials were of course aware of the evil legacy of the Nazi Holocaust, but they also knew that West Germany had attempted to atone for this unbelievable genocide through official remorse, substantial financial reparations, and the prosecution of more than 91,000 persons. Most important, West Germany had developed strong democratic institutions and had become one of the strongest postwar allies of the United States in confronting the evil of totalitarian communism. Nonetheless, West Germany continued to bear the scars from the terrible evil inflicted by Nazis on all of humanity, but especially on Jewish peoples. As one commentator observed at the time of the Bitburg conflict, the Third Reich "was the greatest failure of civilization on the planet."[53]

THE ETHICS OF BITBURG

From a narrowly defined perspective, the issue facing President Reagan was whether to participate in a ceremony of bilateral American–German reconciliation in a cemetery with symbols of evil. For Elie Wiesel and other opponents of the Bitburg visit, the issue was not politics, but "good and evil."[54] Associating even indirectly with Nazi symbols was morally unacceptable. This was a time for protecting and proclaiming the truth, or what Wiesel termed the necessity of speaking "truth to power." While recognizing the development of strong bilateral ties between West Germany and the United States, Bitburg critics argued reconciliation had to be rooted in memory. In particular, any political reconciliation between former enemies had to honor the historical record of the Holocaust and recognize anew the great evil committed by Nazis against the Jews. In Wiesel's words,

> Mr. President, I know and I understand . . . that you seek reconciliation. So do I. So do we. And I, too, wish to attain true reconciliation with the German people. I do not believe in collective guilt, nor in collective responsibility, only the killers were guilty. Their sons and daughters are not. And I believe, Mr. President, that we can and we must work together with them and with all people. And we must work to bring peace and understanding to a tormented world that, as you know, is still awaiting redemption.[55]

In short, critics argued that because remembering is more important than reconciliation and history is more significant than forgiving, President Reagan should have altered his plans and not have gone to Bitburg. Laying a wreath at the Kolmeshöhe military cemetery was wrong, in their view, because it involved an unnecessary association with evil symbols, namely, the burial sites of soldiers who had participated in the Jewish genocide.

From a broadly defined perspective, the issue for President Reagan was whether memory would always define the future or whether it was possible for nations to overcome their evil legacies. Although the Reagan administration never fully explained its moral reasoning behind its actions, it was clear that President Reagan was strongly motivated by the desire to commemorate Germany's moral rehabilitation and U.S.–German reconciliation rather than dwell on the legacies of history. Those who defended the planned trip emphasized two anticipated outcomes. First, because the visit to Bitburg had been developed cooperatively by U.S. and German government officials, the cancellation of the Bitburg ceremony would undoubtedly jeopardize official relations between the two countries. Second, because the ceremony was regarded by many Germans as a symbol of reconciliation between the two former enemy states as well as an expression of Germany's increased acceptance into the international community, some analysts argued that canceling the trip would be psychologically injurious to German political leadership.

After weighing the pros and cons of the Bitburg dilemma, President Reagan decided to follow the original plan and participate in a brief ceremony at the Bitburg cemetery. "I think it is morally right to do what I'm doing," he said, "and I'm not going to change my mind about that." In justifying his decision, President Reagan relied on consequentialist logic:

> But this all came about out of a very sincere desire of Chancellor Kohl and myself to recognize this 40th anniversary of the war's end—and incidentally, it's the 30th anniversary of our relationship as allies in NATO—that shouldn't we look at this and recognize that the unusual thing that has happened, that in these 40 years since the end of that war, the end of that tragedy of the Holocaust we have become the friends that we are, and use this occasion to make it plain that never again must we find ourselves enemies, and never again must there be anything like the Holocaust. And if that is what we can bring out of these observances and the trip that has been planned, then I think everything we're doing is very worthwhile.[56]

One of the ironies of the presidential dilemma over the Bitburg ceremony was that it greatly increased historical awareness of the Holocaust, fostering greater human sensitivity to the psychological pain rooted in the Nazi genocide committed four decades earlier. According to columnist William Safire, Reagan's blunders in dealing with this dilemma turned out to be a blessing in disguise because it made millions of people aware of the costs of reconciliation in a way that no other process could have accomplished. "In seeking at first to sidestep the smoldering resentments," Safire writes, "the President brought on a firestorm 40 years after a Holocaust, which in turn forced a forgetful world through a most necessary grief."[57]

MORAL REFLECTIONS

The Bitburg case study raises a number of issues about the morality of political reconciliation and the nature and feasibility of overcoming past regime offenses. Some of these issues include the following:

- Can nations that have abused power and committed great evils against other peoples be restored into the family of nations? Can a regime that has committed genocide ever overcome its evil past, or must its citizens bear continuing shame and guilt?
- If the bitter, angry past can be overcome, what actions must states fulfill in order to atone for past evils? If international political rehabilitation is possible, what actions must be undertaken in order to heal and restore communal solidarity?
- Has Germany atoned sufficiently for the atrocities of World War II? Given West Germany's postwar history and more particularly the political solidarity and close ties that emerged between the United States and West Germany during the Cold War, was it wrong for President Reagan to visit the German military cemetery at Bitburg? Why or why not?
- In view of the existence of forty-nine SS graves at this cemetery, will the Kolmeshöhe military cemetery always remain a symbol of evil?
- Although Bitburg illustrates the failure to accept collective repentance and grant political forgiveness, should regimes that have accepted culpability and atoned for their offenses be forgiven? Can the process of collective forgiveness contribute to the healing of nations and just, peaceful international relations?
- In a major speech to the Bundestag on May 8, 1985, West German president Richard von Weizsäcker observed that "whoever closes his eyes to the past becomes blind to the present."[58] In light of this claim, how can memory be sustained to honor past suffering while also encouraging reconciliation and the establishment of new political relationships?

SUMMARY

While accountability is important in reckoning with past regime offenses, retribution alone is unlikely to provide justice to victims, healing to offenders, or reconciliation to society. Although legal retribution is essential in the functioning of a developed political community, I have argued that restorative justice provides a preferable strategy because of its emphasis on the restoration of interpersonal and communal relations. Since social solidarity is essential to national peace and prosperity, the healing of communal bonds in the aftermath of systemic crimes and injustices is crucial to the consolidation of democracy and the rule of law. Thus, rather than focusing on the prosecution and punishment of offenders, the restorative strategy focuses on healing and renewal through truth-telling, public apologies, reparations, and political forgiveness. While it is still too early to assess its effectiveness, the South African experiment in amnesty for truth-telling is a bold effort to place communal healing at the heart of a transitional justice process. The Bitburg case study similarly illustrates the promise of healing through moral accountability, reparations, and the pursuit of peaceful, cooperative actions. Despite the consolidation of West German democracy and the establishment of strong bilateral ties between the United States and West Germany, the celebration of German–American reconciliation was problematic because of the symbols associated with the Bitburg cemetery. Even though the Bitburg site was morally problematic, President Reagan decided to follow the planned schedule, believing that it was more important to honor U.S.–German political reconciliation than to cancel a trip because of a tainted cemetery. To Reagan, West Germany had tangibly expressed repentance for Nazi atrocities through collective remorse, tangible reparations, and the consolidation of constitutional government. Although it is important to remember the past, it was time to move forward and honor the significant reforms and changes within Germany.

Chapter Five

The Ethics of International Human Rights

[Human rights] have become a kind of *lingua franca* of ethics talk so that much of the discussion about ethics in international relations takes place making use of the vocabulary of rights.[1]
  —R. J. VINCENT

Considerations of "justice"—democracy, human rights, human welfare—would . . . ordinarily be of a lower priority. . . . The reasoning here is simple. Order is the most basic concern. One can have order without justice but not the other way around.[2]
  —RICHARD H. HAASS

There are goods more important than order. There are wrongs worth righting even at the cost of injuring order.[3]
  —CHARLES KRAUTHAMMER

THE NEWS MEDIA regularly reminds citizens in the developed nations that there is much suffering in many poor, undemocratic states of the Third World. This suffering—manifested by hunger, disease, religious persecution, ethnic conflict, displacement, and mass killing—is often a direct result of political conflict over groups competing for power. For example, the post–Cold War disintegration of Yugoslavia led to a bitter ethnonationalistic war within Bosnia-Herzegovina among Croats, Muslims, and Serbs that resulted in an estimated 300,000 deaths and more than a million refugees. Similarly, the conflict among Somali clans in the early 1990s led to the total breakdown of public order, resulting in a bitter civil war that left hundreds of thousands of Somalis dead, mostly from starvation. In Rwanda, the animosity between Hutu and Tutsi peoples led to a tribal genocide in 1994 that claimed more than 800,000 lives and left more than two million refugees. Individuals, nonpolitical groups, and societies themselves also perpetuate significant suffering when they carry out actions that threaten the dignity of persons. For example, some societies continue to tolerate and even support practices that are widely condemned, such as slavery, child labor, female genital mutilation, and ethnic cleansing.

This chapter examines the quest for human dignity in global society. Because the international community is a society of societies, each with its own social, political, and economic institutions and cultural traditions, defining human rights and the policies likely to enhance human dignity is a daunting task. Even though global society is comprised of many distinct cultures, each with its own traditions and political values, the quest for human dignity is, nevertheless, a global struggle. It is a universal normative task, symbolized by the development of international humanitarian law, because of the shared conviction that each person is entitled to dignity, respect, and equal treatment by government authorities regardless of citizenship or nationality.

Individual rights can be defined and justified in either positive or normative terms. The positive, or empirical, approach describes the individual rights that are already claimed. Positive rights consist of those personal entitlements that are defined by existing domestic statutes or international treaties and conventions. According to the positivist perspective, individuals are entitled to rights because governing bodies have established binding rules and conventions that give effect to such rights. The normative, or moral, perspective defines the rights that ought to be protected. Normative rights include those human rights whose validity depends on the inherent moral legitimacy of the claims. Thus, the normative conception entails rules and principles that are regarded as binding, independent of the statutes and international treaties adopted by states. In sum, whereas positive rights are rooted in fact, normative rights are based on morality.[4]

In defining human rights, it is important to recall that morality can itself be differentiated between positivist and normative conceptions.[5] A normative conception of morality consists of rules and principles that are considered binding regardless of whether they are in fact universally upheld. By contrast, a positivist conception of morality consists of the rules or directives that are in fact upheld as obligatory by what individuals say, believe, or do. However, whether the rules and directives of conventions, such as the Universal Declaration of Human Rights or the International Covenant on Civil and Political Rights, are part of a moral structure will depend on whether persons (as well as groups and states) believe that such rules *ought to be upheld*. As Alan Gewirth has noted, for customs to become morality, there must be a normative component.[6]

The distinction between international morality and international mores is significant because it highlights the important moral role of international treaties and conventions in strengthening the definition and enforcement of human rights in global society. International human rights directives are frequently considered part of international law but not part of international ethics. However, if morality includes rules that people believe should be enforced in global society, such directives are an important part of international morality. Thus, in exploring human rights as a problem of international ethics, this chapter examines the role of international human rights law in the quest for human dignity and global justice.

This chapter has four parts. First, it examines the nature and origins of the human rights doctrine in terms of alternative human rights theories and in light of the problem posed by cultural pluralism. The challenge of competing interpretations of human rights is illustrated with a case study on caning in Singapore. Second, this chapter explores the role of human rights discourse in contemporary international politics, focusing on the international law of human rights. Third, it examines the challenges and opportunities in devising a human rights foreign policy and illustrates some of these moral challenges in using force to protect international human rights with a case study on Rwanda. Finally, it sets forth a number of guidelines that can contribute to the development of a prudent and effective human rights foreign policy.

THE IDEA OF HUMAN RIGHTS

The idea that human beings have individual rights is of comparatively recent origin. Throughout antiquity and the medieval age, Western political thinkers emphasized the development of just political communities by calling attention to the duties and responsibilities of individuals. Human dignity was assumed to be a by-product of participation within and obligations toward a political community. However, with the rise of humanism, the modernization and integration of markets, and the political consolidation of nation-states in the sixteenth and seventeenth centuries, European societies became increasingly urbanized, secularized, and fragmented. In addition, with the consolidation of state power, government authority expanded significantly as it made ever-increasing claims on individuals. At the same time, political thinkers began to emphasize the basic (or natural) rights of persons in political society, the conditional authority of government, and the necessity for limiting the power of rulers to minimize the possibility of tyranny and political oppression. The development of ideas such as these resulted in the theory of political liberalism, a revolutionary doctrine that was to provide the most comprehensive and compelling definition and justification of human rights in the modern world.[7] However, what is important to emphasize at this point is that human rights claims emerged within the context of political liberalism and were expressed fundamentally as claims of individuals against the state.[8]

Although the notion of human rights is a relatively modern political discovery, its development is rooted in a number of major ideas from ancient and medieval political thought. One of the most important of these ideas was the Stoic belief in the universality of moral reason, a concept that reinforced the notions of moral equality of persons and priority of political obligations to all human beings. Because individuals were joined by reason to all persons, their political obligations were not limited to the city-state, as the Greeks had believed, but extended to the universal community.[9] These two Stoic ideas—the universality of moral reason and the priority of the universal community—were significant because they contributed decisively to the rise of natural law, from which the notion of natural rights first emerged in the seventeenth century.

Christianity has also contributed significantly to the human rights idea by emphasizing, among other things, the inherent worth and dignity of every person and the conditionality of temporal obligations.[10] Christianity affirms the dignity of persons not only by claiming that human beings were created in God's image but also by granting the ultimate divine gift—salvation through Jesus' atonement—to all persons. Most significantly, Christianity asserts that God has established a divine, transcendent moral order to which all human beings are subject. In effect, human beings are subject to two authorities: the temporal power of the state and the divine commands of God. According to the Scriptures, citizens should render to Caesar the things that belong to Caesar and to God the things that belong to God. However, when conflict develops between these two realms, citizens should obey God rather than human authorities.

Although some thinkers have argued that human rights are not of Western origin, it is clear that the idea of individual rights is a historical product of European politics and rooted in Western political thought.[11] Some of the most important Western ideas that contributed to the emergence of the human rights idea include the following: 1) a transcendent moral order exists whose norms can be apprehended by reason;[12] 2) human rights are part of the natural order of creation; 3) human beings have inherent worth and need to be treated as ends rather than means; and 4) human beings are fundamentally equal. As originally developed, human rights were rooted in the moral assumptions about human nature. Thus, the notion of human rights was from its inception an ethical idea—a claim based on morality.

Theories of Human Rights

As first articulated, human rights are natural rights rooted in the moral nature of human persons. This perspective can be defined as the *moral theory of human rights*, because the claim that persons are entitled to fundamental claims or rights is grounded in morality. According to this classical theory, persons are entitled to particular benefits or goods by virtue of their humanity, that is, their essential moral worth as human beings. Because human rights are rooted in the fundamental dignity of persons, they are timeless and universal, applicable to all individuals regardless of race, gender, age, ethnicity, or nationality. Moreover, because these rights are rooted in the unique moral nature of persons, they exist independently of the communities, societies, and states in which people live. Thus, human rights are extralegal, deriving their legitimacy from their inherent (or moral) validity, not from constitutional or legal provisions or particular actions by states and international organizations.[13]

In the modern world, the idea of human rights has gained increasing influence. As noted by R. J. Vincent, the idea that human beings have rights as humans "is a staple of contemporary world politics."[14] Whereas the moral theory of human rights provided a convincing argument in the seventeenth and eighteenth centuries, in the modern world that theory has been increasingly challenged by alternative conceptions of rights. The earliest major challenges to the classical doctrine of individual rights were developed in the nineteenth century by such political thinkers as Edmund Burke and Jeremy Bentham. Burke, a late-eighteenth-century British parliamentarian, argued that human rights are rooted in communal customs and traditions, not in abstract reason and universal morality. As a result, human rights are not individualistic claims justified by reason but rather benefits that persons receive through participation in political society. Bentham, a cofounder of utilitarianism, was even more critical of human rights by disavowing the idea altogether.[15] Because Bentham believed that there was no such thing as transcendent morality or natural law, human rights were entirely fictitious. To speak of individual rights was to speak nonsense. Because human rights were rooted in civil laws, the rights derived from the "imaginary" laws of nature were themselves imaginary.

Although political thinkers have continued to challenge the idea of human rights since Burke, Bentham, and others first called into question the morality of individual rights, discourse on human rights continues to dominate contemporary international relations. And notwithstanding the denial of human rights by postmodern scholarship, intellectuals have continued to develop alternative conceptions and justifications of the human rights idea as they seek to develop a more compelling justification for them. To illustrate some of these different perspectives, four alternative human rights theories are briefly sketched here.

One alternative approach seeks to define and justify human rights in terms of basic physical needs. According to the *human needs theory*, persons are entitled to physical survival and security because without them, human life is impossible. Thus, human rights claims are rooted in the requirements of sustaining life and personal well-being.[16] Although this theory has the advantage of focusing on the tangible needs of human life, it fails to illuminate which physical requirements are essential. Moreover, it assumes that human dignity is necessarily achieved by giving priority to the physical dimensions of life.

Charles Beitz has developed a *social justice theory* of human rights that justifies rights in terms of distributive justice rather than the moral nature of persons.[17] According to this theory, human rights are entitlements, based on social justice norms, that ensure the well-being of persons. Beitz claims that because the classical doctrine of natural rights limits entitlements to personal security and fails to include socioeconomic claims, the social justice model provides a more comprehensive account of human rights. Beitz's model, however, has significant limitations. Because distributive justice necessarily depends on the cultures and capabilities of communities, human rights are conditioned by context. Moreover, by defining rights in terms of the distributive capabilities of a particular community, the social justice theory dissolves the fundamental distinction between government goals, such as providing welfare entitlements and individual rights.

A third approach is the so-called *constitutive theory* of human rights, which specifies the rudimentary rights that are necessary for the enjoyment of other human goods. According to Henry Shue, a proponent of this theory, human beings are entitled to those rights without which other desirable goods are impossible to attain. Shue argues that there are three such rights: security, subsistence, and liberty. These rights do not represent a complete list of basic rights, nor are they necessarily more desirable than other rights.[18] Rather, they specify the collective requirements that are necessary in fulfilling other desirable human goods. Although Shue argues that basic rights are collectively necessary to secure other goods, it is clear that individuals frequently enjoy basic rights to different degrees, thereby calling into question the mutual interdependence of basic rights.

A fourth approach, the *social-scientific theory* of human rights, seeks to justify human rights on the basis of cross-cultural consensus. Because of the high degree of cultural pluralism in the contemporary world and because of the continually changing role of mores and values in different societies, finding a high level of consensus on human rights is likely to prove elusive. However, even if significant international agreement were to be found, such an approach would still not offer a compelling argument for human rights, because a moral claim cannot be deduced from empirical facts.

In sum, although scholars continue to differ on how best to define and justify human rights, there is widespread political agreement that such rights claims are legitimate and provide a basis for making demands within states and the international community itself. Before examining the widely accepted international legal principles and conventions on human rights, I briefly address the problem posed by the doctrine of universal human rights in a global community characterized by cultural pluralism.

The Problem of Cultural Relativism

As noted previously, the international community is a society of multiple societies, each with its own languages, historical traditions, cultural norms, and religious and moral values. Cultural pluralism is a fact of global society. However, if moral, religious, and political values differ from society to society, and if human rights conceptions will necessarily reflect the cultural environment in which they are defined and applied, are all cultures equal? If not, whose culture is normative? When values and human rights conceptions come into conflict, who is to determine which interpretation is authoritative?

Because of the widespread relativity of values found in the world, some thinkers have concluded that there can be no international morality. The only morality that can exist is the morality of each particular society. If global society is simply the addition of shared cultures and morality, no doctrine of human rights is possible. The challenge posed by cultural pluralism is how to reconcile universal human rights claims with the fact of cultural and moral relativity.

There are two important points that need to be made about the claims of cultural relativism, one empirical and the other normative. Empirically, the claim of total moral diversity is simply untenable. As A. J. M. Milne has noted, moral diversity cannot be total because "certain moral principles are necessary for social life as such, irrespective of its particular form."[19] Milne argues that there is a common morality shared by all peoples. This morality involves such moral norms as justice, respect for human life, fellowship, freedom from arbitrary interference, and honorable treatment. However, every community also is based on a "particular" morality that is derived from each community's distinctive institutions, social order, and cultural values. As a result, the actual morality of a community involves both a common and a particular morality. Universal human rights are those rights rooted in a shared, or common, morality.

At a normative level, the claims of the doctrine of cultural relativism are similarly untenable because the fact of cultural relativity is not an ethical argument at all. To state that the world is comprised of different cultures is a descriptive statement. Its validity wholly depends on whether the empirical assertion is true. However, the doctrine of cultural relativism claims more than mere description. Because moral values are assumed to be valid only in their particular cultural contexts, cultural relativists claim not only that the values of one society are inapplicable to other societies but that no moral hierarchy among cultural systems is possible. Cultural relativists thus seek to derive an ethical doctrine from the fact of cultural pluralism. But as Vincent has observed, the doctrine of cultural relativism cannot logically rank cultures or pass judgments about them. All the doctrine can do is assert that values are rooted in the particularities of each culture.[20] Cultural values might deserve equal respect, but whether they are worthy of such respect depends on the impact of such norms on persons' behavior and quality of life. In short, because it is impossible to derive morality from empirical conditions, cultural relativism must remain a descriptive fact, not a normative proposition.

In reconciling cultural relativism with the universality of human rights, it is important to emphasize that universalism and relativism are not mutually exclusive categories but rather different ends of a continuum. The choice is not between the extremes of *radical universalism*, which holds that culture plays no role in defining the morality, and *radical cultural relativism,* which holds that culture is the only source of the morality. Rather, the affirmation of human rights in global society will necessarily be based on an intermediary position that recognizes both the reality of cultural pluralism and the imperative of rights claims rooted in universal morality. This is the view taken by Jack Donnelly, who defines his approach as "weak cultural relativism." According to him, such a position recognizes "a comprehensive set of *prima facie* universal human rights" while still allowing "occasional and strictly limited local variations and exceptions."[21] In defining and promoting international human rights, the challenge is to assert and defend the universality of basic rights while recognizing that the formulation and application of rights claims will depend in part on the social and cultural context in which rights claims are asserted.

A case study on flogging in Singapore illustrates the tension between universalism and cultural pluralism.

CASE 5-1: CANING IN SINGAPORE

BACKGROUND

In 1994 Michael Fay, an eighteen-year-old American youth, was found guilty of vandalism in Singapore after he and several other adolescents spray painted about fifty automobiles in a high-income area of the city. Fay was sentenced to six lashes with a cane, four months in prison, and a $2,200 fine—a punishment that was consistent with the severe penalties imposed on lawlessness in the quasi-authoritarian city-state of Singapore but that seemed grossly excessive from an American perspective. Because the punishment involved flogging, a practice long considered inhumane in the West, the Singapore court

verdict precipitated a brief public debate in the United States over the legitimacy of Fay's punishment. The media debate also spread to other related themes, including the relative effectiveness and morality of the Western and Asian approaches to law and order.

Although Singapore is a modern, economically prosperous city-state, it is a tightly regulated society with limited political freedoms and strict social and cultural controls. Economically, Singapore is a relatively free, competitive market system, prospering greatly from global trade; however, politically and socially Singapore is a quasi-authoritarian state, an illiberal society with significant governmental controls over political, social, and cultural life. According to one comparative study of political and civil freedoms, in 1994–1995 Singapore ranked toward the bottom of the countries classified as "partly free."[22] For example, Singapore permits the detention of suspects for up to two years. It also requires organized groups of ten or more to register with the government, and permission from the police is required for any meeting of more than five persons. In addition, Singapore's police must approve speakers at all public functions. Socially, the regulations seem even more draconian: Public acts such as chewing gum, spitting, or feeding birds carry a fine of several hundred dollars; there are even severe penalties for failing to flush a public toilet or eating in the subway.

Flogging, as practiced in Singapore, consists of tying a prisoner to a wooden trestle and striking him or her on the buttocks with a damp rattan cane. Although the effects of caning depend on the number and intensity of the strokes, the punishment involves intense physical suffering, frequently resulting in the tearing of skin tissue that leads to permanent scars. It is a generally accepted principle of international law that torture is an unacceptable form of punishment. For example, Article 7 of the International Covenant on Civil and Political Rights, which went into force in 1976, declares, "No one shall be subjected to torture or to cruel, inhuman or degrading treatment or punishment."

THE MORAL DEBATE OVER CANING

When Fay was sentenced to six lashes, an intense public debate emerged in the United States over the appropriateness of such punishment and the relative effectiveness of Singapore's criminal justice system. The debate increased in intensity when President Bill Clinton condemned the punishment as "excessive" and called on Singapore's president, Ong Teng Cheong, to commute the sentence. In response to Clinton's appeal, President Cheong decreased the caning from six lashes to four, with the punishment being served on May 5, 1994. After an additional month in prison, Fay was released and then returned to the United States to live with his father.

The discourse precipitated by the caning of Fay was fundamentally a public debate of alternative theories of political society and human rights—a debate between the "Asian School" and Western liberalism. Had Singapore been a poor, backward, corrupt society and had the United States not experienced significant social and moral decay in recent years, it is unlikely that the Fay verdict would have erupted in widespread public debate. However, Singapore is not a corrupt Third World nation, nor is the United States an example of civic virtue and social development. Indeed, Singapore has become a modern, dynamic economic society, providing ample economic and social benefits to its people in an urban environment of safety, low crime, social order, and economic prosperity. By contrast, the United States, the leading industrial democratic society in the world, has experienced a dramatic loss of social order, involving the breakdown of family life, the disintegration of neighborhoods, and a rise in crime. The cultural and social decay of the United States is dramatically illustrated by a comparison of Los Angeles and Singapore, cities of roughly the same size: In 1993 Singapore had 58 murders and 80 rapes, whereas Los Angeles had 1,058 murders and 1,781 rapes.[23]

Lee Kwan Yew, the former long-term prime minister of Singapore and the chief architect of the country's political and social system, believes that the social and cultural decline of the West is due to its excessive emphasis on individualism and freedom. The East Asian approach to political society has the advantage, he believes, in more effectively balancing the claims of social and communal goods with the demands of individuals. In his assessment of the social decline of the United States, Kishore Mahbubani, an official of Singapore's foreign ministry, writes, "This social deterioration is so drastic that it cannot possibly be the result of a mere economic downturn or fewer resources for law and order. To Asian eyes, it suggests that something fundamental has gone wrong in the United States."[24] Mahbubani goes on to suggest that the source of social ills in the United States is its ideology of excessive individualism and personal freedom, which has helped to undermine the family and other social institutions. The celebration of individual freedom, in his view, has had an ironic outcome, contributing to social decay and a cultural decline that now threatens the personal security and economic and social well-being of individuals. Mahbubani is critical of Western societies because he thinks that the rights of criminals have been given precedence over the rights of victims. He writes: "It is obvious that this enormous reduction of freedom in America is the result of a mindless ideology that maintains that freedom of a small number of individuals (criminals, terrorists, street gang members, drug dealers), who are known to pose a threat to society, should not be constrained . . . even if to do so would enhance the freedom of the majority."[25] For Mahbubani and other East Asian officials, American culture has become flawed because of its excessive emphasis on individual rights that has, in turn, weakened social institutions and impaired the criminal justice system.

In sum, the moral debate over caning was rooted partly in alternative conceptions of political society and human rights. What was considered cruel treatment in Western societies was regarded as necessary punishment to protect social and political life in Asia.

MORAL REFLECTIONS

This case raises a number of important issues about the conceptualization and implementation of human rights.

- Is caning torture, as the West asserts, or a harsh punishment, as some Third World countries claim?[26]
- When states hold different conceptions of human rights, as was the case in this dispute, which party is to decide whose political morality is correct?
- Does Western political morality emphasize individual rights and freedoms excessively?
- Is the Western emphasis on individual rights claims morally superior to the Asian approach that emphasizes communal obligations? Why or why not?
- How should the West respond to Asian claims that countries such as Singapore have a more stable and secure social order precisely because they emphasize social and community obligations rather than celebrate individual rights?

THE INTERNATIONAL LAW OF HUMAN RIGHTS

Despite the divergent theories, competing ethical and philosophical justifications, and contested interpretations of human rights, there is widespread *political* acceptance of the idea of human rights in the contemporary world. This political agreement is evident in the significant body of international law of human rights that has developed through the codification of norms, rules, and directives in binding conventions. Although international human rights law first began to emerge in the nineteenth century with norms such as the prohibition against piracy and slavery, such laws have developed mainly since the end of World War II.

The first major modern international legal agreement to highlight human rights in contemporary global society was the UN Charter. Although the charter is essentially a constitutional document delineating the institutional structures and functions of the UN system, it is also an important human rights document because it specifies the promotion and protection of human rights as one of the major purposes of the United Nations. In its preamble, the charter reaffirms faith in "fundamental human rights" and then calls on member states to promote and encourage "respect for human rights and for fundamental freedoms" (Article 1). Later, the charter delineates some of the international human rights obligations that member states should promote (Article 55), calling on states to take individual and collective actions in support of these norms.

In 1948, the UN General Assembly adopted the Universal Declaration of Human Rights. Because of its inclusive, comprehensive nature, the declaration is generally recognized as the charter of international human rights, providing its most authoritative global definition.[27] The declaration does not distinguish or rank different types of human rights; rather, it affirms a comprehensive listing of basic, civil, political, social, economic, and cultural rights. The inability to develop a listing of foundational rights and to discriminate between rights and worthy socioeconomic goals was due in great measure to the growing ideological conflict between the two major powers—the United States and the Soviet Union. As a result, the declaration is rooted in a plural conception of human rights, with the West championing civil and political rights and the East championing socioeconomic rights. It is important to emphasize also that although the declaration is not formally international law (it was adopted as a resolution, not as a binding treaty), it is nonetheless viewed as part of the international law of human rights, providing direction in the development and codification of human rights norms.[28]

The international law of human rights is expressed in a number of legally binding agreements. The two most important of these are the International Covenant on Civil and Political Rights and the International Covenant on Economic, Social, and Cultural Rights (see table 5-1), which together essentially legislate what the declaration proclaims.[29] Although the drafters of the declaration had originally intended to follow up their work with a single treaty, Cold War rivalries delayed its development and adoption by more than a decade. Moreover, rather than drafting a single convention, superpower politics resulted in two different agreements, with Western democracies identifying much more with the convention on political and civil rights and the communist states identifying much more with the convention on social and economic rights.

Although the UN has sought to proclaim the interdependence and indivisibility of human rights, political leaders, representing various types of political regimes and diverse cultural traditions, continue to espouse different and at times conflicting conceptions of human rights. International tensions over human rights doctrine are inevitable when statesmen proclaim divergent political ideologies. However, rather than assessing the legitimacy of the different human rights claims and seeking to reconcile the relative merits of conflicting theories, international organizations have simply expanded human rights, incorporating new claims advocated by influential transnational political groups. For example, new rights claims that have been gaining legitimacy in the international community include the "the right to development" and "reproductive rights."[30]

The limited consensus on human rights doctrines, coupled with the ever-expanding list of rights, has had a deleterious effect on the moral foundations and priority of

Table 5-1: Selected International Human Rights

According to the *International Covenant on Civil and Political Rights* (1966), states are obligated to respect and promote a wide variety of basic rights. These include

- the right to life and physical security of the person;
- freedom of thought, religion, and expression;
- freedom of association and peaceful assembly;
- due process of law and a humane penal system;
- freedom from torture; and
- the right to legal equality and nondiscrimination.

According to the *International Covenant on Economic, Social and Cultural Rights* (1966), states are obligated to respect and promote such rights as

- the right to work and to enjoy an adequate standard of living;
- the right to just working conditions, including fair compensation;
- a safe and healthy working environment and periodic holidays;
- the right to form trade unions and to strike;
- the right to education;
- the right to social security; and
- the right to participate in cultural life.

Both covenants emphasize that human rights must be available on the basis of equality and nondiscrimination.

international human rights claims. Because of growing pluralism and confusion about human rights, it has become increasingly difficult to differentiate between basic rights claims (e.g., freedom of conscience and freedom from torture) and secondary rights claims (e.g., the right to work and the right to a jury trial).

This contemporary confusion about human rights was amply evident at the 1993 World Conference on Human Rights, the largest international meeting on human rights in twenty-five years. The aim of this UN-sponsored conference was to bring together governmental and nongovernmental representatives to develop a post–Cold War declaration on international human rights. In preparation for this gathering in Vienna, several regional meetings were held to develop distinctive human rights perspectives and concerns within each geographic region. Whereas Western states did not hold a preparatory meeting, African leaders met in Tunis, Latin American and Caribbean leaders in San Jose, and Asian and Pacific delegates in Bangkok. Each of these meetings issued a declaration named after the city in which officials gathered.

Although each of the regional declarations represented alternative perspectives from the political liberalism championed by the West, the Bangkok Declaration represented a blatant challenge to the idea of basic human rights rooted in limited, democratic government. In that declaration, Asian leaders proclaimed the universality of rights but then argued against such universality by noting that rights "must be considered in the context of . . . national and regional particularities and various historical, cultural and religious backgrounds." Moreover, after affirming the sanctity of state sovereignty, the Bangkok Declaration notes that the promotion of human rights is to be carried out mainly through domestic institutions, not in response to foreign political pressure. Indeed, the declaration emphasizes that foreign aid should not be conditional on the observance of human rights. From an international relations perspective, the Bangkok Declaration is important because it presents a radical departure from the traditional Western conceptualization of human rights, capturing the growing antipathy toward Western democratic values and the priority that the West assigns to political and civil rights.

In view of the increasing conceptual pluralism of human rights, the development of a consensus at the Vienna conference among government representatives from 171 countries proved to be a daunting task. However, what enabled the conference to issue a collective declaration was not the development of greater agreement about the nature of human rights but rather a procedural decision that the Vienna proceedings would be carried out through a "consensus" in which the conference decisions would be based on unanimity. This meant that the final declaration had to be approved by all 171 governments or there would be no final action at all. Because there was significant international pressure to adopt a concluding declaration, efforts to resolve competing and conflicting norms would have delayed the proceedings and possibly threatened the conference itself. As a result, the aim of the conference proceedings was to develop a comprehensive statement that partially satisfied each of the regional groups and many of the 2,000 nongovernmental organizations represented at the conference.

The Final Declaration and Action Program of the World Conference on Human Rights, known as the Vienna Declaration, is a long statement divided into a preamble, a declaration of principles, and a plan of action. The statement of principles, the most important section, includes a reaffirmation of widely accepted political, social, and economic rights but noticeably omits such core rights as freedom of religion, freedom of assembly and association, and freedom of speech. Indeed, the document places its greatest emphasis on social and economic rights, giving at best cursory coverage to civil and political rights associated with limited, democratic government. From a liberal perspective, the major shortcoming of the Vienna conference was the failure of the United States and its allies to press the importance of democratic government in promoting human rights. Thus, one critic suggested that the Vienna Declaration was "a hodgepodge collection of high principles, stolen wording and bad compromises" and was likely to be used by authoritarian rulers "to justify old and new human rights violations."[31]

Because respect for human rights depends in great measure on the underlying political and cultural values of the international community, the Vienna conference is significant because it illuminates the contested and increasingly pluralistic political foundation of global society.[32] However, to the extent that human rights are approached from an increasingly pluralistic or multicultural worldview, the international law of human rights is likely to be regarded as less authoritative. The challenge for the international community is to delimit human rights and to emphasize only those rights considered essential to human dignity.

HUMAN RIGHTS AND FOREIGN POLICY

When gross human rights violations occur in global society, who is responsible for halting and punishing such evil? Are foreign governments morally responsible, individually or collectively, for minimizing human suffering from poverty, hunger, torture, genocide, and war? Do citizens from one state bear moral responsibilities for the personal security and well-being of persons in other states? When governments carry out mass murder and genocide against their own people, how should foreign states respond? As noted earlier, one of the basic ethical norms of global society is that moral obligations are not limited by territorial boundaries. However, if individuals, groups, and states bear moral obligations toward human beings in foreign lands, it is much less evident how such moral obligations should be fulfilled. In the final two sections, I examine the moral responsibility of states in deterring and halting mass murder and genocide and then set forth some principles for advancing human rights in foreign countries. In addressing the first theme, I attempt to illustrate some of the foreign policy challenges in protecting and advancing human rights with a case study on Rwanda.

Although UN membership requires that states promote human rights domestically and internationally, there is no international consensus about the role that human rights should play in foreign policy. Not only do regimes differ as to which human rights are most important, but governments also differ in the priority they assign to human rights goals in international affairs. The United States, which as noted earlier has been inspired periodically by moral idealism in its foreign policy, has undoubtedly been a strong proponent of human rights in world politics. However, its approach has also varied greatly, from the public expressions of humanitarianism by such presidents as Woodrow Wilson and Jimmy Carter to the quiet realpolitik of Richard Nixon and Ronald Reagan. Moreover, northern European countries, such as Norway, Denmark, and the Netherlands, have emphasized socioeconomic rights through their foreign aid and humanitarian assistance programs. Still other major powers, such as Japan and Germany, have deemphasized human rights altogether, believing that the definition and expression of basic rights must be derived from the particular political and cultural environment of each nation-state.

There is no simple way by which states can promote international human rights in other countries. The idea of human rights is, after all, subversive to the idea of an international society of sovereign states.[33] It is subversive for at least two reasons. First, because human rights are, as George F. Kennan has observed, inextricably related to the cultural values and political, economic, and social structures of society, it is impossible to demand human rights reforms without also demanding corresponding changes in other aspects of society on which those rights depend.[34] Some regimes might tolerate human rights violations even though their laws and prevailing cultural and political norms affirm individual rights. However, most human rights abuses involve more than a failure to live up to domestic rules. Instead, they are a direct by-product of a deficient (often an antidemocratic) political culture and an inadequate institutionalization of human rights norms. Thus, when a government demands that another state fulfill its human rights standards more fully, it typically involves a challenge not only to that society's government rules but also to its prevailing cultural mores.

Second, the idea of human rights is subversive because it establishes norms that if not fulfilled by a state can undermine its international legitimacy. Since the international legal order is based upon the sovereign independence of states, each government is responsible for the well-being of its people. When government abuse or disregard the human rights of people, they potentially forfeit their claim to sovereignty. The notion of human rights is therefore subversive to the international legal order, especially when states fail to fulfill their legal obligations.[35] Notwithstanding the widespread popularity of human rights, there is a large gap between the international declarations and conventions on human rights and states' actions in protecting and affirming those rights. As a result, the idea of human rights is potentially revolutionary because its effective application would involve significant behavioral reforms. Moreover, in those regimes where individual rights are systematically abused by the government itself, it would necessitate the radical transformation of both the structures of government and the underlying social, cultural, and political norms and values.

Preventing Mass Murder and Genocide

The international protection of human rights in the modern world is an especially difficult task not only because human rights are regarded as part of the domestic jurisdiction of governments but also because governments themselves abuse rights. Indeed, the most serious human rights violations in the twentieth century have been due not to war, intergroup conflict, or domestic disorder but to deliberate government campaigns of mass murder, or what Stanley Hoffmann terms "the institutionalization of cruelty."[36] In addition, as R. J. Rummel has observed, governments in the twentieth century have been far more brutal to their own people than to foreigners. Whereas international and civil wars have resulted in the death of 35 million persons, Rummel found that domestic killing by authoritarian and totalitarian regimes has claimed the lives of 169 million persons, nearly four and a half times the rate of wartime deaths.[37] Rummel argues that genocide and mass killing by governments—a phenomenon he calls *democide*—is a direct result of the development of authoritarian and totalitarian regimes possessing arbitrary, unconstrained power. The two most destructive regimes have been the Soviet Union and communist China, which together are responsible for murdering 97 million persons, or more than half of all the twentieth century's democide.[38]

In the mid-twentieth century Raphael Lemkin, a Polish Jew, coined the term "genocide" to distinguish killing in wartime from the deliberate effort to exterminate ethnic or religious groups. Limkin had become concerned with ethnic killing when the civilized world failed to hold Turkey accountable for the mass extermination of Armenians during World War I. After Germany invaded his homeland, Lemkin fled to the United States where he continued his single-minded struggle to combat the deliberate and systematic efforts to destroy national, ethnic, racial, or religious groups of people. Since this crime did not have a name, he developed the concept "genocide," rooted in the Greek word *geno*, meaning "race or "tribe," and the Latin suffix *cide*, meaning "killing."

As a result of his tireless efforts, the United Nations General Assembly passed a resolution in December 1946 condemning genocide "as contrary to moral law and to the aims and spirit of the United Nations." More importantly, the measure called for drafting a treaty that would ban this crime. In 1948 the General Assembly approved unanimously the Convention on the Prevention and Punishment of the Crime of Genocide, and two years later the treaty entered into force after a sufficient number of states had ratified it.[39] Although more than 100 states have ratified the treaty, ethnic killing continued throughout the late twentieth century. As Samantha Power notes, in her Pulitzer Prize–winning book "*A Problem from Hell*," the United States, along with other major powers, has generally failed to use its power and influence to halt genocide.[40] For example, in recent decades the United States failed to respond to the mass ethnic killing in Cambodia (2 million deaths), Iraq (100,000 Kurds killed), Bosnia (200,000 deaths), Rwanda (800,000 Tutsi deaths), and Sudan (more than 2 million deaths). Only in Kosovo (see Case 1-1) did the United States, in concert with other NATO powers, resort to war to halt ethnic cleansing and prevent the mass killing of Albanians.[41]

If the promotion of human rights is a legitimate end of foreign policy, surely the protection of life from genocide and mass murder must be regarded as an essential element of a comprehensive human rights policy. Regrettably, however, states have rarely used their individual and collective power to halt the most serious violations of human rights. For example, major powers did not attempt to halt either the Soviet communist government's deliberate starvation of 5 million Ukrainian peasants in the 1930s or to prevent the mass murder of 6.5 million Soviet peasants (kulaks) who were resisting collectivization. Moreover, the international community did nothing to prevent the Chinese communist government from slaughtering more than 20 million of its citizens in the 1950s and 1960s.

From time to time governments have tried to prevent genocide when such mass murder threatens regional security. This was the case with Pakistan's mass murder of 1.5 million Bengalis in Bangladesh (formerly East Pakistan) in 1971, when, in response to this genocidal campaign, some 10 million persons fled to India. This influx of refugees precipitated India's military intervention that ultimately led to West Pakistan's political independence. In 1992–1995, Western powers failed to halt ethnic cleansing in Bosnia, but when the Balkan conflict threatened to expand beyond the Balkans, the United States helped to broker a NATO-enforced cease-fire. Similarly, when Serbs threatened to repeat their ethnic cleansing and killing toward Albanians in Kosovo, NATO used an intense ten-week bombing campaign to force Serb military and police forces from Kosovo.

Why have major powers failed to halt the brutality of modern authoritarian and totalitarian regimes? Why have they failed to protect innocent masses from the breakdown of domestic regimes and the spread of civil strife? To a significant degree, states have been reticent to protect human rights in foreign countries because they have been unwilling to challenge the norm of sovereignty and to risk war over interests not considered vital to the nation. Historically, states have used military force to protect core interests, such as territorial security, but have been reluctant to use force to pursue secondary interests, such as the welfare and humanitarian needs of foreign societies. According to Power, the fundamental reason for the failure of the United States government to respond to genocide has not been lack of knowledge or lack of military and political resources to act. Rather, the main reason why the United States has avoided humanitarian intervention is lack of political will. Powers writes: "American leaders did not act because they did not want to. They believed that genocide was wrong, but they were not prepared to invest the military, financial, diplomatic or domestic political capital needed to stop it."[42] According to Power, what is most shocking about U.S. foreign policy is not its failure to directly intervene militarily. Rather, what is most disturbing is that the U.S. government did almost nothing to deter genocide. Since the country's vital national interests were not threatened by mass killing, Power claims that senior U.S. officials "did not give genocide the moral attention it warranted."[43]

In the final analysis, states must decide whether narrow national goals or broad universal values should guide their foreign policies. Moreover, in pursuing a principled foreign policy, states must face the conflict between two legitimate international norms—sovereignty and human rights. If states have been reluctant to prevent mass murder and alleviate human suffering, it may be because they have given precedence to national interests over cosmopolitan values, sovereignty over humanitarian goals.

To illuminate the tensions between sovereignty and suffering, power and human rights, I next examine the 1994 Rwanda genocide, arguably the most egregious violation of human rights in the post–Cold War era.

CASE 5-2: THE RWANDA GENOCIDE

BACKGROUND

Rwanda is a small nation of about eight million inhabitants in central Africa that is populated by two different peoples: the Hutu and the Tutsi. Although both groups speak the same language, enjoy the same type of food, share similar religious beliefs, and have lived side by side for centuries, they differ in physical appearance and in the vocations they pursue. The Hutu, a short, Bantu people, have historically lived as peasants cultivating the land; the Tutsi, by contrast, are a taller people from northern Africa who have generally worked in cattle grazing. Moreover,

Rwanda's Hutu majority (85 percent of the population) has been historically ruled by the Tutsi minority (15 percent of the population). Even during the colonial rule that began in the late nineteenth century, German and Belgian colonial rulers governed through the Tutsi authorities.

In response to growing demands by the Hutu majority for self-determination, Rwanda gained its independence from Belgium in 1962. After gaining power, the Hutu sought to redress historic political, social, and economic inequalities, resulting in reverse discrimination against the Tutsi. As a result, hundreds of thousands of Tutsis fled Rwanda to neighboring states, especially

Uganda and Burundi. In the 1980s, the Tutsi established a guerrilla force, the Rwandan Patriotic Front (RPF), with the aim of ending Hutu oppression. To halt the cycle of violence, Hutu president Juvenal Habyarimana and Tutsi military leaders signed a power-sharing peace agreement, the Arusha Accords, in Arusha, Tanzania, in 1993. The aim of the accord was to establish a cease-fire between the ruling Hutu and the RPF, develop power sharing among competing groups, carry out internationally supervised democratic elections, facilitate the repatriation of refugees, and encourage the integration of the RPF with the government's armed forces.[44] To ensure the accord's implementation, the UN Security Council established an observer force of 2,500 troops, known as the UN Assistance Mission in Rwanda (UNAMIR).

THE GENOCIDE

On April 6, 1994, as President Habyarimana was returning to Kigali, Rwanda's capital, two missiles hit his jet as it approached the airport. The plane spun out of control and crashed, killing all passengers. Within hours of Habyarimana's death, Hutu militia, led by the Presidential Guard, began a systematic massacre of all Tutsis and some Hutu moderates, including the government's prime minister and ten Belgian members of UNAMIR assigned to protect her. This action led Belgium to withdraw its 400 other troops, virtually paralyzing the UN force.[45] Encouraged by political and civic extremists, Hutu killing spread quickly throughout the land, resulting in the coordinated murder of tens of thousands of civilians. One of the largest massacres occurred in mid-April in the western city of Kibuye, when more than 5,000 Tutsis were rounded up in a stadium and slaughtered. Although the government forces were well equipped with modern weapons, the genocide was carried out by tens of thousands of Hutus at close quarters with primitive weapons. "If people murdered with machetes," writes David Rieff, "it was because the Hutu leadership had conceived of a genocide that would involve the entire Hutu people."[46]

The genocide did not end until the RPF took control of major Rwandan centers by mid-June. By that time, however, the Hutus had killed at least 800,000 Tutsis and moderate Hutus, making this genocide campaign one of the deadliest and most destructive in modern times.[47] One observer has written that the Rwandan genocide "claimed more lives more quickly than any campaign of mass murder in recorded history."[48] Moreover, the RPF's rapid conquest of Rwanda led to one of the largest and fastest refugee movements ever, with more than two million persons fleeing to neighboring states in the immediate aftermath of the collapse of the Hutu regime.

THE FAILURE OF INTERNATIONAL HUMANITARIAN PROTECTION

In view of the disintegration of Rwandan society, the mass killing, and the displacement of some 2.2 million refugees, what actions should neighboring African states have taken to prevent or, at a minimum, limit human suffering? What actions should the major powers have carried out when the evidence of mass killing first came to light? Should an international peacekeeping force have been deployed, and, if so, what should have been its short- and long-term missions? Which states should have participated in and paid for such an operation?

When the genocide began, the only foreign troops in Rwanda were some 1,400 troops of the UN observer force. UNAMIR, created solely to assist implementation of the Arusha Accords, was not authorized to use force to keep peace. Thus, when the genocide began, the UN force was unable to deter mass killing, and after Belgium recalled its troops in mid-April, the remaining UN troops were kept in the barracks. Subsequently, the Security Council, on the recommendation of UN Secretary General Boutros Boutros-Ghali, called for a reduction in the UN observer force to 270 troops.[49] Eventually, Boutros-Ghali reversed his views by calling for the creation of a 5,000-member peacekeeping force. The Security Council, however, refused to support his request. The United States opposed the proposed peacekeeping operation partly because of cost (the U.S. share of peacekeeping operations is 30 percent) but also because of a lack of clarity about the operation's mission and organization. Speaking about the need for a Rwandan peacekeeping operation, President Bill Clinton said that it was important for the United Nations to learn "when to say no."[50] But other major powers on the Security Council, including Britain and France, also had misgivings about military intervention. As Michael Barnett has argued, senior UN leaders could have taken action to either halt or limit the scope of the genocide. In his view, "high-ranking UN staff and some council members either knew of, or had good reason to suspect, crimes against humanity. They had a moral obligation to urge UN action. They did not."[51]

Only one major power (France) temporarily deployed troops after the RPF had gained substantial control of the country. When Hutus began fleeing to surrounding states, France, a supporter of the fallen Hutu regime, carried out a temporary humanitarian intervention to prevent Tutsi military forces from retaliating against fleeing Hutus. The French interventionary force established a security zone in the southwestern part of Rwanda, thereby providing foreign protection for a two-month period (June 23 to August 21). It has been estimated that the French intervention was responsible for saving the lives of tens of thousands of fleeing Hutus.

However, states did provide significant humanitarian assistance to the large Rwandan refugee camps in Zaire, Tanzania, and Burundi.[52] Major international governmental and nongovernmental organizations played a key role in providing humanitarian supplies and medical aid. The U.S. government, in particular, gave significant financial and humanitarian assistance, and when a cholera epidemic began to spread among the 1.2 million Hutu refugees in Goma, Zaire, it authorized the deployment of 4,000 soldiers to assist the relief effort and to prevent the spread of cholera. However, the introduction of U.S. forces was solely for humanitarian relief rather than peacekeeping.

The Rwandan genocide and the subsequent displacement of refugees suggest that, despite the claims and rhetoric of international human rights, foreign states are not eager to intervene to prevent mass killing. Even though international humanitarian law has become increasingly accepted as part of the legal and normative structure of global society, the promotion and protection of human rights is still regarded as an obligation mainly of states. As one scholar has observed, "Until the great powers in the Security Council are willing to act together, and to absorb comparatively small numbers of casualties to prevent the large-scale slaughter of innocent people, there will continue to be after-the-fact hand-wringing and emergency aid efforts. And once again it will have been too late for everything except the grief."[53]

ACCOUNTABILITY

In late 1994 the UN Security Council established the International Criminal Tribunal for Rwanda (ICTR). The court, located in Arusha, Tanzania, was created as an appendage of The Hague-based International Criminal Tribunal for the Former Yugoslavia. Like its Hague counterpart, the Arusha court is charged with prosecuting leaders who have planned or carried out crimes against humanity. For the ICTR, this has meant prosecuting those governmental and nongovernmental leaders with the greatest responsibility for planning and instigating the genocide. Unlike The Hague court, the ICTR has been plagued since its inception with logistical difficulties, bureaucratic inefficiencies, and professional incompetence. Despite a staff of more than 800 persons and an annual budget of $88 million, the court has indicted fewer than 100 persons and convicted only 17 after nine years of work.[54]

Fortunately the primary responsibility for pursuing legal accountability has been the Rwandan courts themselves. Given the small size of the Rwandan judicial system, the country's courts have been overwhelmed by a long backlog of cases. Even though these courts were able to hold trials for some 6,000 alleged offenders through 2002, more than 110,000 Hutus still languished in overcrowded Rwandan prisons awaiting trial. To help alleviate the judicial process, the Rwandan government has begun using traditional communal courts to try lower level cases. This system, known as *gacaca*, calls for elders to dispense justice based upon the hearing and weighing of evidence.[55] In these traditional courts judges and juries sit together on the grass to hear and weigh different sides of a conflict and then determine the guilt or innocence of persons. In these informal hearings, offenders are encouraged to confess and repent of their crimes in the hope that such confession will mitigate punishment and facilitate reconciliation.

MORAL REFLECTIONS

This case raises troubling moral issues about international responsibility for mass atrocities as well as concerns about how best to pursue individual accountability and communal reconstruction.

- Samantha Power writes that the Rwandan genocide was "the fastest, most efficient killing spree of the twentieth century."[56] In view of the widespread commitment by Western nations to the principle "Never Again," how could a genocide that killed persons at a rate faster than the Nazi Holocaust have been allowed to occur in the late twentieth century?
- When it became evident that society-wide killing was underway, should the United States and other major powers have intervened to halt the genocide, even if such intervention would have required a long-term nation-building program?
- During his trip to Africa in 1998, President Clinton expressed regret that the international community had not acted more decisively in halting the Rwanda genocide. In light of his apology, who should bear political guilt over the failure to prevent mass killing—the United States, other major powers, the United Nations, the international community?
- In view of the great demand for trials, is the *gacaca* process morally warranted? Since the traditional courts are authorized only to deal with Hutu crimes, not war crimes that may have been perpetrated by Tutsi guerrillas, is this process still morally justified?
- In light of the analysis in the previous chapter, could political forgiveness contribute to political healing and national reconciliation in a case such as the Rwandan genocide?

PROMOTING HUMAN RIGHTS

Because of difficulties and grave risks entailed in curbing governmental genocide and mass murder, states concerned with human rights have tended to emphasize individual human rights abuses and to neglect systemic, society-wide genocidal campaigns. Western democratic countries have typically promoted civil, political, social, and economic rights selectively. For example, as noted in the previous chapter, the Carter administration's human rights policy focused on individual human rights abuses carried out by authoritarian regimes and neglected the more serious oppression of totalitarian regimes. President Ronald Reagan radically transformed this policy by focusing on the systemic abuses of human rights by totalitarian regimes. Because communist governments were considered a major obstacle to human dignity, the Reagan administration sought to advance human rights by allocating significant aid to anticommunist political groups and Third World regimes threatened by revolutionary Marxist movements. Western European countries, in contrast, have emphasized human rights through quiet diplomacy, giving precedence to social and economic rights through humanitarian programs and foreign aid transfers.

How should major powers promote human rights in global society? What norms should guide their actions? In devising an effective human rights policy, the challenge consists of improving rights without unduly threatening the decentralized nature of global society. The U.S. human rights policies of the 1970s and 1980s offer a number of lessons and insights about the international advocacy of human rights. In light of past experience, the following four principles can contribute to a prudent and effective human rights policy: 1) the priority of actions over declarations, 2) the necessity of developing preconditions for sustaining and protecting basic rights, 3) the superiority of quiet over public diplomacy, and 4) the imperative of humility and modesty. Each is discussed here.

1. Giving priority to actions over rhetoric is important in promoting human rights because the bilateral and multilateral initiatives on human rights have traditionally focused on declarations and conventions. However, the achievement of rights does not depend on pronouncements, constitutions, and international conventions. The emphasis on human rights pronouncements has no doubt contributed to the widespread acceptance of the human rights idea in global political discourse, but it has also had a deleterious effect in fostering the illusion that constitutions, bills of rights, and conventions are sufficient for the implementation of rights. However, declarations and conventions are not self-activating. Robert Goldwin has observed that it is regrettable that so much time and energy has been devoted to creating the illusion that enunciating rights will necessarily lead to their enforcement. He writes that it is either "a conscious fraud, or a naive faith in the magic of words" to assert that recognizing the human right to enough food will resolve the problem of hunger.[57] Thus, some scholars argue that excessive emphasis on the rhetoric of rights can be counterproductive to the advancement of human dignity of persons because it can distract attention from the task of securing basic human rights.

2. Developing socioeconomic and political preconditions is also essential in maintaining a credible and effective human rights policy. As noted earlier, because human rights cannot be separated from the institutions and practices of government or the social and cultural mores of society, it is impossible to promote specific human rights norms in other societies without also changing other dimensions of those societies. Thus, a credible human rights policy must cultivate the essential social, political, and economic preconditions for human rights.

3. Quiet diplomacy is also important in devising a sound human rights policy. The reason that quiet, confidential diplomacy is important in addressing human rights is that states are reluctant to alter their policies solely in response to foreign pressure. Soviet leader Leonid Brezhnev once remarked that "to teach others how to live cannot be accepted by a sovereign state." Although President Carter's highly public human rights policy elevated human rights to a prominent place in U.S. foreign relations, there is considerable disagreement over the extent to which such open diplomacy contributed to an improved observance of human rights. Some scholars argue that public pronouncements, condemnations, and sanctions not only fail to encourage human rights but frequently help to further consolidate oppressive regimes.[58] William Gleysteen, Jr., a former U.S. ambassador, has written that condemnatory public statements about human rights are "one of the most tempting but most coun-

terproductive [foreign policy] instruments."[59] The difficulty of linking human rights to economic interests is also illustrated by the failure of the United States to use most-favored-nation status to foster more humane treatment of dissidents. When President Clinton assumed office, he sought to promote human rights in China by making economic trade conditional on the improvement of human rights. However, as Case 9-1 suggests, the policy of granting China most-favored-nation status backfired and forced the president to delink trade from human rights. Given the complexity and sensitivity of human rights, a prudent foreign policy should be formulated with care and implemented with sensitivity, preferably through confidential channels.

4. Finally, a prudent human rights policy should be modest in scope. This is true for at least two reasons: first, to minimize moral ethnocentrism and, second, to decrease moral self-righteousness and hypocrisy. In calling attention to the dangers of "cultural imperialism," Kennan has written that Americans who profess to know what other people want and what is good for them "would do well to ask themselves whether they are not actually attempting to impose their own values, traditions, and habits of thought on peoples for whom these things have no validity and no usefulness."[60] To be sure, avoiding moral judgments in developing and executing a human rights policy is impossible. However, a state that seeks to foster rights in foreign countries should proceed tentatively, recognizing that international society is comprised of a plurality of cultures and worldviews.

Modesty is especially important in minimizing moral self-righteousness and hypocrisy. Self-righteousness typically arises from excessive confidence in one's own rectitude and the certainty of iniquity in another. However, if a human rights policy is to be credible, the articulation and application of norms must be undertaken dispassionately, remembering that moral indignation itself can impair judgment. Herbert Butterfield wisely noted earlier in the twentieth century that "moral indignation corrupts the agent who possesses it and is not calculated to reform the man who is the object of it."[61] At the same time, human rights also can contribute to hypocrisy when they are not articulated and promoted in a wise, prudent manner. Hypocrisy—the pretentious use of moral slogans for national gain—can arise when a state clothes its national interests in moral (human rights) language, thereby seeking to gain universal approbation. Thus, when human rights are used to justify national interests, the credibility of international morality, and especially of human rights, can be jeopardized.

SUMMARY

Despite the existence of significant pluralism on specific human rights doctrines, there remains widespread international agreement about the utility of human rights claims. This consensus is best affirmed and expressed through the substantial body of contemporary international law on human rights. Because international political society is anarchic, international institutions do not have the authority to ensure compliance with human rights norms. As a result, the international enforcement of human rights ultimately depends on the foreign policies of states, especially major powers, and on the actions of international organizations. However, formulating a credible and effective human rights foreign policy is especially difficult because human rights practices are normally a reflection of the social and cultural values of countries. Because states normally interpret the international enforcement of rights as a qualification of national sovereignty, the international pursuit of human rights will necessarily require modesty of purpose and diplomatic sensitivity.

Chapter Six

The Ethics of Force

Saints can be pure, but statesmen, alas, must be responsible.[1]
— ARTHUR SCHLESINGER

The aggressor is always peace-loving; he would prefer to take over our country unopposed.[2]
— CARL VON CLAUSEWITZ

There is something heroic in the effort to inject morality in the Hobbesian situation par excellence—when states, locked in war, squirm on the floor of survival. It is good to remind statesmen that the ends do not justify all means, that restraints should be observed even in an angry war, that humanity must somehow be preserved.[3]
— STANLEY HOFFMANN

STATES SEEK TO INFLUENCE international affairs through various types of power, ranging from positive sanctions to coercive threats, from "soft power" co-optive strategies that induce desired outcomes to "hard power" strategies that compel through military coercion. Although states rely on different policy instruments to influence the behavior of other states, force—the application of coercive power—remains the ultimate instrument for pursuing vital national interests in global society.

Sometimes international relations are categorized in terms of mutually exclusive conditions of war and peace in which force is applied in the former but not the latter. However, such analysis greatly oversimplifies reality because all interstate relations are in part a by-product of the distribution of power among states. As a result, it is preferable to view the relations among states on a continuum between the extremes of peace and war, with most international relations occurring between these two ideal-type conditions. Although only a small portion of international relations are determined by military force, all relations among states are based partly on coercive power, with most of this power held in reserve as political and military capital. Just as financial capital provides the foundation for investment and economic development, such strategic capital provides the basis for the credible implementation of foreign policy.

This chapter explores the political ethics of force by addressing questions such as the following: In pursuing legitimate national interests in global society, is it morally permissible to threaten and, if necessary, to use force? If force is legitimate, what types of threats and what types of force are morally appropriate? Once war begins, what moral principles should govern the use of force? Is the just war tradition an adequate moral framework for assessing modern war? In view of the rising threat of international terrorism, how should states seek to prevent such violence? Is preemption a morally legitimate strategy for protecting innocent persons from terror?

In examining the ethics of force, this chapter is divided into three parts. In the first part, I briefly sketch the nature and role of force in global politics by focusing on three alternative moral traditions of force: pacifism, amoral realism, and principled realism. In the second part, I examine the ethics of traditional interstate war, focusing on the just war theory. After describing the major elements of this theory, I illustrate the role of just war analysis with a case study on the Persian Gulf War that was precipitated by Saddam Hussein's 1990 invasion of Kuwait. Finally, I explore the role of preemptive force in confronting terrorist threats in the aftermath of the terrorist attacks on September 11, 2001, against the World Trade Center in New York City and the Pentagon in Washington, D.C. In the aftermath of the 9/11 terror attacks, the U.S. government revised its National Security Strategy in September 2002, giving a more explicit role to preemption and prevention. The role of this more vigorous use of force is illustrated by the U.S.-led coalition that toppled the Baathist Iraqi regime in early 2003.

THREE MORALITIES OF FORCE

Historically, three distinct perspectives have dominated the moral analysis of force: pacifism, amoral realism, and principled realism. The first assumes that war and violence are never morally permissible, whereas the last is based on the conviction that military force is politically and strategically necessary to protect vital national interests. Between these two polar positions is an intermediate perspective that assumes that resorting to violence should be a last resort and that, in the event of war, destruction and human suffering should be minimized.

Pacifism

The pacifist approach prohibits the threat and use of force because, in accordance with a rule-based ethic, it assumes that violence can never be a morally legitimate means to provide national security or to secure moral goods such as human rights, international justice, and peace. In its prioritization of values, pacifism holds that peace and nonviolence are the highest norms and can never be compromised to secure other ends, however important they might be. For example, the Dutch Renaissance scholar Erasmus believed that the cost of war was so great that even if a war is won, "you will lose much more than you gain."[4] Thus, for him as well as for other pacifists, force is never a legitimate means by which to protect national interests or to pursue international justice. In sum, the pacifist perspective on global politics offers a simple and categorical rule: Do no violence.

Although pacifism uniformly condemns war and violence, this moral tradition has been expressed in a number of different ways. Four major types of pacifism are pragmatic, humanistic, vocational, and structural. *Pragmatic pacifism* is based on a secular, humanistic worldview, advocating nonviolence in the belief that such a strategy is more effective in promoting long-term global peace. According to this version, modern warfare has become so destructive that it can no longer serve as a vehicle of peacemaking or peacekeeping. Nuclear pacifism, which specifically rejects national security based on nuclear weapons because of their enormous destructive potential, is a particular version of this type of instrumental pacifism.

Humanistic pacifism, another expression of this tradition, assumes that life is sacred and thus that killing is morally impermissible, even in defending other moral values. War is immoral because it destroys that which is sacred. Humanistic pacifism, which is frequently expressed through nonresistance or nonviolent resistance, condemns war and the preparation for war. Like religiously based pacifism, this type of pacifism seeks to protect human life at all costs; however, whereas humanism justifies life through a secular worldview, religious pacifism justifies its commitment to nonviolence and nonresistance through religious convictions.

A third type of pacifism is *vocational pacifism*. According to this perspective, violence and war are morally unacceptable because they are inconsistent with the vocation of Christianity. Some Christians, such as Mennonites and Brethren, believe that the Gospel of Christ calls on Christians to renounce the instruments of power and violence in this world and to model "revolutionary subordination."[5] To follow Christ means to renounce the evil ways of this world, especially its reliance on power and force. Menno Simmons, the founder of the Mennonite sect, once observed, "Our fortress is Christ, our defense is patience, our sword is the Word of God, and our victory is the sincere, firm, unfeigned faith in Jesus Christ. Spears and swords of iron we leave to those who, alas, consider human blood and swine's blood well-nigh of equal value."[6]

James Turner Johnson argues that the roots of vocational pacifism, or what he calls sectarian pacifism, lie in the teaching and witness of the early Christian church, which he suggests called on believers to renounce the world and withdraw from its evil demands.[7] According to Johnson, sectarian pacifists did not seek to resolve the problem of violence in political society; rather, they sought to establish separate communities in which they could live their lives in accord with the demands of their religious convictions. As a result, this tradition expressed itself historically in such sectarian developments as the rise of monastic Christian orders in the medieval era, the spread of Anabaptist sects in sixteenth- and seventeenth-century Europe, and the growth of "peace churches" in contemporary America.

A fourth type of pacifism is *structural pacifism*, or what one scholar calls utopian internationalism.[8] This tradition was first expressed in the Middle Ages in the writings of Dante Alighieri and Marsilius of Padua and subsequently developed by the Renaissance humanist Erasmus and by such modern philosophers as Jean Jacques Rousseau and Immanuel Kant. In the contemporary age, this perspective has been expressed by the World Federalist Movement, which seeks to create a world federalist state as well as by more modest transformational projects, such as the World Order Models Project, guided and elaborated by Richard Falk.[9] According to structural pacifism, because war and the preparation for war are immoral, global institutions need to be transformed so that the risk of war is reduced, if not eliminated. To realize their

utopian dream, structural pacifists favor a radical restructuring of international political society, shifting power from sovereign states to a common global authority. Like
sectarian pacifism, structural pacifism abhors war and seeks its elimination. However,
whereas the former seeks to resolve the problem of violence through withdrawal, the
latter attempts to eradicate war by establishing a more inclusive society based on a
"superstate" that would prevent war altogether.

Although pacifism is an important moral tradition, it provides little help to the soldier or the statesman in structuring moral reasoning about the defense and protection of vital interests in global society. Because the highest priorities are life and
peace, this tradition does not allow for the possibility of using force to pursue other
moral objectives. Pacifism's chief end is the abolition of war and violence. As a result,
it provides a potent moral critique of the security structures of the Westphalian and
post-Westphalian international systems but offers little guidance to decision makers
pursuing justice within and among states.

Amoral Realism

This perspective represents the direct opposite position of pacifism. Whereas pacifism
prohibits war and violence, amoral realism assumes not only that war is a legitimate
instrument of policy but also that morality does not constrain war. Indeed, assuming
the legitimacy of war's ends, amoral realism believes that the only norm governing the
conduct of war is military victory. Moreover, because morality is absent in the international community, global order is achieved not by the pursuit of "moral" foreign
policies but rather as a direct by-product of the balance of power among states.

Although several variants of amoral realism have been developed, two of the most
important are the "cynical" perspective and the "jihad," or religious war, perspective.
Both are similar in that they believe that morality is silent in wartime, denying that
moral limits exist on the conduct of war. Whereas cynics justify force on the basis of
self-interest, adherents to the jihad doctrine justify unlimited violence on the basis of
religious convictions. The cynical perspective is the most radical because it denies
morality altogether, both in the justification and in the prosecution of war. According
to this perspective, because moral values are simply subjective preferences, they have
no constructive role in determining and judging political action in global society. To
the extent that force is justified in international relations, it is based on prudential
judgment divorced from moral values. In addition, because the aim of going to war is
to prevail, there are no inherent moral limitations in defeating the enemy.

The cynical perspective of force is illustrated by Thucydides' account of the Athenian subjugation of the island of Melos in the Peloponnesian War. The Athenians, believing that their own security and well-being lay in a credible balance of power with
Sparta, their arch-rival, sought to extend their imperial control over Melos as they
had over most other islands in the Aegean Sea. The Melians, however, refused Athenian entreaties, desiring instead to remain free from foreign control. After being re-
buffed, the Athenians determined to compel Melos to surrender and become part of
the Athenian empire. Athenian diplomats were sent in an attempt to persuade Melos
to surrender. According to Thucydides, the Athenians cynically told the Melians that
justice depended on the distribution of power, in which "the strong do what they have

the power to do and the weak accept what they have to accept."[10] When the Melians refused to surrender, the Athenians laid siege to the island, eventually forcing their unconditional surrender.

A *holy war* is one that is waged for a religious cause. Because its purpose is assumed to be in accord with the divine will, it involves unlimited use of force for a holy cause. Historically, the two most important expressions of holy wars have been the Islamic jihad and the Christian-inspired crusade. The jihad, or religious war, is rooted in Islam's conviction that the world is divided into two realms—the House of Islam, where Islamic law prevails, and the House of War, comprising the non-Islamic world.[11] Between these two realms there is a "morally necessary, legally and religiously obligatory state of war."[12] Because Islam is assumed to be universally applicable, Muslim believers have a duty to convert or at least to subjugate unbelievers. It is important to emphasize that in Islam the struggle between good and evil is both a spiritual contest and a temporal conflict. As Bernard Lewis notes,

> Muhammad, it will be recalled, was not only a prophet and a teacher, like the founders of other religions; he was also the head of a polity and of a community, a ruler and a soldier. Hence his struggle involved a state and its armed forces. If the fighters in the war for Islam, the holy war "in the path of God," are fighting for God, it follows that their opponents are fighting against God. And since God is in principle the sovereign, the supreme head of the Islamic state—and the Prophet and, after the Prophet, the caliphs are his vice-regents—then God as sovereign commands the army. The army is God's army and the enemy is God's enemy. The duty of God's soldiers is to dispatch God's enemies as quickly as possible to the place where God will chastise them—that is to say, the afterlife.[13]

Although Islamic scholars differ on whether and to what degree morality limits violence in jihad, it is clear that there are comparatively few restrictions placed on the conduct of war, especially when compared with the just war tradition.[14] The aim in the jihad, as in the crusade, is to defeat and destroy the enemies of God. Total war is morally permissible.

The *crusade*, which shares with jihad a divine justification for war, is characterized by a conflict between good and evil in which total force is used to defeat the enemy. Roland Bainton has written that the crusading idea requires that war "be fought under God and with his help, that the crusaders shall be godly and their enemies ungodly, and that the war shall be prosecuted unsparingly."[15] The origins of the crusading idea are found in the biblical accounts of Old Testament religious wars and in particular in the efforts of ancient Israel to gain control of the "promised land." According to Deuteronomy 7, the Lord commanded Israel to expel seven nations or peoples from their territory, giving them the following mandate (v. 2): "Thou shall smite them, and utterly destroy them; thou shalt make no covenant with them nor show mercy unto them." Bainton argues that the crusade goes beyond a holy war in that it was fought "not so much with God's help as on God's behalf, not for a human goal which God might bless but for a divine cause which God might command."[16] The sincerity of the warriors, he goes on to suggest, was evidenced by the fact that war booty was consecrated to God.

The first major religious crusades occurred at the end of the eleventh century, when Pope Urban II called on Christians to recapture the Holy Land from the Turks and in particular to free Jerusalem. Throughout the twelfth and thirteenth centuries, western European military forces carried out numerous expeditions to the Middle East, seeking to reclaim Palestine from the Muslims and seeking to establish strategic centers free from the threat of Muslim forces. The crusading idea was subsequently expressed in a number of different domestic and international conflicts, culminating with the Peace of Westphalia. That treaty brought the Thirty Years' War to a close by giving secular rulers sovereign authority within their states, including the right to determine their country's religion.

Throughout the Renaissance and Reformation, the crusading spirit pervaded many European countries as Christians fought among themselves to establish within society the true religion, to purify their churches from heretical beliefs, and to ensure civil compliance with religious norms. For example, during the Spanish Inquisition in the fourteenth and fifteenth centuries the Roman Catholic Church used torture and violence to punish heretics and to ensure conformity with established religious beliefs. During the conquest of America in the early sixteenth century, Spanish conquerors relied on the crusading idea, modified by the just war theory, to justify the subjugation and Christianization of heathen indigenous peoples. Protestants, too, resorted to military force to ensure compliance with religious beliefs. In sixteenth-century Geneva, Reformation leader John Calvin sought not only to use city government to promote the good and prohibit evil but also to ensure that civil authority reinforced true religion. A century later, Puritan leader Oliver Cromwell sought to institute pietistic Christian norms in one of the most thoroughgoing efforts to legislate morality since the codification of the Mosaic Law.[17] For our purposes, what is significant about Cromwell's Puritan revolution is the extent to which the crusading idea influenced the conduct of military conflict and civil rule. As with other religious wars beforehand, morality was applied to force through a Manichean worldview in which political and military conflict was defined in the religious categories of believer and infidel.

Principled Realism

The third approach, principled realism, represents an intermediary position between the extremes of pacifism and amoral realism. It assumes that all interstate relations, including war, are subject to widely acknowledged moral standards. Because power and force are fundamental realities of the international community, the quest for peace and justice among states can be only imperfectly realized, and then only when power and force are incorporated into the calculus of decision making. Like pacifism, principled realism affirms international moral constraints on war, but whereas pacifism proscribes all war and violence, principled realism assumes that force can be an instrument of justice. Although violence is regarded as evil, it is not necessarily the greatest evil. As a result, some moral values—such as the protection of the innocent, the recovery of something wrongfully taken, the punishment of criminal behavior, and the defense against aggression—may justify the use of force. According to this perspective, just as an individual has the right to resist injustice, so too a state has the right to use force, individually or collectively, to repulse aggression and to resist and punish evil.

The doctrine that best expresses the approach of principled realism is the *just war theory*, an ethic rooted in ancient Greek and Roman philosophy and in the teachings of the early and medieval Christian church.[18] The just war theory is significant because it provides a moral framework for defining and assessing the use of force. Fundamentally, it seeks to limit the violence of war by seeking to restrain the possibility of war and also the destructiveness of war itself. To constrain the possibility and practice of war, the theory provides norms for judging when war might be morally justified and, in the event that a war is justified, how such a war should be limited. The aim of the theory is not to justify war but to bring international relations under the control of morality so that, if moral norms were followed faithfully and consistently by the disputing parties, it would reduce the risk of war.

It is important to emphasize that the origins and development of the just war tradition were rooted not in the limitation of violence but in the quest for political justice. For early and medieval Christian thinkers, the main challenge was to define not how violence might be limited but rather to define the circumstances that might necessitate force in ensuring justice. For example, Ambrose of Milan, an early Christian bishop, argued that when a Christian confronts an armed robber, he may not use force in self-defense, "lest in defending his life he should stain his love for his neighbor." However, if the armed robber attacked a neighbor, the Christian, in fulfilling his duty to love others, had a moral obligation to defend the innocent victim. Failure to defend the neighbor would itself be morally wrong and would make the Christian as culpable for the attack as the robber himself. The principle of charity thus places on believers a major duty to care for others, allowing, as a last resort, limited, proportionate force to halt injustice.[19]

THE THEORY OF JUST WAR

The foundation of just war theory is based on the distinction between the public and private use of force, between warring (*bellum*) and duelling (*duellum*). As George Weigel has noted, *bellum* is the use of force for public purposes by legitimate political authorities that have an obligation to defend the security of persons for whom they have assumed responsibility.[20] *Duellum*, by contrast, is the use of violence by private organizations for private or personal ends. The just war tradition is thus based upon a presumption that coercive power, whether used domestically or internationally, is legitimate when it serves morally legitimate purposes. War, in other words, is not intrinsically evil but rather an instrument of statecraft. Whether armed force is morally justified will depend on the agents, purposes, and methods of those who use it.

The just war theory is comprised of two parts: the *jus ad bellum*, the justice of going to war, and the *jus in bello*, justice in wartime. Because the theory is rooted in natural law, one scholar has defined these two dimensions as "war-decision law" and "war-conduct law."[21] According to this theory, if war is to be considered moral, it must fulfill the norms required for the justification of violence as well as the norms for prosecuting a war. A war might be waged for unjust reasons but still be prosecuted in a just manner. Conversely, even if the reasons for going to war are completely just, the war itself could be prosecuted in an immoral manner, resorting, for example, to indiscriminate attack on civilians. In short, if a war is to be moral, it must satisfy all just war norms.

Although the just war theory has been historically interpreted in a variety of different ways, there is a general consensus about its essential elements. The theory's core norms are listed in table 6-1.

It is important to emphasize that the aims of the *jus ad bellum* are limited in scope. The quest for political justice within states is not a central focus of just war theory. For example, it does not seek to remedy the injustices resulting from the past

Table 6-1 Elements of Just War Theory

I. The *jus ad bellum* has traditionally included the following six norms:

1. *Just cause*: The only legitimate justification for war is to deter aggression, to defend against unjust attack, or to right a grievous wrong. Although the theory does not specify what constitutes a just global order, the effort to alter territorial boundaries by force or to extend political and economic control in foreign lands is considered unjust. Aggression is immoral and gives rise to a just cause to resist by force.

2. *Competent authority*: The use of force is morally permissible only when it is legitimate, that is, authorized by government. Violence prosecuted by nongovernment groups or private individuals is immoral.

3. *Right intention:* A war is just only if it seeks to restore a just peace. The goal of war must be to right the evil that justifies war in the first instance. Because war is, as von Clausewitz once remarked, the pursuit of political objectives by other means, the aim of warfare must be only to alter specific conditions or morally unacceptable actions of an enemy state.

4. *Limited objectives*: A war is just only if its goals are limited. An unconditional, unlimited war of attrition is morally unacceptable. Additionally, goals and means must be proportionate. This means that the good to be realized by prosecuting a war must be commensurate with the probable evil resulting from war, or, as Robert Tucker has put it, "[T]he values preserved through force must be proportionate to the values sacrificed through force."[a]

5. *Last resort:* Before a state can legitimately resort to war, it must exhaust all peaceful means. War can be morally legitimate only when a state has made every effort through measures short of war (e.g., diplomacy, multilateral negotiations, and sanctions) to seek to redress the evil. Before violence can be justified, nonviolent measures must have been exhausted. Like proportionality, this is a difficult norm to apply, requiring uncommon prudential judgment.

6. *Reasonable hope of success*: The use of force against an aggressor must have a reasonable chance of success. Good intentions are not sufficient. A war that is unlikely to achieve its limited goals is immoral.

II. The *jus in bello* establishes norms governing the use of force in wartime. It includes the following two principles:

7. *Discrimination*: Military force must be applied only against the political leadership and military forces of the state. Every effort must be made to discriminate between combatants and noncombatants, soldiers and civilians, to minimize civilian casualties. Direct attacks against civilian targets, such as neighborhoods, hospitals, and schools, are morally impermissible. Indiscriminate mass destruction of cities is similarly impermissible.[b]

8. *Proportionality*: The destruction inflicted by military forces in war must be proportional to the goals they are seeking to realize. An indiscriminate war of attrition that seeks to eliminate the enemy society altogether is not morally justified. The goal should be to use the minimum level of violence to achieve the limited aims of a war.

[a] Robert W. Tucker, "Justice and the War," *The National Interest,* Fall 1991, 111.

[b] Because war frequently results in massive collateral destruction, scholars have developed the corollary principle of *double effect* to define the problem of civilian casualties. According to this norm, civilian casualties are morally permissible only when they are an unintentional by-product of the intentional targeting of military forces.

arbitrary delineation of state boundaries that might have disregarded cultural, linguistic, and ethnic affinities of people, nor does it attempt to relieve the suffering of citizens living in oppressive regimes. Although the absence of political self-rule or the existence of political oppression is morally unacceptable, such injustices do not justify international war. Rather, they give people a right to demand self-determination and just rule. In effect, extreme domestic injustice may justify revolution but not war. I explore exceptions to this conclusion in chapter 7 in discussing the ethics of foreign intervention.

It is also important to note the presumptive conservative character of *jus ad bellum*. Fundamentally, the just war tradition is a status quo doctrine rooted in the existing Westphalian order of sovereign states. Although the theory does not explicitly endorse the anarchic global system, it presumes its moral legitimacy, seeking to advance a just peace within the context of Westphalian norms. For example, the norm of competent authority is typically applied to existing governments, not to potentially legitimate nations seeking to secede from an existing state or to political groups seeking to topple a regime. In addition, the just-cause norm is generally interpreted within the context of territorial international law, which regards aggression—the forceful violation of territorial boundaries—as the most serious justification for war. To be sure, the territorial boundaries of many states have little to do with global justice. In Africa, especially, the boundaries among states were often established arbitrarily by imperial powers without taking into account the distribution of tribal, ethnic, and cultural affinities. Nevertheless, international law accepts the existing order as legitimate, proscribing war as a means to establish more just territorial boundaries.

Because the just war theory seeks to promote a just peace within the international system of nation-states, there is a significant correspondence between the theory and international law, especially the most fundamental norms that govern the rights and duties of states. According to international law, states are entitled to political independence and territorial integrity but also share a duty to respect the sovereignty of other states by not interfering in their internal affairs. Most important, states are obliged to settle disputes peacefully without resorting to force. However, if a state is the victim of aggression, it has the inherent right to use force in self-defense. International law thus shares with the just war doctrine a presumption against force. However, whereas the former provides a legal system for defining states' rights and duties, the latter provides the moral architecture for assessing the morality of force in interstate relations.

To illustrate the role of just war norms in conventional, interstate conflicts, I next examine the ethics of the 1991 Persian Gulf War.

BACKGROUND

On August 2, 1990, Iraq carried out a massive surprise invasion of its tiny neighbor Kuwait. Iraq's much larger and qualitatively superior military forces smashed through Kuwait's defensive positions. Within twenty-four hours, Iraqi forces had taken control of all key Kuwaiti military and government centers and had installed a puppet regime. Within two days, Iraq's initial invasion force had grown to more than 120,000 soldiers and 850 tanks, with a significant portion of those forces stationed along Kuwait's southern border, potentially threatening Saudi Arabia. Within days of the invasion, Saddam Hussein, Iraq's dictator, announced the formal annexation of Kuwait.

Although numerous developments might have contributed to Iraq's decision to attack Kuwait, two factors were especially important. First, Iraq disputed its southern border with Kuwait, claiming that the existing territorial boundary was unjust and historically incorrect. Iraq had periodically pressed Kuwait for a readjustment of the border, seeking in particular to gain sole access to the rich Rumaila oil field along the border and control of two islands at the end of the Euphrates delta. Kuwait had refused Iraq's demands, arguing that the borders were legitimate, having been established by Britain in 1922 in the aftermath of the Ottoman Empire's collapse.

Second, Iraq faced major financial pressures because of its long and costly war with Iran in the 1980s. Although Kuwait had provided Iraq with some $10 billion during the war, when the war terminated in 1988, Iraq had a foreign debt of over $80 billion, making economic reconstruction difficult. If Iraq was to modernize its economy and replenish its military forces, it needed to reduce its oppressive debt, and the only way to do this was to increase its foreign sales of petroleum, its main export. In its effort to increase oil revenues, Iraq claimed that Kuwait was un-dertaking actions that impaired Iraq's economic reconstruction. In particular, it charged Kuwait with two acts of "financial aggression"—selling more than its allotted OPEC quota, thereby depressing petroleum prices, and pumping ("stealing") an excessive amount of oil from the jointly owned Rumaila field. As a result, Iraq demanded that Kuwait not only forgive Iraq's debt of $10 billion but that it pay reparations of $13 to $15 billion. Kuwait refused these demands.

Although Saddam Hussein had no doubt expected that Western nations would oppose his actions, he had calculated that, as the most powerful state in the region, his invasion could not be challenged. However, he failed to anticipate the international condemnation of his action and especially the determination of President George H. W. Bush to redress the aggression. Immediately after the invasion, the U.S. government froze some $30 billion of Iraq's and Kuwait's assets in its jurisdiction. Moreover, with Syria and Turkey closing their Iraqi pipelines and foreign ships refusing to pick up Iraqi oil, Iraqi oil exports came to an abrupt halt.

In a virtually unprecedented action, the UN Security Council passed more than a dozen resolutions opposing Iraq and seeking the restoration of Kuwait's sovereignty. In its first action, the Security Council condemned the invasion and then declared Iraq's annexation of Kuwait null and void. It then adopted numerous actions, including comprehensive sanctions, to force Iraq to withdraw from Kuwait. However, after these actions failed to change Hussein's policies, the Security Council authorized (in Resolution 678) UN member states to "use all necessary means" to force Iraq's withdrawal from Kuwait if it did not do so by January 15, 1991. It is significant also that the Arab League, the principal alliance of twenty-one Arab states, condemned Iraq's action and called for the liberation of Kuwait.

After Iraq failed to comply with the international community's demands, a massive multilateral force, spearheaded by the United States, carried out a forty-six-day war to liberate Kuwait. The allied war began with a massive bombing campaign that eliminated Iraq's air force, destroyed its nuclear weapons development centers and chemical weapons facilities, eliminated the country's military and civilian communications networks, and severely weakened its ground forces. In addition, the bombing damaged the country's infrastructure, especially the transportation system. After six weeks of aerial bombardment, the allied forces launched a ground campaign involving the largest deployment of armored forces in the history of warfare. Within two days allied forces had liberated Kuwait, and within four days they had routed Iraq's armed forces, killing thousands of its soldiers and decimating its armored forces. The ground campaign ended within 100 hours of its beginning as Iraq agreed to cease-fire terms imposed by the allies.

THE JUST WAR DOCTRINE AND THE PERSIAN GULF WAR

Was the Gulf War just? Was the allied military campaign justified, and was it prosecuted in a moral manner? Prior to the allied liberation campaign and in the aftermath of the war, scholars and politicians, especially in the United States, debated these issues, carrying out a vigorous moral debate about the justice of this war. Although there was significant disagreement about which actions were morally appropriate prior to and during the war, the moral debate was framed to a significant degree by just war principles. Even President Bush took pains to use the moral language of just war to justify his decisions.

The case for resorting to force to liberate Kuwait was morally compelling because each of the six *jus ad bellum* criteria was fulfilled. First, because Iraq's invasion was clearly illegal (contrary to international law) as well as unjust (contrary to international political morality), the resort to force was in accord with the "just cause" norm. Regardless of the legitimacy of Iraq's territorial and economic claims against Kuwait, Iraq was duty bound to use peaceful methods to set-

tle its dispute with Kuwait. Iraq's attack was thus an act of war, giving Kuwait the inherent legal and moral right to use individual and collective force to repulse the aggression. Clearly, this conflict provided evidence that the "just cause" criterion had been fulfilled. Indeed, Johnson argues that Iraq's aggression provides "as clear and unambiguous a case as one could hope to find in the real world."[22]

Second, the "competent authority" norm was also fulfilled since the resort to war was authorized by legitimate political authority. In particular, both the U.S. Congress and the UN Security Council authorized military action in the event Saddam did not withdraw from Kuwait. It is important to stress that this norm does not imply that the only legitimate authority for peacekeeping action in the international community is the United Nations. To be sure, since the Security Council is the most authoritative multilateral peacekeeping and peace-enforcing body of the international community, it is desirable for this organ to authorize international peace-enforcement actions. But while such an authorization may be legally desirable, it is not a moral requirement of the just war tradition.

Third, the "right intention" criterion was also fulfilled by the just purpose of liberating Kuwait. The aim was not to conquer Iraq or to topple its dictatorship. The goal was simply to restore Kuwait's sovereignty and to halt the unjust humanitarian and strategic consequences of Iraq's invasion.

Fourth, although it was clear that the allied objectives were consistent with the "limited objectives" norm (liberating Kuwait), determining whether the war's ends and means were proportionate presented particular challenges prior to the war. Although in retrospect it is clear that the liberation of Kuwait and the military defeat of Iraq justified the evil of war, at the time of the crisis it was difficult to be certain of the relationship between means and ends. Would the evil from the liberation campaign be commensurate with the evil already inflicted on Kuwait? What if Saddam resorted to weapons of mass destruction? Despite the potential for significant destruction, the evil inflicted by his regime—an evil involving human rights abuses, the pillaging of Kuwait's treasury, and the violation of core norms of global society—was so extensive that there seemed to be a compelling case for proportionality.[23]

Fifth, the use of force was also in accord with the principle of last resort. This norm is especially difficult to apply because, as Michael Walzer has observed, there is no moral theory to guide its application.[24] As a result, the decision to use force will ultimately be based on political and strategic considerations, areas in which moral philosophers have no special competence. Although critics and advocates of the war were deeply divided on whether this had been fulfilled, it was clear that additional time would not necessarily have resolved the dispute. Throughout the five-month intervening phase between the invasion and the liberation campaign, allies had individually and collectively sought to resolve the conflict through diplomatic negotiation and through the pressure of comprehensive economic sanctions, but Iraq remained belligerent and uncompromising.

Finally, the "probable success" norm was also fulfilled because there was complete certainty about the outcome of the allied liberation campaign. The allies had put together a multilateral force of more than a half million combatants, backed by an extraordinary arsenal of air power and armored forces. There was little doubt that the allies, spearheaded by the United States, would prevail militarily. The only questions were how destructive the war would be and how quickly it would be won.

THE MORAL DEBATE

The most significant moral opposition to the war came from religious and political elites who believed that additional time was necessary to satisfy the "last resort" norm. For them, UN-imposed economic sanctions needed more time to work. However, in their eagerness to avoid war, they failed to appreciate that, from an international legal perspective, the condition of war had already begun when Iraq invaded its neighbor on August 2. More significantly, these elites failed to recognize that sanctions were a source of deep moral harm and were themselves inconsistent with the just war norm of discrimination because the harm fell disproportionately on civilians rather than on the political and military officials of the state. To the extent that comprehensive sanctions would have been given more time to work, they would have imposed an increasingly intolerable burden on the most vulnerable members of society, namely, women, children, and the aged. Walzer has noted that opponents of the war who supported a prolonged blockade of Iraq "seem not to have realized that what they were advocating was a radically indiscriminate act of war, with predictably harsh consequences."[25]

Some religious and political leaders also opposed the war out of fear that the war would be disproportionate. Following a much publicized National Council of Churches (NCC) "peace pilgrimage" to the Middle East in mid-December, leaders of mainline Protestant denominations declared that resorting to force to settle the conflict was "morally indefensible." They claimed that forcibly liberating Kuwait would "unleash weapons of mass destruction" and result in hundreds of thousands of casualties. "It is entirely possible," the NCC leaders noted apocalyptically, "that war in the Middle East will destroy everything."[26] On January 15, the day before the air campaign began, NCC Protestant leaders again urged President Bush not to resort to war because "it is unlikely that this battle can be contained in either scope, intensity, or time." In their view, the risk of war was "out of proportion to any conceivable gain which might be achieved through military action."[27]

The problem with the pacifistic pronouncements of the preachers and the bishops did not lie merely in the inadequacy of their view but also in their failure to morally assess their own position. By failing to seriously consider the use of force to halt oppression and aggression, religious elites were in effect condoning the occupation and annexation of Kuwait. Walzer notes that "it is very bad to make a deal with an aggressor at the expense of his victim," for then we "make ourselves complicitous in the aggression."[28]

Allied military planners also made significant

efforts to apply discriminating force in the war. Indeed, some observers of modern war have suggested that the Persian Gulf War was the most discriminate war ever. Despite the significant destruction involved in both Iraq and Kuwait, allied forces limited civilian casualties and achieved an unprecedented level of compliance with the discrimination norm through the use of precision-guided munitions, such as laser-guided "smart" bombs and cruise missiles. At the same time, however, although Iraq's infrastructure was also classified as a legitimate target, the destruction of communications and transportation systems, electric power centers, water pumping stations and purification plants, and government buildings led some war critics to question the morality of such action.[29] Still, it cannot be denied that from a purely military standpoint, the destruction was almost wholly centered on military targets. By contrast, Iraq's missile attacks on Israel and Saudi Arabia were indiscriminate, intentionally targeting population centers.

The norm of proportionality, the second element of the *jus in bello*, was also fulfilled in significant measure by the allied liberation campaign, which sought to achieve the stated aims of war with the least destruction possible. The goal was to use overwhelming but discriminating force to achieve the liberation of Kuwait as quickly as possible and with the fewest casualties. However, it needs to be emphasized that estimating the proportionality of evil between means and ends is a highly subjective prudential judgment. The difficulty in ascertaining the morality of the means-ends relationship is due in great part to the difficulty in assigning a value to the goal of restoring sovereignty. How can the value of national liberation be determined? Is the restoration of sovereignty worth 1,000, 5,000, or even 50,000 lives?

Some scholars argue that the allies failed to fulfill the proportionality norm because of the disproportionate losses among combatants (50,000 to 75,000 Iraqi deaths vs. several hundred deaths for the allies). Tucker argues that the war's disproportionality was problematic not so much because it was an unfortunate by-product of military battle but because it was di-

rectly intended. The American strategy, influenced by the failure of Vietnam, was designed to use overwhelming force to achieve clear, achievable goals in a short span of time.[30] Jean Bethke Elshtain, for example, attributes the "extraordinary lopsidedness of deaths and casualties" to the use of "excessive firepower," especially in the bombing of "the Highway of Death," on which Iraqis fled Kuwait City with some 15,000 vehicles. In her view, the destruction along that highway was not "a fight by *jus in bello* standards but a massacre."[31] Although Elshtain is correct in emphasizing the just war tradition's insistence on tempering justice with mercy, the proportionality norm applies not to the relationship of combatant casualties but to the relationship between the means and ends of war. As Francis Winters has observed, there is nothing in the moral logic of self-defense that can support the notion that "great powers may justly fight only when they reduce themselves to functional equality with small powers."[32]

MORAL REFLECTIONS

From the foregoing review, it is evident that just war criteria influenced the military liberation of Kuwait. Although some just war elements were fulfilled more fully than others, there is substantial evidence that the resort to force and the prosecution of the air and land wars was unusually consistent with just war principles. Still, some theorists have questioned both the timing and the prosecution of the liberation campaign.

- In light of this case study, was the allied resort to force warranted by Iraq's actions?
- Did the six-month interlude between Iraq's invasion and the commencement of the military liberation campaign provide sufficient opportunity to exhaust nonviolent conflict-resolution alternatives?
- Should more time have been allowed for comprehensive sanctions to affect Iraq's society? Was sufficient time allowed to fulfill the just war's "last resort" principle?
- In terms of *jus in bello* (war conduct) norms, was the targeting of Iraq's economic infrastructure morally legitimate?

- More particularly, was the destruction of communications and power centers, transportation networks, and water stations consistent with the discrimination norm?

- Was excessive force used in defeating Iraq? In view of the allied goals (the liberation of Kuwait), were the military means proportional to the political ends of the war?

THE ETHICS OF PREEMPTION AND PREVENTION

According to international law, states are entitled to the right of political independence and territorial integrity. At the same time, states have a duty to respect the sovereignty and independence of other states, to refrain from intervening in other states' domestic affairs, to settle disputes peacefully, and to abstain from the threat and use of force. If all states and political groups and organizations within states observed these norms, the world would undoubtedly be a far more peaceful and orderly international society. Furthermore, states would feel more secure and be compelled to devote fewer resources to national security. Regrettably, however, the international community, like domestic societies, is characterized by a high level of distrust, competition for scarce resources, and political conflict as states pursue national interests in disregard for, or at the expense of, the interests of other states. Because states have historically resorted to force to pursue vital national interests, and because no international governmental authority exists to assure the political independence and territorial integrity of member states, national security ultimately depends upon each state's power to deter and, if necessary, to repel aggression.

According to international law, every state enjoys the right of self-defense. This right is enshrined in the United Nations Charter, which provides (in Article 51) that states have "the inherent right of individual or collective self-defense if an armed attack occurs." But what if military developments begin to occur that shift the balance of power and thereby threaten the security of individual states or regional stability? How should a state respond to security threats from terrorist groups? Does national self-defense allow for "anticipatory self-defense"—that is, the use of force to prevent aggression before it occurs?

The September 11, 2001, terrorist attack on the World Trade Center in New York City and on the Pentagon in Washington, D.C., mark a major turning point in the evolution of U.S. national security policy. Indeed, some observers classify the 9/11 terror attacks as the beginning of a new global conflict in which nonstate actors can now threaten the security of major states. This new global threat is a direct by-product of the confluence of three developments: the growing availability of modern technology, increasing globalization, and the proliferation of technology and materials used in making weapons of mass destruction (WMD). Whereas the Cold War represented World War III, the third phase of global conflict, World War IV is characterized by a "civilizational" war in which nonstate actors use terror to press their political demands on states.

In the aftermath of the September 11 attacks, the United States declared a "war" on international terrorism. Some have objected to this bellicose approach, however, believing that the more appropriate response to the terror of nonstate actors is to re-gard it as illegal behavior requiring accountability through a state's criminal justice system. But the truck bombings of the Khobar Towers housing complex in Saudi Arabia in 1996 and the nearly simultaneous bombings of the U.S. embassies in Kenya and Tanzania in 1998 were not simply crimes, but large destructive attacks that left hundreds of innocent civilians dead. Moreover, the attack on 9/11 was an act of aggression against the territorial integrity of the United States that killed more persons than the Japanese attack on Pearl Harbor in 1941. This is why Eliot Cohen has written that "September 11 marked the climactic battle in an ill-defined war, but a war nonetheless."[33] It is a "strange" war, he notes, because the enemy is an elusive non-state actor and the conflict itself does not permit simple, neat definitions and classifications of goals, methods, and outcomes. Indeed, the war on terror is likely to be a long-term conflict without an "end state" or "exit strategy."

The enormous impact of the 9/11 terrorist attack on American society, coupled with the potential threat from terrorists' access to WMD, precipitated significant reflection among scholars and public officials about how the U.S. government should undertake to contain future terrorism. Thus, a year after the 9/11 attack, the U.S. government issued a revised national security strategy that directly sought to address this challenge. Titled the *National Security Strategy of the United States* (NSS), the new NSS is noteworthy because of significant modifications in both goals and means to U.S. security policies.[34] In terms of goals, the 2002 NSS redefines and modifies the traditional conception of national interest in moral terminology. Rather than simply pursuing territorial security, however, the new doctrine emphasizes—like the security strategy of the Ronald Reagan presidency in the 1980s[35]—the moral goals that should guide and inspire U.S. foreign policy. In particular it defines the moral vision of the country as the defense of human dignity and the promotion of freedom and democracy.[36] "The great strength of this nation," the NSS asserts, "must be used to promote a balance of power that favors freedom."[37]

The NSS declares that the United States should seek to advance liberty and human rights in the world. To do this, it calls for policies that, among other things, strengthen world order, prevent rogue states from acquiring WMD, inhibit international terrorism, promote the development of democratic states, foster a liberal international economic order, and encourage market strategies that facilitate job creation. In promoting national security, the NSS claims that the United States must be prepared to use its power, unilaterally if necessary. Perhaps the most radical innovation, however, is the claim that the United States will assert the "option of preemptive action" to counter a major threat to its national security. The NSS notes that legal scholars and international jurists have generally regarded preemption as legitimate only when an imminent security threat exists. But the NSS claims that the idea of an imminent threat needs to be modified to confront the growing dangers from terrorists armed with WMD. "The greater the threat," the NSS observes, "the greater is the risk of inaction—and the more compelling the case for taking anticipatory action to defend ourselves, even if uncertainty remains as to the time and place of the enemy's attack."[38]

It is of course important to distinguish between preventive and preemptive war.

Preemption, as a corollary of the right of self-defense, allows for military attack when aggression is imminent. To preempt means to attack before an aggressor strikes. According to Walzer, the legitimacy of the first strike should not be based solely on the imminence of attack but on the level of danger. For him, preemptive attack is morally justified when three conditions are fulfilled: the existence of an intention to injure, the undertaking of military preparations that increase the level of danger, and the need to act immediately because of a higher degree of risk.[39] Walzer argues that since these conditions were fulfilled in Israel's Six-Day War, Israel's preemptive attack on Egypt on June 5, 1967, was a legitimate act of self-defense.

Preventive war, by contrast, occurs at an earlier stage in the evolution of conflict—chiefly in response to a growing imbalance of military power or the development of military capabilities that might pose future security threats. Unlike preemption, however, preventive attack responds not to an imminent threat but to an adversary's increasing military capabilities. The goal of preventive attack is to destroy the enemy's ability to carry out aggression before it can mobilize that capability. This type of action was illustrated in June 1981, when Israel bombed and destroyed an Iraqi nuclear reactor that was about to become operational. It did so because it feared that if the reactor were used to generate nuclear fuel for a weapon of mass destruction, such a development would pose a grave security threat to Israel. Accordingly, Israel destroyed the nuclear reactor to prevent Iraq from acquiring a nuclear bomb. To the extent that preventive military action is consistent with the right of self-defense, this use of force was regarded as morally legitimate but contrary to international law because the attack involved a violation of Iraqi state sovereignty.

From a just war perspective, war is considered morally legitimate if its purpose is self-defense—to inhibit aggression, to protect innocent persons from unjust violence, and to restore conditions existing prior to aggression. Although both preemption and prevention pose moral challenges to the use of force, preemptive war is more easily reconciled with the demands of international political morality when it is based upon an imminent danger whose scope and certainty is empirically demonstrable. By contrast, preventive war is more problematic ethically because the knowledge justifying military action is likely to be more speculative. Even with the best intelligence, determining an adversary's future intentions and capabilities is a difficult and uncertain task in the best of circumstances. The difficulties and challenges of a preventive war are well illustrated in the 2003 war against Iraq by a U.S.-led coalition, a case study to which I now turn.

CASE 6–2: THE U.S. WAR AGAINST IRAQ

BACKGROUND

After the U.S.-led coalition had decisively defeated Iraq in the 1991 Persian Gulf War, the victorious powers imposed a number of demands on the government of Iraq as part of the peace settlement. In particular, Iraq agreed to disarm and to accept economic liability for destruction that it had inflicted by invading and occupying Kuwait. The cease-fire terms were more fully formulated in Security Council Resolution 687, adopted in April 1991, two months after the end of hostilities. Some of its major provisions demanded that Iraq: 1) provide an accurate and complete disclosure about its WMD programs, 2) not use, develop, or acquire WMD and under international inspection, destroy all such weapons, and 3) dismantle and not develop ballistic missiles with a range of more than 150 kilometers. To ensure compliance with these and related provisions, the United Nations established a special commission (UNSCOM) to verify Iraq's disarmament. Although Iraq allowed UNSCOM and inspectors from the International Atomic Energy Agency (IAEA), the institution charged with verifying compliance with nuclear nonproliferation, to carry extensive on-site inspections, Iraqi officials repeatedly delayed, interfered with, and obstructed inspections. As a result of Iraq's continued impediments to the work of inspection teams, both UNSCOM and IAEA ceased their work in 1998. Although inspection teams returned temporarily a year later,[40] they too found it impossible to carry out their work.

Immediately after Iraq invaded Kuwait, the Security Council imposed comprehensive economic sanctions on Iraq but exempted food and medicine, subject to approval by a UN committee tasked to oversee the Oil-for-Food Program. Since Iraq had been exporting petroleum valued at roughly $10-$12 billion annually, the embargo virtually paralyzed the country's economy.[41] After the war had ended, the United Nations continued comprehensive sanctions in the hope that these economic measures would encourage compliance with the disarmament provisions of Resolution 687. As with the original sanctions, the postwar sanctions allowed for limited petroleum sales to meet humanitarian needs and also to pay for war claims and UN operations in Iraq. Beginning in 1991, supervised petroleum sales were authorized to meet humanitarian needs. In its first installment, the Oil-for-Food Program allowed sales of $1.6 billion every six months. This was increased to $2 billion in 1995 and to $5.25 billion in 1998. Although the sanctions imposed significant hardship on the Iraqi people, the regime of Saddam Hussein continued to oppose

accountability and disarmament, as required by the United Nations.

The United States and Britain also used "no-fly" zones over northern and southern Iraq in order to contain Saddam's influence in the aftermath of the war.[42] These zones were initially established in response to Iraqi military repression of Kurds in the north and Shiites in the south after both groups had demanded increased political autonomy. But when Saddam refused to comply with the requirements of the cease-fire, the no-fly zones became a means of surveillance as well as an instrument to check the military power of the regime. Although the cease-fire had ended military operations after a ground war of about 100 hours, Iraq's failure to fulfill the terms of surrender signified that a state of war continued to exist in the region.

By 2000 support for economic sanctions had begun to wane under the weight of human suffering that such measures had imposed on Iraq. Although the Oil-for-Food Program had sought to meet basic human needs, large sectors of society, especially children and the aged, continued to suffer from the lack of adequate nutrition and medical care. Believing that Western economic sanctions would be lifted in the near future, a number of industrial states began investing in Iraq with the anticipation of reaping significant economic advantages when the embargo was lifted. But Saddam Hussein's disregard of the UN disarmament demands would not be allowed to continue indefinitely.

THE CASE FOR REGIME CHANGE

After the 9/11 attacks, the United States began to view Iraq as a far greater menace to global order. Since Iraq had built up stockpiles of chemical and biological weapons, had made substantial progress in developing a nuclear bomb, and had acquired ballistic missiles, Bush administration officials began to regard Iraq's noncompliance with disarmament as a threat to regional stability. And because the Saddam regime had sponsored and harbored terrorists in the past and potentially might help terrorists acquire WMD, senior U.S. government officials began to regard it as a growing threat to U.S. security. Accordingly, President Bush identified Iraq as a part of the "axis of evil" (with the other two states being North Korea and Iran) in his 2002 State of the Union address. Soon after, senior government officials, including Secretary of State Colin Powell, began calling for regime change in Baghdad.[43]

In September 2002, President Bush addressed the United Nations and demanded that the Security Council resolutions be enforced. In his speech Bush claimed that Iraq's conduct was a threat to the authority of the United Nations and to international peace. The president declared:

> All the world now faces a test . . . Are Security Council resolutions to be honored and enforced, or cast aside without consequence? Will the United Nations serve the purpose of its founding, or will it be irrelevant? My nation will work with the UN Security Council to meet our common challenge . . . But the purposes of the United States should not be doubted. The Security Council resolutions will be enforced. The just demands of peace and security will be met, or action will be unavoidable. And a regime that has lost its legitimacy will also lose its power.[44]

In the weeks following the president's UN speech, the United States carried out extensive diplomatic negotiations with other major powers, especially the permanent members of the Security Council, to secure one final resolution that would force Iraq to disclose its WMD programs and fully disarm in accordance with Resolution 687. Negotiations were especially difficult with Russia and France, which were opposed to an Iraqi regime change. But in the end the U.S. diplomatic initiative prevailed, with the Security Council unanimously endorsing Resolution 1441 on November 8, 2002. That resolution charged that Iraq had been "in material breach" of its UN obligations, especially Resolution 687, and that the current resolution represented "a final opportunity to fully comply with disarmament demands." To ensure that Iraq was fulfilling its obligations, Resolution 1441 demanded that Iraq

report to the UN on its WMD programs. Specifically, it called on Iraq to provide "a currently accurate, full, and complete declaration of all aspects of its programs to develop chemical, biological, and nuclear weapons, ballistic missiles, and other delivery systems . . ." within 30 days. The resolution also noted that false declarations or omissions would themselves constitute a material breach of Iraq's international obligations.

Some have claimed that the adoption of Resolution 1441 was a victory for the UN and a triumph for international law. Michael Glennon has argued—correctly, I believe—that this is simply an incorrect reading of Iraqi-UN relations. Glennon writes: "Had the United States not threatened Iraq with the use of force, the Iraqis almost surely would have rejected the new inspections regime. Yet such threats of force violate the charter . . . the council's 'victory,' such as it was, was a victory of diplomacy backed by force—or more accurately, of diplomacy backed by the threat of unilateral force in violation of the charter. The unlawful threat of unilateralism enabled the 'legitimate' exercise of multilateralism. The Security Council reaped the benefit of the charter's violation."[45]

In early December Iraq issued its report on the state of its weapons programs, as called for by Resolution 1441. The 12,000 pages of documents that were released were a disparate collection of files that purported to account for its WMD programs. But within days of receiving the report it was clear to U.S. intelligence agencies that the bundles of papers failed to account for past and present weapons programs. As a result, Secretary Powell declared that Iraq had failed to disclose the required information about its arms programs and was therefore again in "material breach" of Security Council resolutions.[46]

To help enforce the demands of Resolution 1441, UN and IAEA inspectors had resumed on-site inspections for the first time in four years. In late January Hans Blix, the head of the UN inspection team, and Mohamed ElBaradei, the director of the IAEA, provided a preliminary report to the Security Council on the early phase of the inspectors' work. Neither report, however, provided any conclusive evidence that Saddam was carrying out a disarmament program.

In the meantime, the United States increased its pressure not only on Iraq but also on the international community. While military forces were being deployed to the Middle East, President Bush and his senior advisers were repeatedly making the case to Congress, the media, the UN and other international organizations that if the Saddam Hussein regime did not account for WMD it should be replaced. In his January 2003 State of the Union Message, the president set forth the demands bluntly and starkly: "If Saddam Hussein does not fully disarm, for the safety of our people and for the peace of the world, we will lead a coalition to disarm him." Early in February, Secretary Powell addressed the Security Council, giving the most thorough and detailed presentation of any administration official on the dangers posed by Iraq's WMD programs. Speaking in a detailed and impassioned manner, Powell used intelligence to make the case that Iraq was not complying with the UN's demands for disclosure about and destruction of its WMD programs. Powell, however, failed to convince China, France, and Russia that the time had come for military action. France in particular continued to call for more time for further arms inspections. But by the middle of March, Britain, Spain, and the United States had concluded that the time for diplomacy had ended. It was now time to act. Accordingly, the president announced an ultimatum: "Saddam Hussein and his sons," said Bush in a brief televised speech, "must leave Iraq within forty-eight hours. Their refusal to do so will result in military conflict, commenced at a time of our choosing."[47]

On Wednesday morning, March 19, the President met with his National Security Council and after reviewing final preparations issued the order to commence war, dubbed operation "Iraqi Freedom."[48] Since Iraqi forces had carried out significant sabotage against Kuwaiti oil fields in the 1991 war, the U.S. military commander, General Tommy Franks, had ordered covert Special Forces teams into Iraq beforehand to prevent similar sabotage against petroleum depots and other major installations. These teams would play a crucial role in preventing unnecessary destruction, incapacitating ballistic missiles, destroying airfields, preventing sabotage, and taking control of key strategic sites.

Unlike the 1991 Persian Gulf War, which involved nearly a month of aerial bombing, the Iraq war began with combined ground and air operations. The aim was to capture Baghdad and other major urban centers with the least possible destruction. Despite significant obstacles, including an overextended supply line, sporadic battles with regular forces, guerrilla-type attacks by irregular forces, dust storms, and hot weather, the campaign proceeded much more rapidly than military planners had expected. Within three weeks U.S. forces had captured the Baghdad airport and controlled all major roads into the city, and on April 9 U.S. forces entered the city and began taking control of key military and government centers, including most of Saddam's former palaces. Soon thereafter the occupying forces began focusing on the task of state building and nation building in order to provide a new, more legitimate basis of political authority. Given the deep political fragmentation among the Kurds, Shi'a Muslims, and Sunni Muslims, these tasks have proved far more difficult that first anticipated. Moreover, because of the low level of communal trust and social solidarity and the depleted condition of the economy, national reconstruction has remained a daunting challenge.

THE ETHICS OF REGIME CHANGE

U.S. government officials justified the decision to topple the regime of Saddam Hussein with three major claims. First they argued that Iraq had failed to comply with the peace terms of the 1991 Persian Gulf War and more particularly with the disarmament obligations demanded by the Security Council. Second, they claimed that the Saddam government was tyrannical and abusive of human rights, having systematically tortured or killed hundreds of thousands of its own citizens. Third and most important, U.S. officials believed that Iraq's unwillingness to disarm, coupled with its past support of terrorists, made the

Hussein regime a threat to world order and a potential future threat to the United States. Because of Iraq's past offensive military behavior, its development and acquisition of chemical and biological weapons, its acquisition of ballistic missiles, and its failure to account for its past WMD programs, there was widespread concern among Western states that Iraq posed a threat to world order. American government leaders assumed that in the post-9/11 global environment, the conjunction of a tyrannical regime, weapons of mass destruction, and the threat of terrorism created conditions that were a threat not only to the Middle East but also to the world itself. While the threat from Iraq was not considered imminent, it was nevertheless a growing threat, one that was "grave and gathering."

Since the international community is based upon the norm of state sovereignty, the use of force to replace a government is considered an extraordinary step in international politics—one that should be taken only when egregious offenses have been committed and all peaceful alternatives have been exhausted. Moreover, although states are legally entitled to use unilateral force to ensure their own territorial security (Art. 51 of the UN Charter), the enforcement and maintenance of global order is a collective responsibility entrusted to the UN Security Council. In other words, regime change is an exceptional development that should be undertaken only when the Security Council authorizes such action or when legitimate claims of national security are at stake. Of course, the norm of sovereignty is not intended to shield rogue regimes that threaten global order or abuse the human rights of their people. Indeed, the international community can function only if member states fulfill their basic international obligations toward states and their own citizens. As a result preventive or preemptive war may be morally justified when an outlaw state has acquired WMD and poses a significant threat to other states.

Historically, the "just cause" norm of the just war tradition has been interpreted as defense against aggression. But when rogue states like Iraq, Iran, and North Korea acquire highly de-structive armaments, how should the notion of "defense against aggression" be interpreted? Must the United States wait until a rogue state launches a ballistic missile tipped with a WMD before it can legitimately attack such a state? "Can we not say that, in the hands of certain kinds of states," asks Weigel, "the mere possession of weapons of mass destruction constitutes an aggression—or, at the very least, an aggression waiting to happen?"[49] For Weigel, if the decentralized, anarchic world system is to pursue a just international order, the distinction between *bellum* and *duellum* must be preserved by limiting the use of armed force to legitimate, law-abiding states—that is, to those communities that are properly constituted and are fulfilling their international obligations. Outlaw states that condone terrorism or that disregard the demands of the international community should not be entitled to sovereign immunity.

The decision to go to war against Iraq was criticized vociferously by some. Some scholars opposed the war because they believed that the best strategy to inhibit Iraqi aggression was deterrence—that is, maintaining a credible threat of unacceptable punishment. Given the preponderance of American military power, these critics assumed that even if Iraq were to acquire nuclear weapons, the regional and global balance of power would deter Iraqi aggression. According to John Mearsheimer and Stephen Walt, a strategy of "vigilant containment" would ensure that Iraq would not resort to reckless aggression. They explained their confidence in deterrence as follows: "It only takes a leader who wants to stay alive and who wants to remain in power. Throughout his lengthy and brutal career, Saddam Hussein has repeatedly shown that these two goals are absolutely paramount. That is why deterrence and containment would work."[50]

Other critics were opposed to war because they believed that more time was necessary to allow for Iraqi compliance with Security Council resolutions. This was essentially the position of the French and Russian governments, which pleaded for more time for UN inspectors to do their work.[51] It was also the position of numerous scholars and media commentators. Michael

Walzer, for example, argued that other alternatives needed to be pursued before going to war. For him the "last resort" norm of the just war theory had not been fulfilled. While recognizing that "last resort" was a metaphysical condition that could never be fully fulfilled in real life, he believed, nevertheless, that the present system of sanctions, overflights, and UN inspections was working and could be made to work better.[52] But the existing strategy, especially the reliance on economic sanctions, was not without significant moral costs. As noted in chapter 9, economic sanctions are morally problematic because the hardship that they inflict is indiscriminate. While the United Nations had sought to introduce "smart" sanctions under the Oil-for-Food Program, the embargo had, nevertheless, resulted in great suffering to children, the aged, and the sick. UNICEF, the UN children's agency, had estimated that economic sanctions had been responsible for the death of about 5,000 children under the age of 5 per month, or about 60,000 annually.[53] Thus, even assuming that this estimate was inflated, it is not unreasonable to conclude that comprehensive sanctions over twelve years had caused the death of at least half a million children.

Finally, some critics of the war argued that unilateral military action against Iraq, even to enforce the disarmament provisions demanded by the Security Council, was legally offensive because only the United Nations could authorize peace-enforcement action. For them, the pursuit of a stable and peaceful international community required multilateral participation, preferably guided by the Security Council. Since the UN Charter demands that the Security Council authorize the use of force in any cause other than self-defense, the unilateral threat of military action against a member state is normally contrary to the UN Charter and therefore against international law. But while unilateral force on behalf of world order may be inconsistent with international law, such action may nevertheless be morally justified. Indeed, when legal duties confront moral obligations, the cause of justice demands that its moral claims take precedence over structural or legal responsibilities.

Prior to the war former president Jimmy

Carter argued that invading Iraq would be contrary to the just war tradition. He claimed, among other things, that the United States did not have international authority to pursue regime change.[54] But contrary to Carter, the "legitimate authority" criterion of the just war theory does not require international sanction. Rather, what is required is that armed force be used by appropriate political authorities in a proportionate and discriminating manner for the public good. The moral appropriateness of force without UN sanction was illustrated in the Kosovo war of 1999. In that conflict NATO carried out an intensive two-month bombing campaign, even though the Security Council had not authorized the armed action because Russia, Serbia's ally, would have vetoed such a measure. Thus, even though the war was technically illegal, it was subsequently justified as morally legitimate because of the goals and means that were used in the defense of human rights.[55]

MORAL REFLECTIONS

The U.S.-led war against Iraq is challenging to assess morally in 2004 because the relevant knowledge about the Saddam regime and its military capabilities and intentions remains ambiguous and incomplete. Since no WMD have been found in the first year of occupation, some observers have claimed that there was no legitimate reason for going to war against Iraq. Others, however, claim that it is premature to conclude that Iraq had destroyed all existing stockpiles of WMD and that all the prohibited armaments programs had been halted. Moreover, some defense and foreign policy officials argue that even if Saddam had destroyed all of his WMD stockpiles, regime change was nevertheless justified because of the past egregious abuse of human rights and the promise of establishing a more humane, democratic regime.

Regardless of how the WMD debate is settled, the preventive war against Iraq raises several important ethical issues:

- Has modern terrorism made preemptive military action or preventive war more acceptable legally and morally?

- Is the unilateral enforcement of UN Security Council resolutions a morally valid strategy? Although multilateralism might be a prudent approach to international security concerns, is approval by the Security Council a necessary prerequisite for legitimate international peacekeeping or peacemaking initiatives?

- When legal and moral obligations come in conflict, as they did in Iraq and Kosovo, which claims should take precedence? Why?
- Does the failure to find WMD invalidate the moral justification for going to war against Iraq?

SUMMARY

Since war is evil because it leads to killing and destruction, political theorists, theologians, and decision-makers have historically held widely different views about the moral legitimacy of this form of conflict resolution. Of the three important approaches to the problem of war, I argued that just war provides a useful framework by which to judge both the morality of going to war and the morality of war itself. This tradition is not intended to serve as a checklist for government leaders, but rather as a way of thinking about moral statecraft—about bringing moral reasoning to bear on the difficult issues of intractable international conflict.

When states commit aggression against other states, the just war tradition provides principles by which to devise appropriate public policies to defend the legitimate interests of political communities. But when nonstate actors commit terrorist acts, applying just war principles presents a more difficult challenge. Terrorism is of course inconsistent with political morality because the violence it inflicts is perpetrated illegitimately (by nongovernmental organizations) in blatant disregard for the principle of discrimination (intentionally harming innocent civilians). But how should a political community respond to the threat of terror? Must a state wait for major aggression to occur before it can resort to lethal force? While the just war tradition has historically justified war in response to unjust aggression, preemptive or even preventive war may be morally justified in exceptional circumstances, such as to confront the dangers of terrorist groups with WMD.

Regardless of the nature and scope of threats to national security, moral statecraft demands that leaders devise public policies that involve war only as a last resort and that the violence be limited, proportional, and discriminating.

Chapter Seven

The Ethics of Intervention

Probably more lives have been lost to ethnic, religious, or ideological
crusades than to simple [national] greed.[1]
> —LEA BRILMAYER

Respect for sovereignty in itself is not a moral imperative. It cannot
be. The sanctity of sovereignty enshrines a radical moral asymmetry. It
grants legitimacy and thus protection to whoever has guns and powder
enough to be in control of a government.[2]
> —CHARLES KRAUTHAMMER

Humanitarian intervention [is] obligatory where the survival of
populations and entire ethnic groups is seriously compromised. This is
a duty for nations and the international community.[3]
> —POPE JOHN PAUL II

FOREIGN INTERVENTION involves the direct or indirect use of power to influence the affairs of other states.
Intervention can be undertaken openly or covertly, individually or collectively, and involve relatively noncoercive actions, such as propaganda
and official condemnation, to coercive measures, ranging from economic sanctions to
direct military intervention. Moreover, intervention can be undertaken for a variety of
purposes, including economic imperialism, countering prior intervention, promoting
political objectives, protecting human rights, and fostering national security.

In this chapter, I examine the nature, legality, and morality of military intervention—the most extreme type of foreign intervention. Such intervention involves the
individual or collective use or threat of use of force against another state to influence
its domestic affairs. This chapter has three parts. First, it examines the legality of
nonintervention and briefly assesses the extent to which it has been practiced by
states in contemporary international relations. Second, it analyzes some of the arguments used to morally justify state sovereignty and its corollary, nonintervention. Finally, it analyzes and illustrates three types of intervention: political, strategic, and
humanitarian. The first uses military force to promote democracy in foreign countries
or to restore to power an elected government after antidemocratic groups have toppled it. The U.S. intervention in Haiti in 1994, carried out with the authorization of
the UN Security Council, illustrates this type of action. The second, strategic intervention, involves foreign military penetration to advance the security or ideological

goals of the intervening state. Such intervention, commonly used by the superpowers during the Cold War, is well illustrated in the 1983 U.S. intervention in Grenada—an action taken to quell domestic civil strife and to halt the spread of Marxist, revolutionary politics. The third type of action is humanitarian intervention, which involves foreign military action to protect human rights in the face of genocide, famine, war, or anarchy. I illustrate this type of intervention with the UN-sanctioned American intervention in Somalia in December 1992.

INTERNATIONAL LAW AND INTERVENTION

The most fundamental pillar of international society is state sovereignty. This legal right ensures states' juridical equality, political independence, and territorial integrity. Because states have the right to determine their domestic affairs, no foreign state may unilaterally violate the territorial boundaries of another state or interfere in its internal affairs. Moreover, states have a duty to respect the political independence and territorial integrity of other states. Thus, the norm of nonintervention is a corollary of state sovereignty, for without the former the latter is impossible.

The norm of nonintervention has been defined and proclaimed in numerous sources. The most important legal prohibitions against intervention are contained in the UN Charter, which states (Article 2.4) that UN members are obligated to "refrain in their international relations from the use of force against the territorial integrity or political independence of any other state." In 1965, the General Assembly passed Resolution 2131, which states in part, "No State has the right to intervene, directly or indirectly, for any reason whatever, in the internal or external affairs of any other State. Consequently, armed intervention and all other forms of interference or attempted threats against the personality of the State or against its political, economic, or cultural elements are condemned."[4]

Five years later, the General Assembly passed Resolution 2625, titled the Declaration on Principles of International Law Concerning Friendly Relations and Co-operation Among States, which reiterated the nonintervention norm.

Regional international organizations have also affirmed the priority of the nonintervention norm. For example, the Organization of American States (OAS), the regional organ of Latin American states, defines the principle in a highly absolutist, restrictive manner. According to its charter, direct and indirect intervention in the internal affairs of other states is totally prohibited (Article 15). Such prohibition applies not only to armed force but also to other forms of interference or attempted threats against "the personality of the State or against its political, economic and cultural elements" (Article 18).

The norm of nonintervention is so foundational to the contemporary international system that even the United Nations is prohibited by the charter (Article 2.7) from intervening in the domestic affairs of its member states. The United Nations can take actions under Chapter VII of the charter that might involve military operations against the wishes of a state.[5] However, such actions are exceptional and are taken only in response to a serious threat to international peace. In general, international law as expressed in numerous charters and conventions is unambiguous about nonintervention: States and other actors have a duty to respect countries' political independence.

Although nonintervention is the most basic constitutive norm of international society, states have historically intervened in the affairs of other states. Indeed, intervention has been so common in modern international relations, according to Michael Mandelbaum, that the history of global politics is "in no small part the history of intervention."[6] Mandelbaum attributes the prevalence of intervention to the oligarchic distribution of power, which allows strong states to intervene in the domestic affairs of the weak.

Historically, foreign intervention has been undertaken for a variety of reasons, including economic expansion, strategic interests, territorial security, and humanitarianism. For example, during the nineteenth century, major European powers intervened in Asia and Africa to establish colonies that could, among other things, provide a source of raw materials, cheap labor, and a market for goods. In the early part of the twentieth century, the United States intervened in a number of Central American countries (e.g., Cuba, the Dominican Republic, Haiti, Nicaragua, and Panama) to foster domestic political order and reduce economic corruption. Although such interventions were designed to prevent European powers from interfering in the Western Hemisphere, they also served to reinforce the dominant political role of the United States in the region.

During the Cold War, when the two superpowers dominated global politics, the most important motive for intervention was strategic security. Although both the United States and the Soviet Union were more powerful militarily than any other hegemonic powers in history, they nonetheless feared each other and sought to increase their power and influence through bilateral ties and multilateral alliances. Moreover, they intervened militarily in other states to protect and promote vital national interests or to advance ideological goals. Thus, for example, when the Soviet Union intervened in Czechoslovakia in 1968 and in Afghanistan in 1979, it did so to strengthen communism in those states; when the United States intervened in the Dominican Republic in 1965 and in Grenada in 1983, it did so to challenge antidemocratic forces. According to Mandelbaum, during the Cold War, American interventionism was driven almost exclusively by the great rivalry with the Soviet Union: "Korea and Vietnam, where the United States fought the most protracted wars of the Cold War era, were spaces on the board of global geopolitics; the United States was attempting to defend those spaces for fear that, if the Soviet Union and its clients occupied them, the Soviets would be emboldened to challenge Western positions elsewhere."[7]

Territorial security has also been an important motive for military intervention, especially among lesser powers. When a state perceives that its territorial boundaries and economic well-being are threatened by the deliberate actions, political instability, or government oppression in neighboring countries, the threatened state might seek to protect its interests through foreign intervention. For example, when India intervened in East Pakistan (Bangladesh) in 1971 after the Pakistani government began a war against the Bengali people, it did so because India perceived the war and the mass human rights violations as a threat to its own security. Similarly, when Tanzania intervened in Uganda in 1978, it did so, according to its officials, not because the dictatorial regime of Idi Amin was violating human rights but because the record of gross human rights violations was a source of major regional instability, threatening the territorial security of Tanzania. In other words, while gross immorality was being carried out, the rationale that justified foreign intervention was national security rather than the violation of human rights.

However, the gross violation of human rights has served as a justification for some foreign interventions. When the United States intervened in Cuba in 1898 and declared war on Spain, it did so in part to overthrow an oppressive dictatorial regime that was committing gross human rights violations. Moreover, when the United States intervened in Somalia in 1992, it did so mainly to reestablish political order to resume humanitarian relief to millions of people threatened with starvation.

In short, although the international system proscribes foreign intervention, states have, from time to time, violated the sovereignty of other states when they have perceived that their national interests or the global common good would be advanced by such action.[8]

THE ETHICS OF NONINTERVENTION

I suggested previously that international law explicitly affirms state sovereignty and its corollary obligation of nonintervention. However, if the norms of sovereignty and nonintervention have legal validity, do they also possess moral authority? Is state sovereignty a key moral principle of global society? Is nonintervention a foundational norm of global order? What ethical priority do these norms have in international society?

The claim that nonintervention is a morally valid norm in global society is based on several core assumptions and values: (1) the existing anarchic international system is morally legitimate, (2) peoples have a moral right to political self-determination, (3) states have a juridical right to sovereignty and territorial integrity, (4) states have an obligation to resolve conflicts peacefully, and (5) force is an illegitimate instrument for altering existing territorial boundaries. In exploring the moral basis of intervention, I first examine political and moral considerations of this practice and then explore the tension between territorial sovereignty and justice, political independence and the promotion of human rights.

Political Justifications

Political thinkers have offered two types of justifications for sovereignty and nonintervention. One argument is based on the legitimacy of states in the international system; the other is based on the legitimacy of a regime in terms of its people. *International legitimacy* assumes that existing states, as sovereign members of the decentralized, state-centric international community, are entitled to recognition and respect and to the right of political autonomy and its corollary, the right against nonintervention. International legitimacy is not rooted in the character of regimes but in the existing Westphalian order, whose viability depends on the political autonomy of states. If a state is functioning as a politically independent community, it is entitled, according to this perspective, to the rights and obligations of the international society of states.

Domestic legitimacy, by contrast, assumes that states are entitled to respect and support when they fulfill their core obligations as states. According to this perspective, state autonomy is conditional on the fulfillment of basic duties. Fundamentally, this means that states have a responsibility to honor people's collective claim to self-determination and to protect the basic rights of individuals, including freedom of conscience, freedom from torture and arbitrary arrest, and freedom to own property. Given the wide disparity in human rights conceptions, domestic legitimacy is generally defined in terms of the extent to which communal self-determination is practiced. Thus, from a domestic perspective, whether a state is entitled to the right of nonintervention will depend mainly on subjects' approval of the regime itself and to a lesser extent on a regime's protection of basic human rights.

The notion of international legitimacy is generally rooted in the claim that states, like people, have a right to be free and to govern themselves. This argument, based on the application of social contract theory to international relations, assumes that the relationship of persons to domestic society is analogous to the relationship of states to global society.[9] According to this argument, just as individuals have inherent rights such as life and liberty, so too political communities have basic rights, including the freedom and the political independence to define, preserve, and pursue communal interests.

Whereas international legitimacy emphasizes the rights and duties of states, domestic legitimacy emphasizes the rights of persons within communities. Although the comparison of individuals and states can be useful in illuminating and defining ethical rights and obligations within international society, states and persons are not morally equivalent because the former are merely artifacts designed to protect and promote the rights of people they represent. According to this perspective, states are not inherently moral actors but rather conceptual entities whose legitimacy is wholly derived from their ability to sustain and foster the communal well-being of persons. In particular, states derive their domestic legitimacy, that is, their right to rule and to be obeyed, from their capacity to protect and advance people's individual and communal rights.

It is one thing to assert that states, which are entitled to the right of nonintervention, must be legitimate internationally and domestically. It is quite another to define what these notions mean and how they should be applied to contemporary international relations. Are all states and quasi states entitled to sovereignty and nonintervention? If not, how, and by whom, is the legitimacy of states to be determined? What role should foreign actors play in determining state legitimacy, and what should be the role of the people? In times of domestic conflict and civil wars, which political communities are entitled to recognition and thus to political autonomy?

Michael Walzer has provided a useful criterion for judging state legitimacy. For him, states are entitled to political autonomy when they fulfill two conditions—viability and communal support. According to Walzer, a legitimate community is one that can pass the "self-help" test; that is, it must be capable of existing without external aid. He claims, "A legitimate government is one that can fight its own internal wars."[10] Walzer, following John Stuart Mill, argues that the only legitimate self-determination is that which is earned through struggle because only through the long and arduous quest for self-rule will people develop the habits and virtues necessary to sustain political autonomy. One political community cannot give another self-determination; the requirements for authentic self-rule must be indigenous and can be acquired only when individuals and groups struggle to affirm the right of self-determination. Walzer writes, "As with individuals, so with sovereign states: there are things that we cannot do to them, even for their own ostensible good."[11] Although self-help is no doubt important in developing indigenous self-determination, the self-help argument is morally problematic because it runs the risk of equating political success with justice and might with right.

For Walzer, communal legitimacy is based on a community's capacity for self-determination. Such capacity, he suggests, depends on the "fit" between a political community and the government, that is, whether a regime represents "the political life of its people."[12] Walzer writes, "The moral standing of any particular state depends upon the reality of the common life it protects and the extent to which the sacrifices required by that protection are willingly accepted and thought worthwhile."[13] Communal legitimacy is not achieved through periodic elections but rather through the protection and promotion of a people's shared cultural, religious, social, and economic life. For Walzer, communal consent involves representation of a "special sort," rooted in the shared values, experiences, and hopes of a people bonded together through time. Just as individuals have a right to defend their homes, citizens also, he suggests, have a right to protect their homeland and the values and institutions that sustain it politically and economically. However, if this communal life is to enjoy international legitimacy, it must be authentic, which means that solidarity must exist between government and subjects. Thus, a state's right to political autonomy is rooted in the right of individuals to protect their collective life from foreign domination.

Jefferson McMahan has similarly argued that the legitimacy of the state rests on the degree to which a regime protects and promotes "communal self-determination."[14] For McMahan, communal self-determination involves the right of human communities to govern themselves freely and independently. Although democratic practices and institutions would no doubt be conducive to communal self-determination, McMahan argues that democratic government is not a prerequisite. In his view, self-determination does not require self-government. Rather, a political community must be able to control its own destiny and to govern its own affairs independently of external influences while maintaining some level of domestic legitimacy.

For McMahan, two criteria are important in ensuring domestic legitimacy. First, a state must be representative of the political community or communities within its territorial boundaries. Second, it must enjoy the support and approval of the mass of its citizens.[15] According to McMahan, a state that is representative and enjoys the approval of its citizens is domestically legitimate and thus entitled to the right of nonintervention. A state that is not representative and not supported by the people is not a legitimate, self-determining community and therefore not entitled to the right of nonintervention.

In sum, the moral validity of states depends on two types of legitimacy: international and domestic. Internationally, states are presumptively legitimate by virtue of their ability to exist as independent, viable political communities; domestically, states are legitimate to the extent that they affirm communal self-determination—a norm manifested by a regime's representative character and the extent to which citizens approve and support its government. It is important to emphasize that the right of nonintervention does not depend on a regime's democratic self-rule; rather, it depends on two conditions: international viability and the representative character of a regime. Because the domestic legitimacy of states is more restrictive, it is possible for a state to be internationally legitimate, that is, regarded as legitimate by other member states, while still being considered domestically illegitimate by a significant portion of its own citizens.

Moral Justifications

Political thinkers have offered moral and legal arguments for the ethical legitimacy of sovereignty and nonintervention. The most powerful of these is the utilitarian argument that sovereignty and nonintervention must be honored if order is to be maintained in global society. According to this thesis, intervention is wrong (illegal and immoral) because it fosters international chaos and instability by encouraging counterintervention, military conflict, and even large-scale war. This ends-based morality suggests that if global order is to be maintained, it will occur only by honoring the existing cartography. International order cannot be maintained when states fail to respect the territorial integrity and political autonomy of member states. Stanley Hoffmann has argued that whether or not one finds particular states morally acceptable, it is important to uphold the legal rights of states lest international society collapse "into a state of war or universal tyranny."[16]

In her illuminating study on global order titled *Code of Peace*, Dorothy Jones argues that the international community has an ethical framework—a "code of peace," as she calls it—that states have accepted as normative and legally binding in their international relations.[17] These norms are not derived from states' international behavior but rather are rooted in the shared political doctrines and legal and moral principles embodied in widely accepted treaties, conventions, declarations, and other international agreements. According to Jones, the code of peace involves the following nine tenets:

1. Sovereign equality of states
2. Territorial integrity and political independence of states
3. Equal rights and self-determination of peoples
4. Nonintervention in the internal affairs of states
5. Peaceful settlement of disputes between states
6. Abstention from the threat or use of force
7. Fulfillment in good faith of international obligations
8. Cooperation with other states
9. Respect for human rights and fundamental freedoms.[18]

Because this code specifies the acceptable behavioral mores of the international community, it provides not only a regulatory structure but, more significant here, an ethical system. The code is an ethical system because it establishes binding moral obligations on states that, if fulfilled, have the potential of contributing to peace and stability in the international system.

Walzer similarly builds an ethical theory of peace on the basis of sovereignty and other widely accepted states' rights. These foundational norms collectively form a "legalist paradigm," which provides the moral and legal structure for maintaining international peace. The paradigm includes six key principles:

1. An international society of independent states exists;
2. The states comprising the international society have rights, including the rights of territorial integrity and political sovereignty;
3. The use of force or threat of force by one state against another constitutes aggression and is a criminal act;
4. Aggression justifies two types of action: a war of self-defense by the victim and a war of law enforcement by the victim and any other members of the international society;
5. Nothing but aggression justifies war;
6. After the aggressor state has been militarily repulsed, it can also be punished.[19]

Because aggression is contrary to the legalist paradigm, the use of force against a state constitutes an international criminal act, giving rise to the legitimate use of defensive force. Although this legal framework provides the foundational structure for pursuing and maintaining international peace, Walzer recognizes that global order will not necessarily ensure domestic peace and justice. The paradigm might foster international tranquillity and deter aggression, but it will not necessarily ensure justice for individual people. Regimes that are internationally legitimate might be unjust domestically. As a result, Walzer provides for some exceptions to his legalist paradigm.[20] For example, states may carry out an anticipatory military attack if they have conclusive evidence of imminent attack and may intervene militarily in other states to assist viable secessionist movements or rescue peoples threatened with massacre.

For communitarians, models such as Walzer's legalist paradigm and Jones's code of peace are important in global politics because they provide a framework for sustaining international order and promoting international justice. Although some thinkers might consider structural models such as these in purely legal and political terms, Walzer's and Jones's models need to be viewed as ethical systems because they provide norms that, if fulfilled, can contribute to international justice.

Sovereignty versus Justice

Mandelbaum has observed that international boundaries must be based on some principle and that support for the status quo is the simplest one available. If this norm is discarded, all borders become suspect and the potential for international conflict and disorder is considerable. From an ethical perspective, the problem with this status quo argument is that it assumes that the existing cartography is morally legitimate. However, the existing international order has not been fashioned by norms of justice and human dignity but by arbitrary decisions by military and political leaders. As Mandelbaum notes, "Historically, the prize of independence has gone to those powerful or clever or fortunate or merely numerous enough to achieve it."[21] During the Cold War, the sovereignty norm was widely accepted and enforced by the major powers, but in the aftermath of the disintegration of the Soviet Union, the norm of self-determination has become increasingly powerful, challenging the sanctity of existing boundaries. As a result, the post–Cold War era has increasingly witnessed conflict and chaos as ethnic, religious, and political groups demand increasing political autonomy within existing territorial states. The conflict is rooted in the tension between two foundational norms of the post-Westphalian order: sovereignty and self-determination.

As noted earlier, ethics is concerned with the application of multiple and sometimes conflicting moral norms to individual and collective human conduct. Stanley Hoffmann, for example, has suggested that the contemporary international system is based on four norms: sovereignty, self-determination, self-government, and human rights.[22] Although Hoffmann does not prioritize these norms, it is possible to classify them, as shown in figure 7-1, in terms of unit of analysis (the individual and the community) and level of significance (primary and secondary). Because no ethical formula exists by which potential conflict among these norms can be resolved a priori, tensions must be resolved through arguments based on consistency, impartiality, and potential outcomes.

Krauthammer has argued that any foreign intervention should not only meet the test of morality—that is, be judged right in its goals and methods, but also be politically viable domestically—that is, be in the interests of the intervening state. Because intervention uses scarce economic and military resources, states must define those international interests that are important and those that are not. According to Krauthammer, interventions should be undertaken only when key national interests are at stake. He writes, "To intervene solely for reasons of democratic morality is to confuse foreign policy with philanthropy. And a philanthropist gives out his own money. A statesman is a trustee."[23] Thus, for Krauthammer, national goals are not only a legitimate justification for intervention but also a central precondition for any intervention.

Although military intervention can be viewed as a regrettable, last-resort action to protect and advance vital state interests, interventions are morally problematic be-

Figure 7-1: Classification of Global Norms

| | | PRIORITY OF NORMS | |
		Primary	*Secondary*
UNIT OF ANALYSIS	*Individual*	Human Rights	Self-Government
	Community	Sovereignty	Self-Determination

SOURCE: Developed by the author.

cause they violate sovereignty, a cherished norm of the international system. However, because sovereignty is not the sole or even most important norm of global society, the violation of the nonintervention rule might be morally legitimate in exceptional circumstances. Such circumstances might involve protecting a state's vital security interests from destabilizing domestic developments in neighboring states (e.g., civil war, genocide, radical reforms, or revolutionary politics), maintaining a favorable balance of power in a region, or countering strategic initiatives that threaten a state's vital interests. Because the international community recognizes the right of individual and collective defense, interventions carried out to ensure territorial security are thus morally legitimate. Moreover, interventions can also be justified if the values and interests being pursued by the intervening state are regarded as universal and widely accepted in the international community. In short, interventions guided and justified in terms of national interests are not necessarily unethical.

Military intervention poses fundamental moral problems in global society. Because the contemporary international community is regulated by a number of important norms, the dilemma of strategic intervention is basically this: Should the nonintervention norm be violated to advance other legitimate goals, such as human rights or political democracy? Even where compelling evidence exists for overriding sovereignty, scholars have identified norms that should be fulfilled prior to resorting to military action. Some of the most important of these norms, which have been developed from the just war tradition, include: (1) *last resort*—no military intervention should be attempted until all nonviolent alternatives have been exhausted; (2) *proportionality*—the evil done by the military action should be proportional to the good achieved by such action; and (3) *prospect of success*—there must be a high probability of achieving the goals justifying the intervention.[24]

One of the most significant and provocative studies to emerge on the challenge of reconciling sovereignty with the defense of human rights was issued in 2001 by an international commission. In 1999 and again in 2000 UN Secretary-General Kofi Annan called on the international community to seek to develop consensus on when and how foreign intervention on behalf of human rights should be undertaken. In response to this challenge, the Government of Canada, supported by major foundations, established the International Commission on Intervention and State Sovereignty (ICISS) to investigate this issue. After holding extensive discussions throughout the world, the 12-member commission issued its report titled "The Responsibility to Protect."[25] The commission found that a "critical gap" had emerged between the Westphalian rules of global order and the mass human suffering in many parts of the world.

To reconcile the tension between human rights and sovereignty, suffering and international law, the commission proposed that the idea of state sovereignty should be reconceived. Rather than viewing sovereignty as the right to independence and state control, the ICISS boldly recommended that sovereignty be regarded as a duty to care for persons, as a responsibility to protect and promote human rights. If sovereignty is viewed as the "responsibility to protect," when states are unwilling or incapable of fulfilling that responsibility, the commission recommends that this task should be borne by other members of the international community. From the commission's perspective, however, the inability of meeting humanitarian needs does not give rise to a "right of intervention" but rather to the "responsibility to protect."[26] Thus, when a society is suffering from hunger, oppression, genocide, ethnic cleansing, and humanitarian atrocities and a state is unable or unwilling to protect human rights, "the principle of non-intervention yields to the international responsibility to protect."[27] The commission offered several guidelines on how this responsibility should be fulfilled: first, there should be a clear just cause—that is, evidence of mass killing or large-scale ethnic cleansing; second, precautionary principles—such as right intention, last resort, proportionality, and reasonable prospects of success—should be met; and third, military action should be authorized by the Security Council.

The international community has not yet acknowledged or accepted the proposed reconceptualization of sovereignty from control to protection. In the meantime, states will continue to discuss and debate how best to reconcile the moral demands for humanitarian protection with the prevailing rules of international political society.

THREE TYPES OF INTERVENTION

Although foreign intervention is undertaken for a variety of reasons, three major types of intervention are political, strategic, and humanitarian. The first two are undertaken to advance the interests of the intervening powers while the latter is fundamentally concerned with protecting the human rights of citizens of a victim state. When undertaking political intervention, the intervening state uses military force to advance and secure political goals through coercive diplomacy and peace enforcement. The use of NATO forces in Bosnia in the aftermath of the 1995 Dayton Accords, an agreement that effectively partitioned Bosnia, illustrates such intervention. Strategic intervention, by contrast, involves the use of force to compel a foreign state to alter behaviors or conditions against its political will. India's military intervention in East Pakistan (now Bangladesh) in 1971 and the Soviet Union's intervention in Czechoslovakia in 1968 are of this type. Finally, humanitarian intervention involves the resort to military force by one or more states to halt gross human rights abuses by an existing regime. I next examine the ethics of each of these types of military intervention.

Political Intervention

One of the principal ways by which major states seek to advance their political interests in global society is through coercive diplomacy—that is, through negotiations backed by the threat of credible force. Frequently states can achieve their political goals without resorting to war. But when threats fail to alter government actions, they may intervene militarily to compel desired behaviors. One type of political intervention is the use of force to promote democracy. Such intervention can be undertaken to undermine or overthrow a dictatorship in order to create an environment where the development of democratic values and institutions becomes possible. It can also be carried out to restore to power an elected government that has been toppled by the military or antidemocratic groups. To be sure the armed forces of foreign states are unlikely to foster democratic development directly, but they can help create an environment in which the foundation of democratic institutions can be established. As I noted in the previous chapter, the 2003 coalition war against Iraq was undertaken not to promote democracy but to bring down a regime that had failed to account for WMD, had failed to comply with UN Security Council resolutions, and posed a continuing terrorist threat. The restoration of democratically elected leaders is illustrated in the case study on Haiti examined below. As a result of the toppling of the Haitian elected government in 1992, the Clinton administration became increasingly committed to the restoration of democratic rule, especially when growing military repression resulted in a growing exodus of Haitian refugees. Although sovereignty allows states to determine their own government, military coups do not automatically ensure international legitimacy. Thus, when the United States urged the international community to isolate and eventually overthrow an illegal military regime, it received widespread international support, largely because of the growing moral legitimacy of consent as the sole basis of political power.

CASE 7-1: U.S. INTERVENTION IN HAITI

BACKGROUND

Haiti, located some 600 miles south of the Florida coast, is the poorest and most densely populated country in the Western Hemisphere. Although Haiti achieved political independence from France early in the nineteenth century, the nearly two centuries of political self-rule had not resulted in the country's political and economic development. Rather, it had led to cultural decay, economic stagnation, and political oppression. Indeed, because of the country's corruption, political instability, and authoritarianism, conditions in Haiti were, in the words of Thomas Hobbes, "nasty, brutish and short."

In December 1990, Haiti held its first democratic elections, resulting in the overwhelming election of the Reverend Jean-Bertrand Aristide as president. Because the elections were supported by the international community and monitored by foreign officials, many observers were optimistic that the new regime would strengthen democratic institutions and promote human rights while halting the instability, violence, and oppression that had characterized Haitian political life throughout much of the nation's history. However, a year and a half after assuming office, Aristide was overthrown in a military coup and

forced to flee the country. The international community strongly condemned the military's action while states in the Western Hemisphere took more forceful action by imposing a regional trade ban. When these sanctions failed to reinstate Aristide, the UN Security Council imposed a worldwide oil and arms embargo on Haiti, an action that led to immediate oil shortages and forced military leaders back to the negotiating table. Moreover, because of increased economic hardship imposed by sanctions, a growing number of citizens sought to escape the adversity and oppression by seeking illegal entry into the United States. As the number of "boat people" rose, the U.S. government was faced with the difficult moral dilemma of responding to Haiti's rapidly expanding human needs by either sending refugees to a detention camp at the U.S. Naval Base in Guantánamo, Cuba, or returning them to Haiti itself.

As international pressures increased on the Haitian regime, President Aristide and General Raoul Cedras, the head of Haiti's military, met at Governors Island, New York, and concluded an agreement calling for the creation of an interim government, amnesty for military officers involved in the coup, and the return of Aristide as president. Although parts of the agreement were implemented, the military ultimately refused to relinquish power, leading the Security Council to renew the oil embargo. The United States also decided to impose stricter sanctions, including the halting of all commercial air traffic between the United States and Haiti and the banning of all financial transactions between the two countries.

Despite the growing economic adversity within Haiti, the military regime refused to give up power. As a result, in July 1994 the Security Council adopted a resolution authorizing the use of force to reinstate Aristide. Armed with this collective legitimation of force, President Bill Clinton authorized an invasion plan to force compliance with the Governors Island Agreement. However, he also sent a team, headed by former president Jimmy Carter, to seek to convince the Haitian military to comply with the international community's demands. Just as U.S. military forces were about to invade Haiti, General Cedras and the Carter negotiating team reached an accord that averted bloodshed. The agreement required the transfer of political power from the military government to civilian authorities by October 15. Immediately thereafter, a 20,000-member U.S. peacekeeping force began landing in Haiti to ensure the safe return of President Aristide and the peaceful transfer of power. As required by the negotiated agreement, General Cedras resigned on October 10, opening the way for Aristide to return to Haiti to serve out his remaining term as president.

ETHICS AND THE RESTORATION OF DEMOCRACY

After President Aristide was removed from office in 1991, the United States and other leading powers strongly condemned the military's overthrow of the first freely elected government of Haiti. However, after making public declarations and endorsing a number of economic sanctions designed to punish the new regime, they faced the harsh reality of what other actions, if any, should be taken. In the United States, the Haitian imbroglio resulted in two distinct debates, one political and the other moral.

The first debate focused on the relative significance of the political and economic developments within Haiti in light of other competing foreign policy interests. Was the restoration of Haitian democracy of vital significance to the United States, or was the promotion of human dignity and constitutional government merely a secondary interest? If the former case, the U.S. government needed to use its considerable political and economic power to restore the former government and to do so in a timely manner. If the latter case, the U.S. government could pursue its interests in the Caribbean region without urgency or military force.

The second debate focused on international ethics and in particular on what additional actions, including the possible use of military force, should be utilized to restore Aristide to power. Fundamentally, the United States and other members of the international community faced a moral dilemma about how to respond to the new Haitian regime: On the one hand, the United States could view the coup as a domestic political development, protected by the norm of political sovereignty; on the other hand, U.S. government officials could regard the coup as a violation of widely shared moral norms, including human rights and participatory democracy, thereby justifying the use of individual and collective military force to restore the constitutional government of President Aristide. The ethical debate thus involved two moral polarities: national sovereignty on the one hand and human rights and democratic rule on the other.

In devising U.S. foreign policy toward Haiti, administration officials were deeply influenced by the norms of human rights and democratic rule. For the administration, the restoration of democracy was significant because it offered the most promising way of overcoming the legacy of tyranny and oppression that had characterized much of Haiti's history. Moreover, the persistent oppression in Haiti would have continued to cause thousands of refugees to flee the island, resulting in large numbers of asylees (persons who request asylum after they have successfully arrived in a foreign country) and massive refugee dislocations. In short, the determination to restore democratic rule, even if it involved military force, was rooted in a strong moral commitment to the protection and enhancement of Haitians' human dignity.

MORAL REFLECTIONS

This brief case study raises numerous important ethical issues about international moral obligations toward nations suffering from oppressive regimes, human rights abuses, and unconstitutional domestic political change.

- When Third World states such as Haiti suffer from poverty, political oppression, and human rights abuses, which moral values should influence the foreign policies of major states? Which international norm is more important: sovereignty or human rights?

- Do gross human rights violations justify foreign (unilateral or multilateral) intervention? Does international political morality require the removal of illegal military regimes and the restoration of democracy?
- More particularly, did the United States, as the dominant power in the Western Hemisphere, bear special moral obligations to Haiti in the aftermath of the coup that toppled Aristide from power? If so, what were those obligations?
- Although the United Nations legally approved the U.S. intervention, was it moral?
- Given the continued suffering and political instability in the years following the U.S. intervention, was the restoration of Aristide to power morally justified?

Strategic Intervention

Strategic intervention is foreign intervention that seeks to advance the security interests of an intervening state. Since foreign policy is the instrument by which states pursue national interests, every intervention is to some extent an exercise in national self-interest. Thus, the distinguishing feature of strategic intervention is that it seeks to advance the national security of the intervening power.

Some of the major goals pursued through strategic intervention include territorial security, regional stability, restoration or consolidation of democratic government, and regime transformation. For example, the U.S. interventions in the Dominican Republic in 1965 and in Grenada in 1983 were undertaken to prevent the spread of radical revolutionary regimes. The U.S.-led war against Iraq in 2003 was similarly inspired by strategic considerations. Indeed, the decision to conquer Iraq was justified by the conviction that the Saddam Hussein regime posed a security threat not only to the region but also to the United States. The perceived threat, which was documented by Western intelligence organizations and UN inspectors, was based on Iraq's past record in building weapons of mass destruction and its subsequent unwillingness to fully account for its WMD arsenal.

Strategic intervention is also carried out when neighboring states pose a threat to a nation's territorial security. This was the case in 1979 when Vietnam intervened in Kampuchea (Cambodia) and Tanzania intervened in Uganda. In both cases, the military action was justified as a means of promoting the well-being of the citizens of the victim nation and the security of the intervening state. To illustrate the role and problematic nature of strategic intervention, I next examine the U.S. intervention in Grenada in 1983.

BACKGROUND

Grenada, a microstate about twice the size of the District of Columbia, is an island in the south-eastern Caribbean Sea with a population of about 110,000 persons. After receiving political independence from Britain in 1974, Grenada established a parliamentary government, headed by Eric Gairy, an eccentric, populist leader. Gairy sought to consolidate his power by creating paramilitary squads designed to intimidate opposition groups. However, the shift toward more repression backfired and led to even greater opposition from left-wing groups, especially a radical nationalist group known as the New Jewel Movement (NJM). Headed by Maurice Bishop, the NJM emphasized nationalism, mass participation, a Marxist ideology, and closer ties with Cuba.

In March 1979, while Gairy was out of the country, Bishop led a bloodless coup, overthrowing Grenada's weak but increasingly corrupt government and establishing his own People's Revolutionary Government (PRG). Bishop immediately began espousing Marxist ideas and aligned his country with Cuba and other communist regimes. As a result of Grenada's ideological shift, the Carter administration distanced itself from the PRG and even considered blockading the island. After Ronald Reagan became president in 1981, the United States became even more aggressive in its opposition to Grenada's PRG, bringing to a halt virtually all multilateral economic assistance to the island. When Grenada began building a 9,000-foot runway with Cuban assistance, Reagan administration officials regarded this development as part of a strategy to radicalize the Caribbean basin and to directly challenge U.S. efforts to extend democratic capitalism in the region.

Moreover, as a result of growing ideological tensions within the PRG, Bishop was forced to share political power with a hard-line Leninist faction headed by Bernard Coard, the deputy prime minister. When tensions between radical Marxists and hard-line Leninists proved insur-mountable, Coard, with the support of Army Commander General Hudson Austin, carried out a coup against Bishop, placing him under house arrest. The arrest precipitated public demonstrations, riots, and a breakdown in public authority. A mass demonstration in St. George's, Grenada's capital, resulted in the freeing of Bishop, but in the ensuing power struggle Austin's revolutionary guards recaptured and executed Bishop and killed several government and union officials. The guards then turned their guns on the demonstrators, killing up to 100 of them. In the immediate aftermath of Bishop's execution, the new military and political leaders, headed by Coard and Austin, announced the creation of a new government headed by a revolutionary military council.

After the massacre, Sir Paul Scoon, the island's governor-general, concluded that foreign assistance was needed to restore order. At the same time, the elected leaders of five neighboring states (Barbados, Dominica, Jamaica, St. Kitts-Nevis, and St. Lucia), comprising the Organization of Eastern Caribbean States (OECS), concluded that the revolutionary conditions in Grenada were a threat to the region's stability. As a result, two days after the October 19 massacre, the OECS, along with Scoon, requested help from the United States to restore order in Grenada.

THE U.S. INTERVENTION

On October 25, four days after receiving the request for assistance, U.S. military forces invaded Grenada. The military intervention began with the night landing of Navy commandos near St. George's (to protect the island's governor-general). At daybreak, Marines attacked and captured Grenada's sole functioning airport on the eastern side of the island and then proceeded to take control of the southern, more populated area. Some 5,000 U.S. Army Rangers parachuted into Point Salines on the southern tip of the island, where the new airport was being constructed. Although U.S. forces encountered heavy resistance at first, especially from some several hundred armed Cubans, they rapidly consolidated control over the southern region, capturing the island's rebel leaders and securing all key military objectives within three days. Because the U.S. forces had destroyed all military opposition and consolidated power throughout the island by early November, the U.S. government began withdrawing troops so that by early December only token, noncombatant forces remained to assist Grenada in transitioning to democratic rule.

U.S. government officials offered three justifications for taking military action against Grenada.[28] First, U.S. citizens in Grenada had to be protected. In a nationally televised address two days after the intervention had begun, President Reagan stated that the "overriding" reason for authorizing military action was to protect the lives of U.S. citizens seeking to leave the island. Second, the U.S. government was responding to a joint request of eastern Caribbean nations for collective defense, a request that U.S. government officials deemed consistent with Article 52 of the UN Charter, Articles 22 and 28 of the OAS Charter, and Article 8 of the OECS Treaty.[29] Although some international lawyers regarded U.S. action as legally appropriate,[30] others considered the intervention contrary to international law.[31] Third, Grenada's governor-general had requested assistance.[32]

Although government officials publicly defended the intervention of Grenada using these three arguments, the Reagan administration's underlying rationale for the military action, as viewed from a realist perspective, was to halt the spread of Marxism in the Caribbean basin. In particular, the United States intervened to confront the challenge posed by Grenada's radicalization and the threat posed by Soviet-Cuban geopolitical developments within the region.[33] During his first two years in office, President Reagan had repeatedly called attention to Grenada's increasingly radical politics and the threat that its Marxist alignment posed to the region. He believed that Grenada's radicalization threatened not only the Caribbean region but, by extension, U.S. regional interests as well. As he

noted in a speech in March 1983, "It isn't nutmeg that's at stake in the Caribbean and Central America, it's the United States' national security."[34] Thus, after U.S. forces found a large cache of weapons, sufficient to equip a 10,000-person army, and discovered an extensive network of secret bilateral agreements with Soviet-bloc states, Reagan administration officials felt vindicated in their judgment that Grenada's Soviet alignment and increasing militarization had threatened the region's security and the consolidation of democracy in the Caribbean basin.[35]

THE ETHICS OF THE INTERVENTION

Was the intervention legal? Was it moral? From a strictly juridical perspective, the invasion was contrary to international law, notwithstanding the Reagan administration's claim to the contrary. It was illegal because it involved the violation of a country's sovereignty without the authorization of a legitimate international organization. This was the widespread view of most states of the international community, which expressed its overwhelming opposition (108 votes for, 9 against, and 27 abstentions) in a General Assembly resolution deploring the intervention as "a flagrant violation of international law." Even most close U.S. allies failed to support its action by abstaining on this UN action.

The OECS did request U.S. assistance, but it is doubtful that the organization's charter allows for collective security intervention against one of its members. Clearly, the preferable approach to intervention would have been to secure authorization by the United Nations and, failing that, by the OAS. According to Chapter VII of the UN Charter, the Security Council is the main institution responsible for determining when threats to international security exist and what actions are to be taken in response to those threats. When the United States intervened in Somalia in December 1992 to halt starvation and in Haiti in October 1994 to restore to power the elected president, Jean-Bertrand Aristide, it did so with the approval of the Security Council.

Although the OAS and UN charters prohibit foreign military intervention, they do not prohibit the use of force for self-defense. When the destabilizing events were unfolding in Grenada following Bishop's execution, the governor-general, along with OECS leaders, perceived security threats as immediate. Thus, they sought help from the major regional power, the United States. Although intervention critics were correct to point out that legally the OECS lacked a clear mandate to address collective defense, they also failed to appreciate the potential dangers from the unfolding events. As Michael Doyle has noted, critics seemed to have had more confidence in the views of distant states in Asia and Africa than in the views of Grenada's close neighbors, who called for the intervention. "Those are neighbors," writes Doyle, "whose democratic practices reflected Grenadian hopes, whose security was proximately involved, whose economies were closely linked to that of Grenada, whose Afro-Caribbean citizens have friends and relatives in Grenada."[36]

However legally ambiguous the intervention might have been, it is significant that the citizens in Grenada were staunchly in support of the U.S. action. In one poll taken soon after the invasion, 91 percent supported the intervention and the toppling of the Coard-Austin revolutionary regime. In a later, more sophisticated poll, 86 percent of the respondents indicated their approval of the intervention.[37] Although the United States undertook the intervention to support its strategic objectives of containing the spread of Marxist revolutionary regimes, it was also evident to Grenadians that the U.S. action was not designed to control the political destiny of the small island. Rather, the U.S. intervention was carried out solely to depose a revolutionary regime that had not only betrayed the people's trust but also was threatening the order and stability of the Caribbean basin. Thus, the aim of the intervention was to establish domestic order and quickly reestablish the preconditions under which Grenadians could resume their task of self-government.

From a strictly ethical perspective, the Grenada intervention was morally ambiguous. This was so because the ends and the means of the invasion—the conditions giving rise to U.S. action as well as the military force used to imple-ment the policy goals—involved both beneficial and harmful effects. Because the main motives for U.S. action were strategic as well as humanitarian, the basic motives of the liberation operation were not solely moral. Although halting the spread of Marxist regimes, promoting stability in the Caribbean basin, and protecting the lives of U.S. citizens from civil unrest were all legitimate justifications for government concern, they did not give rise to an unambiguous call for foreign military action. Moreover, although Bishop and a number of his supporters had been killed, there had been no genocide, no systematic abuse of basic rights, and no gross violations of international human rights. What Grenadians, along with visiting foreigners, had to face were instability, loss of personal freedoms, growing oppression, and rising fear—conditions that one scholar has categorized as "ordinary oppression."[38] Thus, despite the growing dangers within Grenada, there was no unambiguous justification for humanitarian intervention.

However, legitimate authorities had requested help. Concerned about Grenada's growing ties with Cuba and other Marxist regimes, the massacre, and the demonstrations, the island's governor-general requested help. His call for assistance was a request for a rescue operation to help restore civic order. Moreover, the call for foreign help was supported by Grenada's neighbors, who viewed with growing apprehension the increasing instability and rising threat to human rights. Thus, although no widespread suffering had occurred to justify a humanitarian rescue operation, the Grenadians, through their governor-general, called for foreign assistance to restore legitimate self-rule.

Thus, it can be argued that, from an ends-based moral perspective, the intervention was undertaken for the benefit of most Grenadians. It sought to restore the ability of Grenadians to govern themselves, recognizing that the beneficence of such action also involved detrimental actions, such as the temporary violation of their nation's political sovereignty. As noted previously, public opinion polls strongly supporting U.S. military action suggest that notwithstanding its moral ambiguities, the Grenadians viewed the intervention as politically desirable and morally justifiable. The military action might have been a necessary evil but, according to Grenadians, its good outcomes far outweighed its costs.

Finally, in judging the morality of the American intervention, it is useful to briefly apply the just-war norms of last resort, proportionality, and prospect of success. Because little time was allowed to consider policy alternatives, the last-resort norm was probably not fulfilled. A week after Bishop was placed under house arrest, he was executed, and a week after NJM leaders and supporters were massacred, U.S. forces landed on Grenada. Although the United States had been opposed to Grenada's increasingly radical geopolitical alignment, the precipitating events arose suddenly and unexpectedly, allowing limited time to consider policy alternatives. Although other nonviolent policies could have been pursued, it is doubtful that other strategies would have achieved the desired objectives with less violence and lower political and economic costs. Second, in terms of the norm of proportionality, policy makers and military strategists tended to agree that the suffering and destruction from the anticipated intervention would be far less than the current and future humanitarian suffering and political oppression from a revolutionary regime. For most Grenadians, the estimated costs and destruction from military intervention were clearly justified by the anticipated good to be achieved through the restoration of civic order. Finally, given the extraordinary military power of the United States, there was complete certainty that the military operation would succeed, that is, that the just-war doctrine's "probability of success" norm would be fulfilled.

MORAL REFLECTIONS

This case study raises a number of important ethical issues about the nature and role of military intervention.

- Was the U.S. strategy to contain the spread of Marxism in the Caribbean a morally legitimate foreign policy goal? Can the pursuit of strategic geopolitical goals, such as the containment of Marxism, be morally justified?
- Did the growing instability and repression in Grenada justify U.S. military action? Moreover, because political communities demonstrate communal viability through their capacity for self-government, did the foreign intervention impede or did it help indigenous political self-determination?
- Because U.S. action was taken in response to requests for help from the island's governor-general and the leaders of the OECS, were these requests sufficient to justify U.S. action legally and morally?
- Because it is unlikely that the just-war doctrine's last-resort norm was fulfilled prior to the invasion, should the United States have exhausted other peaceful alternatives, allowing the Coard-Austin junta to consolidate power? Or did extenuating circumstances justify an immediate military response?
- Because Grenada established a peaceful, democratic political system in the aftermath of the invasion, did this outcome justify the morally ambiguous intervention in 1983?

Humanitarian Intervention

According to Jack Donnelly, humanitarian intervention is foreign intervention that seeks "to remedy mass and flagrant violations of the basic human rights of foreign nationals by their government."[39] Although the most flagrant violations of basic rights have historically occurred in oppressive, dictatorial regimes, the most serious human rights abuses since the end of the Cold War have been due to civil war and the breakdown of government authority. Thus, although Donnelly's conceptualization might have been adequate during the Cold War, it is increasingly incomplete in addressing the gross human rights violations of the post–Cold War era. As a result, I define humanitarian intervention as foreign intervention (whether unilateral or multilateral) carried out to limit human suffering and death because of government oppression or because of a country's political disintegration.

In the contemporary era, the major threat to human rights in global society has come from "quasi" or "failed" states, that is, political communities in which government authority is weak or absent. Failed states generally result from two developments: first, the decline in the government's perceived legitimacy because of its unwillingness or inability to respond to popular demands and, second, the growing demands by ethnic, religious, and political minorities for increasing political autonomy. These two developments have led to growing civil strife and the breakdown of government authority in numerous countries, including Liberia, Rwanda, Sierra Leone, Somalia, Sudan, the former Yugoslavia, and former Soviet republics such as Azerbaijan, Georgia, Russia, and Tajikistan. Each of these territories has suffered from human rights abuses involving lawlessness, starvation, genocide, and mass migration. For example, the disintegration of Somalia's political system following the overthrow of the dictatorial rule of Siad Barre resulted in bitter conflict among Somali clan leaders (known as warlords). This conflict destroyed much of Somalia's infrastructure and impeded humanitarian distribution of food, resulting in widespread famine. The tribal conflict between the Hutu and the Tutsi in Rwanda similarly resulted in enormous human violence and suffering, including the death of more than a half million persons and the forced migration of more than two million Hutu. Finally, the disintegration of Yugoslavia in the aftermath of the Cold War resulted in a bitter war among Serbs, Croats, and Muslims, with the most intense fighting taking place over the political future of Bosnia-Herzegovina. This conflict is estimated to have caused some 200,000 deaths and displaced more than one million refugees.

Humanitarian intervention—foreign intervention designed to prevent and minimize gross human rights violations—poses legal and moral problems. Legally, humanitarian intervention challenges the established norm of state sovereignty; morally, it challenges the right of communal self-determination. As noted previously, because nonintervention and self-determination are not the only or even the most important norms in the international system, statesmen must devise prudential policies that take into account competing principles, including the demand for order and justice, stability and human rights. Thus, when gross human rights violations occur in a foreign country, statesmen must determine whether, when, and how their governments should respond.

As with strategic intervention, humanitarian intervention is generally justified if it passes two tests: a political test and an ethical test. First, humanitarian intervention must be in the interests of the intervening state or states. This condition is satisfied when the intervening state perceives human rights abuses in a foreign country as either a general threat to the order, legitimacy, and morality of global society or, as is most often the case, a particular threat to its own economic prosperity, political influence, and territorial integrity. The intervening state might also regard the breakdown in civic order and the growing human rights abuses as a legal obligation in fulfillment of bilateral and multilateral treaty obligations. For example, the United States viewed the political unrest in Haiti in the early 1990s as a major foreign policy responsibility in part because of Haiti's proximity to the United States. Similarly, when war broke out in the former Yugoslavia, it was widely assumed that European states had a special responsibility for containing and resolving the Balkans conflict. Europe's geopolitical responsibilities were assumed to be rooted in geographical proximity, historical ties, and close ethnic and religious bonds between European and Serbo-Croatian peoples.

Second, humanitarian intervention must be in the interests of the people and communities of the intervened state; that is, the evil of military intervention must be justified by the good accomplished in the penetrated state. Because the aim is to relieve the famine, genocide, and human suffering, this condition is satisfied when existing human rights violations are reduced or eliminated and preconditions are established that prevent their immediate recurrence. It is important to emphasize that right intentions are not a sufficient condition to justify humanitarian intervention. As noted in chapter 2, because an ethical policy must be judged in terms of its goals, means, and likely outcomes, a morally legitimate intervention must be just in its goals as well as its methods and results. Noble intentions are not enough. A policy designed to relieve human suffering through military intervention must, if it is to be considered moral, have a high probability of successfully achieving its goals in both the short and the medium term.

Even when these two conditions are satisfied, the decision to intervene is never easy because it normally will involve trade-offs among relevant norms. In particular, humanitarian intervention will involve a choice between nonintervention and human rights, sovereignty and suffering. Nonintervention is an important norm in the international community, but it is not the only, or even most important, moral principle applicable to the foreign relations of states. The challenge for the statesman is to weigh the relative merits of nonintervention, human rights, and other relevant norms to promote both peace and justice.

To illustrate the nature and role of moral values in humanitarian intervention, I next examine the nature, role, and effects of the U.S. intervention in Somalia in 1992.

CASE 7-3: U.S. INTERVENTION IN SOMALIA

BACKGROUND

The U.S. military intervention in Somalia in December 1992 was precipitated by a massive famine that had led to the death of more than 300,000 persons and threatened the lives of another one to two million. The famine was a direct result of a bloody civil war among rival clans that had developed from the ouster of the military dictatorship of General Mohammed Siad Barre, who had ruled Somalia from 1969 until January 1991. Following the overthrow of the Siad Barre regime, civil authority had broken down, and much of the country, especially the Somali capital of Mogadishu, was in virtual anarchy. When lawlessness intensified in late 1991, the United Nations halted humanitarian relief efforts until a cease-fire could be arranged. In April

1992, the UN Security Council authorized a 500-member peacekeeping force—known as UN Operation in Somalia (UNOSOM I)—to protect the relief convoys. When this force proved inadequate, 3,000 more peacekeepers were added. However, even this larger UN force proved incapable of maintaining rudimentary order and could not even ensure the distribution of food in the face of massive starvation.

In light of a deteriorating political situation, President George Bush authorized the intervention of U.S. forces into Somalia to permit the resumption of humanitarian relief.[40] The U.S. intervention was unique in the annals of international relations because it was the first time that the United Nations had authorized a largely single-state military intervention without an invitation or consent of the government. Such consent was impossible because no functioning government existed in Somalia. Indeed, the gross human rights violations were a direct by-product of a civil war among warlords, each vying for the right to rule Somalia. Thus, on December 3, the Security Council adopted Resolution 794, which endorsed the U.S. offer to lead a multinational peacemaking force. Unlike other UN peacekeeping operations, the goal of this interventionary force, justified under Chapter VII of the UN Charter, was not to keep contestants apart but to impose order through military force. The aim, however, was not political but humanitarian because the goal of establishing order was to allow the resumption of humanitarian relief to prevent further starvation.

Operation Restore Hope began in mid-December with the landing of 3,000 U.S. Marines in Somalia. The American military forces quickly increased in size to nearly 28,000 soldiers and in time were supplemented by some 10,000 troops from other countries. Although the Unified Task Force (UNITAF) was formally a multinational operation, in actuality it was a unilateral military operation authorized by the Security Council, for the planning, organization, and execution of the peacemaking force was carried out solely by the United States. Organizationally, the intervention was similar to Desert Storm, the U.S.-led military operation that liberated Kuwait from Iraq in early 1992.

After U.S. Marines landed unopposed, they quickly consolidated control over Mogadishu and its port and airport and then extended control over the urban centers and villages in central Somalia, where the famine was most severe. Within a month, U.S. military forces had established secure transportation links to key urban centers, thereby ensuring the effective distribution of humanitarian relief. After achieving its basic mission of establishing basic political order and ensuring the distribution of famine relief, U.S. forces were gradually reduced, so that by May 1993 only about 5,000 American soldiers remained from the original deployment.

On May 4, the United States ended its peacemaking task and formally transferred authority to a new, large (20,000 soldiers and 8,000 support staff) UN peacekeeping mission—UNOSOM II. Unlike the earlier mission, UNOSOM II had a greatly expanded mandate, authorized not only to maintain order but also to help create the conditions and institutions considered necessary for peaceful self-rule. Whereas the first peacekeeping mission was limited to ensuring famine relief, UNOSOM II, as authorized by Security Council Resolution 814, called for the "consolidation, expansion, and maintenance of a secure environment throughout Somalia" and "the rehabilitation of the political institutions and economy of Somalia." In effect, the original peacekeeping mission was extended from keeping order and facilitating humanitarian relief to nation building. In addition, the new peacekeeping operation is important because it was justified, for the first time in UN history, under Chapter VII of the UN Charter. Finally, UNOSOM II is important because, unlike the first mission, the United States pledged to support this operation with 4,000 soldiers, including a 1,300-member Quick Reaction Force.

In view of UNOSOM II's broader peacekeeping mandate, conflict was inevitable between UN forces and the dominant Somali warlord, General Mohammad Farrah Aideed, and his Somali National Alliance (SNA) forces. After SNA troops ambushed UN peacekeepers, killing twenty-four Pakistani soldiers, the Security Council authorized UN forces to "take all necessary measures" against those responsible for this attack. Over the next four months, conflict between Aideed's SNA and UN peacekeepers intensified, culminating in one of the deadliest battles in UN peacekeeping history. The October 3 firefight, which was precipitated by a surprise raid by U.S. Army Rangers on an SNA center, killed 18 U.S. soldiers and injured 78 and killed or injured between 500 and 1,000 Somalis. Shortly thereafter, President Bill Clinton, under heavy congressional pressure, announced that he was modifying the U.S. role in Somalia from what two U.S. diplomats described as "its admittedly overambitious vision of assertive multilateralism and rebuilding failed states."[41] According to Clinton, U.S. forces would no longer seek to forcefully disarm Somali clans and would withdraw all forces no later than March 31, 1994, even though additional forces were temporarily authorized to increase the security of existing troops deployed in Somalia. Subsequently, UN Secretary General Boutros Boutros-Ghali and the Security Council set March 31, 1995, as the final date for the withdrawal of all UN peacekeeping forces.

THE ETHICS OF THE SOMALIA INTERVENTION

From a legal perspective, there is little doubt that the original Somalia intervention was legitimate. Because all civil authority had broken down in Somalia as a result of war, the Security Council-sanctioned UNITAF provided the necessary legitimacy for the U.S.-led operation to restore order and thereby resume humanitarian relief. However, it is important to emphasize that this UN-sanctioned force was legally unprecedented: It was the first time that the Security Council had authorized intervention in a state without its consent.[42]

From a political perspective, scholars and public officials disagreed over the merits of UNITAF. According to Alberto Coll, these political differences were fundamentally between "interest-driven realists" and "values-driven globalists."[43] For the former, humanitarian intervention was unwise because there were no clearly defined U.S. interests in Somalia. For example, John Bolton, the assistant secretary of state for international organization affairs at the time of the

U.S. operation and an opponent of the action, has suggested that the fundamental failure of U.S. decision makers was the attempt "to adapt the world and U.S. policy to idealized and untested models, rather than to define U.S. interests and then pursue them."[44] For globalists, however, humanitarian intervention was important to prevent the spread of war and suffering in the African continent, because "[i]nternational society, morality, and basic decency form one whole fabric."[45] Despite the high cost of the U.S. intervention ($2 billion for the military operations alone), globalists, such as Chester Crocker, have argued that U.S. action was well justified in protecting life and in temporarily restoring political order to Somalia. For Crocker, U.S. general interests were served by Operation Restore Hope because the United States, as the leading state in the international system, has an interest in the overall stability and well-being of the global society. Crocker writes, "As the end of the century nears, it is surely wise that we and others broaden our understanding of national interest to include consideration of interests related to global order (sanctity of borders, extension of the Nuclear Nonproliferation Treaty) and global standards (avoiding genocide, mass humanitarian catastrophe)."[46]

From an ethical perspective, there is also little doubt that Operation Restore Hope, the first phase of the military intervention, was morally legitimate. Following the tridimensional framework developed in chapter 2, it is clear that the operation's goals (the restoration of order for humanitarian reasons), means (the use of limited, UN-sanctioned force, undertaken as a last resort), and ends (the restoration of order to resume humanitarian relief) were consistent with moral values commonly accepted in global society. However, if the humanitarian intervention under UNITAF was morally compelling, this was not necessarily the case for the expanded mission of the United Nations under UNOSOM II. Because political viability and self-help are important criteria in determining authentic self-determination, the expansion of peacemaking to include nation building, although legally justified by the United Nations, was politically and morally problematic. Politically, it was problematic because it sought to settle an indigenous war among clans by seeking to demilitarize the warring factions while remaining impartial to their claims. However, if wars are to result in a political settlement, the parties themselves must be involved in the settlement. This normally occurs after the warring parties tire of fighting and make a compromise or when the victorious party imposes a settlement on the loser. However, seeking to build a political order without a prior fundamental settlement among the parties is unlikely to foster a long-term peace. Moreover, because nation building requires significant military forces to encourage and if necessary to impose a settlement on the recalcitrant factions, it is a demanding task that is not well suited to lightly armed multilateral peacekeeping forces. In short, because communal solidarity and legitimacy must be earned by the people themselves, the expansion of UNOSOM's mandate was morally problematic because it impaired authentic political development.

MORAL REFLECTIONS

This case study raises a number of critical issues about the ethics of humanitarian intervention.

- Was U.S. intervention morally warranted? Given the many other needs in the world, did the Somali famine present a compelling case for U.S. action?
- In carrying out its foreign policy, should the United States be guided by narrowly defined national interests, or should it seek to carry out initiatives that are consistent with global values?
- This case raises important issues about trade-offs between short-term and long-term goals. Is short-term humanitarian relief morally warranted without also the effort to remedy the underlying conditions giving rise to such needs? Is short-term response to human suffering an adequate moral strategy, or must humanitarian relief also address the fundamental causes of human suffering? More specifically, should U.S. forces have sought to demilitarize the warring factions after successfully establishing the resumption of humanitarian relief?
- Although the U.S. military operation (UNITAF) is generally regarded as morally unassailable and politically legitimate, this is not the case for UNOSOM II. What should have been the mission of this peacekeeping operation? Was the extension of the UN mission to include some nation building tasks a morally and politically prudent action or should the UN operation have simply sought to prevent the resumption of fighting?
- This case raises issues of moral consistency, especially when compared with the U.S. inaction in the Rwanda genocide (see chapter 5). Although the human needs in Rwanda might have been more pressing than those in Somalia, by what moral calculus could the United States have intervened in Somalia but not in Rwanda?

SUMMARY

The nonintervention norm is an important legal and moral rule in the contemporary international system. In light of the decentralized nation-state system, honoring the sovereignty and territorial integrity of states helps maintain international peace. However, nonintervention is not the only or even the most important norm in global society. Conditions might arise that justify military intervention against another state. From a moral perspective, the easiest type of intervention to justify is that which seeks to halt genocide, famine, or civil strife. But intervention for political or strategic reasons can also be morally justified, if the aims of the action advance the fundamental short- and long-term well-being of the people in the victim country. For example, toppling a dictator will not necessarily result in a more stable and humane government, but it creates the possibility for establishing a new political order. Similarly, an intervention that halts genocide and ethnic cleansing, such as India's intervention on behalf of the Bengali people in 1971 and NATO's 1999 Kosovo war against Serbia, can be morally justified.

Whether military intervention is carried out for political, strategic, or humanitarian purposes, it should be undertaken only when the goals are morally legitimate, where intended goals are likely to be realized, and after peaceful alternatives have been exhausted. Military intervention, especially humanitarian intervention, might be morally warranted to prevent widespread human rights atrocities. As a result, the U.S. intervention in Somalia to prevent starvation was morally legitimate because it prevented the deaths of hundreds of thousands of persons. Similarly, although the major powers (with the exception of France) chose not to carry out military action in Rwanda in 1994, military intervention to halt the genocide in that land (Case 5-2) would have also been justified. Still, whether acting unilaterally or multilaterally, states should regard the violation of the nonintervention norm as an exceptional action that is contrary to the long-term interests of the international community.

Chapter Eight

The Ethics of Unconventional Military Operations

Torture is normally a way of waging war, and a way of thinking about one's enemies, not an exceptional response to an exceptional tactical circumstance.[1]

—DAVID RIEFF

The more endangered public safety is thought to be, the more the balance swings against civil liberties. . . . Terrorists are more dangerous than ordinary criminals, and so . . . the dogma that it is better for ten guilty people to go free than for one innocent person to be convicted may not hold when the guilty ten are international terrorists seeking to obtain weapons of mass destruction.[2]

—JUDGE RICHARD POSNER

Terrorist groups refuse to play by the rules of international politics. . . . This refusal to play by the rules, along with the nonterritorial nature of many groups employing such tactics, places state actors in a difficult position in responding. . . . As a result, threatened states may feel pressured to respond with similar tactics.[3]

—WARD THOMAS

THROUGHOUT THE COLD WAR, the United States and the Soviet Union were involved in an all-encompassing ideological conflict that pitted their extraordinary military power against each other. As part of this forty-five-year political contest, each superpower developed and deployed a massive arsenal of conventional and nuclear weapons to deter aggression. A direct war between these two military giants could have led to a nuclear holocaust resulting, in the words of Jonathan Schell, in "the extinction of the species,"[4] so the superpowers avoided direct military confrontation with each other, with the exception of the 1962 Cuban Missile crisis. Instead, they carried out their global competition directly through covert operations and indirectly through proxy wars.

To contain communist expansion and support anticommunist and prodemocratic forces, the United States used a variety of covert and overt strategies, including unconventional military operations, overt military and economic assistance, and direct military intervention.[5] Since covert, unconventional operations were a major element of the superpower conflict, some observers assumed that with the collapse of the Soviet Union in 1991, the role of irregular, unconventional force would soon disappear. But this has not occurred. Indeed, the rise in ethnopolitical conflicts and tribal and religious wars in emerging, developing nations in the post–Cold War era has not only undermined existing governmental authority, but has resulted in new security threats. These threats arise not from the power of states, but rather from the vacuum of power in fragile, fragmented states because the weakness of governments itself has facilitated the rise of radical groups and nongovernmental organizations with access to modern armaments. The proliferation of fragile states is of course significant because such communities may permit the forces of globalization, modern technology, and fundamentalist politics to coalesce into highly destructive terror cells. As regional and global order presuppose the existence of sovereign states that effectively monopolize force within their territorial boundaries, the expansion of weak states potentially threatens not only the well-being and human rights of citizens within those states but also the order and stability of the international system itself.

Despite the growing fragility of many Third World states in the 1990s, the major powers tended to view the international community as a relatively peaceful and secure global order. To be sure, the absence of effective, legitimate authority has resulted in numerous humanitarian crises. But these developments, unlike Third World revolutionary wars and ideological conflicts, resulted in only limited, sporadic involvement by the major powers. The proliferation of weak or even failed Third World states was not a global priority. But the perception of the international community as a relatively peaceful and stable society came to an abrupt end on the morning of September 11, 2001, when four passenger jets were simultaneously hijacked and used to attack New York City's World Trade Center and Washington's Pentagon. This attack turned out to be the deadliest single act of aggression against the United States. Following the 9/11 terrorist attack, the U.S. government declared an all-encompassing war on terrorism. This war would soon lead to the toppling of the Taliban in Afghanistan, a dramatic reorientation in NATO and UN politics, the shifting of Western geopolitical concerns, and the development of a new U.S. national security strategy.

This chapter examines the nature and role of unconventional military force in two distinct contexts—the Cold War revolutionary conflicts and the post-9/11 antiterror campaign. In the first type of conflict, both the United States and the Soviet Union used unconventional military force to seek to influence the outcome of revolutionary insurgencies. In trying to extend their political influence in Third World nations, the superpowers used a variety of economic, political, and military measures, including covert military operations. The reliance on unconventional force was deemed necessary because many of the revolutionary wars were carried out through guerrilla operations and covert terrorism rather than through the conventional military force of states. To be sure, the superpowers facilitated these proxy wars but did so indirectly through economic and military assistance and directly through unconventional military strategies.

In the second type of conflict, the United States has further expanded the use of unconventional military forces to address the threat of international terrorism. Because terror is generally carried out covertly by nonstate actors, the military strategies designed to deter and contain foreign military aggression by enemy states do not apply to the problem of global terrorism. Instead, what is necessary in countering terrorism is a strategy based on accurate and timely intelligence and flexible, covert security operations relying on agents from the Central Intelligence Agency and military Special Forces, or what some have dubbed "shadow warriors."[6] In assessing some of the ethical challenges posed by unconventional military operations in both types of conflicts, I examine first the ethics of counterinsurgency and then the ethics of counterterror warfare.

This chapter has three major elements. I begin by describing the nature and role of covert, unconventional strategies designed to counter revolutionary insurgencies. I then illustrate some of the moral dilemmas about counterinsurgency by describing and morally assessing the Reagan doctrine. In the second section, I explore the threat posed by international terrorism. In the final section, I briefly examine the challenge of devising an effective counterterrorism strategy and the moral challenges involved in gathering accurate and timely intelligence. I explore two particular moral challenges of counterterror warfare: torture and assassination. I argue that while torture and targeted killing might decrease the terrorist threat in the short term, the political, legal, and moral costs of such policies make them unacceptable tactics. I illustrate some key political challenges and moral dilemmas in counterterrorism with a case study on the U.S. war on terror.

THE ETHICS OF COUNTERINSURGENCY

In chapter 6, I examined the ethics of force in conventional interstate wars. I now turn to the role of coercive power involving unconventional military operations—what some strategists have termed "low-intensity conflict" (LIC). Unlike conventional war between the armed forces of two states, LIC operations generally involve small-scale, often covert military actions that seek to undermine and defeat the clandestine forces of states or nongovernmental groups. Although traditional interstate wars have served as the ultimate instrument of conflict resolution in the international system since the nation-state emerged in the mid-seventeenth century, since the end of World War II, covert, unconventional force has become increasingly important in global society. During the Cold War, some of the most significant and persistent military conflicts involved domestic revolutionary wars fought over the nature of the regime. Such wars frequently involved subnational armed forces using covert, guerrilla tactics. In many of these domestic revolutionary conflicts, the superpowers sought to advance their ideological goals by providing overt economic assistance and covert military and strategic assistance. In some cases, the superpowers were directly involved in covert operations.

With the collapse of the Soviet empire, intranational wars have been increasingly based on self-determination claims of ethnonationalist groups demanding either complete secession from a state or increased political autonomy. As a result of these political demands, many states have faced increased political turmoil and instability, resulting in weakened domestic authority or even the complete collapse of internal order. The rise in the number of "quasi" or "failed" states is due principally to this phenomenon. According to one study, of the 164 wars during the 1945–1995 period, only 38 (23 percent) were conventional interstate wars. Of the other 126 internal wars, about half were based on domestic ideological disputes, whereas the other half were based on self-determination claims.[7]

The increase in domestic political violence is significant because most internal wars are carried out with irregular forces using unconventional strategies. As a result, they differ considerably from conventional wars. Whereas classical international wars involve a direct contest between the military forces of two or more states, the revolutionary wars of the Cold War era and the ethnonationalistic wars of the post–Cold War era generally involve military force that is not easily encompassed by the codified rules of war. Moreover, the moral principles used to assess traditional wars are not easily applied to contemporary unconventional wars because classical moral theories, such as the just war doctrine, are concerned fundamentally with interstate violence, not with domestic civil wars. Indeed, internal wars are morally problematic from a just war perspective because the antistate groups are not "competent authorities," and therefore are not permitted to use force. Moreover, the tactics used by irregular forces tend to rely on stealth and secrecy and make civilians key targets of political violence. However, as noted previously, most contemporary domestic wars are fought precisely to determine which groups are entitled to exert political authority within the boundaries of a state.

During the Cold War, the ideological conflicts in the Third World typically involved two major types of action—insurgency and counterinsurgency. *Insurgency*, also known as guerrilla war, involves a protracted political and military effort by irregular forces and illegal political organizations seeking to topple an existing regime. The aim of such a war is to force the collapse of the government through unconventional military tactics, including guerrilla warfare and even periodic terrorist attacks. The strategy of insurgency is not to directly engage a regime's regular forces in battle, but to exhaust them through hit-and-run tactics, low-level military actions, and popular action programs and propaganda campaigns designed to gain the people's political support. *Counterinsurgency*, by contrast, involves a government's effort to counter guerrilla military actions both by maintaining political support of the masses and by overtly and covertly challenging the coercive operations of the insurgent forces.

During the Cold War, both the United States and the Soviet Union were involved, directly and indirectly, overtly and covertly, in these internal wars. The superpowers typically used a variety of coercive instruments short of war to influence the outcome of these conflicts. These unconventional strategies ranged from secret operations (e.g., clandestine raids and covert operations) to overt political, economic, and military support to occasional small-scale military operations. Because many of these Third World conflicts involved insurgency or counterinsurgency, both superpowers participated in these unconventional internal wars.

According to one scholar, the United States utilized four LIC strategies during the Cold War: proinsurgency (supporting insurgent forces), counterinsurgency (fighting against revolutionary guerrillas), peacetime contingency operations (such as police-type actions), and military "shows of force" that display military capabilities.[8] Some of these strategies pose ethical challenges because they involve clandestine operations that rely on irregular forces—that is, troops not distinguished by uniforms and insignia. Insurgencies, as previously discussed, seek to defeat the enemy not through direct military engagements, but rather through wars of attrition based on hit-and-run tactics and attacks on society's infrastructure and on key civilian institutions. A major aim of insurgents' military operations is to foster fear, demoralize citizenship, weaken society, and undermine the economy. To effectively carry out their military operations, insurgent forces rely on secrecy, surprise, and small-scale operations, frequently involving support from civilians. Indeed, insurgencies and counterinsurgencies are morally problematic because, by engaging civilians as supporters and as active participants in the war, they subvert the just war norm of discrimination that differentiates combatants from noncombatants.

Despite the moral challenges posed by unconventional operations, some scholars have defended the right of fighting tyranny with unconventional force. Walzer, for example, argues that, notwithstanding the moral problems of guerrilla war, insurgency can be a morally legitimate means of fighting oppression.[9] Whether fighting against a tyrannical regime is moral will depend on both the conditions that justify violence against a regime and the range of legitimate methods available to rebels. Charles Krauthammer similarly provides a qualified defense of guerrilla tactics when the existing oppression is the greater evil.[10] According to him, while domestic political order is essential for a peaceful, humane society, order is not the only public good by which we judge political communities. As the U.S. Declaration of Independence suggests, when a regime becomes tyrannical, people have a right to rebel and constitute a new, legitimate government authority. In short, internal, unconventional wars, like interstate wars, can be morally permissible, provided that their ends and means are just. However, unlike traditional wars, unconventional military operations present greater challenges in ensuring that the means of violence are morally acceptable.

To explore some of the moral challenges posed by unconventional force, I next describe and ethically assess the Reagan Doctrine, a strategy that supported and justified U.S. participation in Third World unconventional wars.

CASE 8-1: ETHICS AND THE REAGAN DOCTRINE

BACKGROUND

In the November 1980 presidential election, Republican Party candidate Ronald Reagan defeated Jimmy Carter. During the election campaign, Reagan charged that the Carter administration had been "soft" on Soviet communism and had failed to effectively challenge Soviet expansionism in developing countries. In addition, Reagan claimed that Carter had allowed the U.S. military power to deteriorate and had failed to advance America's interests in promoting political and economic freedom in the world. Candidate Reagan promised that, if elected, he would restore American military strength and challenge Soviet expansionism by supporting regimes threatened by revolutionary communism and assisting peoples seeking to overcome tyranny, especially communist oppression.

THE REAGAN DOCTRINE

Unlike other presidential doctrines (e.g., those of Truman and Nixon), the Reagan Doctrine did not emerge from a single speech or initiative, but from a series of addresses, declarations, directives, and policy actions undertaken in the president's first term of office. Krauthammer, who first coined the term in 1985 and was responsible for the concept's popularization, argued that the Reagan Doctrine involved two core features: the rollback of Soviet expansionism and the protection, promotion, and consolidation of democracy.[11] In his view, the doctrine was rooted in the administration's overt support of regimes threatened by Marxist insurgency and in its support of anticommunist liberation movements.

One of the Reagan administration's early initiatives that contributed to the development of this doctrine was its policy toward El Salvador, a country threatened by virulent guerrilla war. Although the U.S. government limited its direct military involvement, it provided substantial economic and military assistance to prevent Marxist revolutionaries from toppling the government. The goal in El Salvador was not only the defeat of the guerrillas but also the strengthening of democracy in that land. Because the U.S. policy toward El Salvador in early 1982 involved both a military strategy of countering insurgency and a political strategy of further institutionalizing democracy, Robert Kagan suggests that the Reagan Doctrine "may have been born in El Salvador in 1982."[12]

One of the most significant expositions of the emerging new doctrine was a speech given by Reagan in June 1982 before the British parliament at Westminster. In that speech, regarded as one of the most important addresses during his eight-year presidency, Reagan proclaimed that the United States would launch a "crusade for freedom," supporting democracy wherever it had a chance to succeed.[13] According to Reagan, the aim of U.S. foreign policy was not simply to contain communist expansion, but to advance the cause of political freedom everywhere, regardless of the ideology of the regime, noting that it would be "preposterous" to "encourage democratic change in right-wing dictatorships, but not in communist regimes." Above all, the long-term goal of the freedom crusade was to "leave Marxism–Leninism on the ash heap of history." The Westminster speech is historically significant because it represented an emerging shift from the traditional Republican foreign policy of containment to a policy of democratic expansion, from realpolitik to an ideological crusade for freedom. As one scholar has noted, Reagan's speech "ventured onto new ideological terrain, leaving traditional Republican foreign policy behind."[14]

Some political leaders and scholars thought that Reagan's pronouncements about the duty to promote democracy and oppose communist regimes were overly simplistic and moralistic. For them, Reagan's foreign policy was unwisely based on a Manichean morality that unnecessarily divided the world into good regimes guided by the "forces of light" and bad regimes guided by the "forces of darkness."[15] Although democracy was regarded as essential in securing human freedom, Reagan's critics argued that foreign policy should be inspired and guided not by a crusading spirit for freedom and democratic institutions, but rather by a more dispassionate and pragmatic assessment of America's national and global interests.

The first Reagan administration initiatives on democratic expansion focused on Eastern Europe. In May 1982, Reagan signed a secret order, National Security Decision Directive (NSDD) 32, setting forth a comprehensive anticommunist national strategy. This directive authorized U.S. officials to challenge the monolithic power of the Communist party rule in Eastern Europe by providing help to antigovernment groups, thereby strengthening the preconditions for democratic rule. In Poland, for example, U.S. officials were authorized to assist such intermediary political groups as the Catholic Church and the union-based Solidarity Movement. A year later, Reagan signed another secret directive (NSDD 75) that further reinforced the U.S. government's commitment to an active anticommunist global campaign. This directive called on the United States to "roll back" the Soviet sphere of influence by seeking to "contain and over time reverse Soviet expansionism."[16]

Although the Reagan administration's anticommunist crusade was proclaimed universally valid, the Reagan Doctrine was applied mainly to the Third World. Such a strategy would permit the United States to challenge by proxy the Soviet Union's Third World influence without directly confronting its military power. The aim was thus to support anticommunist liberation movements without directly challenging the Soviet Union militarily. Not surprisingly, the Reagan administration carried out its anti-Marxist revolutionary campaign in small, developing nations, with the major test cases being Afghanistan, Angola, Cambodia, and Nicaragua.

As it emerged in the mid-1980s, the Reagan Doctrine was characterized by five elements. First, the United States sought to directly challenge and curb Soviet power. Although containment, the dominant U.S. Cold War strategy, tried to limit Soviet expansion, the aim of the Reagan Doctrine was much more expansive, involving the rollback of the Soviet sphere of influence. Second, the United States supported limited, constitutional regimes and helped foster democratic institutions that were conducive to human liberty. Third, the Reagan Doctrine used morality to justify its ideological crusade for liberty. Whereas the Cold War doctrine of containment was defended largely on the basis of national interest, the new doctrine was justified by claims of justice. As one scholar has noted, the doctrine was based on the supposition that "what was necessary had to be coupled with a defense of what was right."[17] According to Reagan, supporting anti-Soviet insurgencies was morally legitimate because human beings were entitled to freedom. Fourth, the Reagan Doctrine was characterized by its "overt and unashamed American support for anticommunist revolution."[18] According to the doctrine, the United States would not directly confront Soviet military power but instead would rely on insurgent forces to carry out anticommunist revolutionary insurgencies. The

United States would provide military, economic, and logistical support to guerrillas fighting Marxist regimes. Finally, the Reagan Doctrine encouraged prudent interventionism to weaken politically oppressive regimes, to support and strengthen anticommunist regimes, and to help consolidate democratic political systems. Such interventionism involved a variety of LIC strategies, ranging from shows of force to limited military operations, from overt economic and military assistance to covert intervention.

THE ETHICS OF THE DOCTRINE

As noted previously, the major foreign policy aims of the Reagan administration as formulated in the Reagan Doctrine were to roll back the geopolitical power of the Soviet Union and promote anticommunist, prodemocratic regimes. In assessing the moral merits of the doctrine's goals, it is clear that Reagan's call for a revolution in liberty—involving increased individual freedom, the spread of democracy, and the reduction of totalitarian control—was morally unassailable. However, if goals are assessed not only in terms of official statements and presidential declarations (declaratory policy) but also in terms of government decisions (operational policy), it is clear that U.S. actions were far more concerned with containing and reducing the power of communist regimes than with promoting and consolidating democracy. As a result, the anticommunist struggles were often invested with more moral content than they deserved.[19] For example, Reagan regularly referred to anticommunist insurgents (in countries such as Afghanistan and Nicaragua) as "freedom fighters," even though such military forces were concerned mainly with political independence and self-determination, not with establishing democratic structures.

Although the Reagan Doctrine's advocates recognized that most of the insurgent forces were not democratic or likely to foster democratic institutions immediately, the destabilization of existing Marxist regimes was considered to be a first step in the development of free, participatory regimes. In their view, undermining the power of oppressive regimes through LIC strategies, although morally problematic, was necessary in promoting personal liberty. For example, Krauthammer, a staunch defender of the doctrine, wrote: "If indigenous rebels, claiming their right to freedom, meet the (lesser) requirements to justify revolution and call for American support, it is hard to see what morally proscribes us from responding."[20] Robert Johnson, however, notes that the doctrine's goal of fostering liberty was an illusory, unattainable ideal in the Third World regions where it was being applied because the notion of popular will has "no clear meaning in pre-modern societies with little or no democratic tradition."[21] Moreover, Johnson argues that in the Reagan administration's eagerness to morally defend and support anti-Marxist insurgencies, it tended to conflate "democracy" and "independence," thereby legitimizing revolutionary struggles that were anticommunist but not necessarily prodemocratic.[22]

Although significant consensus existed over the moral legitimacy of the doctrine's goals, strategists, scholars, and public affairs commentators were deeply divided over the merits of the doctrine's means. The moral ambivalence over methodology was rooted not only in concerns about supporting anticommunist fighters, but also in the legitimation of unconventional guerrilla warfare tactics. From an ethical perspective, the Reagan Doctrine's methods posed two significant problems. First, by supporting covert intervention, the doctrine tended to undermine the territorial integrity and political independence of some Third World countries. Second, by supporting insurgent forces, the doctrine tended to sanction guerrilla warfare tactics. Foreign intervention challenges global order. Support for antigovernment insurgencies is contrary to international law because it compromises a state's right to political sovereignty and its obligation to honor nonintervention. But since international order is not the highest value in global society, respecting sovereignty is not a moral imperative. As Krauthammer has observed, "there are wrongs worth righting even at the cost of injuring order."[23] As foreign military intervention involves actions contrary to the international political architecture of global society, such action is always legally problematic and morally sus-

pect. Nevertheless, as I suggested in the previous chapter, from time to time developments arise that may justify overriding the nonintervention norm, such as the defense of human rights.

Ultimately, whether covert or overt foreign intervention is morally defensible will depend partly on the extent of gross human rights abuses and the prospects for eradicating the tyrannical abuse of power. According to Charles Beitz, if insurgents are worthy of support, they should, at a minimum, be genuinely committed to respecting human rights and should represent "a truly indigenous movement with substantial popular support."[24] Determining whether antigovernment forces have popular support in a tyranny is virtually impossible to ascertain. For example, in his assessment of the Nicaraguan anti-Sandinista insurgents (Contras), Beitz concludes that they did not satisfy the popular-support norm. Similarly, Robert Pastor argues that the application of the Reagan Doctrine in Nicaragua was counterproductive because it was based on policies and tactics that were inconsistent with traditional U.S. foreign policy. "To defeat the Communists," writes Pastor, "Reagan adopted their tactics and jettisoned America's purpose: respect for the rule of law."[25] Still, when citizens were given the opportunity to express their view about the Sandinista regime in presidential elections in 1990, they decisively elected the anti-Sandinista coalition to power.

But even if force is morally justified in challenging communist oppression, is reliance on insurgency a morally legitimate way of advancing justice? For instance, were the U.S.-supported insurgencies in Afghanistan and Nicaragua morally legitimate? As noted previously, guerrilla warfare is morally problematic because it subverts the basic just war distinction between soldiers and civilians, combatants and noncombatants. By their very logic, insurgent forces rely on unconventional warfare using irregular forces and guerrilla tactics that seek to undermine society. Although the discrimination norm is an essential element of the just war theory, it is not the sole criterion. Indeed, since the just war doctrine provides numerous principles for assessing if, when, and how to use military force, ascertaining the moral legitimacy of a particular action—

such as giving military support to the Afghan guerrillas (*mujahedeen*) seeking to topple the Soviet-installed regime in Kabul—must be based in light of all just war norms. In particular, the justice of war must also be assessed in accordance with the legitimacy of the war's goals and the proportionality of the violence inflicted in wartime. Krauthammer, aware of the moral difficulties involved in supporting unconventional warfare, defends the Reagan Doctrine's support for anticommunist insurgencies as "the lesser of two evils," believing that the evils of guerrilla war are justified by the greater good of overthrowing tyrannical regimes.[26]

Did the Reagan Doctrine contribute to the rollback of Soviet influence in the international community? Did it undermine Marxist regimes? Did it contribute to the expansion of democracy, especially in the Third World? The most important test case for the Reagan Doctrine was the U.S. support for the insurgency in Afghanistan, regarded by one scholar as the "cornerstone" of the Reagan Doctrine.[27] In supporting this anti-Soviet insurgency throughout the 1980s, the U.S. government provided nearly $3 billion in covert military assistance, including the transfer of highly sophisticated anti-aircraft Stinger missiles. The success of the *mujahedeen* insurgency, which resulted in major Soviet military losses, eventually forced the Soviet Union to withdraw from Afghanistan and reappraise its foreign policy. Although the insurgency helped defeat the Soviet Union, it contributed little to the development of a more pluralistic society in Afghanistan. Indeed, in the post–Cold War era, Afghanistan was ruled by Islamic fundamentalists, known as the Taliban, who imposed an even more totalitarian government than had been the case under the Soviet-installed puppet regime in the 1980s. The Taliban ruled from the mid-1990s until the regime was toppled by a U.S.-led armed intervention after it refused to turn over Osama bin Laden and other Al Qaeda leaders to the United States in the aftermath of the 9/11 terror attack.

Despite the uneven application of the Reagan Doctrine to Nicaragua, some scholars claim that the Reagan administration's initiatives toward that country might have contributed to its transition from a radical Marxist regime in the early 1980s to a democratic system in 1990. Unlike Afghanistan, in which the Soviet forces were forced to withdraw, the Soviet-supported Sandinista regime was not defeated militarily, in part because of the comparatively modest, sporadic support from the United States.[28] Nevertheless, the Reagan administration's policies contributed to Sandinista reforms, without which the return of democracy in 1990 would have been less likely. "Guns alone could force the Sandinistas from power," writes Kagan, "and guns alone, therefore, provided sufficient pressure to force them to make changes to preserve power."[29] However, if the Contras' military threat was essential to Nicaragua's shift toward democratic rule, Kagan also argues that it was not sufficient to achieve democracy. In his view, the continuation of Reagan administration policies would probably not have resulted in the February 1990 elections, but would have "meant many years of inconclusive struggle."[30] U.S. military support for the Contras was thus a necessary but not a sufficient condition for democratization. Other factors that ultimately contributed to the elections included the Central American Peace Plan initiated by Costa Rican president Oscar Arias, ongoing congressional initiatives and debates, the dramatic decline of Soviet power in the late 1980s, and the renewed commitment of the Bush administration to a peaceful resolution of the regional conflict.

Assessing the international impact of the Reagan Doctrine is especially difficult because practitioners and scholars differ as to how and when the doctrine was implemented. Nevertheless, there can be little doubt that during the 1980s the relative international influence of the Soviet Union declined precipitously. As former secretary of state George Shultz noted in his memoirs, by the end of the 1980s "the Brezhnev Doctrine was dead, with the execution due in some considerable part to its opposite number, the Reagan Doctrine."[31] Some scholars have claimed that the decline of Soviet influence was due mainly to internal economic and political conditions; others, however, have credited the decline of the Soviet Union and the ending of the Cold War to Reagan's vigorous anticommunist campaign.[32] In sum, while scholars and public officials remain divided over the impact of the Reagan Doctrine, there can be little doubt that U.S. foreign policy contributed partly to the decline of communist influence and the expansion of democratic regimes during the 1980s.

MORAL REFLECTIONS

The Reagan Doctrine raises numerous critical issues about the role of moral values and unconventional force. Although there is little doubt that the Reagan Doctrine's aims of democratization and increased individual liberty were morally worthy, it is much less clear that the moral and strategic crusade against communism was similarly justified.

- Were the goals of the Reagan Doctrine morally legitimate? More specifically, did

the belief that communist regimes were the principal obstacle to the promotion of human dignity justify the vigorous anticommunist campaign?

- Was the Reagan Doctrine's reliance on unconventional force consistent with just war norms?
- Was the strategic, military, and political support for anticommunist forces consistent with international law and international political morality?
- In view of the morally problematic nature of guerrilla warfare, was support for insurgent forces morally warranted?
- Would direct U.S. military confrontation with the Soviet Union have been morally preferable to proxy wars?

THE THREAT OF TERRORISM

Terrorism is random violence carried out to communicate a political message. International terrorism, to paraphrase Carl von Clausewitz, is the continuation of politics by other means.[33] Although terrorism, like war, is a form of violence used for political ends, it differs significantly from the armed violence of the state. First, whereas conventional war involves destruction aimed at soldiers and military and political installations, the terrorist makes no distinction between combatants and noncombatants. Second, while war is carried out by the armed forces of a state, terrorism is violence perpetrated primarily by nongovernmental agents. A third difference is that terrorism is essentially "psychological warfare"[34]—that is, violence designed to undermine communal solidarity by fostering fear. As terrorists seek to weaken existing structures and institutions by spreading fear throughout society, they rely on random violence aimed at innocent civilians. Political theorist Michael Walzer writes: "Randomness is the crucial feature of terrorist activity. If one wishes fear to spread and intensify over time, it is not desirable to kill specific people identified in some particular way with a regime, a party, or a policy. Death must come by chance."[35]

Terrorism is illegal and immoral. It is illegal because it does not conform to the codified rules of war, which require that violence be carried out openly by uniformed soldiers of a state. And terrorism is inconsistent with moral law because it refuses to make distinctions between combatants and noncombatants. Indeed, terrorists not only refuse to distinguish between the innocent, who must be spared when carrying out political violence, and soldiers and leaders, who are the legitimate targets of war, but they intentionally seek to kill innocent civilians in order to spread fear. It is not the killing of innocent people per se that is problematic. Rather, the evil of terror lies in the *intention* to kill anybody in the target society, making no allowance for mothers, children, the elderly, and the sick. As the just war tradition reminds us, political violence can be morally legitimate only if the aims and methods of such force are consistent with political morality. As Camus writes in his play *The Just Assassins*, "Even in destruction, there's a right way and a wrong way—and there are limits."[36]

Are some terrorists better than others? Although scholars and public officials generally agree that terrorism is evil because it perpetrates random violence on civilians, there is much less consensus about which individuals and groups are terrorists.[37] One reason for the lack of agreement is the propensity to treat all nongovernmental violence as morally equivalent. As the relativist cliché suggests, "one person's 'terrorist' is another person's 'freedom fighter.'" Another reason for the lack of consensus about which groups are terrorists lies with the political goals being advocated by groups. As people are likely to differ in their perceptions of the moral merits of terrorists' goals, some groups are likely to be regarded as far more evil and offensive than others. An ardent advocate of Palestinian statehood, for example, is likely to view Islamic Jihad or Hamas not as terrorist organizations, but as liberation movements that rely on urban violence to dramatize the injustice of Israel's occupation of Gaza and the West Bank. By contrast, Israeli citizens are likely to view such organizations as evil not only in their methods but also in their goals and tactics. Finally, observers are likely to disagree about terrorism because of different interpretations about motivations. If terrorism is viewed as a by-product of economic deprivation, despair, and powerlessness, such violence will be regarded with more understanding and sympathy than those who view terrorism as simply a tool of power politics. Regardless of the moral merits of terrorists' goals, however, the reliance on terror is inconsistent with international humanitarian law, the laws of war, and international political morality. Terrorism is evil not because of the illegitimacy of its goals but because it uses indiscriminate violence against innocent civilians.

Although terror has existed for a long time, the terrorism of the post–Cold War era differs from the "old" terrorism of the Cold War in several respects.[38] First, the "new" terrorism is more violent because it seeks not only to gain attention but also to inflict mass casualties. Second, whereas the older terrorism was undertaken primarily by revolutionary groups in their quest to transform a domestic political order, new terrorist groups tend to be organizations whose scope and purpose is transnational in character. Their goal is not simply to undermine Western societies but to extend and institutionalize a new political order throughout the world. Third, the new terrorist groups are better organized and better financed than the older groups, which relied primarily on one or more states to provide funding and support. New groups like Al Qaeda derive their income not from states but from their own investments and business operations. Indeed, the resources of Al Qaeda are so extensive that it was able to provide Afghanistan, its primary host state, significant financial resources and serve as a major source of military security and policy planning to its ruling Taliban. Finally, the new terrorist groups have far greater access to weapons of mass destruction (WMD), with the result that dangers from terrorism have increased dramatically. While the destruction of the 9/11 attack was achieved without major weapons, the danger from chemical, biological, and nuclear weapons has greatly increased with the dissemination of information about chemical and biological agents and the proliferation of scientific and technological knowledge about WMD. If trained terrorists can commandeer passenger airplanes to deploy them as large incendiary weapons, presumably they can also threaten nuclear power plants, contaminate the water supply of urban centers, spray toxic agents from airplanes, and place a "dirty" bomb[39] in a major business center.

THE ETHICS OF COUNTERTERRORISM

From an ethical perspective, the major challenge in carrying out a counterterrorism campaign is how to defeat the enemy without resorting to the tactics and strategies of the terrorists themselves. When the Algerian liberation movement—the Front de Libération Nationale (FLN)— resorted to terrorism to end French colonial rule, the French government responded with a brutal war of attrition involving secret killings, torture, and disappearances.[40] Although the French were able to destroy much of the FLN organization in 1957 through a covert counterinsurgency campaign, in the end the brutal tactics of the French were unable to stop the Algerians from gaining independence. The Argentine antiterror campaign of 1975–1979 is similar to the French Algerian experience. In 1975, Argentine military and police forces began a covert war against the Montoneros and other antistate groups, carrying out a counterinsurgency campaign that involved abductions, torture, and secret killings. After democracy was restored in 1983, the new president, Raúl Alfonsín, appointed a truth commission to investigate the fate of the missing. The truth commission, which issued its findings in 1984 in a report titled *Nunca Más* ("never again"), disclosed that nearly four thousand people had been killed by the military and security services and that nearly nine thousand others who had been kidnapped or arrested remained missing. Like the French in Algeria, however, the Argentine military services won the battle against terrorists but lost the war. They did so because by resorting to illegal, morally illegitimate methods, including covert gross human rights abuses, they undermined the armed forces' institutional credibility and public support.

How should a state counter terrorism? How can a government seek to minimize the threat and violence of terrorists, especially the emerging groups that are deeply inspired by religion and are prepared to sacrifice their lives? How can states deter suicide bombings? Since terrorists carry out violence covertly, identifying and locating them is a daunting task. Moreover, since terrorists carry out violence randomly, making no distinction between combatants and noncombatants, devising a counterterror strategy that is consistent with widely accepted principles of humanitarianism and the international law of war presents significant moral challenges. This is especially the case in applying the just war tradition to the problem of terror by nongovernmental agents. This is so because just war norms have been historically applied almost exclusively to states, the only assumed legitimate institutions of coercive power. To be sure, the tradition can be extended and applied to the problem of terror, but it presents daunting challenges.[41]

When facing security threats from other states, states have historically relied on coercive diplomacy, deterrence, and defensive power to prevent and, if necessary, repulse aggression. But these conventional strategies are unlikely to protect society from fanatical fighters committed to terror. Since terrorists are disciplined, well organized and deeply committed to their goals, and because they undertake violence with secrecy and stealth, combating terrorism presents enormous challenges. To begin with, conventional strategies that rely on military power to deter, defend, or punish aggression are unlikely to protect society from the random, indiscriminate violence of terrorists. Because terrorists are members of an elusive revolutionary movement or small covert organization, identifying and locating its members is a difficult challenge. More importantly, because terrorists are fanatical in their devotion to the political cause they serve, the threat of retaliatory military punishment is unlikely to dissuade action. The contemporary phenomenon of suicide bombings, where terrorists willingly kill themselves in carrying out bombing missions, illustrates this high level of fanaticism.

Since containment through deterrence is unlikely to protect society, combating terrorism will involve a two-pronged strategy, one defensive and the other offensive. The defensive strategy, known as *antiterrorism*, seeks to protect society by establishing policies, regulations, structures, and other initiatives that help to reduce a society's vulnerability to terror. Its aim is to protect people and, in the event of an attack, minimize the effects of terror. Antiterrorism is illustrated in the initiatives and reforms instituted by the U.S. government in the aftermath of the 9/11 terrorist attack. Some of these include the centralization of security and intelligence responsibilities in a new department (Homeland Security), increased surveillance in major transportation centers, increased border controls, more stringent security regulations at airports, and increased authority for law enforcement officials. Since protective measures alone are unlikely to protect society from terror, a second strategy seeks to undermine terrorist networks and organizations before they are able to carry out their mission. This strategy, known as *counterterrorism*, uses the military and economic power of the state to attack, weaken, and destroy terrorist organizations and movements. While such a strategy is appealing, it is extraordinarily difficult because terrorist networks function covertly.

Given the elusive character of terrorism, an effective counterterrorism strategy will require, at a minimum, accurate and timely intelligence and small, covert unconventional force. As terrorists carry out their missions with great secrecy, the most important requirement in countering terrorists is knowledge about the nature, mission, structure, funding, personnel, capabilities, and future targets of the terrorist group. Second, a sound strategy will involve highly trained counterterrorist agents who can carry out secret missions with stealth and effectiveness. The two tasks of intelligence-gathering and fighting terrorists are highly intertwined, so many of the agents will be involved in both tasks simultaneously. Of course, when a terrorist network establishes its base of operations within a state, as was the case with Al Qaeda in Afghanistan, conventional military power can be employed to destroy the base of operations and topple the government harboring the terrorists. This is, of course, the action that the United States took in the aftermath of the 9/11 attack, a case study I examine below. Typically, however, terrorist networks operate with great stealth, making identification difficult.

In seeking to defeat terrorism, democratic states face enormous challenges. Since an effective counterterrorist strategy will require patience, stealth, and intelligence, state security forces may be tempted to counter terrorism with means used by terrorists themselves. But if a democratic state is to maintain its legitimacy and credibility, it must not succumb to illegal and immoral tactics. In carrying out their unconventional, covert war against terrorists, they must use proportionate violence only as a last resort and solely against legitimate targets. In particular, states must refrain from using tactics that undermine human rights and call into question the moral authority of the state. In devising and carrying out a counterterror strategy, constitutional governments face two important moral challenges. The first major issue is whether torture is ever morally permissible in gaining intelligence, especially in a "ticking bomb " case where major destruction is involved. The second concern is whether targeted assassination of senior military or political leaders can be justified. Because both of these topics have been important concerns in developed democratic states, I next examine the ethics of each.

The Ethics of Torture

One of the most difficult moral challenges in devising an effective and legitimate counterterrorism strategy is how to gain reliable, accurate, and timely intelligence through moral means. Historically, states and nonstate actors have been tempted to inflict physical pain to acquire information about the capabilities, organization, personnel, and potential targets of terrorist groups. But torture is contrary to the widely accepted norms of international political morality and international law. As Henry Shue observes, torture is "contrary to every relevant international law. . . . No other practice except slavery is so universally and unanimously condemned in law and human convention."[42] In 1984, nations adopted the Convention Against Torture (formally known as the Convention Against Torture and Other Cruel, Inhuman, or Degrading Treatment or Punishment) and three years later it became effective after sufficient states had ratified the treaty.[43] While international law prohibits torture, some governments, especially dictatorships and authoritarian regimes, have used and continue to use torture in the belief that such a practice is necessary for countering security threats. Even democratic regimes have periodically resorted to torture when facing intractable political violence. Israel, for example, used modest torture—or what was termed "moderate physical pressure"—until its Supreme Court declared such action illegal in September 1999.

Perhaps the major challenge in seeking to eliminate the practice of torture is the lack of consensus on what the term prohibits. How much coercion is permissible? Is psychological manipulation a form of torture? While the distinction between legitimate and illegitimate coercion may be unclear at times, there is broad consensus among democratic societies that such violence as caning, use of electrical shock, pulling fingernails, and sticking pins through fingers is morally reprehensible and prohibited by international law. In his 2003 State of the Union address, President Bush identified some of the torture techniques used by Iraq's security agents, including electric shock, burning with hot irons, dripping acid on the skin, and mutilation with electric drills. Bush then observed, "If this is not evil, then evil has no meaning." But are less coercive methods—or what Mark Bowden terms "torture lite"[44]—also legally and morally unacceptable? Such pressures can involve sleep deprivation, exposure to cold and heat, rough physical treatment such as slapping and shaking, making a prisoner stand for a long time or sit in an uncomfortable position, or manipulating the psychological state of the prisoner through fear.

Perhaps the most notorious example of a democracy using torture was the French war against the Algerian FLN in the late 1950s. When Algerian forces resorted to terrorism to undermine French colonial rule and to press their demand for Algeria's political independence, the French authorities responded with a brutal counterinsurgency strategy involving torture and secret killings. The French security forces justified the use of torture through utilitarian, consequentialist logic: torture was a necessary evil in order to prevent a much more significant injustice—the deliberate killing of innocent civilians through terrorism. General Jacques Massu, a French commander in Algeria, articulated the cost-benefit logic of this view by claiming that "the innocent [the next victims of terrorist attacks] deserve more protection than the guilty."[45]

The noted criminal lawyer Alan Dershowitz argues that "the tragic reality is that torture sometimes works."[46] But the belief that torture works is itself a dubious claim because the efficacy of such action is at best likely to be a short-term success. While torture might help defeat an immediate terrorist threat, the historical record suggests that the abuse of human rights to gain national security is likely to be at best a Pyrrhic victory. Indeed, the use of illegal and immoral means is likely to have deleterious effects not only on the terrorists, but also on those who carry out the terror and on the society itself. In other words, torture might help win a particular conflict, but it is unlikely to contribute to the defeat of a terrorist movement. For example, while the French were able to destroy the FLN terrorist network through their brutal antiterrorist campaign, the harsh strategy of repression and torture turned out to be counterproductive, eventually undermining French moral and political authority not only in Algeria but also in France itself. Bruce Hoffman, a leading scholar of terrorism, has written that the French army's counterinsurgency campaign alienated the Muslim masses, transformed their passive and apathetic response into political activism, swelling the popularity of and support for the FLN, and increasingly undermined French public support for continued colonial control. "The army's achievement in the city," writes Hoffman, "was therefore bought at the cost of eventual political defeat."[47] The deleterious effects of torture are also evident in Argentina and Chile, where military governments resorted to torture and secret killings in order to defeat antistate revolutionary groups.

Even if Dershowitz is correct that torture sometimes "works," constitutional regimes face the challenge of defining under what exceptional national security threats such violence might be justified. Since the law is the basis of a constitutional order, torture will necessarily represent a violation of both domestic and international law. But torture is also morally unacceptable because it uses human beings as a means to an end, allowing violence to be inflicted on prisoners in order to gather information—that is, using evil (physical torture) for moral ends (preventing terror).

Since Dershowitz wants to offer societal protection from terrorism without undermining the rule of law, he argues that when open, democratic nations are facing extreme security threats, such as the prospective destruction from a "ticking-bomb," nonlethal torture may be morally justified, provided it is authorized by judicial authority. For Dershowitz, nonlethal torture can be justified in exceptional circumstances if the agents seeking the desired information secure a "terror warrant."[48] The problem with courts authorizing torture, however, is that such action will undoubtedly encourage and regularize a behavior that is considered immoral and illegal. According to Judge Richard Posner, a better way to address extenuating security challenges is to allow "executive discretion"—that is, to leave in place existing legal prohibitions against torture with the understanding that they will not be enforced in extreme circumstances. Posner fears that if courts are allowed to legitimate nonlethal torture in extraordinary circumstances, such a practice will become institutionalized and in time will become commonplace.[49]

The United States ratified the Convention Against Torture in 1994, and the U.S. government has steadfastly maintained, especially in the aftermath of the 9/11 terrorist attack, that it is deeply committed to the prohibition of this practice. After many Al Qaeda prisoners were brought to the military base in Guantánamo, Cuba, numerous allegations were made that the U.S. government was itself using torture or condoning the use of torture by other states in the campaign against Al Qaeda fighters. But the government has consistently denied this. After Amnesty International protested U.S. treatment of detained captives, President Bush reaffirmed American opposition to torture. He said, "I call on all governments to join with the United States and the community of law-abiding nations in prohibiting, investigating, and prosecuting all acts of torture . . . and we are leading this fight by example."[50] But this claim ceased to be credible when graphic photography of U.S. prisoner abuse at Baghdad's Abu Ghraib prison became widely available in May 2004, resulting in widespread media coverage.[51]

The digital photographs, taken by military police, showed prisoners being sexually humiliated and threatened with dogs. Some soldiers charged that these actions were taken to "soften up" prisoners for subsequent interrogation. Others argued that the mistreatment was due to lack of professionalism and a failure of military leadership, while still others claimed that the sadistic actions had been orchestrated for the guards' entertainment. Whatever the reasons for the mistreatment, it was evident that the human depravity depicted in the widely circulating images was contrary to humanitarian law and the common morality of civilized people and a deep embarrassment to the American people and its government. President Bush vigorously denounced the Abu Ghraib abuses, saying that such actions did not represent the values of the United States, while Senator John Warner (R-Va.), the chairman of the Senate Armed Services Committee, declared that the photographs represented the worst "military misconduct" that he had seen in sixty years. Some political leaders demanded the resignation or firing of the secretary of defense, Donald Rumsfeld. However the scandal is defined and explained, the prison abuses undermined the U.S. initiative to promote a more humane and democratic Iraq along with the values necessary to sustain such a political order. As one commentator noted, "the Abu Ghraib photographs and the terrible story they tell have done great damage to what was left of America's moral power in the world, and thus its power to inspire hope rather than hatred among Muslims."[52]

Although the nature of, and responsibility for, prisoner mistreatment has been, and continues to be, investigated by the U.S. government, it is clear that American soldiers have mistreated captives in detention centers and prisons in both Afghanistan and Iraq.[53] While overcrowded prison conditions, inadequate resources and personnel, poor training, and tensions between interrogators charged with intelligence-gathering and military police tasked with prison security may have contributed to the mistreatment of detainees, two factors appear to have been especially important in the breakdown of military discipline. First, the U.S. government decision to treat Al Qaeda operatives as "unlawful" combatants meant that such detainees would not be accorded the legal protection normally given soldiers. Even though detainees were to be treated humanely, the removal of international legal protection may have introduced unnecessary uncertainty and flexibility in the rules governing nonstate insurgents. Second, in response to the growing Iraqi insurgency in 2003 that had resulted in hundreds of American casualties, U.S. military leaders relaxed the rules of interrogation in order to increase "actionable intelligence" from captured insurgents.[54] Although these adjustments in interrogation tactics focused on psychological techniques and excluded physical torture, they may have nevertheless undermined existing prohibitions against torture and thereby facilitated prisoner mistreatment.

The Ethics of Targeted Assassination

The second major moral issue in a counterterror campaign is the question of targeted killing, or assassination. As terrorism is generally carried out secretly through non-state actors, some thinkers have argued that an effective way of defeating terrorism is by killing individual terrorists, especially its leaders.[55] Legitimate state violence must target only combatants and seek to protect innocent civilians, so a strategy of targeted assassination provides an effective way of fulfilling the discrimination norm of just war theory. Sir Thomas More is believed to have defended assassination as a means of warfare, since it spared ordinary citizens from the suffering of war for which political leaders were responsible.[56] Similarly, for numerous ancient, medieval, and Renaissance thinkers—such as Aristotle, Cicero, John of Salisbury, and John Milton—the killing of a tyrant (tyrannicide) by his own subjects was a legitimate means of ending oppression. For defenders of tyrannicide, as with advocates of international assassination, the killing of evil rulers is justified by the prospects of promoting a more just, humane political order.

Historically, groups and states have used international assassination as an instrument of statecraft. Even though chivalry may have restrained the violence in war in ancient and medieval times, killing political, religious, and military leaders was, nevertheless, widely practiced. During the fifteenth and sixteenth centuries, when religious and political rivalries intensified in Europe, targeted assassination became even more commonplace. Philip II of Spain, for example, was an ardent advocate of assassination of Protestant leaders, sponsoring numerous plots against William of Orange in Holland and Queen Elizabeth I in England. Indeed, in the 1570s and 1580s the English queen was subject to at least twenty assassination plots, while she herself plotted assassinations in Ireland. Targeted killing was so widespread that the emerging international law of war tended to accept assassination as a legitimate instrument, making no distinction between killing the enemy on the battlefield or elsewhere. Hugo Grotius, the distinguished seventeenth-century Dutch jurist, for example, believed that it made no difference where an enemy was killed.[57] Assassinating enemy leaders, however, was not regarded as an unlimited state right. Indeed, many writers following the chivalric code assumed that targeted killing was permissible only if it was undertaken without treachery. The seventeenth-century jurist Alberico Gentili believed that treachery was so contrary to the moral law that assassination involving fraud and deceit was contrary to the emerging international law of war. This distinction between legitimate and illegitimate means of killing the enemy later served as a basis for the modern laws of war.

The norm against targeted killing began to emerge in the seventeenth and eighteenth centuries as European political and intellectual leaders sought to limit the widespread practice of assassination. By the mid-nineteenth century, the murder of enemy leaders was widely regarded as an unacceptable way of resolving political disputes. The U.S. Army's Lieber Code of 1863, which provides one of the earliest American documents setting forth norms governing war, condemned the assassination of enemies, viewing such killing as a relapse into barbarism.[58] Additionally, the Code prohibited the arbitrary classification of prisoners as "outlaws," so that they could be killed without trial. Some four decades later, representatives from most states gathered in The Hague for a series of conferences that led to two major conventions. In the 1907 Hague Convention, signatories agreed, among other things, to attack only combatants, spare civilians, refrain from inflicting unnecessary suffering, and treat prisoners humanely and the wounded with compassion. Killing prisoners and the wounded was prohibited, while the killing of combatants or civilians through "treachery" was similarly forbidden. The 1956 U.S. Army Field Manual (27–10) on land warfare incorporates this later prohibition and links it with assassination. In sum, while the laws of war greatly expanded throughout the twentieth century, the norm prohibiting assassination has remained intact.

In 1975, the Senate Foreign Relations Committee held hearings that led to the shocking disclosure that the Central Intelligence Agency (CIA) had tried to kill a number of political leaders, including Congo's Patrice Lumumba and Cuba's Fidel Castro. As a result of the disclosure of past assassination attempts, President Gerald Ford issued an executive order banning such action. The order, which has been reaffirmed by every subsequent president, reads: "No person employed by or acting on behalf of the United States Government shall engage in, or conspire to engage in, assassination." Domestic U.S. law thus reinforces the international legal ban on assassination.

Despite the pervasive consensus on the prohibition of targeted killing, there is much confusion over what this rule entails. The confusion arises in part from the fact that in war (or in covert military operations short of war), the aim is to defeat an enemy—a goal accomplished by killing combatants. But killing in war is carried out not by targeting persons per se, but by attacking and destroying what are euphemistically termed "military targets." Such terminology sanitizes the killing, making it general and abstract. Indeed, killing in war is made palatable by the fiction that international war is waged by states, not persons. So long as the killing is not personalized, the discriminating and proportionate use of force against state security structures is deemed acceptable. For example, when the United States carried out retaliatory military raids against Libya in April 1986 in response to Libyan sponsorship of terror, it bombed various military and political installations, including Col. Muammar Qaddafi's house. Although the U.S. government denied that it had intended to kill the Libyan dictator, the bombing sites suggest that the U. S. government would have been pleased had he been killed in the bombing of its military targets.[59] Similarly, in March 2003 the United States commenced war against Iraq not by trying to assassinate Saddam Hussein, Iraq's dictator, but by bombing a Baghdad residential site in which he was thought to be spending the night. Since intelligence had suggested that the site had an underground bunker, the attack on Saddam could not be carried out with cruise missiles but necessitated the use of bombers equipped with laser-guided two-thousand-pound bombs.[60]

Is killing people with missiles and bombs different from killing a person with a sniper's rifle or pistol? Those who defend the ban on assassination think so. They argue that the prohibition helps maintain a clear distinction between the impersonal violence of the state and the targeted violence of private agents. In addition, the ban ensures that the humane, democratic values of constitutional regimes are maintained. Finally, since the major powers, especially the United States, have highly trained military forces to carry out special operations, the use of covert military operations may prove sufficient to undermine terrorism.

But what if the terror persists, as has been the case in Israel, where hundreds of Israelis have been killed in the new millennium by suicide bombers? How should the U.S. military respond to the ongoing bombings by Sunni Baathist fighters, who continue in their covert insurgency against the American occupation of Iraq? Is the killing of terrorist leaders desirable? Is it morally permissible, especially if capture is not possible? Does the threat of terror allow states to carry out anticipatory self-defense?

To illuminate some of the challenges of countering terror, I next turn to the U.S. campaign against Islamic fundamentalism, focusing on the military efforts against Al Qaeda, arguably the world's leading and most dangerous terrorist organization. This terrorist network is inspired by a devotion to Muslim fundamentalist tenets and relies on modern technology to carry out its operations throughout the world. It is headed by Osama bin Laden, a sophisticated terrorist CEO who uses modern communication and financial techniques to operate this transnational terrorist organization.

BACKGROUND

In 1993, Muslim militants tried but failed to destroy New York City's World Trade Center. Three years later, an explosive-laden truck destroyed the Khobar Towers hotel in Saudi Arabia that was occupied by U.S. military personnel. The attack killed nineteen airmen and injured countless others. On August 7, 1998, two massive truck bombs nearly simultaneously destroyed the American embassies in Kenya and Tanzania. After recognizing that these terrorist attacks had killed 301 people and injured another 5,000, and after identifying Al Qaeda as the primary organization responsible for this violence, President Bill Clinton ordered retaliatory strikes against suspected Al Qaeda sites. Using cruise missiles, the U.S. armed forces destroyed Al Qaeda training camps in Afghanistan, where bin Laden was known to be living, and a pharmaceutical plant in Sudan suspected of making chemical agents for WMD. When U.S. authorities discovered that bin Laden had escaped from the bombing, they began demanding that the Taliban, the ruling regime in Afghanistan, turn him over for prosecution. When this failed, the Clinton administration froze all Taliban assets in the United States. In the meantime, various covert efforts were made to capture and, if necessary, kill bin Laden, but these efforts were unsuccessful. According to some officials, part of the failure stemmed from the White House demand that bin Laden be brought to justice rather than be assassinated—a demand that greatly complicated the CIA covert mission.[61]

A year later—on October 12, 2000—a suicide bomber ran his explosives-laden boat against the American destroyer USS Cole while it was refueling in Port of Aden, Yemen. The attack killed and injured many sailors and led to the near loss of the vessel. After this attack, President Clinton vowed to bring those responsible to justice, but once again no effective action was taken. As Charles Hill, a former U.S. diplomat, observes,

the U.S. pattern of reaction to terror was "to act quickly but without a sustained effort."[62]

All this changed on September 11, 2001, when nineteen Muslim fanatics hijacked four jumbo jets in a well-coordinated terrorist act. Two of the wide-bodied jets were forcibly flown into the twin towers of New York City's World Trade Center, causing massive fires that led to the collapse of both 110-story buildings and the death of some three thousand persons. The third jet crashed into the Pentagon in Washington, D.C., killing nearly two hundred additional persons, while the fourth plane crashed in rural Pennsylvania after some passengers struggled with the hijackers to prevent a further deadly attack. This surprising and unprecedented terrorist attack, carried out by a small group of Muslim fanatics, turned out to be the deadliest single act of aggression against the territory of the United States—an attack more destructive and more costly psychologically than the Japanese attack on Pearl Harbor in December 1941.

THE RESPONSE

Soon after the 9/11 attack, President George W. Bush declared a war on terror, noting that the United States would use armed force not only against terrorists themselves but also against the states that harbored them. To reinforce the president's call for action, Congress authorized the president to use "all necessary and appropriate force" to destroy those responsible for the attack. After identifying Al Qaeda as the prime suspect of the attack, U.S. government officials called on other states to participate in this campaign against terrorism. In particular, it requested the assistance of Afghanistan, where the Al Qaeda terrorist network was headquartered, and Pakistan, Afghanistan's neighbor and a country that helped the Taliban, the fundamentalist Muslim regime, gain and maintain power.

Soon thereafter, the U.S. government announced that it had incontrovertible evidence that Al Qaeda was responsible for the attack and demanded that the Taliban turn over Osama bin Laden and his key aides. While Pakistan's military ruler, Pervez Musharraf, publicly promised to assist the United States in its military campaign against terrorism, the Taliban balked at severing ties with Al Qaeda. As a result, the United States commenced armed hostilities determined to replace the regime and destroy the elusive Al Qaeda terrorist cells located in the mountainous regions of eastern Afghanistan.[63] Given Afghanistan's inhospitable terrain, the military campaign (Operation Enduring Freedom) was essentially an air war supported by a small number of Special Forces that relayed targeting information to bombers flying overhead. Additionally, covert teams provided significant tactical support to a coalition of anti-Taliban fighters known as the Northern Alliance.

This large and diverse coalition of Tajik, Turkmen, and Uzbek fighters from Afghanistan's northern region had been battling the Taliban ever since the Pashtun Muslim fundamentalists had taken control of the country in 1996. Thus, when the United States began its war with the Taliban, it immediately began collaborating with the Northern Alliance, providing it with military assistance and tactical guidance. This close cooperation, backed by a large and highly intensive bombing campaign, allowed the Northern Alliance forces to rapidly extend control over the region north and west of Kabul, the country's capital. By December 2001, three months after the war had begun, the Taliban had been defeated. While a variety of factors contributed to the unexpectedly rapid collapse of the Taliban, some developments were especially decisive. These include the collaboration of Pakistan and the Northern Alliance, humanitarian assistance designed to win the "hearts and minds" of the Afghan people through food shipments and economic aid, and the use of highly accurate bombing.[64]

The military victory over the Taliban did not represent a defeat of Al Qaeda. Indeed, two years after the Taliban had been removed from power, the most senior Taliban and Al Qaeda leaders, including Mullah Muhammad Omar and Osama bin Laden, remained at large. As a result, remnants of the Taliban and Al Qaeda continued

to inflict periodic violence against coalition forces and especially against Afghan citizens who were participating in the U.N.-sanction project of nation building. Despite multilateral support, including assistance from NATO and the UN, the process of consolidating a constitutional regime continued to face significant challenges in the face of ongoing political violence. As the country prepared for UN-supervised elections in 2004, the Taliban continued to inflict periodic violence, thereby inhibiting participation in the electoral process.[65]

THE ETHICS OF THE WAR

When a nonstate actor like Al Qaeda commits terror, two moral offenses are committed. First, the violence is a moral offense because nonstate organizations are not legitimate political actors that can use armed force. Following the just war tradition (see chapter 6), the *jus ad bellum* specifies that force can be authorized only by properly constituted political institutions—that is, by legitimate governments.[66] The just war tradition begins with the presumption that force is acceptable only when it is carried out by public authority for the common good of society. Private, nonstate actors do not possess "right authority" to wield the sword. The second offense committed by terrorists is that the violence and destruction is perpetrated randomly against civilians. Because such violence disregards the *jus in bello* norms of discrimination and proportionality, terror is clearly an affront to civilized peoples and to the international community of states.

How should states respond to terrorism, especially large-scale terror like major urban bombings? Two options are available: the first is to view terror as a law enforcement problem; the second is to view it as an act of aggression against a political community, requiring the use of legal, political, and military institutions in punishing and deterring future terrorism. The first approach assumes that the violence perpetrated by terrorists is a crime against individuals that needs to be redressed through a state's retributive legal system. Because individuals commit terror, the criminal justice system of states must be responsible for identifying, capturing, prosecuting, and punishing those persons who are guilty of committing such acts. According to this approach, terrorism is not a collective crime but an act committed against the state and individual victims.[67] Thus, rather than viewing terror as a collective offense that seeks to undermine existing political authority through fear, the criminal justice approach seeks accountability for the offense through the state's courts.

Others, however, argue that violence perpetrated by well-established organizations like Hamas and Al Qaeda cannot be viewed solely as a violation of state law or a crime against victims but, more significantly, as an attack on the entire political community. According to this perspective, the terror of 9/11 was a hideous act of aggression against American society, requiring a collective response by the nation's president. Courts are designed to ensure compliance with the law, but the president is charged with the protection of society from aggression. As Eliot Cohen has noted, "September 11 marked a climactic battle in an ill-defined war, but a war nonetheless."[68]

In defining the U.S. national security strategy in the aftermath of the 9/11 attack, President Bush approached the threat as a political rather than a criminal justice problem. Instead of defining the terrorist threat as a law and order problem, Bush declared a war on terror. Since serious terrorism would not exist without the support of some states, the president indicated that the military would be used to pursue those nations that provide aid or safe haven to terrorists. Bush then said: "Every nation in every region now has a decision to make: either you are with us or you are with the terrorists. From this day forward, any nation that continues to harbor or support terrorism will be regarded by the United States as a hostile regime."[69] In his joint address to Congress on September 20, 2001, he declared: "Great harm has been done to us. We have suffered great loss. And in our grief and anger we have found our mission and our moment." He then went on to define the post-9/11 national security mission as follows: "The advance of human freedom . . . now depends on us. Our nation, this generation, will lift the dark threat of violence from our people and our fu-

ture. We will rally the world to this cause by our efforts, by our courage. We will not tire, we will not falter, and we will not fail."

In developing its counterterror strategy in the post-9/11 context, the U.S. government was inspired by the so-called Bush doctrine[70] and guided by the 2002 National Security Strategy (NSS). This doctrine is significant because it sets forth the core principles governing American power, while the NSS defines the means and methods by which the goals are to be pursued. Fundamentally, the Bush doctrine makes two basic claims: first, a universal political morality exists that affirms the dignity and worth of all persons, and second, the United States will use its power to promote and defend regimes that secure individual freedom and human dignity. At the 2002 West Point commencement, President Bush articulated his conviction on the universality of international political morality by declaring:

> Different circumstances require different methods, but not different moralities. Moral truth is the same in every culture, in every time, and in every place. Targeting innocent civilians for murder is always and everywhere wrong. Brutality against women is always and everywhere wrong. There can be no neutrality between justice and cruelty, between the innocent and the guilty. We are in a conflict between good and evil, and America will call evil by its name. By confronting evil and lawless regimes, we do not create a problem, we reveal a problem. And we will lead the world in opposing it.[71]

As all persons are entitled to human dignity, the Bush doctrine pledges that the U.S. government will seek to advance individual freedom internationally and foster constitutionalism and democratization where liberty is absent or threatened. The second element of the doctrine calls for the use of American power to secure its own national security and to promote a stable, peaceful global order. According to the doctrine, the United States will pursue a national security strategy that deters and, if necessary, prevents aggression, whether by states or nonstate actors.

The 2002 NSS sets forth the challenges and methods for applying the normative principles of the Bush doctrine in the post-9/11 global context. As indicated in chapter 6, the revised strategy defines the operational principles by which power will be used to promote territorial security and foster a just global order. In carrying out this objective, especially against terrorist nonstate actors, the NSS declares that the United States will not hesitate to use its power unilaterally and, if necessary, preemptively.[72]

MORAL REFLECTIONS

Containing and preventing terrorism presents significant strategic challenges because terrorism is generally carried out secretly by nongovernmental actors. Most importantly, devising a morally appropriate counterterror strategy is especially challenging because of the elusive nature of terrorism. Following are some important ethical concerns raised by the U.S. war on terror:

- Terrorism involves the random, indiscriminate use of violence for political ends by nonstate actors. Is war an appropriate metaphor for a counterterror strategy? Or should the antiterror campaign be viewed as a police action, designed to apply a state's criminal justice system to alleged perpetrators of violence?

- If counterterror strategy is defined as a war, how should the military carry out its mission? Should it pursue the enemy through conventional strategies or should it rely on covert, unconventional force? Moreover, war implies a military contest that results in victory or defeat, so is the metaphor of war useful for an activity likely to have no clear outcome and no finality?

- The United States has detained a large number of Al Qaeda and Taliban fighters. How should such prisoners be classified: as "unlawful combatants," as the U.S. government contends, or as prisoners of war (POWs), entitled to protection under the laws of war and, more particularly, the Geneva Convention on POWs?

- U.S. law prohibits the assassination of political leaders. Should leaders of terrorist groups, such as Osama bin Laden, be exempted from this prohibition? Prior to the 9/11 attack, should the U.S. government have sought to capture or assassinate bin Laden?

SUMMARY

During the Cold War, the superpowers resorted to unconventional force in carrying out proxy wars. Guerrilla war, the most widely used strategy in developing nations, was morally problematic because civilians were encouraged to support and directly participate in these operations, thereby blurring the distinction between combatants and noncombatants. In confronting guerrilla wars, the United States pursued LIC strategies that relied on conventional and unconventional force. Although LIC strategies pressed the limits of the rules of war, counterinsurgency strategies that conformed to the norms of just war doctrine were regarded as morally legitimate.

The rise of international terrorism has resulted in the reinvigoration of unconventional military strategies. Terrorism is elusive; countering terror will require accurate and timely intelligence and covert operations that can identify and destroy terrorist networks. If a counterterror campaign is to succeed in a democratic society, it will have to conform to domestic and international law as well as international political morality. In particular, states must resist the temptation of resorting to torture and targeted assassination when confronting major terrorist threats, for terrorism will be undermined and defeated only through methods that are consistent with values that can sustain a free, democratic society. Thus, eliminating the terrorist menace must be carried out with tactics and strategies that conform to the law and to international political morality.

Chapter Nine

The Ethics of Economic Sanctions

A nation boycotted is a nation that is in sight of surrender. Apply this economic, peaceful, silent, deadly remedy and there will be no need for force. It is a terrible remedy. It does not cost a life outside the nation boycotted, but it brings pressure upon that nation that, in my judgment, no modern nation could resist.[1]

—WOODROW WILSON

Wreaking economic havoc on an impoverished developing country that is already unable to meet the basic needs of its people hardly commends itself as appropriate action, even if the foreign or domestic policy of the country concerned merits an international response.[2]

—MARGARET DOXEY

I do not understand how your Christian conscience allows you [Bishop Tutu] to advocate disinvestment. I do not understand how you can put a man out of work for a high moral principle. You put a man out of a job and make his family go hungry so that some high moral principle could be upheld. I think your morality is confused just as was the morality of the church in the Inquisition, or the morality of Dr. Verwoerd in his utopian dreams. You come near to saying that the end justifies the means, which is a thing no Christian can do.[3]

–ALAN PATON

STATES USE A VARIETY of foreign policy instruments to influence the behavior of foreign countries. These include, in order of increasing coerciveness, secret diplomacy, speeches, public condemnation, mild sanctions, comprehensive sanctions, limited military action, military intervention, and war. From an ethical perspective, the most desirable method of pursuing foreign policy goals and of resolving interstate conflicts is through peaceful negotiation. However, when states are unable to resolve disputes through reason and persuasion, they frequently resort to coercive measures, including the use of economic pressures and military force. In the previous three chapters, I examined different dimensions of force; here, I analyze the nature, role, and morality of economic sanctions.

The first part of this chapter examines the major goals of economic sanctions and their effectiveness in achieving them. In assessing the relative effectiveness of sanctions, I differentiate between the success in imposing economic hardship and the success in achieving behavioral reform. I then illustrate some domestic political dimensions of economic sanctions and more particularly the challenge in promoting human rights through trade sanctions with a case study on China. The case raises questions about the feasibility and desirability of fostering political reforms through the threat of economic penalties. In the second section I examine the effectiveness of economic sanctions, and illustrate the limitations of this foreign policy tool with a case study on the U.S. economic embargo against Cuba. The third part of the chapter examines the ethical legitimacy of economic sanctions by applying moral norms derived from the just war doctrine. Although economic sanctions are normally viewed as an alternative to war, just-war norms provide a useful moral structure by which to judge the ethics of sanctions. I illustrate some of the major moral ambiguities in economic statecraft with a case study on comprehensive sanctions against South Africa.

THE AIMS AND EFFECTS OF ECONOMIC SANCTIONS

Economic sanctions are a particular type of statecraft used to advance foreign policy goals. According to David Baldwin, sanctions are "influence attempts" in which states seek to exert power over other international actors, that is, to get them to do what they otherwise would not do.[4] The major difference between economic statecraft and military statecraft does not lie in the level of coercion or destructiveness involved but in the nature of the tools used: Military statecraft relies on force to influence other states (through rewards or punishment) whereas economic statecraft relies on economic instruments.

Strictly speaking, economic sanctions can involve positive incentives ("carrots") designed to induce or reward desirable behaviors or negative actions ("sticks") designed to punish actors for illegal or undesirable behaviors, to deter unwanted behavior, and to compel desired political change. According to the logic of positive sanctions, an effective way to influence the behavior of other states is to provide economic rewards, such as an increase in foreign aid, the expansion of foreign loans at concessionary rates, or the granting of preferential trade treatment. By contrast, the logic of negative sanctions assumes that the most effective way to deter unwanted actions or to compel behavioral change is through the imposition of economic penalties. These sanctions might range from modest actions, such as selected quotas, limited tariff increases, or the reduction of foreign aid, to more extreme measures, such as a freeze of foreign assets, a halt of foreign investment, a ban on technology transfers, or a total economic blockade. Although some scholars have suggested that positive sanctions are much more likely to induce behavioral change than threats or punishment, negative sanctions have been used more commonly in contemporary international relations than positive inducements.[5] Because most economic sanctions are negative in character, the discussion here is limited to this type of statecraft.

The Goals of Sanctions

Historically, states have used economic sanctions for a variety of reasons. James Lindsay, for example, has identified five reasons that states have imposed trade sanctions: (1) *compliance*—forcing a state to alter its behavior in conformity with the sanctioning state's preferences; (2) *subversion*—seeking to remove particular political leaders from office or attempting to overthrow a regime; (3) *deterrence*—dissuading a target state from carrying out unacceptable behavior; (4) *international symbolism*—sending a message to other governments; and (5) *domestic symbolism*—increasing domestic political support by undertaking a popular public policy initiative.[6] In addition, sanctions are imposed as punishment for actions perceived as objectionable. As Kim Nossal has noted, states use economic punishment as retribution for prior harmful or evil acts in the hope that such penalties will rectify past injustices and deter future objectionable behaviors.[7]

Although most major powers have historically used economic sanctions as an instrument of foreign policy, the United States, more than any other country, has relied on economic statecraft in recent decades to seek to influence the behavior of foreign states. For example, one study of U.S. economic sanctions in the post–Cold War era found that during the 1993–96 period, the government imposed sanctions or passed legislation to do so sixty times against thirty-five countries. The major reasons for imposing unilateral sanctions were to promote human rights and democratization (twenty-two times), to punish and deter terrorism (fourteen), to curb and deter nuclear proliferation (nine), to curb drug trafficking (eight), to foster political stability (eight), and to promote workers' rights and condemn prison labor (six). The principal countries targeted with sanctions were Iran (eleven times), Cuba (nine), Sudan (seven), and China (six).[8]

The Impact of Sanctions

One of the most widely accepted ideas about international statecraft is that economic sanctions are an ineffective instrument of foreign policy. Economist Charles Kindleberger asserts that "most sanctions are not effective,"[9] whereas Margaret Doxey concludes her analysis of sanctions by noting that "in none of the cases analyzed . . . have economic sanctions succeeded in producing the desired political result."[10] In light of the perceived ineffectiveness of sanctions, David Baldwin observes that "[i]t would be difficult to find any proposition in international relations literature more widely accepted than those belittling the utility of economic techniques of statecraft."[11] Moreover, after reviewing seven decades of public statements and scholarly literature, M.S. Daoudi and J.S. Dajani conclude that the idea that sanctions do not work is so widespread that this notion has become nearly axiomatic.[12]

In assessing the effectiveness of sanctions, it is important to distinguish between their economic success and political success, between the economic hardship imposed on the target state through sanctions and the degree of political compliance realized through such penalties.[13] Because a major assumption of economic statecraft is that changes in economic welfare in a target state will induce desired policy changes, economic success is generally regarded as a precondition for political effectiveness.

Economic success: What factors influence the economic success of sanctions? According to one major study of 115 sanctions episodes from 1914 to 1990, economic sanctions have achieved their greatest economic harm when the following conditions were met:

- The target state was economically weaker and politically less stable than the sender; in effect, the relationship was asymmetrical. In successful sanctions episodes, the average sender's economy was 187 times larger than that of the average target state.
- The target and sender had a high level of economic interdependence. In successful sanctions cases, the target state depended on the sender for an average of 28 percent of its total trade.
- Sanctions were imposed quickly and decisively, thereby enhancing the political credibility of the sanctions and increasing the potential for economic harm by preventing the target state from effectively adjusting to the imposed hardship.
- The cost of the sanctions to the target state was significant, generally exceeding 2 percent of its gross national product (GNP).[14]

Another factor that can influence the economic effectiveness of sanctions is the level of multilateral participation. Because most economic goods and services are highly fungible (i.e., can be replaced or substituted), broad participation, especially from the major powers, is normally a prerequisite for imposing the desired hardship on the target state. The importance of collective action was illustrated in 1990–91 during the Persian Gulf crisis, when the United Nations imposed comprehensive economic sanctions against Iraq. Because nearly every country honored the embargo, Iraq's GNP declined by nearly 50 percent. By contrast, the U.S.-led economic embargo against Cuba has been relatively ineffective because few major states have supported this thirty-five-year old policy.

Finally, significant participation by nongovernmental actors can also increase the economic success of sanctions. Given the increasing independent power of multinational corporations and other private actors, their support for sanctions can greatly reinforce and intensify sanctions. For example, in response to growing U.S. domestic opposition to South African apartheid, private actors encouraged private divestment and directly pressured American banks and corporations to institute disinvestment programs.[15] These private initiatives not only reinforced the policies of Western governments but also greatly intensified them. Indeed, private disinvestment by American financial institutions and corporations brought far greater harm to the South African economy in the 1980s than did government-imposed sanctions.

Political Success: Political success refers to the probability that economic sanctions will lead to desired behavioral changes in the target state. The fundamental assumption of economic sanctions is that negative penalties will discourage existing policies and foster behavioral reform. Although economic "sticks" can no doubt affect the behavior of foreign actors, it is doubtful that economic coercion alone will determine the political decisions of foreign states. For one thing, foreign policy decision making is a multidimensional process that is subject to numerous domestic and international influences. Moreover, as noted previously, some scholars have questioned the belief that economic adversity encourages behavioral reform, arguing that positive inducements are far more likely to achieve desirable policy objectives than economic penalties.

What is the historical record on economic sanctions? According to one comprehensive study, economic sanctions during the 1914–90 period were successful in bringing about desired reforms in about one-third of the cases.[16] However, another scholar, using the same data, has argued that the success rate is less than 5 percent![17] Regardless of whether one accepts the optimistic or pessimistic measures of political success, it is clear that the application of economic hardship has not often resulted in desired political outcomes. Although it is clear that major economic sanctions can result in significant hardship to the target state, such adversity does not automatically translate into desired policy reforms. However, to the extent that sanctions foster desired outcomes, their political effectiveness is likely to depend on three factors: the openness of the target society; the scope and significance of the demands placed on the target state; and the level of multilateral participation.

First, economic sanctions are likely to have far more impact on democratic systems than on autocratic regimes. Because military governments and dictatorial regimes depend less on public opinion, international economic pressures are generally ineffective in influencing regime decision making. For example, the economic sanctions imposed by the United States against Cuba, Iran, Iraq, and Libya have failed either to achieve desired policy goals or to undermine these regimes, in great part because they are undemocratic and largely unresponsive to public pressures.

Second, because economic sanctions are a "marginal" tool of statecraft,[18] they are most effective when applied to nonvital issues. When the aim is to topple an existing regime or to compel major changes in international behavior they are likely to be strongly resisted by the target state. For example, the economic sanctions imposed on Rhodesia in the 1970s to foster democratic rule, on Nicaragua in the 1980s to promote political pluralism, and on Iraq in the mid-1990s to comply with UN-imposed weapons disarmament were largely ineffective because the target governments considered such statecraft a direct affront to national sovereignty.[19] The case study on the U.S. policy debate over granting most-favored-nation (MFN) trading status to China illustrates the limitations of sanctions in fomenting major domestic reforms.

Finally, political success requires international support, especially from the major powers and from neighboring states. Global support is important because it increases the political credibility of sanctions. A lack of international cooperation will not only impair the economic effectiveness of the sanctions but also compromise the perception of resolve. A major reason for the failure of economic sanctions against Cuba has been the unwillingness of other major powers to support the U.S. embargo.

BACKGROUND

As a result of its normalization of bilateral relations in 1978, the United States began granting China most-favored-nation (MFN) trade status.[20] The granting of MFN, coupled with China's domestic economic liberalization, contributed to China's significant economic expansion and led to a dramatic increase in trade between the two states. By the early 1980s, the Chinese economy was growing at nearly 10 percent per year, the highest rate in the world and one that persisted for another decade. By 1994, the value of annual trade between China and the United States had grown to more than $40 billion, with China's exports to the United States accounting for more than 40 percent of its total trade.

According to the amended Trade Law of 1974, the renewal of MFN depends on a state's honoring the human right of emigration.[21] Because China, unlike the Soviet Union, had not sought to restrict emigration, the United States regularly renewed its MFN status. However, when Chinese authorities massacred an untold number of demonstrators in Beijing's Tiananmen Square in 1989 and instituted their crackdown on dissidents pressing for democratic reforms, the United States imposed modest sanctions but did not withdraw MFN.

The underlying assumption of the Bush administration was that increased U.S. engagement and continued economic expansion through market reforms would help create the social and economic preconditions conducive to greater democratization and increased respect for human rights. Isolating China through economic sanctions would only impede potential reforms. As James Lilley, a former U.S. ambassador to China, observed, the United States could best foster democratic forces and enhance human rights by broadening American involvement in China's economy. "Rapid economic growth and joint ventures," he writes, "have done more to improve the human rights situation in South China than

innumerable threats, demarches, and unilaterally imposed conditions."[22]

HUMAN RIGHTS AND TRADE

During the 1992 presidential campaign, Bill Clinton repeatedly charged that President George Bush was neglecting human rights and was coddling China's tyrants. Clinton promised that, if elected, he would confront China about its disregard for international human rights. Thus, when he was elected president, he was confronted with how to reconcile his campaign pledges on human rights with the continuation and expansion of U.S.-China economic relations. Officials within his own administration were deeply divided, with the Department of State being most strongly committed to the enforcement of human rights and the Departments of Treasury and Commerce being far more sympathetic to the demands for strong bilateral economic ties. As the May 1993 MFN deadline approached, both human rights activists and corporate organizations intensified their government lobbying. To reinforce corporate influence, the Chinese government went on a U.S. buying spree, placing orders for more than $1.1 billion in goods: $800 million for Boeing aircraft, $160 million for automobiles, and $200 million for oil drilling equipment.

Rather than giving precedence to either trade or human rights, President Clinton decided in May 1993 to partially satisfy both human rights goals and business interests. He did so by renewing MFN but also by imposing stricter human rights conditions on future MFN renewals. Thus, when the president announced the continuation of MFN, he issued an executive order declaring that future MFN renewals would depend on "significant progress" in selected human rights areas.[23] Because China's trade balance with the United States exceeded $23 billion at the time, U.S. government officials were hopeful that China's large trade surplus would foster greater compliance with human rights norms.

As anticipated by some, Clinton's confrontational policy did not lead to improved human rights conditions in China. Indeed, the human rights policy was accompanied not only by increasingly repressive treatment of political dissidents and religious minorities but also by strained U.S.-China relations. One scholar estimates that more political arrests and trials occurred in 1994 than in any year since the Tiananmen Square crackdown began in 1989.[24] The policy of threatening the withdrawal of MFN status if human rights abuses were not reduced was clearly not working. As a result, President Clinton announced in June 1994 the "delinking" of MFN renewal from China's human rights record. Although the United States would continue to promote human rights, it would not make the continuation of MFN status conditional on China's human rights record. Thus, despite Clinton's condemnation of the "engagement" strategy of previous administrations, his administration not only a similar policy but in fact increased economic trade between countries, ultimately supporting China's membership in the World Trade Organization.

THE SANCTIONS DEBATE

The continued human rights abuses by the government of China presents a classic dilemma between two approaches to economic statecraft: isolation and engagement, or what one scholar has termed strategies of "asphyxiation" and "oxygen."[25] The first strategy assumes that the United States should hold China accountable for human rights violations and abuses. Because China has failed to improve its human rights record since the 1989 Tiananmen Square massacre, the United States should impose economic penalties, withdrawing MFN status at a minimum. The second strategy assumes that notwithstanding human rights violations, the United States should maintain and increase economic contact, using international economic relations to foster economic development and encourage political liberalization.

Although the continuation of MFN status might not lead to human rights improvements,

the previous analysis casts doubt on the effectiveness of economic sanctions in fostering behavioral change. Sanctions critics argue that an isolation strategy is likely to be ineffective in fostering Chinese human rights reforms for three reasons. First, if the United States were to seek to isolate China, it would stand largely alone. European countries, as well as China's East Asian neighbors, strongly support a strategy of engagement and are unlikely to support an alternative policy. Second, although withdrawal of MFN might result in China's loss of $15 billion in U.S. trade revenue, this total would represent a small fraction of China's economy (less than one-half of 1 percent of China's $3 trillion GNP). Third, and most important, because a nation's ideology, structure of government, and conceptualization of human rights are deeply rooted in its core values, the attempt by a foreign state to influence human rights practices is likely to be interpreted as an affront to national sovereignty and would thus be resisted.

MORAL REFLECTIONS

This case raises a number of important questions about the appropriateness of economic sanctions as a policy instrument.

- If the aim of the United States is to foster democratic reforms and to help consolidate democratic capitalism in China, what is the most effective strategy to advance these goals: isolation or engagement, punishment or positive incentives? When is isolation and economic coercion preferable to engagement and positive incentives?

- During the mid-1980s, this issue was widely debated with regard to U.S. policy toward South Africa. The Reagan administration's policy of constructive engagement was based on the assumption that the most effective way to weaken the apartheid regime and foster democracy was to maintain a high level of interaction with South Africa. Administration critics, by contrast, argued that the Afrikaner regime needed to be punished, weakened, and isolated by the imposition of comprehensive economic sanctions. The aims of such sanctions were to limit trade, reduce foreign direct investment, and isolate the country from the international community of states. Was the imposition of sanctions against South Africa warranted? Should a similar strategy be pursued against China? Why or why not?

■ The China-MFN debate also suggests the difficulty of imposing sanctions when the target and the sending states have a high level of economic interaction. Since the 1980s, U.S. foreign direct investment and trade have grown significantly. In the mid-1990s, the volume of annual trade between the two countries exceeded $50 billion while foreign direct investment continued to rise. As a result, investors, traders, and consumers had a significant and growing stake in the policy debates over China. In view of the high level of economic interdependence with China, was it morally appropriate to allow commercial interests to influence human rights policy?

■ This case raises questions concerning the effectiveness of unilateral sanctions, especially when the target state is a strong economic power and unilateral sanctions are likely to lead to trade diversion and thereby result in limited economic harm. In view of alternative sources for imports and exports, is the imposition of unilateral sanctions a prudent policy? Should economic sanctions, especially against a major economic power, be based on multilateral participation?

THE EFFECTIVENESS OF ECONOMIC SANCTIONS

The previously noted general skepticism about the overall effectiveness of sanctions does not derive from the inability to impose economic hardship on the target state but from the dubious assumption that punishment encourages behavioral reform. Although adversity can encourage capitulation, it can also increase resolve and determination, especially if the target state considers the issues of vital national interest. In addition, sanctions can be politically ineffective because economic harm frequently falls disproportionately on the average citizen while only marginally affecting a regime's political and military leadership. For example, when the United States imposed comprehensive sanctions against Panama in 1988 to topple the government of General Manuel Noriega, the sanctions brought severe hardship to Panamanian civilians but had limited impact on government and military officials.[26]

Perhaps one of the reasons that sanctions have generally been considered ineffective tools is that they have been judged successful only when the desired political goals are achieved. As noted earlier, one major study of economic sanctions found that during the 1946–89 period, sanctions achieved behavioral changes in only 34 percent of the cases. Moreover, the study found that during the first half of this period, sanctions were far more effective politically than in the second half, with the success rating declining from a pre-1973 average of 44 percent to an average of only 25 percent in the 1973–89 period.[27]

However, if the success of sanctions is determined solely by the extent of political change, then sanctions are unlikely to be regarded as an effective foreign policy tool. But if sanctions are viewed as part of a state's overall repertoire for communicating interests and exercising international influence, then sanctions can be considered a useful instrument of statecraft. Indeed, Baldwin argues that the received wisdom that sanctions are ineffective is wrong because sanctions can serve as effective communications symbols in interstate bargaining.[28] Lisa Martin similarly suggests that the role of economic sanctions has been underestimated and argues that sanctions can be especially effective in demonstrating resolve and in sending signals.[29] In her view, such signaling is most effective when carried out multilaterally and when senders demonstrate resolve by their willingness to suffer economic loss. In addition, it is important to note that the effectiveness of sanctions as instruments of communication need not be based on the direct economic harm inflicted by sanctions. As William Kaempfer and Anton Lowenberg have noted, the impact of signals and threats communicated through sanctions is "unrelated to their market or income effects" because private actors can carry out actions that hasten the desired political reforms.[30]

The important role of sanctions as symbols and instruments of communication has been illustrated in many recent sanctions episodes. For example, when the United States imposed economic sanctions on South Africa in 1985 and 1986, it did so to communicate its opposition to apartheid, not for the instrumental purpose of fostering domestic reforms in the apartheid regime. Additionally, when the United States, supported by the Organization of American States and the United Nations, imposed increasingly stringent sanctions against the military regime in Haiti for failing to restore elected president Jean-Bertrand Aristide to power, it did so mainly to signal its commitment to democratic government.

Sanctions imposed as punishment are also generally perceived as successful because all that is required for them to be effective is to cause significant economic hardship on a target state. When the international community imposed major economic sanctions against Haiti in 1991, the hardship was perceived as a legitimate price for the toppling of the elected government. When the United Nations imposed comprehensive sanctions against Serbia in 1992 in response to its continued military aggression against Bosnia and Croatia, the sanctions were considered effective because of the hardship they imposed on Serb society, even though they did not lead to behavioral changes by Serb authorities.

Finally, sanctions are regarded as successful when they inhibit or delay the use of force. Because war is generally far more destructive than economic sanctions, the latter are generally considered a morally preferable tool of statecraft to military force. As a result, economic sanctions can be viewed as successful when they allow the sending state to impose harm on the target state without resorting to military force.[31] However, in using this minimalist standard, virtually all sanctions episodes are likely to be viewed as successful, whether or not the target state modifies its policies.

In short, economic sanctions remain a popular tool of statecraft not because they are effective tools of deterrence and compliance but because they are cheap and powerful symbols of communication. Although the instruments of economic coercion might not lead directly to behavioral reform, they can galvanize domestic and international public opinion, thereby weakening the government's authority in the target state. To the extent that economic sanctions weaken and isolate a regime, as was the case with governmental and nongovernmental sanctions toward South Africa in the

1980s (see case 9-3), they can encourage the target state to alter its unacceptable structures and policies. Ironically, economic sanctions are likely to be most effective against small, moderately developed democratic states in which the citizenry is informed and involved in the affairs of state but least effective in authoritarian regimes based on limited political participation. But as the following case study on Cuban economic sanctions suggests, even comprehensive sanctions by the United States, the world's richest, most powerful state, against a small, nearby island of eleven million people, does not necessarily assure compliance with political objectives.

CASE 9-2: U.S. ECONOMIC SANCTIONS AGAINST CUBA

BACKGROUND

In January 1959, Fidel Castro, the leader of a revolutionary movement, took control of the government of Cuba after forcing strongman Fulgencio Batista from office. Although Cuba had maintained close political and economic ties with the United States ever since Spanish colonial rule had ended with the Spanish-American War in 1898, from the outset of Castro's dictatorship the new regime sought to end those close ties, which it viewed as a continuation of imperialism. Accordingly, the new government announced in April 1959 that it did not want U.S. economic aid. Two months later it enacted a far-reaching agrarian reform law that subsequently led to the expropriation of U.S.-owned sugar plantations and mills. While Cuba was seeking to reduce its economic dependence on the United States, it pursued closer ties to the Soviet Union. This initiative led to a sugar-for-oil barter accord in which the Soviet Union agreed to trade petroleum for sugar. Since the imported oil was unrefined, Cuban authorities asked the U.S. oil corporations to refine Soviet petroleum, and when they refused, Castro nationalized the companies.

The expropriation of the petroleum industry greatly angered U.S. government officials, leading them to suspend the Cuban sugar quota. Since the United States had historically imported more than half of Cuba's sugar production, the ending of the sugar quota had catastrophic economic consequences on the nation's economy. But while the collapse of U.S.-Cuban commercial ties was economically costly to Cuba, Castro was nevertheless committed to reducing the island's historic dependence upon the United States and to simultaneously replacing capitalist structures and policies with state socialism. Not surprisingly, when the United States cut sugar imports, Castro retaliated by nationalizing all remaining American-owned properties, including electricity and telephone companies and nickel mines. It has been estimated that at the time of expropriation U.S. assets were valued at roughly one billion dollars, or about 40 percent of the country's gross national product.[32]

The final step in the complete breakdown of U.S.-Cuban relations occurred in January 1961, when Cuba demanded that the U.S. drastically reduce the size of its embassy staff. When the Castro government demanded that the United States reduce its embassy staff to eleven persons, the Eisenhower administration decided to break diplomatic relations altogether. Subsequently, Castro confirmed the deep ideological rift between the United States and Cuba by declaring that Cuba was a "socialist state" and that he was, and would remain, a "Marxist-Leninist." And because of Cuba's growing commitment to revolutionary communism, coupled with its commitment to export its radical policies to other Western Hemisphere states, President John F. Kennedy imposed a comprehensive economic embargo on Cuba in February 1962, barring all U.S. exports to and shipping with Cuba. As a result of the collapse of U.S.-Cuban economic ties, trade that had been valued at $577 million in

1957 fell to less than $1 million in 1962.[33]

When economic sanctions were first imposed on Cuba they were unilateral in nature. But as Castro's influence grew in the region, other Latin American countries became concerned. As a result, Western Hemisphere foreign ministers met under the auspices of the Organization of American States (OAS) in January 1962 and agreed to join the United States in imposing limited sanctions on Cuba and, more importantly, to exclude Cuba from participating in the inter-American system. Two years later—in response to evidence that Cuba had shipped weapons to guerrillas in Venezuela—the OAS voted to demand that its members break diplomatic relations with Cuba and to impose a collective trade embargo. The multilateralization of sanctions, however, was short-lived. When Cuba reduced its support of social revolution in the region, Latin American countries began normalizing relations with the Castro government, which later resulted in the resumption of modest economic trade. Thus by the early 1970s, regional sanctions had all but collapsed.

In response to superpower détente, the United States began to explore normalization of relations with Cuba in the mid-1970s. But soon after undertaking modest sanctions reforms, Castro complicated political accommodation by deploying troops to Angola. When President Carter initiated further normalization by establishing diplomatic representation (interest sections) in Havana and Washington and by allowing Americans to travel to Cuba, Castro once again undermined the Carter initiatives by deploying some 20,000 Cuban troops to Ethiopia. Tensions with Cuba escalated again in the early 1980s when Castro increased aid to revolutionary political movements in Central America, especially Nicaragua and El Salvador. As a result, the Reagan administration imposed further controls on Cuban travel and shipping and initiated a major anti-Castro media campaign through radio broadcasts beamed to the island. Perhaps the most significant modifications in the sanctions regime developed in the 1990s, when legislators decided that the end of the Cold War provided a propitious time to once again increase economic pressures on Cuba.

Because of the dramatic fall in Soviet aid, American leaders decided that a new opportunity had developed to impose significant economic hardship to promote democratic change in Cuba. Accordingly, the U.S. Congress passed the 1992 Cuba Democracy Act (known as the Torricelli bill for its author, Rep. Robert Torricelli) and the 1996 Cuba Liberty and Democratic Solidarity Act (known as the Helms-Burton Law for its two authors, Sen. Jesse Helms and Rep. Dan Burton). The first act prohibits American subsidiaries from trading with Cuba and restricts ships involved in Cuban tourism or commerce from docking in U.S. ports for at least 180 days. The second act, which is far more punitive, allows U.S. citizens with claims to property expropriated by the Cuban government to sue for damages. According to Title III of the Helms-Burton Law, persons or corporations that "traffic" (i.e., use, lease, manage, or buy) in such property can be sued for damages. This means that persons and corporations of third countries that use confiscated property are liable to suits from former property owners.[34] Since Title III imposes U.S. law on foreign states, it is highly controversial, calling into question the right of sovereign states to judge the legitimacy of expropriations by foreign governments.[35] Given the extraterritorial nature of this measure, the law provides that the president can delay implementation of this provision (in 6-month intervals) if he deems that the delay is in the American national interest or is likely to contribute to the democratization of Cuba. Although no president has allowed the implementation of Title III, the threat of legal liability has, nonetheless, appeared to have limited direct foreign investment in Cuba. At a minimum, the Helms-Burton Law appears to have dampened investor confidence, resulting in a decline of economic growth, from 7.8 percent in 1996 to 2.5 percent in 1997, a year after the law went into effect.[36] Finally, the Law (Title IV) authorizes the U.S. government to ban entry into the United States to senior officials and their families of any company that is found to be trafficking seized property. This measure has been applied to a number of persons working for Canadian and Mexican corporations.

In short, while U.S. economic sanctions

against Cuba have shifted from time to time in response to the evolution of global political dynamics, the fundamental policy of economic asphyxiation has remained unchanged for more than forty years.

THE EFFECTIVENESS OF CUBAN SANCTIONS

To measure the effectiveness of sanctions it is imperative to identify the goals being pursued through the imposition of economic hardship. This is difficult to do in this case because the aims of the sanctions against Cuba have changed over time. According to Kaplowitz, U.S. sanctions have pursued the following six major objectives: 1) symbolic opposition, 2) overthrow of the Castro regime, 3) retaliation, 4) containment, 5) rupture of Cuban-Soviet ties, and 6) democratization.[37] When U.S. relations with Cuba began deteriorating in 1959 and 1960, American foreign policy pursued the first three objectives—namely, communicating U.S. condemnation of the radical transformation of Cuban institutions, seeking to topple the regime, and imposing economic penalties for the expropriation of U.S. property. When Cuba began supporting social revolution in other countries in the mid-1960s, the United States used sanctions to try to contain Cuban revolutionary activities in foreign states. Additionally, as Cuba increased its economic and political dependence on the Soviet Union, the United States used sanctions to seek to undermine the Soviet-Cuban partnership. Finally, and most recently, sanctions have been used as a tool to promote the democratization of Cuba.

According to sanctions theory, the economic effectiveness of sanctions is likely to increase if the target country is highly dependent on trade with the sanctioning or sending state. Since Cuba had historically depended upon sugar exports for the bulk of its foreign exchange, and because roughly two-thirds of Cuba's trade was with the United States, the structure of Cuba's economy was highly conducive to the imposition of economic hardship through comprehensive sanctions. But Cuba's economic dependency on the United States did not translate into significant influence on the behavior of the country. A principal reason for this is that sanctions did not lead to significant long-term economic hardship. After imposing sanctions, Cuba was able to compensate for the economic loss by gaining access to Soviet aid and trade.

Thus, rather than imposing significant hardship, sanctions encouraged and accelerated stronger ties with the Soviet Union. As one scholar observes, far from threatening Cuba's revolutionary policies and its growing ties with communist states, the embargo "locked Cuba more tightly into the Soviet Union's trade and assistance sphere."[38]

Throughout the Cold War years, the Soviet bloc countries accounted for more than 80 percent of Cuban trade, while the USSR is estimated to have directly invested from $60 to $80 billion in the Cuban economy.[39] It has been estimated that when the Soviet bloc began to reduce its economic commitments to Cuba in 1990, the Soviet Union had been providing direct and indirect subsidies valued at about $8 billion annually, or roughly $800 per Cuban inhabitant.[40]

After the disintegration of the Soviet Union in 1991, not only did its direct annual subsidy of $5–6 billion come to a halt, but investment from and trade with COMECON, the Eastern European trading bloc, collapsed as well.[41]

Since the collapse of Soviet-bloc aid, Castro has been forced to undertake significant reforms to compensate for lost income. Some of the most important initiatives involve increased small-scale private enterprise in such areas as farming, transportation, and restaurants, increased foreign direct investment, especially in the tourist sector, and the legalization of the U.S. dollar.[42] To foster economic growth, Castro welcomed foreign investment, allowing foreign corporations to gain up to 49 percent ownership, with a promise to repatriate profits fully. Thus, from 1990 to 1997 foreign companies invested more than $700 million out of a total planned investment of $5.3 billion, much of it in tourism.[43] Not surprisingly, the tourist sector has grown at an astounding rate, with income rising from $243 million in 1990 to $1.8 billion in 1997.[44]

Despite the growth in revenues from the

tourist trade, Cuba's economy remains one of the poorest in the Western Hemisphere. And while the intensification of U.S. sanctions has dampened foreign direct investment and inhibited tourism and Cuban exports, the economic impact of sanctions has been less than anticipated in part because of the significant financial transfers of Cuban-Americans to their families in Cuba. Ironically, the country that has imposed comprehensive sanctions to force a change has also permitted, for humanitarian reasons, financial transfers to family members in Cuba.[45] Indeed, it has been estimated that U.S. private financial transfers account for the largest single source of Cuban foreign exchange, even exceeding tourism revenues.[46]

A second reason for the ineffectiveness of Cuban sanctions is that Castro has been able to use the economic adversity to rally domestic political support. When the U.S. Congress increased the severity of economic sanctions with the passage of the Torricelli and Helms-Burton laws, Castro used these measures to rekindle revolutionary fervor and further consolidate power. Thus, rather than undermining the Castro communist regime, the Torricelli and Helms-Burton laws have not only failed to encourage a democratic transition but have, paradoxically, strengthened Cuban resolve and further isolated the United States from its Western allies. Jatar-Hausmann has written that while the Helms-Burton Law was designed to destroy Fidel Castro, it has "done wonders to rally support for his regime at home and abroad."[47]

Since sanctions have not worked in bringing about democratization, why are they continued? To a significant degree, the answer is domestic politics. Cuban populations are concentrated in two states (New Jersey and Florida) and have well-organized lobbies to pressure Congress and the executive to continue economic sanctions. Additionally, Castro's policies and actions have also made any normalization exceedingly difficult. When President Carter sought to improve relations in the late 1970s, for example, Castro increased his revolutionary activities in Ethiopia and Angola, all but ending President Carter's initiative. And even though some initiatives were undertaken during the Reagan and Bush admin-

istrations, little progress was achieved toward normalization of relations. When Congressman Torricelli introduced legislation to stiffen Cuban sanctions, President Bush felt compelled to support and sign the bill in 1992, especially after Bill Clinton had endorsed the measure as part of his presidential campaign. Four years later, President Clinton signed the Helms-Burton Act into law, even though he was opposed to the measure. He did so after the Cuban air force downed two American civilian planes off the Cuban coast, precipitating strong anti-Castro sentiment among Cuban-Americans. More recently, Castro's crackdown on political dissidents in 2003 made it all but impossible for the U.S. government to ease sanctions.[48]

MORAL REFLECTIONS

Although the four-decades-old economic sanctions policy of the United States has shifted over time, its fundamental objectives have remained the same: to end the communist dictatorship, to restore democratic government, and to ensure restitution or adequate compensation for property losses by U.S. citizens. Some key moral issues raised by this case study include the following:

- If the aim of economic sanctions is to compel a government to change its policies, how much hardship is morally justified to achieve the desired goals? Must the hardship be proportional to the benefits resulting from behavioral change? Is an unconditional demand for change ever morally justified?
- How long must a country endure economic asphyxiation? From a moral perspective, does a statute of limitations exist on the imposition of sanctions?
- Leaders are frequently able to protect themselves from the pain of economic sanctions, while the masses frequently bear the bulk of the hardship from sanctions. If "smart," discriminating sanctions cannot be imposed, should sanctions be avoided altogether as a policy instrument? Since the United States has permit-

ted private financial transfers that have eased the economic hardship for many Cuban families, does this policy make the comprehensive trade and investment sanctions more morally legitimate?

- The U.S. government has claimed that sanctions can be eased only if Cuba moderates its authoritarian policies and allows greater freedom in society. But if Cuba continues to deny pluralism and freedom, is there a moral justification for lifting the sanctions nonetheless?
- Finally, it is estimated that Cuba confiscated U.S. property valued at roughly $1

billion in the immediate aftermath of the Castro takeover in 1959. These assets have increased in value over time and were estimated to be worth $1.8 billion in 1972 and $5.7 billion in 1994.[49] When normalization occurs, how should economic claims be addressed? Does justice demand full compensation, or should partial debt forgiveness be instituted in the hope of quickly restoring the political and economic health of the country and restoring cooperative U.S.-Cuban relations?

THE MORALITY OF ECONOMIC SANCTIONS

Unlike international relations issues such as human rights, intervention, and war, scholars have undertaken comparatively little moral analysis of economic statecraft. The limited moral scrutiny given economic sanctions is no doubt due to the belief that sanctions are preferable to force. However, economic sanctions are not morally neutral foreign policy instruments but rather indiscriminate tools that impose harm on the target state to foster desired political changes. As a result, the conditions and manner justifying the imposition of sanctions involve a variety of ethical issues, ranging from the moral appropriateness of such instruments to the manner in which such instruments are applied. Because sanctions are morally ambiguous policy instruments, it is important, as Baldwin and others have emphasized,[50] that economic statecraft be judged not solely in terms of political and economic criteria but also in terms of international political morality.

One potentially useful approach in assessing the morality of sanctions is to apply principles of the just-war doctrine. Although application of just-war norms to economic statecraft is based on an analogy of two different decision-making environments, just-war theory can nonetheless offer an invaluable ethical structure by which to morally assess economic sanctions. In particular, just-war principles can provide moral standards for judging economic sanctions policies and for assessing issues such as the following: When is economic coercion justified? Are economic sanctions always morally preferable to military force? Does morality require that economic sanctions be targeted directly on a regime's decision-makers? How much collateral harm (i.e., harm to civilians) is morally permissible? Must the anticipated harm from sanctions be proportional to the political good they are expected to achieve?

The principles of the just-war doctrine provide a framework for morally assessing economic sanctions. In applying just-war norms to sanctions, it is important to emphasize that the environments giving rise to war and economic statecraft are radically different. The just-war doctrine is mainly a defensive theory of force applicable to states victimized by aggression, whereas economic sanctions are instituted as an alternative to force to punish third parties for objectionable behaviors. Because the environments of war and peace present radically different decision-making contexts, some scholars have suggested that the just-war doctrine is "an ultimately inadequate paradigm for moral analysis of comprehensive sanctions."[51] Others, by contrast, argue that just-war morality can strengthen the ethical assessment of the role of economic sanctions.[52] The following analysis is based on the latter conviction.

The Just-Sanctions Doctrine

The just-war tradition, as noted in chapter 5, involves two dimensions: the justice of going to war (*jus ad bellum*) and justice in wartime (*jus in bello*). Although these norms were developed to inhibit war and, in the event of war, to inhibit human suffering, they nonetheless provide a useful framework for judging the morality of economic sanctions. All eight principles (see table 6-1), with the exception of the competent-authority norm, can be applied to economic statecraft. Because private actors can contribute significantly to a sanctions regime, the requirement that governments impose sanctions is unnecessary.[53]

Based on the just-war theory, a *just-sanctions doctrine* can be developed involving two dimensions: the justice of whether to use sanctions and the justice of how to apply them. Of the seven principles of the just-sanctions doctrine, the first five provide a moral framework for determining when economic coercion is morally permissible; the last two specify how sanctions should be applied. The following norms comprise the just-sanctions doctrine:

1. *Just cause*: The aim of economic sanctions must be just. This can involve promoting peace among states, but it can also involve promoting human dignity within states when regimes systematically abuse basic rights.
2. *Right intention*: Sanctions are legitimate only if they are imposed to promote just structures and policies. Sanctions are not justified to increase national power or extend economic influence.
3. *Limited objectives*: Sanctions must have limited goals, involving behavioral reform of only those behaviors and institutions that are unjust and evil. In addition, the objectives of sanctions must be proportional to the good that they are seeking to achieve.
4. *Last resort*: The imposition of sanctions must be preceded by other, less coercive instruments. Only when peaceful negotiations have failed is resort to comprehensive economic sanctions morally warranted.
5. *Probability of success*: The resort of economic sanctions must have a reasonable chance of success. That is, there must be a reasonable hope that the economic hardship inflicted on the target state will result in greater justice.
6. *Discrimination*: Economic hardship must be targeted on the government and the elites that support it. Economic hardship should not be imposed directly on innocent civilians. Following the principle of double effect, economic harm on the masses can be justified only as a by-product of the unintended effects of legitimately targeted sanctions.[54]

7. *Proportionality*: The good intended from sanctions must be proportional to the harm inflicted on the target state.

The application of the just-sanctions doctrine will depend greatly on the particular circumstances in which economic sanctions are employed as well as the specific purposes that they are designed to serve. Earlier, I noted that sanctions are applied for a variety of reasons. If the aim of sanctions is to bring about political reforms or policy changes in the target state, the just-sanctions doctrine can provide an invaluable moral structure for judging policies. However, if the aim of sanctions is simply to punish or to signal resolve, the doctrine's usefulness in moral analysis of sanctions will be limited. As a result, the analysis here focuses solely on sanctions as a tool of behavioral reform.

The Role of Just-Sanctions Norms

In chapter 2, I suggested that an ethical foreign policy must be judged in terms of its intentions, means, and outcomes. The just-sanctions doctrine provides norms by which to judge sanctions at each of these three levels. The first two norms—just cause and right intention—provide the principles for judging the moral legitimacy of sanctions goals. According to these two norms, the imposition of major economic suffering is morally legitimate only if its aims are morally right. The doctrine also provides principles for judging the policy instruments themselves. Specifically, the doctrine provides three norms by which to judge the moral legitimacy of sanctions— proportionality, last resort, and discrimination. Sanctions are just when (1) the harm they impose is proportional to the good they are likely to achieve; (2) other, less destructive alternatives have been exhausted; and (3) economic penalties are discriminatory, targeting harm on political and government officials responsible for a state's decisions and actions. If sanctions are imposed to influence the political behavior of the target state, it follows that the pain and suffering of economic statecraft should be borne mainly by those responsible for government decision making. Finally, the sanctions doctrine addresses the level of outcomes by specifying that sanctions should be applied only if there is a strong likelihood that the political goals will be realized.

Undoubtedly, the most important yet most morally challenging principle of the sanctions doctrine is discrimination. Indeed, one scholar argues that the major moral problem posed by sanctions is their inability to fulfill the discrimination norm.[55] This principle, which demands protection of innocent persons from the harm being imposed by ruling elites, is significant because it establishes limits on the means that can be utilized in pursuing a moral end. However, reconciling economic sanctions with discrimination is difficult because sanctions are blunt policy instruments. Although sanctions remain a popular tool of statecraft because they provide an alternative to force, sanctions are also a morally problematic instrument because they cannot discriminate between civilians and public officials.

Who are the innocent and who are the culpable? As noted previously, the just-war tradition holds that innocent persons are those who have not participated in societal evils giving rise to war or have not been involved in ordering, prosecuting, and supporting war. Because such persons do not bear direct responsibility for instigating and conducting war, the just-war tradition holds that such persons are "innocent" and should not be subject to intentional attack. Thus, the distinction between combatants and noncombatants is rooted in the notion that harm should be inflicted only on those who bear responsibility for the public actions of government. As Michael Walzer has observed, innocent people are those who "have done nothing, and are doing nothing, that entails the loss of their rights."[56] Thus, they are entitled to be free from direct attack.

If we apply these wartime distinctions to sanctions episodes, who are the innocent civilians and responsible decision-makers, the sanctions' "noncombatants" and "combatants"? From a simplistic perspective, the latter are those who have ordered, implemented, and supported actions deemed illegal and morally reprehensible by the sending state. Innocent civilians are those who have not supported or participated in such actions. Thus, as Lori Fisler Damrosch has noted, the discrimination norm calls on policy makers to "target the perpetrators of violence or other wrongdoing and minimize severe adverse consequences on civilians who are not in a position to bring about cessation of wrongful conduct."[57]

There can be little doubt of the importance of the discrimination norm in developing a morally just sanctions policy. However, applying such a norm is especially challenging because economic sanctions, as noted earlier, are fundamentally nondiscriminatory instruments of statecraft. Indeed, the hardship imposed by sanctions frequently falls disproportionately on low-income sectors of society. "The principal moral dilemma posed by sanctions," write Drew Christiansen and Gerard Powers, "is that the more effective they are, the more likely that they will harm those least responsible for the wrongdoing and least able to bring about change: civilians."[58] In addition, even when efforts are made to target a regime's leadership, political, economic, and government elites are frequently able to divert resources to minimize the hardships brought about by sanctions.

Despite their indiscriminate nature, economic sanctions remain a popular instrument of foreign policy. To a significant degree, the Western elites' preference for sanctions over force is rooted in the belief that the former is almost always morally preferable. For example, during the Persian Gulf crisis, religious elites opposed force, arguing repeatedly that more time was needed for sanctions to work. In making this argument, however, such elites failed to realize, as Walzer has noted, that "what they were advocating was a radically indiscriminate act of war, with predictably harsh consequences."[59] Because of the morally ambiguous nature of sanctions, some scholars have suggested that economic sanctions should be imposed only when humanitarian measures are undertaken to protect innocent civilians. Such measures might include the exemption of essential goods, such as food and medicines, and the distribution of aid to vulnerable groups.[60]

The next case study, on sanctions and South African apartheid, illustrates the morally ambiguous nature of economic sanctions. Although such statecraft no doubt contributed to the abolition of apartheid, economic sanctions also inflicted significant harm on the black workers.

BACKGROUND

After the Afrikaner National Party gained control of the South African government in 1948, it began to further institutionalize racial separation (apartheid). Racial segregation was well entrenched in South Africa's social, political, and economic structures when the National Party assumed power, but the effort to establish a comprehensive legal system of racial separation was unprecedented, leading to significant international condemnation.

International opposition to South Africa's apartheid policies began in the early 1960s. For example, in 1962, the UN General Assembly passed a nonbinding resolution condemning apartheid, calling on states to break diplomatic relations with South Africa and to stop trading with it. Subsequently, the Security Council authorized a ban on arms shipments to South Africa and in 1977 imposed a total arms embargo. Another important action taken against South Africa in the early 1970s was the imposition of an oil embargo by OPEC, forcing South Africa to pay much higher costs for petroleum. None of these actions, however, had much impact on South Africa's government decision making. Indeed, the oil embargo led South Africa to pioneer in the development of oil extraction from coal, whereas the arms embargo encouraged the development of a major military arms industry, providing a significant source of foreign exchange.

In response to growing American public opposition to apartheid, some municipalities and universities began demanding divestment of stock in companies involved in South Africa. The aim of the divestment campaign was not only to force institutions to sell their stock but also to ultimately force companies to withdraw from South Africa through disinvestment (i.e., selling or closing their operations). By 1982, several state legislatures and city councils had approved measures mandating divestment, and by 1984 more than forty-five colleges and universities had adopted divestment programs. The divestment campaign accelerated in the mid-1980s, culminating with California's adoption of a $12 billion divestment program, calling for the sale of South African holdings in state pension funds and in the endowment of the state's university system.[61] It has been estimated that by 1991, more than twenty-eight states, twenty-four counties, and ninety-two cities had adopted divestment measures, resulting in the sale of some $20 billion of stock.[62]

In response to growing public opposition to apartheid, congressional support for economic sanctions began to increase in the mid-1980s. To forestall more severe sanctions being considered by Congress, President Reagan instituted modest sanctions in September 1985. The following year, however, Congress, overriding a presidential veto, passed legislation instituting more drastic economic sanctions. The 1986 Comprehensive Anti-Apartheid Act, among other things, banned new investment in South Africa, prohibited new U.S. commercial loans and the export of petroleum and computers, banned selected South African imports, and terminated landing rights for South Africa's airlines. The European Community and the British Commonwealth also instituted similar, although more modest, sanctions at this time.

Although government-imposed economic sanctions were symbolically significant, the most influential economic measures were the actions of the international business community, especially the disinvestment by major corporations and the ban on new bank loans. One scholar writes, "The real actors who overturned constructive engagement [the official U.S. foreign policy toward South Africa] were not public, but private—namely, U.S. commercial banks and foreign investors responding to economic and political risks and nongovernmental anti-apartheid organizations that magnified corporate responses to those risks."[63] It has been estimated that of the almost 400 U.S. companies doing business in South Africa in 1984, only 124 remained in 1989. Moreover, the decision by international banks to call in their loans and close their operations had an especially devastating impact. When the Chase Manhattan Bank announced in 1985 that it would no longer make new loans to South Africa, other foreign banks quickly followed suit, leading to an immediate tightening of domestic credit markets. As a result of the cutoff of loans and direct foreign investment, South Africa experienced massive capital outflows and a sharp weakening of its currency. It has been estimated that from 1985 to 1989 net capital outflows were $11 billion, leading to a significant contraction of the South African economy and a loss of at least $4 billion in export earnings.[64]

THE MORAL AMBIGUITY OF SANCTIONS

The principal justification offered by public officials and interest group leaders for the imposition of economic sanctions against South Africa was the belief that apartheid was evil and needed to be abolished. Sanctions advocates argued that economic penalties should be imposed on South Africa to punish the regime and compel the government to alter its social and political structures. Some, such as Archbishop Trevor Huddleston and Archbishop Desmond Tutu, argued that sanctions were necessary to convey a moral message, that is, to express outrage at the inhumane and discriminatory system of apartheid. Others advocated sanctions for strategic reasons, basing their argument on consequentialist logic: Economic hardship and international isolation, they believed, would compel structural reforms.

Most sanctions opponents, including British prime minister Margaret Thatcher and President Reagan, also shared the conviction that apart-heid was discriminatory, undemocratic, and unjust but believed that the application of comprehensive economic sanctions was an unacceptable policy. Sanctions were opposed for two major reasons: first, because they were considered ineffective in fostering domestic reforms and, second, because they imposed unnecessary

economic harm on the black labor class.

Some leaders believed that externally imposed hardship was unlikely to encourage domestic structural changes. Indeed, some sanctions critics argued that economic harm and isolation would only encourage Afrikaner resistance. A far better approach, in their view, was to foster increased participation in the global political economy. Chester Crocker, the assistant secretary of state for African affairs who was responsible for developing President Reagan's African policy of constructive engagement, believed that U.S. influence toward South Africa would be realized only by maintaining strong political and economic ties. Similarly, Helen Suzman, a long-term member of the South African parliament and a leading apartheid critic, repeatedly claimed that only a strategy of economic expansion could foster humane social change. Indeed, she argued that the major improvements in the living and working conditions for South Africa's blacks had been achieved through economic growth. According to Suzman, economic expansion was responsible for increased skilled jobs for blacks, improvements in education and training, recognition of black trade unions, acceptance of black urbanization, and the abolition of "pass laws" regulating the movement of people among different racial communities.[65] If Western states wanted to help South Africa establish the preconditions for liberal democratic society, they needed to facilitate economic expansion, without which no improvement in the black majority's living standards could be achieved. Moreover, only through a strategy of engagement could foreign states help foster capitalistic and democratic norms in preparation for establishing a more just post-apartheid regime.

A second major reason for opposing sanctions was the belief that they were harmful to the economic and social well-being of the nonwhite working class. Alan Paton, author of the influential book *Cry, the Beloved Country* and one of the first major critics of apartheid, repeatedly condemned sanctions, especially disinvestment, for causing unjust harm to black workers. He explained his moral opposition to disinvestment as follows:

It is my belief that those who will pay most grievously for disinvestment will be Black workers of South Africa. I take very seriously the teachings of the Gospels, in particular the parables about giving drink to the thirsty and food to the hungry. It seems to me that Jesus attached supreme—indeed sacred—significance to such actions. Therefore, I will not help to cause any such suffering to any Black persons.[66]

From the perspective of the just-sanctions doctrine, two major shortcomings of South African economic sanctions were the failure to target economic harm on decision makers and the failure to protect the black majority from unnecessary hardship. In seeking to weaken and isolate the apartheid regime, economic sanctions led to a major contraction of the South African economy that resulted in mass unemployment and underemployment among blacks. Even targeted sanctions, such as those imposed on the mineral and fruit industries, imposed especially harsh costs on black laborers, as the retrenchment in these labor-intensive industries significantly increased unemployment. Scholars differ significantly over the negative impact of sanctions on the South African labor market. One study predicted that from 1986 to 1990, comprehensive sanctions would lead to more than 1.1 million lost jobs;[67] another scholar estimates the number of lost jobs at 100,000.[68]

Sanctions, especially divestment (the liquidation of foreign assets), also had perverse, unanticipated effects. Rather than strengthening the economic power of the black majority, the sale of foreign subsidiaries, for example, resulted in increased white ownership of major foreign corporations. For example, when Barclays Bank (London) decided to pull out of South Africa in 1987, a large South African conglomerate (the Anglo-American Corporation) acquired the bank, paying substantially less than it was worth.[69] In 1986 alone, the Johannesburg stock market increased in value by nearly $9 billion, in great part because of the purchase of foreign assets at "fire-sale" prices. Moreover, divestment resulted in increasing concentration of South African wealth. According to Merle Lipton, in 1983 four

major South African conglomerates (Anglo-American, Sanlam, South African Mutual, and Rembrandt) controlled 70 percent of the Johannesburg stock exchange; four years later, in response to divestment, these groups accounted for 83 percent of all South African stock.[70] In addition, the contraction of the South African economy led to an increase in the economic power of the state. For example, the UN-imposed petroleum and arms embargoes resulted in the expansion of major industries in synthetic fuel (from coal) and armaments. It has been estimated that from 1977, when the UN arms embargo became mandatory, until 1989, the South African arms industry (Armscor) increased employment by more than 100,000 jobs.[71] Moreover, during the 1980s, while the South African economy was experiencing a major slowdown, South Africa's government employment actually increased by 18 percent![72]

In 1990, President F.W. de Klerk freed Nelson Mandela and other political prisoners, unbanned the African National Congress and other black opposition parties, and set in motion a process of radical change that culminated with the election of Mandela as president in 1994. In response to these developments, Western countries gradually eliminated all official sanctions. However, as of 1997, many multinational corporations that had terminated their South African operations in the 1980s either had not returned or had failed to reestablish successful enterprises.

Although many observers now believe that economic sanctions contributed (symbolically, if not substantively) to political change in South Africa, scholars continue to disagree about the role of sanctions in bringing about an end to apartheid and the moral legitimacy of such a policy. As noted previously, there is little doubt that economic sanctions—especially those nongovernment initiatives such as divestment and disinvestment that led to massive capital outflows—were harmful to the South African economy. However, the key issue is not whether sanctions were costly to South Africa but whether they were responsible for ending apartheid. Some anti-apartheid leaders, such as Tutu and Mandela, believe that economic sanctions were essential in ending white-minority rule. Others, especially National Party officials, have suggested that sanctions played a minimal role in bringing about political reform. De Klerk, for example, has observed that although sanctions disrupted the South African economy, "it was not sanctions that brought about change."[73]

MORAL REFLECTIONS

The South African case study on sanctions raises a number of important ethical issues.

- Sanctions are morally problematic because they generally impose hardship disproportionately on innocent civilians and leave political leaders and military officials largely untouched. In view of this, can the use of this nondiscriminatory tool be morally justified?
- Can a morally dubious policy be justified to bring about a morally just goal? Can an immoral means (comprehensive economic sanctions) be used to promote justice (the ending of apartheid)?
- From an ends-based approach (consequentialism), the use of economic sanctions is a morally legitimate policy alternative, provided that the intended goals are just and that the likelihood of achieving the desired goals is high. From this perspective, the goal of ending a racially unjust regime is morally just. Moreover, economic sanctions are superior to military force because they involve much less destruction. From a rule-based approach, however, economic sanctions are morally problematic because they fail to protect innocent persons from economic hardship. Thus, because sanctions impose hardship on civilians, should policy makers get their hands "dirty" by using sanctions to foster a more just world, or should they attempt to keep their hands "clean" by refusing to use immoral means to pursue political justice?
- Was the economic hardship brought about by sanctions proportional to the good achieved by the collapse of the apartheid regime? Was the hardship imposed on poor, unemployed blacks justified by the victory in ending a regime based upon racial discrimination?

SUMMARY

Because force is considered the most extreme and least desirable foreign policy instrument, economic sanctions offer a useful instrument short of war. However, as the previous analysis suggests, the use of sanctions as an alternative to force is morally problematic, in part because the effectiveness of such tools is uncertain but, more importantly, because the impact of such economic hardship can itself lead to unjust results. Since the hardship of sanctions cannot be easily targeted, the suffering from sanctions is frequently disproportionately borne by innocent civilians. Not only can governments divert resources to mitigate the hardship on soldiers, government officials, and other state agents, but the imposition of sanctions can provide opportunities for government leaders to prosper from sanctions by establishing enterprises that circumvent sanctions. Thus, although economic sanctions are a potentially useful instrument of statecraft, their role and impact are often morally ambiguous, frequently involving legitimate ends but dubious means.

Chapter Ten

The Ethics of Global Society

We should not view national boundaries as having fundamental moral significance. Since boundaries are not coextensive with the scope of social cooperation, they do not mark the limits of social obligation.[1]
—CHARLES R. BEITZ

How well we come through the era of globalization (perhaps whether we come through it at all) will depend on how we respond ethically to the idea that we live in one world. For the rich nations not to take a global ethical viewpoint has long been seriously morally wrong. Now it is also, in the long term, a danger to their security.[2]
—PETER SINGER

The extent of a country's respect for personal self-determination says something very basic about how it is governed. It is an index of a state's responsiveness to its citizens and, by extension, a measure of overall social health.[3]
—ALAN DOWTY

THE EMPHASIS in the previous chapters has been on the nature and role of moral norms in the development and execution of foreign policy. In this final chapter, I examine and attempt to offer a preliminary assessment of the moral legitimacy of the international system itself, especially in light of some of the major problems of our contemporary world. A cursory glance at global society suggests that there is great suffering in the modern world, stemming from factors such as war, forced displacement, ethnic and religious discrimination, starvation, poverty, disease, and ecological degradation. Although such evil is caused by many factors, the international system itself is a major source of human suffering. Because global structures permit war, tolerate egregious international economic inequalities, neglect human rights, and abuse the global environment, some scholars and political leaders have concluded that the contemporary system is seriously flawed and morally unjust.

The structures of global society pose major ethical questions. For example, how should the world system be conceived—as a single community or as a group of national societies? Does the moral legitimacy of states depend on their willingness and ability to protect human rights? Who is responsible for the well-being of migrants and refugees? Are the structures, rules, and procedures of global society fundamentally just? Finally, who is responsible for protecting the global commons, that is, the atmosphere, oceans, and land shared by all member states of global society?

Although such questions might seem esoteric and far removed from the realities of global political life, it is clear that the international order has been increasingly challenged because of perceived wrongs and injustices. Some of the international community's major limitations and problems include the arms race, global inequalities, environmental pollution, and human rights abuses. According to some critics of the existing neo-Westphalian order, the international community's structures are morally bankrupt because they have been incapable of regulating military competition and inhibiting war. Because there is no common authority, global society encourages states to give excessive emphasis to military security, encouraging arms races among states. This tendency was vividly illustrated during the Cold War, when the superpowers greatly expanded the size and power of their conventional and nuclear forces, diverting scarce economic resources toward military competition and threatening the world with mass destruction.

Another limitation of the international community is the perceived injustices between rich and poor nations. Because of growing international economic disparities, Third World leaders began challenging the legitimacy of the global economic order in the late 1970s and 1980s. They argued that its structures and procedures were morally flawed, if not fundamentally unjust, because of the large income inequalities perpetuated between the industrial states in North America and Western Europe and the developing nations in Asia, Africa, and Latin America. As a result, Third World leaders advocated a transformation of the global economic system, proposing a set of reforms, known as the New International Economic Order (NIEO), that would shift economic power and resources from the rich, developed North to the underdeveloped South. With the collapse of the Cold War, the pace of economic globalization greatly increased, resulting in significant economic improvements in many modernizing Third World countries coupled with rising income inequalities both within and between states.

Another significant challenge to the global order emerged in the mid-1980s, when scientists and activists began calling attention to the decay of the global environment because of misuse or overuse of common resources. Scholars refer to shared resources like water, the atmosphere, and fishing stocks as "collective goods" because persons from all nations are entitled to them. Unlike domestic environmental protection, protecting the "global commons" is a daunting challenge because there is no common authority in the international system to make and implement binding rules that protect shared resources. Although numerous multilateral efforts have been undertaken to protect endangered animal and plant species and to minimize land, water, and air pollution, international system critics have argued that greater political centralization of authority is essential to ensure "sustainable development," that is, environmentally safe economic growth. Although some treaties and conventions have been adopted on global environmental protection, critics still claim that much more needs to be done.

Finally, the moral legitimacy of the existing world order has been challenged because of its failure to protect human rights. Because states bear the primary responsibility for the welfare of persons, the neglect of human rights is directly attributable to them. At the same time, the international community itself is also responsible for the well-being of persons. This is especially the case for the 25 million refugees and other displaced persons who have been forced to flee their homelands since the end of the Cold War because of political oppression, civil war, or ethnic and religious persecution.

This chapter has three sections. In the first part, I examine the ethics of protecting the global commons and illustrate this concern with a case study on global warming. In the second part, I examine the complex nature and role of justice in international society through two different paradigms of global society—communitarianism and cosmopolitanism. I then illustrate the role of these alternative perspectives with a case study on foreign aid. In the third part, I examine the role of the individual in the international community, focusing on persons who migrate from one state to another and on the moral status of refugees.

PROTECTING THE GLOBAL COMMONS

Because no central authority exists in global society to make and enforce rules that manage and preserve the earth's shared resources, protecting the atmosphere, oceans, and soil beyond the jurisdiction of individual states is ultimately a cooperative enterprise among state and nonstate actors. As expected, states maintain widely varied policies and practices on domestic environmental protection. Some modern industrial states have developed a significant body of rules to reduce pollution, regulate waste disposal, and protect biodiversity. By contrast, other states, mostly poor, developing nations, have neglected pollution control, focusing instead on promoting economic growth. The extent to which states implement sustainable development strategies domestically is vitally important because domestic practices will profoundly affect transboundary air and water pollution and thus impact the quality of the earth's atmosphere and oceans as well as the prospect for long-term economic growth.

Global Environmental Protection

In the early nineteenth century, English political economist William Foster Lloyd developed the "tragedy of the commons" metaphor to explain the dangers of parochial, short-term practices.[4] According to the metaphor, village farmers allow livestock to graze on private and public pastures. Whereas each farmer carefully regulates grazing on private land, communal land is used freely by all community participants. As a result, the pasture on private plots is well maintained, whereas the village green suffers from overgrazing.

The commons metaphor is helpful in assessing collective-agency issues because it illuminates the dilemma of protecting resources owned or used in common. Because the village commons can sustain only a limited number of animals (this is defined as the commons' "carrying capacity"), the challenge for village farmers is to maximize their individual well-being without destroying the shared land. If each villager defines his interests in terms of the common good, he will allow only limited grazing by his animals. However, if farmers pursue their immediate self-interest and disregard the interests of others, the communal property will deteriorate and eventually be destroyed through overuse.

If the earth is viewed as a global commons, where the soil, atmosphere, and water are collective goods, developing long-term, cooperative strategies might help prevent the misuse or overuse of the earth's shared resources.[5] As with the village green, the challenge for states is to manage the earth's bountiful resources by wisely protecting global resources and devising rules and cooperative strategies that foster sustainable economic development. Additionally, states have regional and international accords to help prevent transboundary pollution and to protect natural resources.[6]

Perhaps the most significant international initiative to promote global environmental protection was the 1992 UN Conference on Environment and Development in Rio de Janeiro. Billed as the "last chance to save the planet," the conference, generally referred to as the Earth Summit, was the largest international conference ever held, bringing together more than 25,000 participants. In addition to 172 official government delegations, the summit also involved some 15,000 representatives from over 2,000 environmentally related nongovernmental organizations (NGOs). It is important to emphasize that, although government officials played a decisive role in negotiating various declarations and conventions, NGOs carried out most of the preparatory work on global environmental protection. By developing awareness and concern about global environmental protection, these organizations fostered international collective action on the earth's resources, biodiversity, and environment. Two major treaties were signed at the Earth Summit: the UN Framework Convention on Climate Change (also known as the Climate Treaty) and the Convention on Biological Diversity (also known as the Biodiversity Treaty). In addition, officials adopted three nonbinding agreements: a declaration of principles for establishing national environmental conservation programs, a statement of how to sustain forests, and a blueprint for promoting environmentally sustainable economic development.

The Ethics of Global Environmental Protection

Protecting the earth's biodiversity, environment, and resources presents political, technical, and moral challenges. Politically, environmental protection requires a mature collective will. Because protecting species, reducing pollution, and conserving resources involve long-term, elusive payoffs, the development and implementation of transnational environmental strategies is difficult, especially when the political decision-making process is focused on short-term goals. However, if the protection of global resources is important, all members of the international community must implement environmentally safe policies. Economic development strategies must be sustainable. As with the protection of the village green, countries must avoid the overuse or misuse of shared resources.

Technically, sustainable development requires the development of new technologies that reduce pollution, conserve energy, and foster the development of alternative energy sources. Most western European and North American governments have greatly reduced the proportion of pollution in generating energy through the application of new technologies. Although industrial production in these countries has been made more environmentally safe, much more remains to be done to strengthen the environmental protection and conservation regime. Developed countries need to continue to devise new technologies and encourage more efficient use of energy. Third World nations, for their part, need to become more aware of the effects of industrialization on the environment and to apply energy conservation policies and environmentally safe technologies as a means of encouraging sustainable economic development.

Finally, environmental protection presents a moral challenge by requiring states to balance their national interests with global interests, current economic needs with those of future generations. An ethical approach to energy consumption will demand that the pursuit of immediate national economic well-being take into account the interests of future generations as well as those coupled of other nations. If development is to be sustainable—that is, available to future generations—economic growth must involve careful use of renewable and nonrenewable resources, ensuring that present demands are balanced against the potential needs and wants of future generations. In addition, a moral approach to environmental protection must ensure that access to the global commons is fair and that the distribution of the commons' resources is similarly perceived as just. This is a most difficult challenge not only because decision-makers perceive political and economic reality differently but also because they hold different conceptions of justice. But regardless of how justice is defined (whether as a fair distribution of benefits or fair application of procedural rules), egregious inequalities in the use or misuse of global resources is morally problematic.

To illustrate some of the ethical challenges in promoting environmental protection in the contemporary international system, I next examine and assess the politics and ethics of global warming.

CASE 10-1: THE KYOTO PROTOCOL AND THE ETHICS OF GLOBAL WARMING

BACKGROUND

The earth's climate is determined principally by the balance between energy received from the sun, largely as visible light, and the energy radiated back to space as invisible infrared light. Water vapors and human-made gases (mainly carbon dioxide), however, can impair this balance by trapping solar radiation, much like the glass of a plant-breeder's greenhouse. The "greenhouse effect" thus occurs because vapors and gases allow more of the sun's heat to be absorbed by the earth than is released back into space. Although human-made gas emissions are responsible for only a small part (estimated at less than 5 percent) of the greenhouse effect, they nonetheless play a critical role in influenc-ing the earth's climate because carbon dioxide and other gases linger for long periods of time in the atmosphere before dissipating.

At the 1992 Earth Summit, some 166 countries signed the Climate Treaty, establishing a framework for reducing the growth of greenhouse gas emissions. This action was taken in the belief that stabilization of atmospheric pollution was essential to reducing the potential of further global warming. At the time that this agreement was signed, there was some scientific uncertainty about the role of human-made gases in climate change. Subsequently, however, the UN Intergovernmental Panel on Climate Change (IPCC), a group of about 2,500 distinguished scientists, issued a report on climate change that, although tentative and cautious in its conclusions, left little doubt about the role of greenhouse gases in climate change. According to the IPCC report, greenhouse gas emissions will continue to rise if there is no drop in the use of fossil fuels (coal and petroleum). As a result, the earth's temperature is projected to increase from 2–5 degrees (C) over the next century. Subsequently, the IPCC issued reports in 1996 and 2001 that similarly predicted temperature increases of 1–3.5 degrees and 1.4–5.8 degrees, respectively.[7] Although global warming could cause some beneficial developments, such as an increase in agricultural land in the Northern Hemisphere, environmentalists have warned that climate change could also bring about significant harm, including a rise in the sea level due to thermal expansion. Such a development would lead to the flooding of coastal lowlands and the destruction of numerous tropical islands.

Although the 1992 Climate Treaty called attention to the need to reduce greenhouse gas emissions from the burning of fossil fuels, it did not establish binding targets for states. As a result, signatory states implemented few if any structural reforms to reduce greenhouse gas emissions. By 1995 it was clear that the 1992 convention was having little impact on global carbon emissions. In view of a growing international awareness that climate change could result in highly destructive developments, a global consensus began to emerge in the mid-1990s that a stricter, more demanding treaty was needed. Thus, after holding eight major preparatory meetings, some 5,000 delegates gathered in Kyoto, Japan, in December 1997 to develop a more authoritative global warming regime.

After intense negotiations, Kyoto conference delegates established a framework accord that delineated specific cuts in greenhouse gas emissions. The Kyoto Protocol—essentially an addendum to the 1992 Climate Treaty—required that industrialized countries reduce their greenhouse emissions by about 5 percent below their 1990 level no later than the year 2012. To achieve this goal, the protocol established significant cuts in pollution—8 percent for the European Union, 7 percent for the United States,

and 6 percent for Japan. Significantly, no binding targets were established for China and India or other developing nations. Because the accord called for a reduction of roughly 30 percent in the projected carbon emissions of industrialized countries, the Kyoto framework represented a significant challenge to energy consumption patterns of industrialized states, especially the United States, a country that accounts for nearly one-fourth of the world's greenhouse emissions.

Since the Kyoto accord established only a general framework for action, the specific compliance mechanisms had to be worked out in subsequent meetings. This proved to be far more difficult than anticipated, in great part because the contemplated pollution reductions imposed significant economic burdens on the major industrial states. This was especially the case for countries like Canada, Norway, and the United States, which, unlike most European Union member states, had fewer energy conservation measures in place. To facilitate compliance with the protocol's stringent emissions targets, some industrial states demanded flexibility in meeting their obligations. The protocol had stipulated (Article 17) that rich countries could meet their obligations by buying "emission rights" from developing countries that had below average greenhouse emissions. Similarly, the protocol had provided that reforestation programs, known as carbon "sinks,"[8] could contribute to "emission credits" (Article 3), thereby allowing states to offset excessive greenhouse gases.

In March 2001, shortly before compliance issues had been fully resolved, the Bush administration announced the United States' withdrawal from the Kyoto Protocol. It did so because it considered the economic costs of implementation excessive but also because the accord exempted Third World countries, especially the two most populous states, China and India.[9] U.S. officials claimed that the United States strongly supported sustainable economic development, provided a balance was maintained between environmental protection and job creation. After rejecting the Kyoto framework, the Bush administration set forth a more flexible approach that called for an 18 percent reduction in greenhouse gas intensity—that is, the ratio of emissions to economic growth. Thus, rather than seeking specific curbs in total carbon emissions, the new approach sought to provide a dynamic way of relating economic expansion to global warming by focusing on reducing the overall percentage (intensity) of harmful pollution.

According to Kyoto guidelines, the protocol was to become binding international law when 55 countries accounting for at least 55 percent of the world's 1990 greenhouse emissions had ratified it. Although more than 80 countries had ratified the treaty by 2003, these states had failed to meet the 55 percent emissions threshold. Since the United States accounted for nearly one-fourth of the world's carbon emissions, its withdrawal from the Kyoto accord meant that Japan and Russia had to adopt the agreement if it was to become binding. After receiving significant concessions for its carbon sinks,[10] Japan ratified the protocol in 2002. Subsequently, however, Russia announced that it would not support the accord, thereby all but ending the prospects for the treaty's formal adoption.

While the Kyoto Protocol has not become binding international law, the accord is nevertheless important to the collective efforts to limit pollution. Indeed, the provisions of the protocol have influenced and will continue to guide environmental policies of states. The countless conferences, academic discussions, and international negotiations over global warming have resulted in increased global awareness of, and sensitivity to, the harmful effects of greenhouse gases. Thus while the global warming discourse has not resulted in a formal treaty, the diplomacy over the Kyoto Protocol has undoubtedly helped to shape values, attitudes, and public policies that contributed to lower levels of carbon pollution than might have been the case otherwise.

Despite the difficulties and limitations of the Kyoto process, some environmental officials have expressed confidence in the emerging climate change regime. Margo Wallström, the E.U. commissioner for the environment, for example, observed at the successful completion of Kyoto compliance measures in Bonn in 2001 that "now we can go home and look our children in the eye and be proud of what we have done."[11] Michael Meacher, Britain's environment minister, was similarly enthusiastic about the environmental agreement reached at Bonn. He said: "Climate change is the single greatest threat to the human race. This agreement is a historic day that all of us will remember."[12] Others, however, regard the proposed efforts to limit greenhouse emissions as woefully inadequate. Barrett, for example, claims that the Kyoto accord does not provide the supporting incentives required to bring about significant behavioral change in energy consumption patterns.[13] And Gardiner claims that Kyoto is problematic because it fosters the illusion that serious progress is being made to confront climate change.[14]

THE ETHICS OF STABILIZING GREENHOUSE GAS EMISSIONS

The question of how best to confront the problem of global warming raises numerous moral concerns. Below I briefly explore four different issues. First, I examine the intergenerational problem posed by global warming in which the failure to reduce greenhouse pollution in the present generation is likely to impose significant harm on future societies. Because the costs and benefits of collective action are separated by time, there are few incentives to protect the environmental commons. Second, I explore the moral validity of buying and selling pollution "rights." Third, I describe and assess the differential burdens placed on rich and poor states in seeking to reduce total global greenhouse emissions. Unlike the first concern, this is an intragenerational problem that explores how the burdens of reducing total greenhouse gases should be distributed among states. Finally, since nuclear power can provide energy without the undesirable atmospheric emissions that foster global warming, I briefly explore the ethics of shifting energy production from the burning of fossil fuels to nuclear power.

One of the most important ethical issues raised by the debate over greenhouse emissions is the conflict between economic development and environmental sustainability, between meeting current human needs and protecting the environment for future generations. Ideally, economic development should be sustainable—that is, conducive to the short- and long-term protection of the environment. But if a choice must be made between limiting economic growth or preventing global warming, fostering job creation or protecting the environment, which goal should take precedence? This dispute is morally complex because it involves an intergenerational conflict between the current wants and needs of people with the claims of future generations. Since fossil fuels have served as the principal energy source for industrialization and economic development, there is a significant incentive to continue using such fuels to promote further economic modernization. Although the burning of such fuels leads to immediate energy benefits, the costs of carbon emissions, the major cause of global warming, are transferred to the future. Indeed, since the cumulative destructive impact of carbon dioxide is not felt immediately, there is little incentive for countries to restrict the use of such fuels. This is especially the case for low-income countries that are eager to increase their standard of living through modernization.

Besides the challenge of how best to reconcile the intergenerational trade-offs between present and future needs, devising a morally appropriate policy is morally ambiguous and difficult because public policy making is probabilistic. The lack of consensus over which strategies are most conducive to achieving desired outcomes frequently derives from conflicting interpretations of scientific knowledge as well as uncertainty over the effects and results of different public policies. This uncertainty principle is clearly evident in the scientific and public policy debates over climate change.[15] For example, while there is a significant consensus over the fact of global warming, there is much less agreement over its causes, timing, and magnitude.[16] Thus, while public officials may agree that a harmful by-product of industrial pollution is the spread of greenhouse gases, they may hold radically different perspectives about how best to control and reduce greenhouse emissions.

A second important ethical issue involved in the global debate over climate change is the trading of emissions rights. According to the Kyoto accord, industrial states with excessive levels of carbon emissions, such as Greece, Ireland, Norway, and the United States, may pay countries with low levels of emissions as a way of meeting Kyoto obligations. Although the introduction of market forces could possibly contribute to the reduction of total world greenhouse emissions, the commercialization of pollution is itself a dubious ethical development. For one thing, it removes the stigma that is normally associated with pollution.[17] When an industry violates pollution regulations, a government agency fines the industry. Such a fine is not simply a financial cost to business but also represents a community's moral judgment that the industry's action (excessive pollution) was wrong. However, when pollution is commercialized, it destroys the moral stigma associated with unacceptable behaviors. Moreover, the trading of emission rights is morally problematic because it weakens communal solidarity required in the collective management of global resources. When some countries can fulfill their communal responsibilities toward the global warming regime by buying the right to pollute, global solidarity is weakened, ultimately making the fulfillment of other global commitments more difficult. If the international community is to remain a community, state actors must all participate in fulfilling shared responsibilities.

A third important ethical issue concerns how the burden of pollution reduction should be allocated among states. Should the costs of cutting carbon dioxide be borne by the rich, developed nations (North), as some thinkers and environmentalists have claimed, or by all states, including the poor, developing nations (South)? The Kyoto framework assumes that major responsibility for curbing carbon emissions should fall on industrial states, the countries that are chiefly responsible for the bulk (more than 60 percent of the total) of world greenhouse emissions. Moreover, because developed states have superior technology, they are better equipped to generate economic growth with technologies that are environmentally friendly. In addition, since the North's economic development has caused most of the accumulated atmospheric greenhouse gas emissions, Third World officials claim that they should be permitted to modernize without restricted use of fossil fuels. However, even if Third World countries adopt fuel-efficient technologies, further economic development in the South will lead to increased fuel consumption and thereby to a rise in greenhouse emissions.

Although developing nations are now responsible for about one-fifth of the world's total carbon emissions, the growth of atmospheric pollution in the developing world is not an insignificant issue. It has been estimated that, in the absence of any restrictions on coal burning or petroleum use, greenhouse emissions will more than double in the South in the next two decades in response to increased industrialization. According to one estimate, the developing world's share of global gas emissions is expected to rise from about 20 percent in the mid-1990s to more than 50 percent by the year 2025.[18] Developing nations do not assert that climate change is solely the responsibility of the developed states. Instead, they claim that since current atmospheric pollution is a direct by-product of the North's industrialization, the high-income countries must bear the primary responsibility for reducing greenhouse emissions. Since poor countries with little pollution can sell emissions rights, the North can meet reductions in emissions by making payments to the South. Some scholars have suggested that if climate change is managed in this manner, the cost to the North will greatly exceed any previous international wealth transfer in modern history.[19]

Finally, the effort to curb fossil fuel use raises ethical issues about relying on alternative energy sources, especially nuclear power. Although the Kyoto Protocol does not address the ethics of nuclear energy, the issue is significant because a number of countries—notably France, Spain, South Korea, Sweden, and Switzerland—have increased reliance on nuclear power to re-duce carbon emissions. During the 1980s, France carried out a massive national effort to reduce the burning of fossil fuels by converting to nuclear power, thereby reducing carbon dioxide emissions by 40 percent. By 1994, 78 percent of France's electricity was being generated by nuclear power. Although the United States has been much more hesitant to rely on nuclear power, by 1993 it had 109 nuclear-powered electricity-generating plants that collectively were responsible for lowering carbon dioxide emissions by 30 percent. It has been estimated that in the absence of some 450 nuclear power plants throughout the world, global greenhouse emissions would be about 10 percent higher.[20] The moral problem posed by increased reliance on nuclear energy is that nuclear power itself involves significant, albeit rare, environmental dangers and risks. The question of whether shifting from fossil fuels to nuclear power, as France has done, is a wise and morally correct strategy is still open to debate, especially in view of the continuing uncertainty about the cost, feasibility, and safety in the disposal of nuclear waste.

MORAL REFLECTIONS

The Kyoto Protocol raises a number of important ethical questions.

- Ideally, development should be sustainable. But to the extent that economic development and reduction in carbon dioxide emissions are in conflict, which goal should take precedence—job creation or pollution control, economic growth or global warming?
- Because the North is responsible for most of the existing greenhouse gas emissions, should developed countries bear the principal cost of curbing greenhouse emissions? Is the protocol's imposition of different standards on the North and the South morally just?
- Because the developed countries have established high standards of living while implementing various types of policies

and strategies that encourage environmental protection, should they transfer
these technologies to the poor countries?
Should developed countries (North) pay
developing nations (South) to reduce
their emissions?

- Is it moral to buy or sell pollution rights?
  Why or why not?
- Given the risks and dangers associated
  with nuclear power, is the shift from car-
  bon-burning plants to nuclear power
  plants morally warranted?

THE NATURE OF INTERNATIONAL JUSTICE

To assess international society in light of political morality, it is necessary to have a
normative standard by which to judge the rightness or justness of the structures and
policies of that society. In effect, what is needed is a conception of international justice. However, defining the nature of international justice and its essential principles
is a daunting task. Several factors contribute to this difficulty.

Defining International Justice

First, global political justice is difficult to ascertain because of the lack of agreement
about such a norm. This is due partly to the absence of an authoritative conception of
political justice. Although justice is one of the most frequently examined themes in
Western political philosophy, the different normative theories and conceptualizations
of political justice have not yet yielded an authoritative definition of the term. Rather,
Western political scholarship has provided a multitude of theories and perspectives
about different dimensions of the quest for political justice. For example, some theories emphasize the rights and obligations of individuals in developing a just political
society, whereas others emphasize the character and responsibilities of government
and other public institutions. Still other thinkers approach justice by seeking to identify foundational principles of political society, whereas others focus on the policy outcomes of government. It is significant that throughout most of Western civilization the
quest for political justice was viewed as a by-product of the fulfillment of moral obligations. As a result, most classical political theory emphasized the role of duties and
obligation in cultivating political justice. Contemporary thinkers, by contrast, have
placed priority on rights. In sum, normative political thought provides insights, perspectives, and theories about the nature of political justice but no authoritative framework for determining justice.

A second reason for the elusive nature of international justice is that global society
is comprised of a plurality of cultures and moralities. Whereas domestic societies typically are characterized by comparatively coherent and authoritative decision-making
structures, the international community has no comparable legal or political institutions. Moreover, domestic societies are typically based on a more coherent political
morality. As Stanley Hoffmann has observed, although there is generally a consensus
within national communities about what constitutes justice, in the international community there is "a cacophony of standards." Because of the moral pluralism of global
society, justice becomes either "a matter of sheer force—carried at the point of a

sword—or, when force does not prevail, a matter of fleeting bargains and tests of fear or strength."[21] It is also important to recognize that the quest for international justice is difficult because such a quest might involve conflict with other normative goals. More specifically, as I note in the case study below, the quest for international order might not be consistent with the quest for justice either within or among states.

Finally, determining international justice is difficult because the notion of political justice can be interpreted in two very different ways. One approach associates political justice with the rightness and fairness of the rules, procedures, and institutions of political communities and the consistent and impartial application of such norms. This perspective is sometimes called *procedural justice* because it defines justice in terms of processes rather than outcomes. According to this approach, political justice involves the impartial and nondiscriminatory application of rules and procedures, not the determination of particular desirable goals or moral outcomes. In effect, justice is realized not by pursuing particular ends but by ensuring the fairness of the system. Such an approach is illustrated by the American judicial system, which pursues justice through impartial courts. To ensure impartiality, a judge maintains strict neutrality as he or she enforces strict compliance with norms governing the presentation of evidence and arguments by the prosecution and defense before an impartial jury.

The second approach defines political justice in terms of the rightness and fairness of outcomes. Justice is that which promotes good or right ends. Because this perspective associates morality with particular distributions or results, it is frequently referred to as *substantive*, or *distributive justice*.[22] Although this approach has become increasingly influential in contemporary political ethics, it is significant that traditional international morality was defined mainly in terms of procedural norms and in particular "the laws of nations." As Terry Nardin has observed, the association of international justice with particular outcomes is a relatively recent development, dating to the current century when the notion of distributive justice began to be applied to international relations.[23]

A sound, comprehensive approach to international ethics should be rooted in both procedural and substantive norms. Procedural norms are important because they emphasize the impartial application of authoritative rules and principles of global society; substantive norms, however, are also important because their perception of justice is partly rooted in the perception of just outcomes. To be sure, the application of distributive justice among member states presents significant challenges. However, the increased moral sensitivity to egregious inequalities within and among nations has fostered a more robust moral assessment of international relations.

Liberalism and Political Justice

From a normative perspective, the dominant ethical paradigm utilized in assessing twentieth-century international relations has been political liberalism. As noted in chapter 3, this tradition emerged in the seventeenth and eighteenth centuries with the political writings of theorists such as John Locke, Jean Jacques Rousseau, James Mill, Jeremy Bentham, and John Stuart Mill. Fundamentally, liberalism espouses two basic principles. First, because human beings possess rights, the primary task of government is to secure and protect those rights. Second, the most effective way to inhibit tyranny and promote the common good is through limited government based on consent.

Because liberalism first developed as a domestic political theory, its application to international society was, as Hoffmann has noted, "little more than the projection of domestic liberalism on a world scale."[24] Indeed, liberals have argued on the basis of the "domestic analogy" that states possess rights and duties comparable to those of individuals in political society.[25] The application of liberalism to global society has resulted in the development of *liberal internationalism*—a doctrine that emphasizes the peacefulness of democratic regimes, a belief in the fundamental harmony of interests among different peoples, and the universality of human rights. In addition, this doctrine, following the claims of early-twentieth-century American liberals such as Woodrow Wilson, asserts that peoples (nationalities) have an inherent right to political self-determination and that this political right is not only consistent with but also conducive to global order.

Liberal internationalism has contributed to the development of two meta-ethical perspectives on international justice: communitarianism and cosmopolitanism. *Communitarianism* accepts the existing community of states as normative, believing that the quest for human dignity is best secured within and through each of the distinct political societies of the international system.[26] Although the state can be an impediment to justice, it also serves as the primary political agency for ensuring human rights domestically and peace and tranquility internationally. However, the communitarian approach recognizes that establishing legitimate order domestically is not sufficient to ensure human dignity; what is also required is that conditions in global society of states be conducive to peace and justice among states and, derivatively, to the well-being of persons. Thus, a central concern of the communitarian perspective is to define the obligations that foster and maintain a just order among member states.

Cosmopolitanism, by contrast, seeks to promote human dignity by giving priority to global or cosmopolitan bonds.[27] Its major focus is on the pursuit of just political relations within all relevant communities, including global society itself. Although this perspective views the state as an important structure in fostering human rights, it also recognizes that states can and do abuse rights. Indeed, because states have been a major source of tyranny and human suffering, cosmopolitans believe that the moral legitimacy of states is conditional on their protection of human rights. In effect, they assume that international morality requires the subordination of state boundaries to human dignity. Thus, whereas communitarianism accepts the legitimacy of the existing international order, the cosmopolitan approach denies the moral significance of the structures of the existing neo-Westphalian order. Because of its idealistic orientation, cosmopolitanism is sometimes referred to as global utopianism.

In comparing communitarianism and cosmopolitanism, it is significant that both perspectives assert the primacy of human dignity but differ in how best to secure and protect human rights.[28] Whereas the former assigns primary responsibility to the state in securing and protecting individual rights, the latter assigns primary obligation to global society itself. In addition, it is significant that both approaches assume the primacy of morality. Indeed, both traditions are rooted in the tradition of "common morality," which regards ethical norms as rationally accessible and universally binding. Despite cultural pluralism in global society, common morality assumes that the quest for peace and human dignity must be based on moral norms that are transculturally authoritative.

International Justice versus Cosmopolitan Justice

Communitarianism and cosmopolitanism give rise to two distinct emphases on political justice. For the communitarian, states are the primary actors in global society and thus are presumptively legitimate and entitled to sovereignty, that is, political independence and self-rule. Because communitarianism is concerned mainly with the promotion of a just peace among states, global political ethics is approached as a quest for *international justice,* involving equity and peace among member states. Because states vary considerably in their size, power, and economic resources, the quest for interstate justice is a daunting task. Moreover, because there is no common power within international society to resolve conflicts, the establishment and maintenance of order is similarly a difficult task. Thus, when a state commits aggression, communitarians believe that force can and should be used to defend the legitimate rights of states.

Communitarians recognize that the quest for interstate justice will not ensure justice within states. Some governments might be unwilling to protect the rights and liberties of persons. Indeed, some regimes might deliberately pursue policies that inflict great harm on their people. However, when gross injustices occur, the communitarians and cosmopolitans differ in their readiness to use external force to correct the alleged injustices. Because communitarians believe that the protection of existing rules of global society is foundational to domestic and international order, they are reluctant to override the sovereignty norm in the name of human rights, believing that in the long run global order is essential to human rights. As a result, communitarians are willing to intervene only as a last resort. At the risk of oversimplification, it can be said that liberal communitarians are eager to affirm individual rights but are reluctant to protect or advance such rights through foreign intervention.[29]

Cosmopolitanism, by contrast, is concerned mainly with the well-being of persons. Cosmopolitan thinkers argue that states have a moral obligation to defend and protect basic rights and that when they fail to do so they lose their moral standing within international society. Because cosmopolitans view nation-states as legitimate political actors only to the extent that they protect and secure human rights, state boundaries are not morally significant.[30] While affirming the legal principle of nonintervention, *cosmopolitan justice* assumes that the existing structures and rules of international society should not be used to protect injustice within states. Thus, when gross human rights occur, foreign intervention, whether individual or collective, is not only permissible but also, in exceptional circumstances, morally obligatory. Accordingly, when states are unable or unwilling to secure citizens' rights and, more important, when they intentionally violate universally accepted human rights norms, they lose their moral standing in the international society of states. In short, sovereignty is subordinate to human rights.

These two conceptions of political justice provide alternative approaches to the pursuit of world order and the protection of human rights. Because the communitarian approach emphasizes the role and legitimacy of states, it is more likely to foster international stability. The cosmopolitan approach, by contrast, focuses on individual welfare and thus is more likely to encourage the protection of human rights. Moreover, because the quest for global order and the protection of human rights are not complementary processes, the pursuit of order will often come at the expense of human rights and vice versa. If the pursuit of world order is primary, honoring state autonomy may require tolerating domestic injustices. However, if human rights claims are primary, sovereignty might have to be compromised through humanitarian intervention to halt the gross violation of human rights. Thus, because the pursuit of international justice frequently involves a trade-off between sovereignty and human rights, between autonomy and suffering, the quest for a just international order can be realized only imperfectly, most often by giving precedence to either a cosmopolitan or a communitarian perspective.

On the basis of the concepts and approaches developed previously, I next examine the ethics of foreign aid, seeking to illuminate some of the important dilemmas and issues involved in foreign economic assistance.

CASE 10-2: THE ETHICS OF FOREIGN AID

BACKGROUND

Do rich societies have a moral obligation to provide economic assistance to poor countries? If developed nations have a moral responsibility to alleviate hunger, human suffering, and poverty, how much economic aid should states provide, and to whom should the aid be given—to people directly (through NGOs) or to their governments?

In addressing the ethics of foreign aid, it is important to distinguish between emergency relief and development assistance. The former involves assistance to meet humanitarian needs arising from droughts, earthquakes, tribal wars, and other disasters. The latter concerns aid to foster economic growth and thereby decrease poverty. Although humanitarian relief and development aid are both praiseworthy, the former is more morally compelling because it seeks to meet immediate human needs directly rather than through long-term processes of economic growth. Indeed, since human dignity is a universal norm of global political ethics, emergency relief to sustain life and relieve suffering may be morally obligatory on rich, developed nations.

Unlike relieving human suffering with emer-

gency aid, reducing poverty through development aid is a difficult, complex process that presupposes the existence of cultural, legal, political, and economic preconditions. As a result, foreign aid is unlikely to bring about job creation in an economic environment that inhibits productive enterprise. Moreover, since foreign aid is not the only, or even most important, factor affecting the nature and rate of economic expansion, such assistance can help, but not assure job creation. Development aid can of course facilitate economic growth and thereby contribute to a more just international system. But whether such aid contributes to this task will depend upon the conditions and policies of the receiving state as well as how the assistance is used.

DEVELOPMENT AID

The modern foreign aid regime began in 1949, when the United States inaugurated a foreign economic assistance program to foster economic growth and development in the developing nations of Asia, Africa, and Latin America. In launching the U.S. foreign aid program (called Point Four), President Harry S. Truman noted that the United States "should make available to peace-loving peoples the benefits of our store of technical knowledge in order to help them realize their aspirations for a better life." Truman asserted that "[g]reater production is the key to prosperity and peace. And the key to greater production is a wider and more vigorous application of modern scientific and technical knowledge. Only by helping the least fortunate of its members can the human family achieve the decent, satisfying life that is the right of all people."[31]

Although the Point Four program was modest in its inception, U.S. economic assistance expanded greatly during the 1950s and 1960s. Moreover, beginning in the late 1950s, other developed democratic states joined the United States in providing development assistance to poor nations. Although their contributions were modest at first, they increased both absolutely and relatively throughout the 1970s and 1980s. Whereas the United States provided more than half of all development aid in the 1950s and 1960s, by 1975 it had declined to 30 percent and by 1989 to only 16 percent.[32]

Foreign aid, generally referred to as official development assistance (ODA), involves loans and grants provided bilaterally and multilaterally to assist the economic development of poor countries. During the Cold War era, developed democratic countries gave more than $1.1 trillion (constant 1988 dollars) in ODA. Because such aid includes only official financial transfers to poor countries and does not include foreign direct investment, commercial loans, or nongovernmental financial assistance and humanitarian relief, it greatly understates the net transfer of financial resources from Western societies to developing nations. For example, 1982 ODA was estimated at $18 billion, while total net financial transfers from rich to poor countries were estimated at almost $80 billion, or more than four times the size of ODA.[33] Assuming that total net financial transfers have been roughly three times the size of ODA, it would be reasonable to assume that during the 1950–1990 period total net financial aid to the Third World was at least $3 trillion, or about three times the estimated official aid. Moreover, since the end of the Cold War, the share of private financial transfers to poor countries relative to total foreign aid has greatly increased, especially in the United States. For example, of the total U.S. international assistance to developing nations in 2000 ($58 billion), Carol Adelman estimates nearly 60 percent ($35 billion) involves private giving from individual remittances, religious organizations, foundations, corporations, universities, and private voluntary organizations (PVOs).[34]

Although numerous justifications have been given for granting foreign aid, David Lumsdaine argues convincingly that humanitarian concerns have provided the major impetus for economic assistance to the Third World. After examining Western economic assistance during the 1949–89 period, Lumsdaine concludes that donor countries' "sense of justice and compassion" provided the major reason for giving aid. He writes, "Support for aid was a response to world poverty which arose mainly from ethical and humane concerns and secondarily, from the belief that long-term peace and prosperity was possible only in a generous and just international order where all could prosper."[35]

The purpose of ODA is to improve living conditions of low-income nations and thereby foster global economic justice. Has foreign aid succeeded in promoting economic development? Moreover, has foreign economic assistance fostered international or distributive justice by reducing economic inequalities among states? There can be little doubt that substantial sums of public and private assistance have been given to poor nations in the second half of the twentieth century, but the effects of those transfers have been mixed at best. To begin with, since reduction in poverty is strongly correlated with economic growth rates, economists have concluded that a major requirement for the improvement of people's living conditions is economic growth. Moreover, since economic studies have shown that there is no link between aid and growth, foreign aid can assist economic development but only if other economic, social, and political preconditions are present.

In an important study, two World Bank economists found that aid has a positive effect on growth when a favorable economic environment exists—that is, when inflation is low, when government budget deficits are low, and when a country is open to foreign trade. Between 1970 and 1993 developing nations with favorable economic conditions grew at an annual rate of 2.2 percent per person, while developing nations with a favorable economic environment and significant foreign aid grew nearly twice as fast (at an annual rate of 3.7 percent).[36] But the absence of a favorable domestic economic environment can impede poverty reduction even when large aid transfers are involved. For example, Zambia's real per capita income declined by one-third between the early 1960s and the early 1990s, even though the country received some $2 billion in foreign aid during this time. According to economist William Easterly, had Zambia been successful in using this capital for development purposes, annual per capita income would have increased dramatically (to about $20,000) rather than declined to $600.[37]

Despite the needs of low-income countries, some scholars and public officials argue that aid can be harmful to growth. Aid critics claim that ODA encourages waste, strengthens corrupt regimes, overpoliticizes the process of economic growth, and results in inefficient and at times counterproductive investments. Most importantly, some economists, including P.T. Bauer, argue that official aid to developing nations harms job creation by reinforcing inefficient practices and economic dependency.[38] The failures of ODA are well illustrated in the economic performance of sub-Saharan Africa, a region that received more than $22 billion in aid in the 1970s, yet was unable to increase agricultural production, its chief source of income, during that time. Indeed, because of economic stagnation and an absolute decline in agricultural production, to prevent starvation in the mid-1980s the West began pouring in more than $7 billion per year.[39]

In chapter 2, I observed that an ethical foreign policy was one whose intentions, means, and results were moral. Noble goals might inspire the human spirit but they are not enough to ensure global justice. Although humanitarian intentions (e.g., relieving poverty through growth) are necessary in developing a moral foreign economic policy, they will not alone ensure

ethical outcomes. What is essential in reducing poverty is the promotion of sustainable economic growth that results in improved living conditions for those with human needs.

MORALITY, JUSTICE, AND FOREIGN AID

Since political philosophers distinguish human actions that are morally obligatory from those that are praiseworthy, foreign aid can be similarly justified as a moral duty or as a morally desirable act. From the latter perspective, foreign aid can be given as an act of charity or benevolence to reduce poverty and promote job creation through economic growth. According to the charity thesis, rich societies should provide economic assistance to poor nations to help reduce extreme poverty and make the world a more humane environment. Since acts of charity are voluntary, they do not impose moral obligations on aid-granting nations. Thus, when foreign aid is conceived as an act of charity, societies that do not transfer resources to those in need are not morally blameworthy for such assistance is a "supererogatory" act that is expected only of saints and other moral exemplars, not of average human beings.[40] Historically, since foreign development aid has been viewed from the charity perspective, it has been regarded as desirable public policy but not necessarily an ethical imperative.

An alternative approach to foreign economic assistance is one that regards aid as morally obligatory. Such moral imperatives can be justified on the basis of either claims of justice or claims of humanity. The former imposes moral duties to promote international justice among people of the international community, while the latter imposes duties to affirm the inherent worth of persons. According to Brian Opeskin, the justice thesis claims that foreign aid must be given in order to meet two types of international obligations: corrective claims and distributive claims.[41] Because corrective, or restitutive, justice involves reparations for past wrongs, such justice requires that the prior injustices be clearly delineated before appropriate action can be taken. Claims of distributive justice, on the other hand, are rooted in the conviction that social and economic goods within a community should be distributed equitably. Although there is widespread support for the notion that the state has a moral obligation to ensure distributive justice within domestic society, there is much less support for the idea that distributive justice should be applied within the fragile international community. [42]

Perhaps the more compelling argument for foreign aid is the humanity thesis, which asserts that because human beings are moral agents, they are entitled to universal protection regardless of proximity, ethnicity, nationality, or citizenship. When people suffer from hunger, disease, malnutrition, and other calamities, their fundamental worth as moral agents is compromised. Historically, emergency relief has been justified primarily on this basis. In an influential essay written in response to the massive famine in Bangladesh, Peter Singer illustrates this approach by arguing that societies with resources have a moral obligation to relieve human suffering regardless of where it is found. According to this argument, if people have the ability to prevent something bad from happening without sacrificing anything of comparable moral importance, they also have a moral obligation to help relieve suffering.[43] This moral obligation to strangers is illustrated in the biblical parable of "the Good Samaritan," an account of how a stranger meets the human needs of an injured traveler.[44] When applied to international affairs, the logic of the parable can be expressed in the following propositions: 1) X nation has experienced a human disaster and its people are suffering; 2) the citizens of Y have knowledge of X's human needs as well as the resources to relieve X's suffering; 3) even though the people of X and Y are strangers, they share a common humanity; and 4) the people of Y have a moral obligation to help the citizens of X.

I noted previously that justice in global society can be defined either from the perspective of states (communitarian justice) or from the perspective of persons (cosmopolitan justice). From a communitarian perspective, rich states have a moral obligation to assist the economic development of poor countries to relieve poverty and human suffering in those lands. However, to whom is this moral duty owed—to poor states,

to peoples in poor lands, or to both? Moderate communitarians assume that developed states have a moral obligation to both peoples and states in meeting immediate humanitarian needs as well as in fostering their economic development. Although nongovernmental actors can facilitate the distribution of short-term aid and contribute to long-term job creation, the development of national infrastructure and the establishment of structures and policies conducive to job creation are essential in stimulating national economic expansion. As a result, moderate communitarians strongly support development aid to governments.

The radical communitarian perspective, however, gives priority to distributive justice over job creation. As a result, it believes that developed states should seek to reduce international economic inequalities through substantial financial transfers from the rich to the developing nations. This approach was illustrated in the proposed New International Economic Order (NIEO), a reform plan devised by the developing nations in the late 1970s. The aim of the NIEO was to shift economic resources and power from the North to the South. Although the NIEO was a relatively modest proposal, the underlying premises were rooted in the radical claim that the existing international economic system was morally bankrupt because of excessive and continually expanding international economic inequalities. By the late 1980s, however, the NIEO had lost much of its appeal, in great part because economic liberalism had become the prevailing international economic ideology and also because many developing nations had achieved a significant rise in national income through export-led growth.

Of course, the most extreme approach to economic assistance is the cosmopolitan perspective. Because cosmopolitanism regards human welfare within global society as the principal determinant of justice, state and nonstate actors have a moral obligation to relieve hunger and poverty wherever it occurs. Because state boundaries are not morally significant, foreign economic assistance should be provided until basic needs of all human beings have been met. Some thinkers, following the logic of cosmopolitanism, have argued that the welfare policies of modern democratic states should be applied to global society. However, political leaders have not seriously considered such speculative notions because governments from both poor and rich countries have remained staunchly committed to the decentralized system of sovereign states.

MORAL REFLECTIONS

This case study raises a number of critical issues.

- Because the international community is a global society of many different nations, are developed countries morally obligated to assist poor nations?

- If a moral obligation exists, to whom should the aid be given—the people directly, NGOs, or governments?
- Since resources can be transferred to poor nations through public and private channels and used for a variety of purposes, which aid strategies are morally preferable?
- If economic growth reduces absolute poverty but also exacerbates international economic inequalities, should growth be pursued nevertheless?
- What should be the aim of foreign aid— to reduce global economic inequalities, foster national economic development, or meet basic human needs?

THE INDIVIDUAL AND GLOBAL SOCIETY

Historically, liberal political thought has been concerned mainly with defining the rights and duties of citizens within the boundaries of states. From the perspective of political liberalism, theorists have consistently asserted that just as citizens have the rights of freedom of speech or freedom of assembly, they have a right to freedom of movement within territorial boundaries. However, classical thinkers did not extend this argument to international society. Although international law has provided some regulatory principles governing emigration and immigration, transnational migration was left largely to the discretion of states. At the same time it is important to emphasize that the classical perspective did not assert unbridled nationalism. It did not claim, as Garrett Hardin has, that nations are like "lifeboats," each with a limited carrying capacity that requires that states impose strict limits on immigration.[45] All that the traditionalist perspective asserted was that states should take into consideration national and international claims when establishing rules governing migration.

However, as global interdependence has increased the ease of transnational migration, the traditional view of absolute control over borders has been increasingly challenged. Some theorists, such as Joseph Carens and Peter Singer, have argued that international justice requires an open admissions policy.[46] Since birth and citizenship are entirely a matter of chance, they claim that the distribution of economic, social, and political benefits through states is morally unwarranted. Following the cosmopolitan perspective, these thinkers have argued that the rights of persons must take moral precedence over the political claims of national autonomy. More particularly, they have suggested that citizens' economic, social, political, and cultural claims must be subordinated to the basic needs of foreigners and especially to the fundamental human rights claims of migrants.

The Ethics of Migration

Are the territorial subdivisions of the international community morally important? More particularly, are the rights and interests of states morally significant, as communitarians suggest, or must national interests be subordinated to the claims of individuals, as cosmopolitans suggest? How should the needs of migrants be morally reconciled with the claims of national autonomy?

From the perspective of international political morality, individuals have an inherent right to leave their homeland. This right, which has become increasingly accepted as a fundamental human right in the contemporary international system, is defined in categorical and unqualified terms by the Universal Declaration of Human Rights (Article 13): "Everyone has the right to leave any country, including his own." The moral basis of the right of emigration is rooted in the voluntary character of democratic societies. Alan Dowty explains the priority of the right to emigrate as follows:

> The right to leave thus gets at the very essence of government by consent—a concept that has achieved near universal acceptance in principles, even amongst states that rarely abide by it. Since government by consent holds that citizenship is a voluntary act, the right to leave a country implicitly serves to ratify the contract between an individual and society. If a person who has the right to leave chooses to stay, he has signaled his voluntary acceptance of the social contract. From this follows his obligation to society. But if he does not have the option of leaving, then society's hold on him is based only on coercion.[47]

Dowty argues that the character of a regime is revealed by the respect that it accords to personal self-determination and, in particular, to the right of emigration. As Dowty's statement at the beginning of this chapter suggests, the degree of personal autonomy is a measure of a country's "overall social health."

Individuals also have the right of emigration from an international legal perspective. Although some European states extended the doctrine of sovereignty in the seventeenth and eighteenth centuries to prohibit emigration (to increase their population base), it is clear that contemporary international law provides states with no such right.[48] From an international legal perspective, persons have the right to leave their homeland or country of residence. Thus, when East Germany erected the Berlin Wall to keep its people from migrating to West Berlin, this action was considered morally and legally reprehensible. Similarly, when the government of the Soviet Union refused exit visas to Soviet Jews, this action was widely condemned as an affront to international human rights. Fundamentally, then, individuals, not governments, have the right to decide whether and when they will leave their country of residence. Moreover, although states have the legal and moral right to expel illegal aliens (i.e., foreign persons whose entry into a country was not legally approved), it is legally and morally impermissible for governments to deport their own people.

Although individuals have the right to emigrate, they do not necessarily have the right to immigrate to a particular state. This is because governments, not international organizations or migrants themselves, determine admission into sovereign countries.[49] Although the Universal Declaration of Human Rights (Article 15.1) affirms the right to a nationality, this claim does not entitle a person to reside in a country of his or her choice. As Brian Barry has noted, "It is a general characteristic of associations that people are free to leave them but not free to join them."[50] Thus, emigration and immigration are morally and legally asymmetrical. The moral asymmetry between exit and entry, departure and arrival, is illustrated in everyday social and economic life. For example, workers have a right to leave their place of employment but are not entitled to another job of their own choosing. Employers, not prospective employees, determine employment. Similarly, students may withdraw from colleges and universities at any time, but their desire to continue their studies at another academic institution depends wholly on their admittance to that institution.

Michael Walzer has set forth one of the most powerful arguments about the ethics of border regulation. He argues that regulating membership through admission and exclusion is essential in preserving "communities of character," that is, "historically stable, ongoing associations of men and women with some special commitment to one another and some special sense of their common life."[51] Walzer explains the necessity of regulating migration as follows:

> The distinctiveness of cultures and groups depends upon closure and cannot be conceived as a stable feature of human life without it. If this distinctiveness is a value . . . then closure must be permitted somewhere. At some level of political organization something like the sovereign state must take shape and claim the authority to make its own admissions policy, to control and sometimes restrain the flow of immigrants.[52]

Walzer illustrates the nature and importance of membership by comparing political communities with neighborhoods, clubs, and families. States, he suggests, are like neighborhoods in that national cohesion depends significantly on common cultural, social, and ethnic bonds. Just as neighborhood unity is rooted in shared values and customs, national cohesion similarly derives from common cultural and political norms and widely shared communal aspirations. States are also like clubs in that membership is entirely up to the members themselves to decide. Admissions policies, like immigration laws, are a significant feature of communal life because they contribute to the maintenance of cohesion and a sense of shared purpose. Finally, states resemble families in that they can help meet the human needs of nonmembers. Although family commitments are generally directed toward next of kin, families also provide periodically for the well-being of strangers; similarly, states frequently extend refuge to persons in need even when there is no religious, ethnic, or political bond between the refugees and the state's citizens.

Walzer's analysis suggests that political communities have the right to protect their distinctive cultural, social, and political features and to seek to perpetuate those distinctive qualities through immigration controls. At the same time, political communities, he suggests, have a moral obligation to strangers, especially those who suffer persecution and destitution. Walzer's arguments are significant because they provide moral justification for the contemporary immigration regime based on widely shared rules and procedures governing migration flows. Myron Weiner characterizes this emerging consensus as follows:

That no government is obligated to admit migrants, that migration is a matter of individual national policy, that most governments need more effective control over their borders, that more forceful measures are needed to halt illegal migration and the growth of worldwide migrant smuggling, that improved procedures are needed to distinguish genuine asylum seekers and refugees suffering from persecution and violence from individuals who use these procedures to migrate, that "temporary" guestworker policies do not work.[53]

One of the challenging issues in immigration politics is determining how open borders should be. This issue involves two fundamental policy concerns—the number of immigrants to be admitted annually into states and the criteria governing the selection process. Immigration pressures, which are much greater than at any time in either the nineteenth or the twentieth centuries, are a result of several developments. First, as international economic inequalities have increased, people suffering from poverty have tried to escape their relative economic deprivation by seeking entry into more economically prosperous countries. The phenomenon of "boat people"—citizens seeking to escape poverty and oppression by sea travel—is a dramatic illustration of this development. Second, as globalization has increased, information and transportation networks that facilitate international human migration have similarly increased. Even though border regulation is controlled more tightly than ever before, the means by which people can bypass such controls have also expanded.

Undoubtedly the most challenging problem in migration politics is the question of responsibility for the care and protection of refugees. Fundamentally, refugees are persons who have fled their homeland because of war, ethnic strife, religious persecution, political oppression, or other significant threats to personal security and human dignity.[54] When people flee their communities because of security threats but remain within their own country they are classified as "internally displaced persons," or IDP's. Over the past two decades the persistence of ideological, religious, and ethnic conflict has resulted in many bitter wars. Since these conflicts have brought about discrimination, ethnic cleansing, political oppression, and even the collapse of state authority, they have resulted in enormous human suffering and systematic abuse of human rights. In 2003 the number of refugees who had fled their homeland because of war and persecution was about 13 million. The number of persons that had been domestically displaced because of war and persecution was estimated at nearly 22 million.[55]

The Ethics of Asylum

Among the many moral challenges posed by migration politics, none is more complex and morally vexing than the issue of refugees or "forced migrants."[56] Several factors make the plight of refugees especially challenging legally and morally. First, because refugees fall, as Louis Henkin has noted, "in the interstices of state boundaries," they suffer from a lack of protection from authoritative institutions.[57] While international humanitarian organizations, such as the Office of the UN High Commissioner for Refugees (UNHCR), play a major role in caring for refugees, it is states that serve as the principal structures for caring of refugees. To begin with, states decide whether to admit refugees, to permit them to remain, or force them to return to their homeland.

Second, determining which persons are entitled to refugee status is difficult. Although there is broad consensus that a refugee is any person living outside his or her homeland because of a "well-founded fear of persecution," governments have applied widely different admission criteria for asylum seekers. Determining which asylum seekers have legitimate claims is frequently complicated by the large number of refugees making claims on particular states as well as by the rising number of claims regarded as unwarranted and unfounded. Because western European countries, especially Germany, have historically maintained generous asylum policies, it is not surprising that tens of thousands of persons sought protection in these states in the wake of increasing civil strife and economic turmoil in the former Yugoslavia and the former Soviet-dominated countries. It has been estimated that from 1988 to 1992, the number of refugees in western Europe increased from 230,000 to 660,000, resulting in a major migration crisis.[58] This was especially the case in Germany, the country with the largest number of refugees. Because government officials considered many of the refugees' claims to be unfounded, governments, led by Germany, established more restrictive refugee policies to manage and reduce the number of asylum seekers.[59]

Third, because the number of persons desiring asylum greatly exceeds the supply of authorized visas, governments establish preferential criteria for determining refugee admissions. During the Cold War, for example, the United States gave preferential treatment to political refugees (persons fleeing tyrannical regimes, especially Communist countries) over economic refugees (persons fleeing desperately poor nations). More recently, the United States has stressed geographic diversity in its refugee admissions.

Although scholars and public officials generally concur that states bear a moral obligation to care for foreigners in need, there is little agreement on the nature and scope of humanitarian assistance that should be provided, especially to refugees.[60] Cosmopolitans, for example, argue that refugee resettlement should be greatly increased,[61] whereas nationalists would prefer to limit such practices in the belief that significant refugee flows undermine national economic, social, and cultural well-being. Communitarians, holding to an intermediary position, assume that states have a moral obligation to provide humanitarian assistance but not necessarily an obligation to accept refugees. Human suffering requires that states care for strangers but not that they grant membership. Myron Weiner has described the intermediary position as follows: "If someone is in urgent need and the risks and cost of giving aid are low, we ought to help the injured stranger—not on the basis of justice but on the basis of charity."[62]

In addressing the needs of refugees, it is generally acknowledged that for communal reasons the most desirable long-term solution for refugees is repatriation back to the home country. Although the Universal Declaration of Human Rights enshrines the right of return (repatriation), the ability and willingness of people to avail themselves of this right depends largely on local political conditions. Repatriation can be impaired when the political instability, oppression, and enmity that originally forced people to flee continue. As a result, refugee protection sometimes involves long-term humanitarian assistance by the UNHCR or even requests for permanent resettlement. Third-country resettlement, however, is generally regarded as the least desirable solution, in part because of the great cultural, social, and economic challenges that refugees themselves must overcome in becoming fully integrated into the new society.

Although international migration pressures are being faced by many developed states, they are especially acute in the United States, a country that has historically maintained one of the most liberal immigration and refugee policies in the world. For example, the foreign-born population in the United States increased by 57 percent between 1990 and 2000, rising from 19.8 million to 31.1 million.[63] But America's historic openness has been challenged in the new millennium by two developments. First, the government has greatly intensified border controls and tightened immigration regulations in the wake of the September 11 terrorist attacks. Second, there is a growing awareness that the high rate of illegal migration across the 2,000-mile Mexico-U.S. border—a migration that has resulted in an estimated 7 million unauthorized residents[64]—poses significant challenges to existing immigration policies and threatens the cohesion and stability of American society.[65] To illuminate some of the moral dilemmas involved in contemporary migration politics, I next explore some of the immigration policies and practices of the United States.

CASE 10-3: THE ETHICS OF U.S. IMMIGRATION POLICY

BACKGROUND

Historically, the United States has been a nation of immigrants. The growth and early development of the country are closely bound to immigration. From 1820 to 1860, nearly 5 million immigrants came to the United States. During the next twenty years, another 5 million foreigners arrived, principally from England, Ireland, and Germany. The growth of immigration culminated in the 1900–20 period, when more than 14.5 million persons, principally from southern and eastern Europe, settled in the United States. This mass migration was facilitated in part by the relatively modest regulations governing immigration. However, this open and largely unregulated approach changed abruptly in the aftermath of World War I, when Congress turned inward by first passing temporary immigration restrictions in 1921 (the Temporary Quota Act) and then adopting the Immigration Act of 1924. The 1921 law established strict national immigration controls for the first time, reducing total annual immigration and creating a national origins quota system to maintain the country's ethnic and cultural distribution. The new law set the annual immigration quota at 3 percent of a given nationality residing in the United States in 1910; the 1924 Immigration Act reduced the quota to 2 percent and moved back the target year to 1890. Because these laws sought to maintain the ethnic and cultural status quo, they favored the early immigrant peoples of northern and western Europe and discriminated against newcomers, such as Italians, Spaniards, Russians, and especially Asians, Africans, and Latin Americans.

In time, the national quota system was perceived as politically and morally unacceptable. As a result, Congress passed the 1965 Immigration and Nationality Act (INA), replacing nationality with family reunification and employment-based immigration criteria. In addition to giving priority to relatives of citizens or permanent residents and to immigrants who possessed skills needed in the American economy, the law granted preferences to refugees. As expected, the new legislation resulted in major changes in immigration patterns, including a significant rise in the number of non-Europeans. At the same time, illegal immigration began to grow, especially from Mexico and other Central American countries. To reduce the growth of undocumented aliens, Congress passed in 1986 the Immigration Reform and Control Act (IRCA), which required employers to verify the legal status of workers. At the same time, IRCA granted amnesty to all undocumented aliens who could prove that they had been living in the United States prior to January 1, 1982—a development that resulted in some 2.7 million illegal aliens gaining citizenship eligibility.[66]

The basic statutory guidelines for admitting refugees were first established in the Refugee Act of 1980. This legislation is significant because it greatly expanded refugee admissions and established greater order in refugee resettlement. The latter was achieved by requiring annual executive-legislative consultations to establish the maximum number and geographical distribution of refugees. The Refugee Act also authorized the Immigration and Naturalization Service (INS),[67] the federal agency responsible for implementing immigration and refugee policies, to annually grant asylum to a specified number of eligible asylees—that is, refugees who seek permission to remain permanently in the receiving state. In 2002 and 2003, the admissions ceilings for refugees and asylees was about 70,000 and 10,000, respectively. Although refugee admissions averaged about 75,000 during the 1996–2000 period, this number fell dramatically to less than 30,000 in 2002 and 2003, even when the ceiling remained at 70,000. This was undoubtedly due to the effects of the 9/11 terrorist attack, which resulted in much more intensive scrutiny of immigrants and increased regulation governing international travel.

The most recent law governing U.S. immigration policy is the 1990 Immigration Act (IMMACT). This law establishes the priorities regulating annual immigration admissions and defines groups that are to receive special humanitarian consideration, such as Amerasians (children of American fathers and Vietnamese mothers), refugees, and asylees. In 2003, the statutory ceiling for new immigrants (known as legal permanent residents or LPRs) was set at 675,000, of which about 70 percent were allocated for family reunification and 20 percent for desired employment.[68] To foster geographic diversity, the U.S. government annually holds a lottery for aliens from underrepresented nations. The lottery allows 50,000 aliens to become legal residents.

THE ETHICS OF U.S. IMMIGRATION POLICY

During the early 1990s, total annual legal admissions were about 800,000, of which roughly 15 percent were refugees. From an ethical perspective, were such admission ceilings morally appropriate? Is the preferential treatment accorded aliens with close family ties to a U.S. citizen or those with needed job skills morally warranted? Clearly, there are no "right" moral answers to such questions, because they depend on prudential judgments rooted in a variety of competing and conflicting claims, especially between the claims of nationals and those of migrants. Moreover, the admissions policies will involve moral ambiguity because of the inevitable trade-off between the moral claim of compassion and the legitimate responsibility to protect communal rights and interests.

I have argued that the existing international system gives sovereign states the legal and moral right to regulate immigration. It follows that governments are entitled to establish immigration ceilings and to implement preferential treatment that they believe will contribute to the social, political, economic, and cultural development of their nations. Ethical traditions and moral values are essential in developing admissions policies because they provide the normative structure for defining and assessing the means and goals of government action. However, although morality is important in developing a prudent admissions policy, it is not alone sufficient. Indeed, because moral considerations are but one element of a multidimensional process, migration and refugee issues cannot be defined solely in terms of morality.[69]

From a moral perspective, the persons with

the strongest claim to admission in the United States are likely to be refugees. Because such individuals have fled their homeland to avoid persecution, there is a general consensus that such persons are entitled to special protection. However, their need of refuge does not entitle them to admission into the United States (or, for that matter, any other state), because admission in the contemporary international system is normally regarded as a humanitarian act, not a binding moral obligation. This is the underlying principle of the 1980 Refugee Act, which views refugee admissions as "an exceptional *ex gratia* act provided by the United States in furthering foreign and humanitarian policies."[70]

Although the United States follows international law in defining refugees as those persons who have fled their homeland because of "a well-founded fear of persecution," the circumstances justifying refugee status have expanded in light of growing admissions pressures. During the Cold War, the United States granted refugee claims largely on the basis of political oppression, but in the post–Cold War era, other factors, such as religion, ethnicity, and cultural mores, have been accepted as legitimate justifications for persecution. For example, a young Muslim woman successfully claimed refugee status because female circumcision was required of all young women in her homeland.[71] Moreover, because refugee admissions are governed by geographical and preferential criteria, the changing application of refugee status has resulted in different admissions policies that have modified but not necessarily increased refugee admissions.

The difficulty in responding to refugee claims is illustrated by the moral challenge posed by the tens of thousands of Haitians who have sought to enter the United States illegally since the early 1980s. Throughout the 1970s, a growing number of Haitians migrated to the United States, most of them legally. However, in the 1980s, a large number of Haitians sought to flee their homeland not only because of its abject poverty, civil unrest, and political oppression but also because of the desire to find refuge in a developed country. The number of Haitian "boat people" increased dramatically in the early

1980s, in part because of growing leniency toward Haitian asylees (Haitian refugees in the United States) and because of the success of some 125,000 Cubans fleeing their homeland in the 1980 Mariel boatlift.[72] To stem the tide of Haitian illegal immigration, the Reagan administration made an agreement in 1981 with Haiti's dictator, Jean-Claude Duvalier, permitting the U.S. Coast Guard to interdict Haitian vessels, screen refugees at sea and then return them to their homeland.[73]

However, following the 1991 military coup that overthrew the elected government of President Jean-Bertrand Aristide, the number of Haitian refugees increased once again, especially after the international community's economic sanctions began to inflict significant hardship on the citizens of Haiti, especially its poor. Indeed, the number of Haitians being interdicted was so high by late 1991 that the United States established a temporary processing center in Guantánamo, Cuba, that was filled to capacity by mid-1992. Because of the overwhelming flow of refugees, President George Bush issued an executive order authorizing the U.S. Coast Guard to halt all Haitian boat people and return them, as well as those held in Guantánamo Bay, to Haiti.[74] Although Bill Clinton criticized the Bush administration's policy of repatriating Haitian refugees, he followed a similar policy after he assumed office, and when the flow of Haitian boat people increased again in 1994, the United States forced the removal of the military government and the reinstatement of President Aristide. This development contributed greatly to the reduction in Haitian illegal immigration.

The moral assessment of U.S. immigration policy will depend in great measure on what ethical traditions and methodologies are utilized. For example, since cosmopolitanism regards state boundaries as morally insignificant, cosmopolitan thinkers are likely to conclude that U.S. immigration statutes are of dubious moral validity because they subordinate refugee claims to the national interest. On the other hand, nationalists (amoral realists) will similarly disapprove of American immigration policies, but for opposite reasons, namely, because citizens' claims are unnecessarily subordinated to those

of immigrants and refugees. Only principled realists, that is, those who seek to reconcile national claims with global needs, power with
morality, are likely to endorse the American approach to immigration because it seeks to protect the legitimate interests of domestic society
while also providing humanitarian care.

However, because principled realists hold a
wide variety of conceptions of the nature, role,
and priority of political morality, their ethical
perspectives on American immigration policy differ as well. For example, some principled realists, such as Walzer, have justified the American
communal approach by claiming that states are
entitled to regulate migrant and refugee admissions and that no person, even a refugee, is
morally entitled to admission in a foreign state.
Walzer suggests that although political communities, following the principle of "mutual aid,"
should provide humanitarian aid as the need
arises and as resources permit, refugees have no
right to expect admission.[75] Other principled realists, such as Weiner, have sought to defend
regulatory immigration policies while de-empha-
sizing morality. Although Weiner recognizes that
migration and refugee issues involve both moral
and political considerations, he emphasizes the
prudential nature of public policies, arguing that
immigration policies are "not a matter of general
moral principles but of politically defined national interests and values, that is, in the broad-
est sense, national sovereignty."[76]

MORAL REFLECTIONS

This brief examination of U.S. immigration policy
raises a number of critical moral issues about
migration politics.

- What are the nature and scope of a
  state's moral obligations toward migrants
  and especially refugees? Do the moral obligations toward foreigners depend on an
  individual's country's social and economic
  resources?
- Is U.S. immigration policy consistent with
  international morality? In light of the U.S.
  admission of about 800,000 migrants and
  refugees annually, does U.S. policy ade-
  quately protect the communal solidarity
  of the American nation while also ade-
  quately caring for the needs of immigrants?
- Is the U.S. policy of granting preferential
  treatment to families and, to a lesser degree, to workers with particular job skills
  morally justified?
- What policy should the United States pursue toward illegal aliens? Should such
  aliens be deported? If not, how should
  the U.S. government seek to incorporate
  them into American society or encourage
  them to return voluntarily to their homeland? What policies should be adopted to
  reduce illegal immigration?

SUMMARY

The quest for international justice is elusive not only because governments fail to for-
mulate and implement policies that advance the common good but also because analysts and public officials hold different and frequently conflicting conceptions of
global justice. Because of competing conceptions of justice as well as alternative views
of international society, public officials must frequently choose between the shared interests of global society and the national interests of states, the common good for the
world and immediate interests of nations. As the case studies on climate change, foreign aid, and international migration suggest, the claims of sovereignty are frequently
in conflict with the interests of foreign states and the legitimate transnational claims
of people. Indeed, the three cases show that an ethical foreign policy will necessitate
a balancing of present and future needs, national and transnational obligations.

Conclusion: Ethics Matters

> Politics will, to the end of history, be an arena where conscience and power meet, where the ethical and coercive factors of human life will interpenetrate and work out their tentative and uneasy compromises.[1]
> —REINHOLD NIEBUHR

> There is no single operational international code of behavior. There are competing codes, rival philosophical traditions, clashing conceptions of morality. . . . It is true, as some point out, that all statesmen use the same moral language. . . . Unfortunately, from the point of view of moral harmony, this is meaningless. A community of vocabulary is not the same thing as a community of values.[2]
> —STANLEY HOFFMANN

ETHICS MATTERS. Although most international relations are carried out by complex entities called states, these political communities bear moral responsibilities domestically and internationally. Domestically, states are just and legitimate to the extent that they fulfill widely accepted international moral obligations, such as the protection of human rights and the promotion of the social and economic well-being of persons. Internationally, states are morally legitimate to the extent that they fulfill their legal and ethical responsibilities as members of global society. These duties include honoring the sovereignty and territorial integrity of other states, the pursuit of peaceful foreign relations, the promotion of international stability and global justice, and the protection of the global environment.

The realist tradition has commonly regarded international relations as an arena dominated by the quest for security and by the instruments of power and force. Although security is a core national interest, survival is not the only goal of states. Indeed, most global politics involves the pursuit of many different individual and collective interests through a variety of means other than power. Because the conceptualization of national interests and the development and implementation of policies are based on moral values and ethical judgments, political decision making is of necessity a moral enterprise—a truth that is regularly confirmed by contemporary international events. For example, after India and Pakistan carried out nuclear tests in mid-1998, thereby confirming their status as nuclear powers, the U.S. government was faced with the challenge of responding to this dangerous development. Political calculations were involved in determining how the U.S. government should confront

India and Pakistan in their violation of the nonproliferation regime. However, moral reasoning was also involved as decision-makers pondered the short- and long-term implications of these developments. The U.S. government's decisions to provide famine relief to North Korea in 1997 and 1998 and to continue comprehensive economic sanctions against Iraq in the aftermath of the Persian Gulf War were similarly rooted in moral judgments. Clearly, the claim of moral skeptics that power and necessity alone dictate international politics is unpersuasive.

As Reinhold Niebuhr's statement at the beginning of this chapter suggests, political decision making is a domain in which morality and power coalesce. This study has sought to defend the Niebuhrian claim by exploring the nature and role of moral values in international relations. The aim has not been to provide "moral" solutions to major international issues. Rather, the goal has been to define concepts, strategies, and ethical traditions that facilitate moral reflection about international relations and to illustrate the role of political morality in global politics with case studies in five major problem areas: human rights, force, intervention, economic sanctions, and global issues.

As noted throughout this study, moral values are essential in developing a sound foreign policy and creating norms and structures that are conducive to a more peaceful and just global society. As ancient philosophers long ago observed, the good life (*summum bonum*) is based on individual and communal justice. A major aim of international ethics is to foster political justice within and among states by illuminating relevant moral norms and structuring moral reasoning. This task is especially daunting because global society is comprised of many states, each with its own cultural norms and conceptions of morality. However, the existence of cultural pluralism does not invalidate either the quest for international justice or the legitimacy of political morality. Rather, the reality of competing cultures and moral traditions provides an environment for encouraging a deeper, more reflective political morality and a more self-critical application of such morality to international affairs.

One of the reasons for scholars' and decision makers' limited concern with international ethics is the belief that politics and moral reasoning are two distinct realms that should not be integrated: politics is a domain of power and community-wide decision making, whereas ethics, as a branch of philosophy, is a domain of speculative reasoning. It is commonly assumed that whereas the task of the moral philosopher is to explore the nature of morality and the basis of moral obligation, the task of the statesman is to foster global order, facilitate transnational cooperation, and promote peaceful conflict resolution. These two tasks, it is sometimes argued, should not be combined if analysis and decision making are to remain logical and internally consistent. However, applied ethics, by definition, seeks to develop moral reasoning in specific areas of public and private life. Thus, international ethics is concerned with the interrelationship of moral values and foreign policy, ethics and international politics.

Of course, not all issues, claims, and arguments in international relations are concerned with ethics. As noted in chapter 1, ethics involves the identification, critique, and application of moral values to human life. International ethics is thus concerned solely with the normative realm, that is, with choices and actions involving right and wrong, good and evil. Nonmoral concerns—such as historical facts about territorial boundary claims or the international law of the sea or empirical facts about the balance of trade, weapons development programs, or environmental protection rules—are not a central focus of international ethics because descriptive issues do not involve normative judgments. Thus, in bringing moral reasoning to bear on international affairs, it is important to distinguish between the empirical and normative realms and then to identify and apply political morality to particular foreign policy issues or global concerns.

The challenge of differentiating between the empirical and normative realms is illustrated by the phenomenon of global warming, a development brought about partly by human-made greenhouse gases that trap solar heat. Knowledge about the nature, causes, and potential effects of global warming is based on science and thus is not subject to moral judgment. By contrast, defining the nature and extent of states' responsibilities for global warming is a normative issue because the individual and collective behaviors of states are partly responsible for the earth's climate. In view of the effects of greenhouse emissions on the earth's temperature, continued industrialization is likely to encourage further climate change. Thus, the potential adverse effects of increased global warming pose significant moral issues about states' individual and collective responsibility for past greenhouse emissions and for curbing future pollution.

In fostering moral reasoning and ethical decision making, statesmen and moralists employ a variety of approaches that rely on different methodologies, strategies, and ethical traditions. In classifying moral decision making, it is helpful to distinguish between those approaches that apply political morality deductively and those that do so inductively. The first approach is essentially a "top-down" methodology, bringing first principles to bear on specific issues and problems. Fundamentally, it is based on a rule-based strategy and is characterized by a highly structured decision-making process, relying heavily on moral theories. This approach is deductive because it begins with core norms and then applies them to particular issues and problems.

The application of the just-war tradition to issues of war and peace illustrates this approach. As one of the most sophisticated and comprehensive moral theories in international relations, the just-war tradition defines norms by which to assess when and how states may employ force in pursuing political justice. As a moral theory of decision making, the just war tradition provides an understanding of statecraft in which the use of force in the service of justice is "both permitted and restrained."[3] Because the just-war doctrine is based on the quest for interstate justice, the doctrine's concepts and propositions are useful in assessing not only issues of war and peace but also other international relations concerns, such as economic sanctions and humanitarian intervention.[4]

The second approach to ethical decision making is inductive and informal, relying on a variety of concepts and strategies. It is a "bottom-up" methodology that applies morality flexibly to the goals, means, and results of decisions, relying mainly on the ends-based and tridimensional strategies described in chapter 2. Because this approach is eclectic, it is less structured than the deductive application of moral principles. Moreover, unlike the deductive method, this approach does not seek to apply rules and norms directly to issues but instead relies on prudence, allowing decision-makers to define and select actions in light of potential alternatives. According to Robert Kagan, this inductive, prudential approach to decision making is politically and morally superior to an approach based on a priori guidelines because it permits flexibility in addressing the dynamic, ever-changing events of global society.

Both the deductive and the inductive decision-making models are ideal types, representing extremes along a continuum. Because most moral reasoning and decision making in international affairs involve elements from both models, most international ethical analysis will be found in the middle of the continuum. In implementing eclectic decision making rooted in deductive and inductive approaches, it is desirable to adhere to procedural rules that ensure moral accountability. As noted in chapter 2, a flexible, inductive approach can quickly lead to consequentialism if the integrity of decision making is not protected.

Regardless of which decision-making approaches and ethical traditions are applied to international affairs, it is clear that virtually all important foreign policy issues and global concerns involve moral values. Although politically salient issues such as disarmament, Third World poverty, gross human rights abuses, air and water pollution, and war clearly involve political morality, even technical problems and politically neutral issues might involve moral judgments. Indeed, because political life is based on human choices, few national and international concerns can bypass normative judgments. Moreover, in bringing political morality to bear on public policies, decision makers must judge moral action not only in terms of outcomes, as is commonly the case, but also in terms of the intended goals and methods used. Thus, developing a moral foreign policy is challenging precisely because few issues are likely to comply completely with all the demands of the tridimensional model of political ethics sketched in chapter 2.

Given the complexity of most global issues, ethical reasoning in international affairs seldom results in simple moral verdicts. Indeed, the explicit integration of political morality with the development and implementation of foreign policies rarely results in consensus among public officials and citizens. However, this lack of agreement does not imply (as some cynics have suggested) that moral standards do not exist in global politics, that moral reflection is unnecessary in foreign affairs, or that ethical decision making is a wholly subjective, relativistic enterprise. To be sure, the absence of agreement in international ethics is sometimes due to the underdeveloped nature of global morality. However, the lack of consensus in international ethics is often based on conflicts and disagreements over facts and interests, not moral values. As a result, what appears to be a dispute over political ethics might be, in reality, a conflict over different interpretations of facts or different assessments of political strategies.

For example, the mid-1980s global debate over the moral appropriateness of economic sanctions against South Africa was rooted mainly in different views of the political effectiveness of such statecraft, not in different perspectives on apartheid. Some apartheid critics favored sanctions in the belief that they would hasten democratic reform in South Africa; others opposed sanctions because they believed that isolating South Africa would only delay political change. Similarly, the failure of the United States and other major Western powers to respond to ethnic cleansing in the

Bosnian war was partly due to strategic calculations about the costs, feasibility, and likely consequences of military intervention and partly due to a lack of moral courage to act on behalf of the common good. However, the international community's inaction toward the Bosnian genocide was also influenced by the widely disparate interpretations about the nature and causes of the war and the nature, sources, and scope of ethnic violence. Some viewed ethnic cleansing mainly as a Serb strategy to destroy the Muslim people and their culture; others viewed ethnic violence as part of a war among Croats, Muslims, and Serbs over whether and how to construct a multiethnic Bosnian state.[5] Although most Western observers viewed Serbs as the major perpetrators of Bosnian violence, by 1995 it was evident that Croats and Muslims had also carried out significant ethnic killing. Thus, the reticence and ineffectiveness of the United Nations in halting Bosnian violence was based in part on the perceived complexity and ambiguity of the conflict itself.

Although lack of knowledge might inhibit people from confronting gross evil in global society, the main obstacle to a vigorous application of international political ethics is behavioral, not intellectual. It is not the absence of empirical and moral knowledge that contributes to injustice and instability in global society; rather, leaders themselves fail to fulfill perceived moral obligations. One scholar has observed that in moral life "ignorance isn't all that common; dishonesty is far more so."[6] Thus, in developing a more humane and just global society, the great challenge is to develop both moral knowledge and personal character that leads to the fulfillment of foundational moral obligations. Applying international ethics will require knowledge of relevant concepts, strategies, and theories of international political morality. However, it will also involve the cultivation of moral character and human virtue that are essential in the moral life. If international ethics is to contribute to a more humane and just world order, citizens and leaders must possess the wisdom to define international justice and the courage to fulfill its moral obligations.

Notes

INTRODUCTION

1. George F. Kennan, "Morality and Foreign Policy," *Foreign Affairs* 64 (Winter 1985/ 1986): 206.

2. Arnold Wolfers, *Discord and Collaboration: Essays on International Politics* (Baltimore: Johns Hopkins University Press, 1962), 58.

3. The Dayton Peace Accord was a U.S.-brokered agreement among Muslim, Serb, and Croat leaders that brought an end to the fighting in Bosnia. The agreement, signed in November 1995, calls for a federal Bosnian state comprised of two government entities, one Serb and the other Muslim-Croat. To maintain order during a transitional phase, a 65,000-member NATO military force, led by the United States, was introduced to keep the belligerents apart and to ensure compliance with the accord's electoral and political provisions.

4. Although states are entitled under the norms of the international community to develop military capabilities to ensure their national security, the nonproliferation regime prohibits nonnuclear states from developing or acquiring nuclear arms.

5. Passengers on the fourth jet struggled with the hijackers, causing the plane to crash in rural Pennsylvania. Some commentators have speculated that had passengers not acted against the terrorists, the fourth plane would have been used as an incendiary bomb against another major governmental institution in Washington, D.C.

CHAPTER 1: MORALITY AND FOREIGN POLICY

1. Arnold Wolfers, *Discord and Collaboration: Essays on International Politics* (Baltimore, Md.: Johns Hopkins University Press, 1962), 58.

2. James Q. Wilson, "What Is Moral and How Do We Know It?" *Commentary* (June 1993): 43.

3. Sir Harold Nicolson, *Diplomacy*, 3d ed. (New York: Oxford University Press, 1973), 147.

4. Dean Acheson, "Ethics in International Relations Today: Our Standard of Conduct," *Vital Speeches of the Day* 31 (February 1, 1965): 227.

5. Thomas Donaldson, "Kant's Global Rationalism," in *Traditions of International Ethics*, ed. Terry Nardin and David R. Mapel (Cambridge: Cambridge University Press, 1992), 137.

6. R. M. Hare, *Freedom and Reason* (Oxford: Oxford University Press, 1963), 15.

7. John Rawls, *A Theory of Justice* (Cambridge, Mass.: Harvard University Press, 1971). For a further elaboration of Rawls's conceptualization of morality, see "The Nature and Bases of Political Morality" in this chapter.

8. Lord Moulton of Bank, "Law and Manners," quoted in Rushworth M. Kidder, *How Good People Make Tough Choices* (New York: Morrow, 1995), 67.

9. For a discussion of the distinction between moral and nonmoral decision-making realms, see William Frankena, *Ethics*, 2d ed. (Englewood Cliffs, N.J.: Prentice Hall, 1973).

10. Lea Brilmayer, *American Hegemony: Political Morality in a One-Superpower World* (New Haven, Conn.: Yale University Press, 1994), 25.

11. It is interesting to note that a major aim of normative political theory has been to define the nature, scope, methods, duties, and constraints involved in just or legitimate political rule. Political thinkers have given many different justifications for political hierarchies, including knowledge, power, consent, social class, and religious fidelity.

12. Michael Walzer, *Just and Unjust Wars: A Moral Argument with Historical Illustrations* (New York: Basic Books, 1977).

13. Charles Beitz, *Political Theory and International Relations* (Princeton, N.J.: Princeton University Press, 1979).

14. George Kennan, *Realities of American Foreign Policy* (New York: Norton, 1966), 48.

15. John Rawls, "The Law of Peoples," in *On Human Rights: The Oxford Amnesty Lectures, 1993*, ed. Stephen Shute and Susan Hurley (New York: Basic Books, 1993), 41–82. For a penetrating critique of Rawls's argument, see Stanley Hoffmann, "Dreams of a Just World," *New York Review of Books*, November 2, 1995, 52–56.

16. John Rawls, "The Law of Peoples," 55.

17. See, for example, David Gauthier, *Morals by Agreement* (Oxford: Oxford University Press, 1986).

18. Terry Nardin, "Ethical Traditions in International Affairs" in Nardin and Mapel, eds., *Traditions*, 12–13.

19. Dorothy V. Jones, *Code of Peace: Ethics and Security in the World of Warlord States* (Chicago: University of Chicago Press, 1992).

20. Michael Walzer, *Thick and Thin: Moral Argument at Home and Abroad* (Notre Dame, Ind.: University of Notre Dame Press, 1994), 1–19.

21. Walzer, *Thick and Thin*, 8.

22. Francis V. Harbour, "Basic Moral Values: A Shared Core," *Ethics and International Affairs* 9 (1995): 155–70.

23. A. J. M. Milne, "Human Rights and the Diversity of Morals: A Philosophical Analysis of Rights and Obligations in the Global System," in *Rights and Obligations in North–South Relations: Ethical Dimensions of Global Problems*, ed. Moorehead Wright (New York: St. Martin's Press, 1986), 21.

24. Walzer, *Just and Unjust Wars*, 19.

25. Thomas Donaldson, *The Ethics of International Business* (New York: Oxford University Press, 1989), 1.

26. John C. Bennett, *Foreign Policy in Christian Perspective* (New York: Scribner's, 1966), 36.

27. David Halloran Lumsdaine, *Moral Vision in International Politics: The Foreign Aid Regime, 1949–1989* (Princeton, N.J.: Princeton University Press, 1993), 283.

28. Lumsdaine, *Moral Vision*, 287.

29. Robert W. McElroy, *Morality and American Foreign Policy* (Princeton, N.J.: Princeton University Press, 1992), 30.

30. William Wilberforce labored for nearly fifteen years in the House of Commons before the slave trade was outlawed in 1807; he then devoted his remaining eighteen years in Parliament to the emancipation of slaves within the British Empire. On July 29, 1833, eight years after Wilberforce retired from Parliament, the House of Commons passed a bill abolishing slavery.

31. Robert Kennedy, *Thirteen Days* (New York: Norton, 1968), 27.

32. Arthur Schlesinger, Jr., "The Necessary Amorality of Foreign Affairs," *Harper's Magazine*, August 1971, 73.

33. Stanley Hoffmann, *Duties Beyond Borders* (Syracuse, N.Y.: Syracuse University Press, 1981), 33.

34. For a description of the nature and effect of Serb conquest of Kosovo, see Noel Malcolm, *Kosovo: A Short History* (New York: HarperPerennial, 1999), 238–63.

35. Warren Zimmerman, "Milosevic's Final Solution," *New York Review of Books* (June 10, 1999), 41.

36. Misha Glenny, *The Fall of Yugoslavia: The Third Balkans War*, 3d rev. ed. (New York: Penguin Books, 1996), 67.

37. Tim Judah, *Kosovo: War and Revenge* (New Haven, Conn.: Yale University Press, 2000), 65.

38. Since Germany was home to more than 200,000 Kosovar refugees, Germany became the de facto home of the Kosovar "phantom" government.

39. The disintegration of Albania occurred in response to the collapse of the nation's economy after citizens discovered that their retirement savings had been squandered in fictitious, pyramid-type (Ponzi) investment schemes.

40. It is estimated that when war erupted in March 1999, there were more than 40,000 Serb military and police personnel in Kosovo.

41. Stanley Hoffmann, "What Is to Be Done?" *New York Review of Books* (May 6, 1999), 17.

42. Besides the United States, this group included Britain, France, Germany, Italy, and Russia.

43. The Rambouillet accord was based in great part on a plan developed by Christopher Hill, the U.S. ambassador to Macedonia. The plan, which was rooted in the Serb-Kosovar negotiations that he had carried out in 1998, called for Kosovo's autonomy but left the issue of sovereignty undefined. See, Malcom, *Kosovo*, "Preface."

44. See Michael Mandelbum, "Leave Kosovo Issue on the Table," *Newsday*, March 9, 1999, 35.

45. Zimmerman, "Milosevic's Final Solution," 41.

46. While the total Serb population remained constant at around 200,000 throughout the Cold War, the percentage of Serbs in Kosovo fell from 27.5 percent in 1948 to 10.9 percent in 1991. Fundamentally, this demographic shift has been achieved because Albanians have had a much higher birth rate than Serbs.

47. Julie A. Mertus, *Kosovo: How Myths and Truths Started a War* (Berkeley: University of California Press, 1999), 11.

48. The Christmas threat, communicated by acting secretary of state Lawrence Eagleberger read in part: "In the event of a conflict over Kosovo carried by Serbian action, the U.S. will be prepared to employ military force against Serbians in Kosovo and in Serbia proper." See Barton Gellman, "How We Went to War," *Washington Post National Weekly Edition* (April 26, 1999), 7. See also Judah, 73.

49. Judah, *Kosovo,* 84.

50. Quoted in Mark Danner, "Kosovo: The Meaning of Victory," *New York Review of Books* (July 15,1999), 53.

51. Michael Ignatieff, "Annals of Diplomacy: Balkan Physics," *The New Yorker* (May 10, 1999), 78.

52. Vaclav Havel, "Kosovo and the End of the Nation-State," *New York Review of Books* (June 10, 1999), 6.

53. Vaclav Havel, "Kosovo and the End of the Nation-State," 6.

54. Henry A. Kissinger, "New World Disorder," *Newsweek* (May 31, 1999), 43.

55. Some have argued that Operation Horseshoe was part of a Serbian long-term strategy of forcefully deporting Albanians from Kosovo in order to make the province a more homogenous ethnic community and thereby prepare it to be incorporated into an ethnically pure community prior to its integration into a Greater Serbia. While Serbia may have planned to carry out this operation irrespective of NATO action, it is clear, nevertheless, that if NATO's air war did not initiate widespread ethnic cleansing it at least greatly accelerated the systematic deportation of hundreds of thousands of Kosovars.

56. Judah, *Kosovo,* 250.

57. Leon Wieseltier, "Force without Force: Saving NATO, Losing Kosovo," *The New Republic* (April 26 and May 3, 1999), 29.

58. Paul W. Kahn, "War and Sacrifice in Kosovo," *Report from the Institute for Philosophy & Public Policy* (Spring/Summer 1999), 4.

59. Kissinger, "New World Disorder," 43.

60. Timothy Garton Ash, "Anarchy & Madness," *New York Review of Books* (February 10, 2000), 50.

61. Havel, "Kosovo and the End of the Nation-State," 6.

CHAPTER 2: STRATEGIES OF ETHICAL DECISION-MAKING

1. Peter Berger, "Moral Judgment and Political Action," *Vital Speeches of the Day* 54 (December 1, 1987): 179.

2. Owen Harries, "First Kosovo. Then Russia. Now China," *New York Times,* May 16, 1999, 17.

3. Stanley Hoffmann, *Duties Beyond Borders: On the Limits and Possibilities of Ethical International Relations* (Syracuse, N.Y.: Syracuse University Press, 1981), 143–44.

4. Jeremy Bentham, "Principles of Morals and Legislation," in *Great Political Thinkers: Plato to the Present,* 4th ed., ed. William Ebenstein (Hinsdale, Ill.: Dryden Press, 1969), 515.

5. Jonathan Schell, *The Fate of the Earth* (New York: Avon Books), 152.

6. Bernard Brodie, "Implications for Military Policy," in *The Absolute Weapon: Atomic Power and World Order,* ed. Bernard Brodie (New York: Harcourt Brace, 1946), 76.

7. Henry Kissinger, *The Necessity for Choice: Prospects of American Foreign Policy* (Garden City, N.Y.: Doubleday, 1962), 12.

8. George F. Kennan, *The Nuclear Delusion* (New York: Pantheon, 1982), 202.

9. Michael Walzer, *Just and Unjust Wars: A Moral Argument with Historical Illustrations* (New York: Basic Books, 1977), 282.

10. Such conditions can involve norms for going to war (e.g., pursuit of a just cause, limited wartime goals, and exhaustion of alternatives before resorting to war) and norms for conducting the war (e.g., the use of proportional violence and the protection of civilians).

11. Michael Mandelbaum, *The Nuclear Revolution* (Cambridge: Cambridge University Press, 1981), 4.

12. National Conference of Catholic Bishops, *The Challenge of Peace: God's Peace and Our Response* (Washington, D.C.: United States Catholic Conference, 1983), 41–42.

13. The concept of firebreak, used by firefighters to denote land that is cleared to prevent the escalation of forest fires, refers to the physical and psychological area of demarcation between conventional and nuclear arms.

14. During the 1970s and 1980s, U.S. military strategists debated the relative merits of limited, nuclear warfighting threats versus massive assured destruction threats. The first strategy, known as counterforce, or nuclear utilization theory (NUT), emphasized the actions that would

be taken in the event of a failure in deterrence; the other strategy, known as countervalue, or MADvocy, emphasized the prevention of nuclear conflict altogether by emphasizing the unacceptability of nuclear conflict and by opposing nuclear warfighting options that made retaliation more credible.

15. John Mearsheimer, "Why We Will Soon Miss the Cold War," *The Atlantic Monthly*, August 1990, 37.

16. Thomas Schelling, "What Went Wrong with Arms Control," *Foreign Affairs* 64 (Winter 1985/1986): 233.

17. Walzer, *Just and Unjust Wars*, 382.

18. National Conference of Catholic Bishops, *The Challenge of Peace*, 54–55.

19. John Lewis Gaddis, *The United States and the End of the Cold War* (New York: Oxford University Press, 1992), chap. 10.

20. Schelling, "What Went Wrong with Arms Control," 233.

21. See, for example, John Mueller, "The Essential Irrelevance of Nuclear Weapons: Stability in the Postwar World," *International Security* 13 (Fall 1988): 55–79, and John A. Vasquez, "The Deterrence Myth: Nuclear Weapons and the Prevention of Nuclear War," in *The Long Postwar Peace: Contending Explanations and Projections*, ed. Charles W. Kegley, Jr. (New York: HarperCollins, 1991), 205–23.

22. Thomas Donaldson, "Kant's Global Rationalism," in *Traditions of International Ethics*, ed. Terry Nardin and David R. Mapel (Cambridge: Cambridge University Press, 1992), 137–38.

23. David Halloran Lumsdaine, *Moral Vision in International Politics: The Foreign Aid Regime, 1949–1989* (New Haven, Conn.: Yale University Press, 1993), 283.

24. Frederick Lewis Schuman, *American Policy toward Russia since 1917* (New York: International Publishers, 1928), 277.

25. Thomas A. Bailey, *America Faces Russia: Russian–American Relations from Early Times to Our Day* (Ithaca, N.Y.: Cornell University Press, 1950), 253.

26. For an analysis of Herbert Hoover's role in the Russian famine relief, see Benjamin M. Weissman, *Herbert Hoover and Famine Relief to Soviet Russia: 1921–1923* (Stanford, Calif.: Hoover Institution Press, 1974).

27. Schuman, *American Policy toward Russia*, 204.

28. Weissman, *Herbert Hoover and Famine Relief*, 199.

29. Robert W. McElroy, *Morality and American Foreign Policy* (Princeton, N.J.: Princeton University Press, 1992), 86.

30. George F. Kennan, *Russia and the West under Lenin and Stalin* (Boston, Mass.: Little, Brown, 1960), 180.

31. Hoffmann, *Duties beyond Borders*, 190–91.

32. Alberto R. Coll, "Normative Prudence as a Tradition of Statecraft," *Ethics & International Affairs* 5 (1991): 33.

33. Joseph S. Nye, Jr., *Nuclear Ethics* (New York: Free Press, 1986), 22.

34. Ronald Reagan, "Launching the SDI," in *Promise or Peril: The Strategic Defense Initiative*, ed. Zbigniew Brzezinski (Washington, D.C.: Ethics and Public Policy Center, 1986), 49.

35. William E. Burrows, "Ballistic Missile Defense: The Illusion of Security," *Foreign Affairs* 62 (Spring 1984): 844.

36. McGeorge Bundy, George F. Kennan, Robert S. McNamara, and Gerard Smith, "The President's Choice: Star Wars or Arms Control," *Foreign Affairs* 63 (Winter 1984/1985): 265.

37. Leon Wieseltier, "The Ungrand Compromise," *The New Republic*, November 16, 1986, 31.

CHAPTER 3: THE ROLE OF ETHICAL TRADITIONS

1. Charles R. Beitz, "The Reagan Doctrine in Nicaragua" in *Problems of International Justice,* ed. Steven Luper-Foy (Boulder, Colo.: Westview Press, 1988), 194.

2. Joseph S. Nye, Jr., "Redefining the National Interest," *Foreign Affairs* (July/August 1999), 24.

3. Peter Berger, "Moral Judgment and Political Action," *Vital Speeches of the Day* 56 (December 1, 1987): 120.

4. Gordon A. Craig and Alexander L. George, *Force and Statecraft: Diplomatic Problems of Our Time,* 2d ed. (New York: Oxford University Press, 1990), 275–88.

5. Terry Nardin, "Ethical Traditions in International Affairs," in *Traditions of International Ethics,* ed. Terry Nardin and David R. Mapel (Cambridge: Cambridge University Press, 1992), 6.

6. Nardin, "Ethical Traditions," 6.

7. Nardin, "Ethical Traditions," 6. Interestingly, the tradition of prudence, rooted in the political thought of Aristotle and Aquinas and developed subsequently by Edmund Burke and others, is omitted in this study.

8. David A. Welch, "Can We Think Systematically about Ethics and Statecraft?" *Ethics & International Affairs* 8 (1994): 26–27.

9. Welch, "Can We Think Systematically about Ethics and Statecraft?" 33.

10. See J. L. Mackie, *Ethics: Inventing Right and Wrong* (New York: Penguin, 1977), 64.

11. Hans J. Morgenthau, *Politics Among Nations: The Struggle for Power and Peace*, 5th ed., rev. (New York: Random House, 1978).

12. Morgenthau, *Politics Among Nations,* 5.

13. Kenneth Waltz, *Theory of International Politics* (Reading, Pa.: Addison-Wesley, 1979), 118.

14. Steven Forde, "Classical Realism," in Nardin and Mapel, eds., *Traditions of International Ethics,* 63.

15. Jack Donnelly, "Twentieth-Century Realism," in Nardin and Mapel, eds., *Traditions of International Ethics,* 93.

16. George F. Kennan, "Morality and Foreign Policy," *Foreign Affairs* 64 (Winter 1985/1986): 206.

17. Morgenthau, *Politics Among Nations,* 12.

18. Thucydides, *History of the Peloponnesian War*, trans. Rex Warner (Harmondsworth: Penguin, 1972), 23.

19. Donald Kagan, *On the Origins of War* (New York: Doubleday, 1995), 57, 69.

20. Robert Gilpin, *War and Change in World Politics* (Cambridge: Cambridge University Press, 1981), 227–28.

21. Thucydides, *History of the Peloponnesian War,* 402.

22. For an alternative assessment of idealism, see Michael W. Doyle, *Ways of War and Peace: Realism, Liberalism, and Socialism* (New York: Norton, 1997), pt. 2. Doyle differentiates among three types of liberalism in international relations thought: first, institutionalists, such as Locke and Bentham, who emphasize the role of human nature and the necessity of institutions to constrain human passions; second, commercial pacifists, such as Adam Smith and Joseph Schumpeter, who believe that trade is conducive to peace; and third, internationalists, such as Kant and Hume, who emphasize the pacific nature of international relations among constitutional regimes.

23. Doyle, *Ways of War and Peace,* 230–31.

24. For a discussion of Kant's system, see Doyle, *Ways of Peace and War,* 252–58.

25. Joseph M. Grieco, "Anarchy and the Limits of Cooperation: A Realist Critique of the Newest Liberal Institutionalism," in *Controversies in International Relations Theory: Realism and the Neoliberal Challenge,* ed. Charles W. Kegley, Jr. (New York: St. Martin's Press, 1995), 153–54.

26. John J. Mearsheimer, "The False Promise of International Institutions," *International Security* 19 (Winter 1994/95): 15.

27. For a discussion of political idealism in international affairs, see Michael Joseph Smith, "Liberalism and International Reform," in Nardin and Mapel, eds., *Traditions of International Ethics,* 201–24.

28. Nardin and Mapel, eds., *Traditions of International Ethics,* 203.

29. E. H. Carr, *The Twenty Years' Crisis, 1919–1939: An Introduction to the Study of International Relations* (New York: Harper Torchbooks, 1964), 41–60.

30. Zbigniew Brzezinski, *Power and Principle: Memoirs of the National Security Adviser, 1977–1981* (New York: Farrar, Straus & Giroux), 49.

31. R. J. Vincent, "The Response of Europe and the Third World to United States Human Rights Diplomacy," in *The Diplomacy of Human Rights,* ed. David D. Newsom (Lanham, Md.: University Press of America, 1986), 36.

32. For a description and assessment of congressional human rights initiatives throughout the 1970s, see John P. Salzberg, "A View from the Hill: U.S. Legislation and Human Rights," in Newsom, ed., *The Diplomacy of Human Rights,* 13–20.

33. Jimmy Carter, "Power for Humane Purposes," in *Morality and Foreign Policy: A Symposium on President Carter's Stance,* ed. Ernest Lefever (Washington, D.C.: Ethics and Public Policy Center, 1977), 4–5.

34. Hendrik Hertzberg, quoted in Joshua Muravchik, *The Uncertain Crusade: Jimmy Carter and the Dilemmas of Human Rights Policy* (New York: Hamilton Press, 1986), 1.

35. The increased importance of the report is partly evident by its expanded breadth and depth, growing from about 137 pages in 1977 to more than 1,100 pages in 1981.

36. Quoted in Muravchik, *The Uncertain Crusade,* 24.

37. Irving Kristol, "Morality, Liberalism, and Foreign Policy," in Lefever, ed., *Morality and Foreign Policy,* 69.

38. Brzezinski, *Power and Principle,* 126.

39. Brzezinski, *Power and Principle,* 528.

40. Muravchik, *The Uncertain Crusade,* 53–73.

41. Jeane Kirkpatrick, "Human Rights and American Foreign Policy: A Symposium," *Commentary,* November 1981, 43.

CHAPTER 4: THE ETHICS OF POLITICAL RECONCILIATION

1. Walter Wink, *When the Powers Fall: Reconciliation in the Healing of Nations* (Minneapolis, Minn.: Fortress Press, 1998), 54.

2. Pope John Paul II, "Offer Forgiveness and Receive Peace," Message for World Day of Peace, January 1, 1997.

3. Carlos Santiago Nino, *Radical Evil on Trial* (New Haven, Conn.: Yale University Press, 1996), 187–88.

4. The inquiry into this topic has spawned extensive scholarly literature. The best general introduction to this subject is the three-volume study titled *Transitional Justice: How Emerging Democracies Reckon with Former Regimes,* edited by Neil J. Kritz and published by the United

States Institute of Peace Press. Volume 1 deals with general considerations, volume 2 concerns country studies, and volume 3 covers relevant laws, rulings, and reports.

5. José Zalaquett, "Balancing Ethical Imperatives and Political Constraints: The Dilemma of New Democracies Confronting Past Human Rights Violations," in *Transitional Justice: How Emerging Democracies Reckon with Former Regimes*, ed. Neil J. Kritz, vol. 2, Country Studies (Washington, D.C.: United States Institute of Peace Press, 1995), 496.

6. Timothy Garton Ash, "The Truth about Dictatorship," *New York Review of Books* 45 (February 19, 1998): 35.

7. For a discussion of this point, see Miroslav Volf, "The Social Meaning of Reconciliation," *Interpretation* 54 (April 2000): 158–68.

8. Trudy Govier and Wilhelm Verwoerd, "Trust and the Problem of National Reconciliation," (unpublished paper).

9. Francis Fukuyama, *Trust: The Social Virtues and the Creation of Prosperity* (New York: The Free Press, 1995).

10. Michael Feher, "Terms of Reconciliation," in *Human Rights in Political Transitions: Gettysburg to Bosnia,* ed. Carla Hesse and Robert Post (New York: Zone Books, 1999), 325–28.

11. Abraham Lincoln, "Second Inaugural," in *Lend Me Your Ears: Great Speeches in History,* ed. William Safire, (New York: W. W. Norton, 1992), 441.

12. George Weigel, *Tranquillitas Ordinis: The Present Failure and Future Promise of American Catholic Thought on War and Peace* (New York: Oxford University Press, 1987).

13. Diane F. Orentlicher, "Settling Accounts: The Duty to Prosecute Human Rights Violations of a Prior Regime," *Yale Law Journal* 100 (1991): 2542–44.

14. "Argentina: Presidential Pardons" in *Transitional Justice: How Emerging Democracies Reckon with Former Regimes*, ed. Neil J. Kritz, vol. 3, Laws, Rulings, and Reports (Washington, D.C.: United States Institute of Peace Press, l995), 528–32.

15. According to Elizabeth Kiss, restorative justice is an approach that emphasizes the healing of victims, legal accountability for offenders, preventing future human rights abuses, and promoting reconciliation. Since the first three norms are also given priority in retribution, the distinctive feature of the restorative approach is reconciliation. See Elizabeth Kiss, "Moral Ambition within and beyond Political Constraints: Reflections on Restorative Justice," in *Truth v. Justice: The Morality of Truth Commissions,* ed. Robert I. Rotberg and Dennis Thompson (Princeton, N.J.: Princeton University Press, 2000), 79.

16. Robert Meister, "Forgiving and Forgetting: Lincoln and the Politics of National Recovery," in *Human Rights in Political Transitions,* ed. Hesse and Post. For a further discussion of the Lincolnian strategy, please see chapter 9.

17. Mahmood Mamdani, *When Victims Become Killers: Colonialism, Nativism, and the Genocide in Rwanda* (Princeton, N.J.: Princeton University Press, 2001), 272–73.

18. "Argentina: *Nunca Más*—Report of the Argentine Commission on the Disappeared" in *Transitional Justice*, vol. 3, 6.

19. Some of the most important legislation fostering racial segregation in the early twentieth century included a 1913 law defining where blacks and whites could live and work, the 1913 Pass Laws that regulated the movement of blacks, and the 1923 Native (Urban Areas) Act that extended the principle of racial segregation to urban areas. For a comprehensive overview of all major South African statutes enacted from 1910 through the early 1980s that institutionalized racial segregation, see Truth and Reconciliation Commission, *Truth and Reconciliation Commission of South Africa Report*, vol. 1 (London: Macmillan Reference Limited, 1999), 450–66.

20. Some of these included: the Mixed Marriages Act (1949), which made interracial mar-

riage illegal; the Population Registration Act (1950), which required that all persons be classified by race; the Group Areas Act (1950), which specified where members of each race could
live; the Reservation of Separate Amenities Act (1953), which required that public facilities be
racially segregated; and the Black Authorities Act (1951), which, together with subsequent legislation, established black homelands. For a discussion of the apartheid ideology and its practices, see Leonard Thompson, *A History of South Africa*, 3d ed. (New Haven, Conn.: Yale University Press, 2000).

21. One of the most important of these was the creation of a tricameral parliament, giving
Indians and Coloureds, but not Africans, their own legislature along with some participation in
executive power-sharing.

22. Piet Meiring, *Chronicle of the Truth Commission: A Journey through the Past and Present—Into the Future of South Africa* (Carpe Diem: Vanderbijlpark, S.A., 1999), 146.

23. Alex Boraine, "Truth and Reconciliation in South Africa: The Third Way," in *Truth v.
Justice: The Morality of Truth Commissions,* ed. Robert Rotberg and Dennis Thompson (Princeton: Princeton University Press, 2000), 143.

24. According to the TRC Report, *ubuntu* is generally translated as "humaneness," and expresses itself in the phrase "people are people through other people."

25. Desmond Tutu, *No Future without Forgiveness* (New York: Doubleday, 1999), 19.

26. Tutu, *No Future without Forgiveness*, 23.

27. As conceptualized by the TRC, the approach of restorative justice involves a number of
distinctive features. First, it calls for a redefinition of crime that focuses on personal injuries
and human suffering rather than on impersonal rule breaking. Second, it emphasizes reparations for victims in order to facilitate their restoration into the fabric of communal life, while
also emphasizing the rehabilitation of perpetrators based on full accountability for past offenses. Third, it encourages direct conflict resolution among victims, offenders, and the community. And finally, it calls for "a spirit of understanding" between victims and offenders, without mitigating or undermining offenders' accountability for wrongdoing. Such accountability is
not only legal and political but also moral. TRC, *Truth and Reconciliation Commission of South
Africa Report*, vol. 1 (London: Macmillan Reference Limited, 1999), 126–31.

28. The commission's specific tasks were to 1) uncover the truth about gross human rights
violations perpetrated from March 1, 1960, to May 10, 1994; 2) establish the fate or where-
abouts of victims; 3) assist in restoring the dignity of victims by giving them an opportunity to
testify about their suffering; 4) recommend a set of measures of reparation that would help restore the human dignity of victims; 5) grant amnesty to those who confessed their crimes; 6)
prepare and disseminate a comprehensive report on the commissions' findings; and 7) make
recommendations that contribute to the establishment of a humane society and prevent the future violations of human rights. TRC, *Commission Report*, vol. 1, 55.

29. The members represented a broad cross-section of South African society, and included
seven women, ten men, seven Africans, two Indians, two Coloureds, six whites, six lawyers, and
four church ministers. Most had been strongly identified as opponents of the apartheid regime.

30. The full report and supporting documents are available on the Web at www.truth.org.za.

31. According to the TRC process, amnesty depended solely on three conditions: 1) full
confession of crimes; 2) crimes had to be a part of the political struggle over apartheid; and 3)
the crimes must have been carried out during the legally prescribed time frame specified by
parliament (March 1960 to May 1994).

32. More than one-third of these applications were rejected because they failed to fulfill the
objective criteria necessary for eligibility.

33. The TRC officially began its work in December 1995 and concluded most of its operations in July 1998, when three of its four offices (Johannesburg, East London, and Durban)

were closed. After the TRC's final report was published in October 1998, the Cape Town office continued to function with a small staff to support the ongoing amnesty hearings and the drafting of a supplementary report, released in early 2003.

34. Since victims' testimony was not subject to cross-examination, a South African court ruled that the TRC could not arbitrarily identify alleged offenders without first warning them of the charge and allowing sufficient time to contest it in court.

35. John Dugard, "Retrospective Justice: International Law and the South African Model," in *Transitional Justice and the Rule of Law in New Democracies*, ed. A. James McAdams (South Bend, Ind.: University of Notre Dame Press, 1997), 284–86.

36. McAdams, *Transitional Justice and the Rule of Law in New Democracies*, 23.

37. Rajeev Bhargava, "Restoring Decency to Barbaric Societies," in *Truth versus Justice*, ed. Rotberg and Thompson, 60.

38. David A. Crocker, "Retribution and Reconciliation," *Report from the Institute for Philosophy & Public Policy* 20 (Winter/Spring 2000): 6.

39. Fareed Zakaria, *The Future of Freedom: Liberal Democracy at Home and Abroad* (New York: W. W. Norton, 2003).

40. D. A. Rustow has observed that the first step in establishing a democratic regime is the development of national unity. He argues that communal solidarity must precede the other three phases of democratization—namely, the acceptance of political conflict, the institutionalization of rules governing political conflict, and the habituation of political struggle. See D. A. Rustow, "How Does a Democracy Come Into Existence?" in *The Practice of Comparative Politics: A Reader*, ed. Paul G. Lewis and David C. Potter (Bristol: The Open University Press, 1973), 120–30.

41. Michael Ignatieff, *The Warrior's Honor: Ethnic War and the Modern Conscience* (New York: Henry Holt & Co., 1997), 168.

42. The name of the revolutionary group means "spear of the nation."

43. Following the just war doctrine, the laws of war comprise two dimensions—the principles of going to war (justice of war) and the rules of war (justice in war). A war may be morally legitimate but prosecuted in a criminal manner. Similarly, an unjust war can be carried out legally and justly by, for example, targeting only military personnel or using only the minimum force to achieve military objectives. Thus, the ANC's military purposes (the destruction of the apartheid regime) may have been just but the resort to terror, indiscriminate bombings, and the killing or torture of informants was contrary to the laws of war.

44. Alex Boraine, *A Country Unmasked* (Oxford: Oxford University Press, 2000), 326.

45. Quoted in Boraine, *A Country Unmasked*, 317.

46. The court justified its ruling based on the postamble of the Interim Constitution, which set forth the argument for the political and moral reconstruction of the nation. The court argued that amnesty for civil and criminal liability was justified by the postamble's claim that amnesty would encourage truth-telling and by the promise of reparations to victims. Additionally, the court found that the amnesty provision was not inconsistent with international law, nor did it violate the country's treaty obligations. For a further discussion of the court's ruling, see Boraine, *A Country Unmasked*, 118–21.

47. Boraine, *A Country Unmasked*, 341.

48. *New York Times*, November 1, 1998.

49. Hannah Arendt, *The Human Condition* (Chicago: University of Chicago Press, 1958), 238–40.

50. Patrick Glynn, "Toward a New Peace: Forgiveness as Politics," *Current* (March/April 1995): 19.

51. For an illuminating study of the potential role of forgiveness in politics, see Donald W.

Shriver, Jr., *An Ethic for Enemies: Forgiveness in Politics* (New York: Oxford University Press, 1995).

52. Elie Wiesel, "Remarks of Elie Wiesel at Ceremony for Jewish Heritage Week," in *Bitburg: In Moral and Political Perspective*, ed. Geoffrey Hartman (Bloomington: Indiana University Press, 1986), 243.

53. Lance Morrow, "Forgiveness to the Injured Doeth Belong," *Time*, May 20, 1985, 90.

54. Wiesel, "Remarks," 242.

55. Wiesel, "Remarks," 243–44.

56. Interview of President Reagan by Representatives of Foreign Radio and Television," in *Bitburg*, ed. Hartman, 250–51.

57. William Safire, "'I Am a Jew . . .'" in *Bitburg*, ed. Hartman, 214.

58. Quoted in Shriver, *An Ethic for Enemies*, 110.

CHAPTER 5: THE ETHICS OF INTERNATIONAL HUMAN RIGHTS

1. R. J. Vincent, "The Idea of Rights in International Ethics" in *Traditions of International Ethics*, ed. Terry Nardin and David R. Mapel (Cambridge: Cambridge University Press, 1992), 267.

2. Richard N. Haass, *The Reluctant Sheriff: The United States after the Cold War* (New York: Council on Foreign Relations), 69.

3. Charles Krauthammer, "Morality and the Reagan Doctrine," *The New Republic*, September 8, 1986, 20.

4. For further discussion of this distinction, see Maurice Cranston, *What Are Human Rights?* (New York: Basic Books, 1962), 8–12.

5. Alan Gewirth, "Common Morality and the Community of Rights," in *Prospects for a Common Morality*, ed. Gene Outka and John P. Reeder, Jr. (Princeton, N.J.: Princeton University Press, 1993), 30–31.

6. Gewirth, "Common Morality and the Community of Rights," 30–31.

7. Rhoda E. Howard and Jack Donnelly, "Human Dignity, Human Rights, and Political Regimes," *American Political Science Review* 80 (September 1986): 802.

8. Howard and Donnelly, "Human Dignity, Human Rights, and Political Regimes," 804.

9. R. J. Vincent, *Human Rights and International Relations* (Cambridge: Cambridge University Press, 1986), 21.

10. For a contrary view, see Arthur Schlesinger, Jr., "Human Rights and the American Tradition," *Foreign Affairs* 57, 3 (1979): 504. Schlesinger argues that because religion had traditionally rejected the notion that people were entitled to earthly happiness, Christianity had little to do with the rise of the idea of human rights.

11. Eugene Kamenka, "The Anatomy of an Idea," in *Human Rights*, ed. Eugene Kamenka and Alice Erh-Soon Tay (London: Edward Arnold, 1978), 5–6. See also Jack Donnelly, *Universal Human Rights in Theory and Practice* (Ithaca, N.Y.: Cornell University Press, 1989), 50.

12. The transcendent moral order applicable to political society has historically been defined as natural law. To simplify my argument, I avoid using this concept altogether, although it is clear that the foundation of classical human rights was the notion of natural law.

13. For an excellent overview of the meaning of the human rights doctrine, see Donnelly, *Universal Human Rights*, 9–27.

14. Vincent, *Human Rights and International Relations*, 7.

15. According to the philosophy of utilitarianism, decisions should seek to maximize "util-

ity" by making choices that provided "the greatest good for the greatest number."

16. Christian Bay, "Self-Respect as a Human Right: Thoughts on the Dialectics of Wants and Needs in the Struggle for Human Community," *Human Rights Quarterly* 4 (February 1982): 53–75.

17. Charles R. Beitz, "Human Rights and Social Justice," in *Human Rights and U. S. Foreign Policy*, ed. Peter G. Brown and Douglas MacLean (Lexington, Mass.: Lexington Books, 1979), 45–63.

18. Henry Shue, *Basic Rights: Subsistence, Affluence, and U.S. Foreign Policy* (Princeton, N.J.: Princeton University Press, 1980), 13–34.

19. A. J. M. Milne, "Human Rights and the Diversity of Morals: A Philosophical Analysis of Rights and Obligations in the Global System," in *Rights and Obligations in North-South Relations*, ed. Moorehead Wright (New York: St. Martin's Press, 1986), 21.

20. Vincent, *Human Rights and International Relations*, 54–55.

21. Donnelly, *Universal Human Rights in Theory and Practice*, 112–14.

22. James Finn, ed., *Freedom in the World: The Annual Survey of Political Rights and Civil Liberties, 1994–1995* (New York: Freedom House, 1995), 505–508.

23. Michael Elliott, "The Caning Debate: Should America Be More like Singapore?" *Newsweek*, April 18, 1994, 22.

24. Kishore Mahbubani, "The United States: 'Go East, Young Man,'" *Washington Quarterly* 17 (Spring 1994): 11.

25. Mahbubani, "The United States," 21.

26. A different but related question concerns capital punishment. Most European countries have outlawed such punishment, while the criminal justice system of the United States provides for its continued use. Is death by lethal injection or electrocution a barbaric practice, as European human rights leaders claim, or is it a legitimate deterrent to violent crime?

27. Jack Donnelly, *International Human Rights* (Boulder, Colo.: Westview Press, 1993), 7.

28. Louis Henkin, *The Age of Rights* (New York: Columbia University Press, 1990), 19.

29. Other important international human rights agreements include the International Convention on the Prevention and Punishment of the Crime of Genocide (1948); the International Convention on the Elimination of All Forms of Racial Discrimination (1965); the Convention against Torture and Other Cruel, Inhuman or Degrading Treatment or Punishment (1984); and the Convention on the Rights of the Children (1989).

30. The right to development became an official part of the UN lexicon in 1986 when the General Assembly adopted the Declaration on the Right to Development. Among other things, the statement proclaims that "the right to development is an inalienable human right by virtue of which every human person and all peoples are entitled to participate in, contribute to, and enjoy economic, social, cultural and political development, in which all human rights and fundamental freedoms can be fully realized."

31. Charles J. Brown, "In the Trenches: The Battle over Rights," *Freedom Review*, September–October 1993, 9.

32. Since the Vienna meeting, several other conferences have reinforced the growing cultural and political pluralism in the international community. The three most important were the International Conference on Population and Development in Cairo (1994), the World Summit on Social Development in Copenhagen (1995), and the Fourth International Conference on Women in Beijing (1995).

33. Vincent, *Human Rights and International Relations*, 142.

34. George F. Kennan, "Ethics and Foreign Policy: An Approach to the Problem," in *Foreign Policy and Morality: Framework for a Moral Audit*, ed. Theodore M. Hesburgh and Louis J. Halle (New York: Council on Religion and International Affairs, 1979), 44.

35. Stanley Hoffmann, "Reaching for the Most Difficult: Human Rights as a Foreign Policy Goal," *Daedalus* 112 (Fall 1983): 33.

36. Hoffman, "Reaching for the Most Difficult," 28.

37. R. J. Rummel, *Death by Government* (New Brunswick, N.J.: Transaction Publishers, 1994), 15.

38. Hoffmann, "Reaching for the Most Difficult," 4.

39. Interestingly, the United States did not formally ratify the Genocide Convention until 1988, some nineteen years after Senator William Proxmire of Wisconsin began to call for senatorial endorsement.

40. For a compelling account of the United States failure to respond to genocide, see Samantha Power, *"A Problem from Hell": America and the Age of Genocide* (New York: Basic Books, 2002).

41. Although it can be argued that the U.S.-led wars against the Taliban in Afghanistan in 2001 and the Baathist regime in Iraq in 2003 were undertaken to end tyrannical governments, the fundamental purpose of both wars was to eliminate the direct and indirect threat of terrorism.

42. Power, *"A Problem from Hell,"* 508.

43. Power, *"A Problem from Hell,"* 504.

44. For a detailed examination of these and other developments prior to the genocide, see Gérard Prunier, *The Rwanda Crisis: History of a Genocide* (New York: Columbia University Press, 1995), esp. 159–92. See also Philip Gourevitch, *We Wish to Inform You That Tomorrow We Will Be Killed with Our Families: Stories from Rwanda* (New York: Farrar Straus and Giroux, 1998) and Linda R. Melvern, *A People Betrayed: The Role of the West in Rwanda's Genocide* (New York: Zed Books, 2000). For an interpretive historical account of the factors that contributed to the origins and evolution of Hutu-Tutsi animosity, see Mahmood Mamdani, *When Victims Become Killers: Colonialism, Nativism, and the Genocide in Rwanda* (Princeton, N.J.: Princeton University Press, 2001).

45. The ineffectiveness of UNAMIR after the genocide began was also due to the fact that the original mission was limited to being an observer force. Even after evidence became available that a major genocide was underway, the UN Security Council refused to increase the size of UNAMIR or to expand its mandate.

46. David Rieff, "The Age of Genocide," *The New Republic*, January 26, 1996, 31.

47. The most complete and dispassionate account of the genocide is Prunier, *The Rwanda Crisis*.

48. Rieff, "The Age of Genocide," 31.

49. In view of this UN initiative, UNAMIR was reduced to a force of less than 500 soldiers.

50. Milton Leitenberg, "Anatomy of a Massacre," *New York Times*, July 31, 1994, sec. 4, 15.

51. Michael Barnett, *Eyewitness to a Genocide: The United Nations and Rwanda* (Ithaca, N.Y.: Cornell University Press, 2002), 155.

52. One of the moral ambiguities about this humanitarian aid was that it gave assistance and protection to Hutu leaders and fighters who had inspired and carried out the genocide.

53. Barnett, *Eyewitness to a Genocide*, 155.

54. *New York Times*, December 4, 2003, 1 and 10.

55. For a discussion of the *gacaca* process, see Samantha Power, "Rwanda: The Two Faces of Justice, *New York Review of Books* (January 16, 2003), 47–50. For a critique of this process see Allison Corey and Sandra F. Joireman, "Retributive Justice: The *Gacaca* Courts In Rwanda," *African Affairs* 103 (2004), 73–89.

56. Power, *"A Problem from Hell,"* 334.

57. Robert Goldwin, "Human Rights and American Policy, Part IV—Arguments and Afterwords," *The Center Magazine*, July–August 1984, 59.

58. For a criticism of the Carter administration's human rights policy, see Joshua Muravchik, *The Uncertain Crusade: Jimmy Carter and the Dilemmas of Human Rights Policy* (New York: Hamilton Press, 1986).

59. William H. Gleysteen, Jr., "Korea: A Special Target of American Concern," in *The Diplomacy of Human Rights,* ed. David D. Newsom (Lanham, Md.: University Press of America, 1986), 99.

60. George F. Kennan, *The Cloud of Danger: Current Realities of American Foreign Policy* (Boston: Little, Brown, 1977), 43.

61. Herbert Butterfield, *History and Human Relations* (London: Collins, 1951), 110.

CHAPTER 6: THE ETHICS OF FORCE

1. Arthur Schlesinger, Jr., "The Necessary Amorality of Foreign Affairs," *Harper's Magazine*, August 1971, 72.

2. Carl von Clausewitz, *On War,* trans. Michael Howard and Peter Paret (Princeton, N.J.: Princeton University Press, 1976), 370.

3. Stanley Hoffmann, *Duties Beyond Borders: On the Limits and Possibilities of Ethical International Politics* (Syracuse, N.Y.: Syracuse University Press, 1981), 81.

4. Quoted in James Turner Johnson, "Threats, Values, and Defense: Does the Defense of Values by Force Remain a Moral Possibility?" in *The Nuclear Dilemma and the Just War Tradition,* ed. William V. O'Brien and John Langan (Lexington, Ky.: Lexington Books, 1986), 36.

5. John Howard Yoder, *The Politics of Jesus* (Grand Rapids, Mich.: Eerdmans, 1972).

6. Cited in Roland H. Bainton, *Christian Attitudes toward War and Peace: A Historical Survey and Critical Re-evaluation* (New York: Abingdon Press, 1960), 153.

7. James Turner Johnson argues that although first-century Christians avoided military service, they did so not out of convictions about the evil of violence but because they held themselves "aloof from the kingdom of Caesar in expectation of the imminent coming of the kingdom of Christ." See James Turner Johnson, *The Quest for Peace: Three Moral Traditions in Western Cultural History* (Princeton, N.J.: Princeton University Press, 1987), 42.

8. Johnson, *The Quest for Peace,* xiii–xv.

9. Johnson, *The Quest for Peace,* 267–75.

10. Thucydides, *The Peloponnesian War,* trans. Rex Warner (New York: Penguin, 1954), 402.

11. Since *Islam* is used to denote "the faithful," *House of Islam* thus means the "house of the faithful" whereas those opposed to Islam are part of the "house of the unfaithful."

12. Bernard Lewis, *The Political Language of Islam* (Chicago: University of Chicago Press, 1988), 73.

13. Bernard Lewis, "The Roots of Muslim Rage," *The Atlantic Monthly,* September 1990, 49.

14. See, for example, John Kelsay, *Islam and War: The Gulf War and Beyond* (Louisville, Ky.: John Knox Press, 1993), chap. 4.

15. Bainton, *Christian Attitudes,* 148.

16. Bainton, *Christian Attitudes,* 45.

17. Will and Ariel Durant, *The Story of Civilization: Part III. The Age of Louis XIV* (New York: Simon and Schuster, 1963), 195.

18. For a comprehensive account of this theory, see Paul Ramsey, *The Just War: Force and*

Political Responsibility (New York: Scribner's, 1968). For a historical account of the origins and development of this theory, see James Turner Johnson, *Ideology, Reason, and the Limitation of War: Religious and Secular Concepts, 1200–1740* (Princeton, N.J.: Princeton University Press, 1975), and James Turner Johnson, *Just War Tradition and the Restraint of War: A Moral and Historical Inquiry* (Princeton, N.J.: Princeton University Press, 1981).

19. James Turner Johnson, "The Concept of Just Cause," *American Purpose* 10 (Spring 1996): 4; see also James Turner Johnson, "The Broken Tradition," *The National Interest,* Fall 1996, 27–30.

20. George Weigel, "Moral Clarity in a Time of War," *First Things* (January 2003): 22. Rowan Williams, the Archbishop of Canterbury, has critiqued some of Weigel's arguments and the author responds with a vigorous defense of his claims. See "War & Statecraft: An Exchange," *First Things* (January 2004): 14–21.

21. William V. O'Brien, *The Conduct of Just and Limited War* (New York: Praeger, 1981).

22. James Turner Johnson, "The Just War Tradition and the American Military," in *Just War and the Gulf War,* ed. James Turner Johnson and George Weigel (Washington, D.C.: Ethics and Public Policy Center, 1991), 22.

23. This evil became especially apparent when Iraq used civilians as protective shields during the air war, dumped large quantities of petroleum into the Persian Gulf, and destroyed nearly a thousand Kuwaiti oil fields.

24. Michael Walzer, "Perplexed," *The New Republic,* January 28, 1991, 14.

25. Michael Walzer, "Justice and Injustice in the Gulf War," in *But Was It Just? Reflections on the Morality of the Persian Gulf War,* ed. David E. DeCosse (New York: Doubleday, 1992), 3.

26. Quoted in George Weigel, "The Churches and War in the Gulf," *First Things* 11 (March 1990): 39.

27. Message from Thirty-Two Church Leaders to President Bush," in *Just War and the Gulf War,* ed. James Turner Johnson and George Weigel (Washington, D.C.: Ethics and Public Policy Center, 1991), 137.

28. Walzer, "Perplexed," 13.

29. See, for example, Walzer, "Justice and Injustice," 12–13.

30. Robert W. Tucker, "Justice and the War," *The National Interest,* Fall 1991, 111–12.

31. Jean Bethke Elshtain, "Just War and American Politics," *The Christian Century,* January 15, 1992, 43.

32. Francis X. Winters, "Justice and the Gulf War," *The National Interest,* Winter 1991/92, 104.

33. Eliot A. Cohen, "A Strange War," *The National Interest* (Thanksgiving 2001), 12.

34. The NSS is available on the web at www.whitehouse.gov/nsc/nss.html For an analysis and assessment of the NSS, see John Lewis Gaddis, "A Grand Strategy," *Foreign Policy* (November/December 2002): 50–57 and Philip Zelikow, "The Transformation of National Security: Five Redefinitions," *The National Interest,* Spring 2003, 17–28.

35. This strategy, known as the Reagan doctrine, called for the vigorous promotion of democratic institutions and practices and the rollback of Soviet communism. See chapter 8 for a discussion of the nature and impact of this doctrine on U.S. foreign policy in the 1980s.

36. In the 2002 NSS, the term "freedom" appears 46 times, while the terms "democracy," "liberty," and "human dignity" appear 13, 11, and 9 times, respectively. See the "National Security Strategy of the United States," September 2002.

37. National Security Strategy of the United States," Section I.

38. National Security Strategy of the United States," Section V.

39. Walzer, *Just and Unjust Wars,* 81.

40. A year after UNSCOM's work came to a halt, the United Nations established a succes-

sor inspection organization known as the UN Monitoring, Verification and Inspection Commission, or UNMOVIC.

41. For an excellent overview of the nature and evolution of economic sanctions on Iraq after the Persian Gulf War, see Erik D. K. Melby, "Iraq," in *Economic Sanctions and American Diplomacy*, ed. Richard N. Haass (New York: Council on Foreign Relations, 1998), 107–28.

42. The enforcement of no-fly zones, which involved some 350,000 sorties during the twelve years that they were in force, cost the U.S. some $20 billion.

43. Michael R. Gordon and David E. Sanger, "Powell Says U.S. Is Weighing Ways to Topple Hussein," *New York Times*, February 13, 2002, A1.

44. *New York Times*, September 13, 2002, A10.

45. Michael J. Glennon, "Why the Security Council Failed," *Foreign Affairs* 82 (May/June 2003): 26–27.

46. Todd S. Purdum, *A Time of Our Choosing: America's War in Iraq* (New York: Times Books, 2003), 65.

47. Purdum, *A Time of Our Choosing*, 91.

48. It was expected that the war would begin several days later, thereby allowing time so that more Special Forces teams could secretly enter Iraq to make preparations for combat. But the CIA received current intelligence indicating that Saddam Hussein would be meeting in a particular building on that same night. On the advice of Secretary of Defense Donald Rumsfeld and CIA director George Tenet, the president authorized a bombing attack on the Baghdad site that evening.

49. Weigel, "Moral Clarity in a Time of War," 25.

50. John J. Mearsheimer and Stephen M. Walt, "An Unnecessary War," *Foreign Policy* (January/February 2003): 59.

51. Of course, the only reason why Iraq had accepted the resumption of UN inspection teams in December 2002 was that the United States, along with Britain and Spain, had begun making preparations for war. It was the growing threat of war that had compelled Saddam Hussein to take seriously Security Council Resolution 1441.

52. Michael Walzer, "The Right Way," *New York Review of Books* (March 13, 2003), 4.

53. "Why War Would Be Justified," *The Economist*, February 22, 2003, 13.

54. Jimmy Carter, "Just War—or a Just War?" *New York Times*, March 9, 2003.

55. Anne-Marie Slaughter, "Good Reasons for Going Around the U.N.," *New York Times*, March 18, 2003, 31.

CHAPTER 7: THE ETHICS OF INTERVENTION

1. Lea Brilmayer, *American Hegemony: Political Morality in a One-Superpower World* (New Haven, Conn.: Yale University Press, 1994), 154.

2. Charles Krauthammer, "Morality and the Reagan Doctrine," *The New Republic*, September 8, 1986, 21.

3. Quoted in Drew Christiansen and Gerard F. Powers, "The Duty to Intervene: Ethics and the Varieties of Humanitarian Intervention," in *Close Calls: Intervention, Terrorism, Missile Defense, and "Just War" Today*, ed. Elliott Abrams (Washington, D.C.: Ethics and Public Policy Center, 1998), 183.

4. Quoted in Kelly Kate Pease and David P. Forsythe, "Human Rights, Humanitarian Intervention, and World Politics," *Human Rights Quarterly* 15 (1993): 292.

5. According to Chapter VII, the Security Council can take whatever political and military actions it designates to respond to "a threat to peace, breach of the peace or act of aggression." In effect, the United Nations can, when the Security Council so decides, intervene against the

wishes of a member state. Such action was undertaken in 1992 when the United Nations authorized U.S. military intervention in Somalia.

6. Michael Mandelbaum, "The Reluctance to Intervene," *Foreign Policy*, no. 95 (Summer 1994): 14.

7. Mandelbaum, "The Reluctance to Intervene," 6.

8. For an informative collection of essays on emerging norms governing international boundaries, see *Emerging Norms of Justified Intervention,* ed. Laura W. Reed and Carl Kaysen (Cambridge, Mass.: Committee on International Security Studies, American Academy of Arts and Sciences, 1993).

9. Michael Walzer calls this approach the "domestic analogy." For a discussion of this argument, see Michael Walzer, *Just and Unjust Wars: A Moral Argument with Historical Illustrations* (New York: Basic Books, 1977), 58.

10. Walzer, *Just and Unjust Wars*, 101.

11. Walzer, *Just and Unjust Wars*, 88.

12. Michael Walzer, "The Moral Standing of States: A Response to Four Critics," *Philosophy & Public Affairs* 9, no. 3 (Spring 1980): 214.

13. Walzer, *Just and Unjust Wars*, 54.

14. Jefferson McMahan, "The Ethics of International Intervention," in *Political Realism and International Morality: Ethics in the Nuclear Age*, ed. Kenneth Kipnis and Diana T. Meyers (Boulder, Colo.: Westview Press, 1987), 82–83.

15. McMahan, "The Ethics of International Intervention," 85.

16. Stanley Hoffmann, *Duties beyond Borders: On the Limits and Possibilities of Ethical International Politics* (Syracuse, N.Y.: Syracuse University Press, 1981), 58.

17. Dorothy Jones, *Code of Peace: Ethics and Security in the World of Warlord States* (Chicago: University of Chicago Press, 1992).

18. Jones, *Code of Peace*, xii, 163–64.

19. Walzer, *Just and Unjust Wars*, 61–63.

20. Walzer, *Just and Unjust Wars*, 90–108. A number of scholars have challenged Walzer's international relations paradigm as being too statist and insufficiently sensitive to the injustices that arise within states. For a critique of Walzer's argument, see Gerald Doppelt, "Walzer's Theory of Morality in International Relations," *Philosophy & Public Affairs* 8, no. 1 (1978): 2–26; Charles R. Beitz, "Bounded Morality: Justice and the State in World Politics," *International Organization* 33 (Summer 1979): 405–24; and David Luban, "Just War and Human Rights," *Philosophy & Public Affairs*, 9, no. 2 (1979): 161–81. For Walzer's response to his critics, see Michael Walzer, "The Moral Standing of States: A Response to Four Critics," *Philosophy & Public Affairs* 9, no. 3 (1980): 209–29.

21. Mandelbaum, "The Reluctance to Intervene," 8.

22. Stanley Hoffmann, "Delusions of World Order," *New York Review of Books,* May 28, 1992, 37–43.

23. Charles Krauthammer, "When to Intervene," *The New Republic*, May 6, 1985, 11.

24. For a discussion of the role and relevance of the just war doctrine to military intervention, see Kenneth R. Himes, "Just War, Pacifism and Humanitarian Intervention," *America*, August 14, 1993, 15, 28–29.

25. International Commission on Intervention and State Sovereignty, *Responsibility to Protect: Report of the International Commission on Intervention and State Sovereignty.* See www.idrc.ca

26. According to the ICISS, the principle of protection demands that: 1) the assessment of humanitarian needs should be undertaken from the perspective of the victim, not the concerns of the intervening state, 2) the primary responsibility for meeting human needs should rest

with each state concerned, and 3) the duty to protect should not only respond and react but also prevent and rebuild. ICISS, *Responsibility to Protect*, 17.

27. ICISS, *Responsibility to Protect*, xi.

28. For a clear articulation of these three justifications, see U.S. Department of State, Bureau of Public Affairs, "The Decision to Assist Grenada," January 24, 1984. In this statement, Langhorne Motley, the assistant secretary of state for inter-American affairs, explains to the House Armed Services Committee why the United States intervened in Grenada. ·

29. Terry Nardin and Kathleen D. Pritchard, "Ethics and Intervention: The United States in Grenada, 1983," *Case Studies in Ethics and International Affairs*, no. 2 (New York: Carnegie Council on Ethics and International Affairs, 1990), 16.

30. See, for example, John Norton Moore, "Grenada and International Double Standard," *American Journal of International Law* 78 (January 1984): 153–59.

31. See, for example, Christopher C. Joyner, "The United States Action in Grenada," *American Journal of International Law* 78 (January 1984): 131–44, and Francis A. Boyle et al., "International Lawlessness in Grenada," *American Journal of International Law* 78 (January 1984): 172–75.

32. Moore, "Grenada and International Double Standard," 148–49.

33. Alberto R. Coll, "Why Grenada Was Important," *Naval War College Review* 40 (Summer 1987): 4–13.

34. Nardin and Pritchard, "Ethics and Intervention," 7.

35. Coll, "Why Grenada Was Important," 7–8.

36. Michael W. Doyle, *Ways of War and Peace: Realism, Liberalism, and Socialism* (New York: Norton, 1997), 415.

37. Ibid., 413.

38. Ibid., 411.

39. Jack Donnelly, "Human Rights, Humanitarian Intervention and American Foreign Policy: Law, Morality and Politics," *Journal of International Affairs* 37 (Winter 1984): 313.

40. For an excellent discussion of the U.S. military and diplomatic operation in Somalia, see John L. Hirsch and Robert B. Oakley, *Somalia and Operation Restore Hope: Reflections on Peacemaking and Peacekeeping* (Washington, D.C.: U.S. Institute of Peace Press, 1995).

41. Hirsch and Oakley, *Somalia and Operation Restore Hope*, 145.

42. It is important to emphasize that the Security Council authorized this action in great part because of the total breakdown of government authority. Because there was no effective government in Somalia, the UN Charter's prohibitions against UN intervention in the domestic affairs of states (Article 2.7) were not applicable.

43. Alberto R. Coll, "Somalia and the Problems of Doing Good: A Perspective from the Defense Department," in *Close Calls: Intervention, Terrorism, Missile Defense, and 'Just War' Today*, ed. Elliott Abrams (Washington, D.C.: Ethics and Public Policy Center, 1998), 177–81.

44. John R. Bolton, "Somalia and the Problems of Doing Good: A Perspective from the Department of State," in *Close Calls*, ed. Abrams, 157.

45. Coll, "Somalia and the Problems of Doing Good," 179.

46. Chester Crocker, "The Lessons of Somalia," *Foreign Affairs* 74 (May/June 1995): 7.

CHAPTER 8: THE ETHICS OF UNCONVENTIONAL MILITARY OPERATIONS

1. David Rieff, "The Bureaucrat of Terror," *World Policy Journal* (Spring 2002), 108.

2. Richard A. Posner, "The Best Offense," *The New Republic* (September 2, 2002), 30.

3. Ward Thomas, "Norms and Security: The Case of International Assassination," *International Security* 25 (Summer 2000): 127–28.

4. Jonathan Schell, *The Fate of the Earth* (New York: Avon Books, 1982), 172.

5. Examples of these types of American foreign policy initiatives during the Cold War include: military and economic assistance to Greece in the late 1940s, military efforts to undermine the Cuban communist regime of Fidel Castro in the early phase of the Cuban revolution (1960–1961), a covert counterinsurgency campaign against communist forces in Laos in 1969–1971, military assistance to the anti-Soviet forces in Afghanistan in the 1980s, and economic and military assistance to the anti-Sandinistas forces throughout the 1980s in order to undermine the Marxist regime in Nicaragua.

6. See Jennifer D. Kibbe, "The Rise of the Shadow Warriors," *Foreign Affairs* 83 (March/April 2004): 102–115.

7. Kalevi J. Holsti, *The State, War, and the State of War* (Cambridge: Cambridge University Press, 1996), 22.

8. Michael T. Klare, "Low-Intensity Conflict," *Christianity and Crisis*, February 1, 1988, 11–14.

9. Michael Walzer, *Just and Unjust Wars: A Moral Argument with Historical Illustrations* (New York: Basic Books, 1977), 179–96.

10. Charles Krauthammer, "Morality and the Reagan Doctrine," *The New Republic* (September 8, 1986), 23.

11. Charles Krauthammer, "The Reagan Doctrine," *Time* (April 1, 1985), 54–55. For a more extensive elaboration of the doctrine, see Charles Krauthammer, "The Poverty of Realism," *The New Republic* (February 17, 1986), 14–22.

12. Robert Kagan, *A Twilight Struggle: American Power and Nicaragua, 1977–1990* (New York: The Free Press, 1996), 209.

13. Reagan's Westminster speech can be accessed on the Internet at www.reagan.utexas.edu/resource/speeches/1982/60882a.htm (accessed July 23, 2004).

14. Kagan, *A Twilight Struggle*, 211.

15. For an illuminating moral assessment of optimistic and pessimistic worldviews, see Reinhold Niebuhr, *The Children of Light and the Children of Darkness: A Vindication of Democracy and a Critique of Its Traditional Defense* (New York: Scribner's, 1944).

16. James M. Scott, *Deciding to Intervene: The Reagan Doctrine and American Foreign Policy* (Durham, N.C.: Duke University Press, 1996), 20–21.

17. Scott, *Deciding to Intervene*, 223.

18. Krauthammer, "The Reagan Doctrine," 54.

19. Robert H. Johnson, "Misguided Morality: Ethics and the Reagan Doctrine," *Political Science Quarterly* 103 (Fall 1988): 512.

20. Krauthammer, "The Reagan Doctrine," 19–20.

21. Johnson, "Misguided Morality," 520.

22. Johnson, "Misguided Morality," 512.

23. Krauthammer, "Morality and the Reagan Doctrine," 20.

24. Charles R. Beitz, "The Reagan Doctrine in Nicaragua," in *Problems of International Justice,* ed. Steven Luper-Foy (Boulder, Colo.: Westview Press, 1988), 189.

25. Robert A. Pastor, *Whirlpool: U.S. Foreign Policy toward Latin America and the Caribbean* (Princeton, N.J.: Princeton University Press, 1992), 82.

26. Krauthammer, "Morality and the Reagan Doctrine," 23.

27. Scott, *Deciding to Intervene*, 79.

28. Indeed, the Afghan guerrillas received more ($500 million) in 1986 than the Nicaraguan Contras received from 1981 to 1988, the period of U.S. assistance.

29. Kagan, *A Twilight Struggle*, 722.

30. Kagan, *A Twilight Struggle*, 723.

31. George Shultz, *Turmoil and Triumph: My Years as Secretary of State* (New York: Scribner's, 1993), 1129.

32. For an interpretation of the USSR's decline because of domestic political and economic developments, see Raymond L. Garthoff, *The Great Transition: American–Soviet Relations and the End of the Cold War* (Washington, D.C.: The Brookings Institution, 1994), 754–55. For an alternative account that emphasizes the U.S. foreign policy initiatives as important factors contributing to the end of the Cold War, see Jack F. Matlock, Jr., *Autopsy on an Empire: The American Ambassador's Account of the Collapse of the Soviet Union* (New York: Random House, 1995), 668–70.

33. Carl von Clausewitz, *On War*, trans. Michael Howard and Peter Paret (Princeton, N.J.: Princeton University Press, 1976), 87.

34. Bruce Hoffman, "Rethinking Terrorism and Counterterrorism since 9/11," *Studies in Conflict & Terrorism* 25 (2002), 313.

35. Walzer, *Just and Unjust Wars*, 197.

36. Quoted in Walzer, *Just and Unjust Wars*, 199.

37. Historian Timothy Garton Ash has identified four criteria by which to judge and classify terrorists. He suggests that in evaluating the moral and political legitimacy of alleged terrorists, we should focus on biography, goals, methods, and context. See Timothy Garton Ash, "Is There a Good Terrorist?" *New York Review of Books* (November 29, 2001), 30–33.

38. The following insights are taken from Russell D. Howard, "Preface," in Russell D. Howard and Reid L. Sawyer, *Defeating Terrorism: Shaping the New Security Environment* (Guilford, Conn.: McGraw-Hill, 2004), ix–xi.

39. A "dirty bomb," also called a radiological weapon, is a conventional explosive with radioactive material that is dispersed with the bomb explosion. Such a weapon kills or injures from the initial blast and from the residual radiation and dispersed contamination.

40. It is estimated that this war resulted in the death of about 400,000–500,000 Algerians, 27,500 French soldiers, and between 3,000 and 9,000 French civilians. See Rieff, "The Bureaucrat of Torture," 105.

41. For an illuminating assessment of U.S. counterterror policies in light of just war principles, see Neta C. Crawford, "Just War Theory and the U.S. Counterterror War," *Perspectives on Politics* 1 (March 2003): 5–25.

42. Henry Shue, "Torture," *Philosophy & Public Policy* 7 (Winter 1978): 124.

43. The Torture Convention defines torture as "any act by which severe pain or suffering, whether physical or mental, is intentionally inflicted on a person for such purposes as obtaining from him or a third person information or a confession, punishing him for an act he or a third person has committed or is suspect of having committed, or intimidating or coercing him or a third person, or for any reason based on discrimination of any kind, when such pain or suffering is inflicted by or at the instigation of or with the consent or acquiescence of a public official or other person acting in an official capacity."

44. Mark Bowden, "The Dark Art of Interrogation," *The Atlantic Monthly* (October 2003), 53.

45. Bruce Hoffman, "A Nasty Business," *The Atlantic Monthly* (January 2002), 51.

46. Alan M. Dershowitz, *Why Terrorism Works: Understanding the Threat, Responding to the Challenge* (New Haven, Conn.: Yale University Press, 2002), 137.

47. Hoffman, "A Nasty Business," 51.

48. Hoffman, "A Nasty Business," 141.

49. Richard A. Posner, "The Best Offense," *The New Republic* (September 2, 2002), 30.

50. Bowden, "The Dark Art of Interrogation," 56.

51. For early, detailed coverage of the Abu Ghraib scandal, see Seymour M. Hersh, "Torture at Abu Ghraib," *The New Yorker* (May 10, 2004), 42–47; Seymour M. Hersh, "Chain of Command," *The New Yorker* (May 17, 2004), 38–43; and Seymour M. Hersh, "The Gray Zone," *The New Yorker* (May 24, 2004), 38–43.

52. Mark Danner, "The Logic of Torture," *New York Review of Books* (June 24, 2004), 74.

53. When U.S. military authorities first learned of prisoner abuses at Abu Ghraib in January 2004, they immediately established a task force, headed by Major General Antonio Taguba, to investigate the allegations. In his secret report, issued at the end of February, General Taguba found that military personnel had committed "sadistic, blatant, and wanton criminal abuses"— a conclusion that led to the removal of the general in charge of prison security and to the court martial of several soldiers charged with criminal wrongdoing. For a brief discussion of the Taguba report, see Mark Danner, "Torture and Truth," *New York Review of Books* (June 10, 2004), 46–50. In July 2004 the Army's inspector general, Lieutenant General Paul T. Mikolashek, issued a detailed report on Iraqi prisoner abuses. In his report, General Mikolashek argued that, contrary to General Taguba's conclusions, the mistreatment of prisoners was not due to systemic problems. Instead, he claimed that the abuses were the result of "unauthorized actions taken by a few individuals, coupled with the failure of a few leaders to provide adequate monitoring, supervision, and leadership over those soldiers." While acknowledging that U.S. military detention operations in Iraq and Afghanistan were plagued with poor training, haphazard organization, and outmoded policies, General Mikolashek claimed that those flaws did not directly contribute to the mistreatment of prisoners at Abu Ghraib. *New York Times*, July 23, 2004, 1 and 9.

54. For a discussion of the struggle over interrogation techniques, see Anthony Lewis, "Making Torture Legal," *New York Review of Books* (July 15, 2004), 4–8; and Dana Priest and Bradley Graham, "A Struggle over Interrogation Tactics," *Washington Post National Weekly Edition*, June 28–July 11, 2004, 15.

55. For example, in March 2004 the government of Israel assassinated the senior leader of Hamas, a radical Palestinian group demanding statehood over all Palestine, because of the organization's reliance on terror. In view of the continuing civilian deaths from suicide bombings, Israeli officials vowed that they would attempt to assassinate all other senior leaders as well.

56. Ward Thomas, "Norms and Security: The Case of International Assassination," *International Security* (Summer 2000): 110.

57. Mark Vincent Vlasic, "Cloak & Dagger Diplomacy: The United States and Assassination," *Georgetown Journal of International Affairs* (Summer/Fall 2000): 96.

58. Quoted in Thomas, "Norms and Security," 113.

59. Journalist Seymour Hersh argues that the aim of the U.S. bombing mission was to kill Colonel Qaddafi. See Seymour Hersh, "Target Qaddafi," *New York Times Magazine* (February 22, 1987), 17–26.

60. Evan Thomas and Daniel Klaidman, "The War Room," *Newsweek*, March 31, 2003, 26.

61. For a brief overview of the CIA's search for bin Laden as well as CIA–White House tensions over his capture, see Steve Coll, "The CIA's Secret Hunt" and "Legal Disputes Paralyzed Clinton's Aides," *Washington Post National Weekly Edition*, March 1–7, 2004, 6–9.

62. Charles Hill, "A Herculean Task: The Myth and Reality of Arab Terrorism," in *The Age of Terror: America and the World after September 11*, ed. Strobe Talbott and Nayan Chanda (New York: Basic Books, 2001), 87.

63. For an account of the U.S. war against the Taliban, see Norman Friedman, *Terrorism,*

Afghanistan, and America's New Way of War (Annapolis, Md.: Naval Institute Press, 2003).

64. The effectiveness of the bombing campaign was accomplished through ground spotters who identified targets and relayed GPS coordinates to aircraft carrying laser-guided bombs. Of the twelve thousand bombs dropped in the war, more than half were guided by laser.

65. As of February 2004, only about one million citizens had registered to vote out of an eligible population of more than ten million. Registration among women and in Kandahar and other Pashtun areas was especially low.

66. For a discussion of this point, see George Weigel, "The Just War Tradition and the World after September 11th," *Catholic University Law Review* 51 (Spring 2002): 703.

67. From this perspective, public judicial authority responds by bringing criminal charges against the accused, while the victims pursue civil claims in their private capacity.

68. Eliot A. Cohen, "A Strange War," *The National Interest* (Thanksgiving 2001), 12.

69. President Bush's address to Congress, September 20, 2001.

70. For a description of the key elements of this doctrine, see Norman Podhoretz, "In Praise of the Bush Doctrine," *Commentary* (September 2002): 19–28. For a critical assessment of the doctrine, see Robert Jervis, "Understanding the Bush Doctrine," *Political Science Quarterly* 118, 3 (2003): 365–88.

71. George W. Bush, "Remarks by the President at 2002 Graduation Exercise of the United States Military Academy, West Point, New York." See www.whitehouse.gov/news/releases/2002/06/20020601–3.html (accessed July 23, 2004).

72. For an assessment of the notion of preemption, see Lawrence Freedman, "Prevention, Not Preemption," *The Washington Quarterly* (Spring 2003): 105–14.

CHAPTER 9: THE ETHICS OF ECONOMIC SANCTIONS

1. Quoted in Barry E. Carter, *International Economic Sanctions: Improving the Haphazard U.S. Legal Regime* (Cambridge: Cambridge University Press, 1988), 9.

2. Margaret P. Doxey, *International Sanctions in Contemporary Perspective* (New York: St. Martin's Press, 1987), 145.

3. Quoted in Richard E. Sincere, Jr., *The Politics of Sentiment: Churches and Foreign Investment in South Africa* (Washington, D.C.: Ethics and Public Policy Center, 1984), v.

4. David A. Baldwin, *Economic Statecraft* (Princeton, N.J.: Princeton University Press, 1985).

5. See, for example, Roger Fisher, *Conflict for Beginners* (New York: Harper & Row, 1969).

6. James M. Lindsay, "Trade Sanctions as Policy Instruments: A Re-examination," *International Studies Quarterly,* no. 30 (June 1986): 155–56.

7. Kim Richard Nossal, "International Sanctions as International Punishment," *International Organization* 43 (Spring 1989): 313–14.

8. National Association of Manufacturers, *A Catalog of New U.S. Unilateral Economic Sanctions for Foreign Policy Purposes, 1993–96* (Washington, D.C.: National Association of Manufacturers, 1997), 1–4.

9. Charles Kindleberger, *Power and Money: The Economics of International Politics and the Politics of International Economics* (New York: Basic Books, 1970), 97.

10. Margaret P. Doxey, *Economic Sanctions and International Enforcement* (New York: Oxford University Press, 1971), 139.

11. Baldwin, *Economic Statecraft,* 57.

12. M. S. Daoudi and J. S. Dajani, *Economic Sanctions: Ideals and Experience* (London: Routledge & Kegan Paul, 1983).

13. Donald L. Losman, *International Economic Sanctions: The Cases of Cuba, Israel and Rhodesia* (Albuquerque: University of New Mexico Press, 1979), 1, 124.

14. Gary C. Hufbauer, Jeffrey J. Schott, and Kimberly Ann Elliott, *Economic Sanctions Reconsidered: History and Current Policy*, 2nd ed. (Washington, D.C.: Institute for International Economics, 1990), 49–73.

15. For a discussion of the relationship between private and public actors, see Kenneth A. Rodman, "Public and Private Sanctions against South Africa," *Political Science Quarterly* 109 (Summer 1994): 313–34.

16. Hufbauer, Schott, and Elliott, *Economic Sanctions Reconsidered*.

17. Robert A. Pape, "Why Economic Sanctions Do Not Work," *International Security* 22 (Fall 1997): 90–136.

18. Franklin L. Lavin, "Asphyxiation or Oxygen? The Sanctions Dilemma," *Foreign Policy* 104 (Fall 1996): 153.

19. Kimberly Ann Elliott, "Factors Affecting the Success of Sanctions," in *Economic Sanctions: Panacea or Peacebuilding in a Post-Cold War World?*, ed. David Cortright and George A. Lopez (Boulder, Colo.: Westview Press, 1995), 53.

20. The MFN principle, the most basic norm of the world economy, requires that trade be carried out in a reciprocal and nondiscriminatory manner, so that any trade preferences must be extended to all member states.

21. The Jackson-Vanik amendment (to the Trade Act) was adopted to encourage the Soviet Union to allow greater freedom of Jewish emigration. Although the amendment's sponsors assumed that the threat of economic penalties would encourage greater emigration liberalization, in actual fact the law had the direct opposite effect, resulting in a significant decline in the number of emigrants.

22. James Lilley, "Freedom through Trade," *Foreign Policy* 94 (Spring 1994): 40.

23. According to the order, the improvement in human rights had to be realized in seven areas, two of them mandatory. The two mandatory areas were emigration of dissidents' family members and termination of prison-made exports to the United States. The five other areas were (1) allowing Voice of America broadcasts to China, (2) accounting for political prisoners, (3) improving prison conditions, (4) easing political repression in Tibet, and (5) providing better treatment of religious minorities.

24. Richard Dicker, "The U.S. Business Community and Human Rights in China," *Current History*, September 1994, 253.

25. Lavin, "Asphyxiation or Oxygen?" 140.

26. In December 1989, the United States intervened militarily to oust the Noriega government and to capture and bring the dictator to trial.

27. Hufbauer, Schott, and Elliott, *Economic Sanctions Reconsidered*, 53–54.

28. Baldwin, *Economic Statecraft*, 96–114.

29. Lisa Martin, *Coercive Cooperation: Explaining Multilateral Economic Sanctions* (Princeton, N.J.: Princeton University Press, 1992).

30. William Kaempfer and Anton Lowenberg, *International Economic Sanctions: A Public Choice Perspective* (Boulder, Colo.: Westview Press, 1992), 133.

31. For a discussion of this point with reference to selective cases (the Megarian decree, the League of Nations sanctions against Italy, and the trans-Siberian pipeline sanctions), see Stefanie Ann Lenway, "Between War and Commerce: Economic Sanctions as a Tool of Statecraft," *International Organization* 42 (Spring 1988): 409–19.

32. U.S. investment dominated many sectors of the Cuban economy, including utilities (90 percent), hotels (80 percent), oil production (80 percent), pharmaceuticals (80 percent), rail-

ways (50 percent), sugar production (40 percent), and banking (25 percent).

33. Donna Rich Kaplowitz, *Anatomy of a Failed Embargo: U.S. Sanctions aagainst Cuba* (Boulder, Colo.: Lynne Reinner Publishers, 1998), 42.

34. Although most property owners were Cuban citizens at the time that their property was nationalized, the largest number of potential suits are likely to come from Cubans who have become U.S. citizens since fleeing Cuba. It is estimated that some 430,000 naturalized citizens of Cuban origin could file suit. Potential property claims could exceed $100 billion.

35. The extension of legal jurisdiction to third states is known as the practice of extraterritoriality. Whereas traditional international relations is based upon the acceptance of state sovereignty, the Helms-Burton Law extends the reach of American jurisdiction to third parties, denying in effect the validity of nationalization by the Cuban state. This act has resulted in vigorous condemnation by Mexico, Canada, as well as the OAS and the European Union.

36. Susan Kaufman Purcell, "Cuba," in *Economic Sanctions and American Diplomacy*, ed. Richard N. Haass (New York: Council on Foreign Relations Book, 1998), 52.

37. For a discussion of major sanctions objectives, see Kaplowitz, *Anatomy of a Failed Embargo*, 3–9.

38. Kaplowitz, *Anatomy of a Failed Embargo*, 6.

39. Kaplowitz, *Anatomy of a Failed Embargo*.

40. Ana Juli Jatar-Hausmann, *The Cuban Way: Capitalism, Communism, and Confrontation* (West Hartford, Conn.: Kumarian Press, 1999), 57.

41. Purcell, "Cuba," 44.

42. For an excellent description of Cuba's efforts to introduce some free enterprise initiatives in the post–Cold War era, see Jatar-Hausmann, *Cuban Way*, 67–89.

43. Of more than twenty countries involved in Cuban investment, the largest foreign investors were Mexico, Canada, Italy, and Spain.

44. Jatar-Hausmann, *Cuban Way*, 141.

45. According to U.S. statutes, U.S. citizens may remit up to $300 per Cuban household every three months. In effect, families can contribute a maximum of $1,200 annually for relatives in Cuba.

46. This claim was made by a U.S. government representative at the U.S. interest section in Havana in March 2002. Ana Jatar-Hausmann, by contrast, estimates private financial transfers from Cuban-Americans at about $800 million, or roughly one-half of the income generated from tourism.

47. Jatar-Hausmann, *Cuban Way*, 136.

48. For an informative overview of the nature and impact of Castro's spring 2003 crackdown on dissidents, see Theresa Bond, "The Crackdown in Cuba," *Foreign Affairs* (September/October 2003): 118–30.

49. Kaplowitz, *Anatomy of a Failed Embargo*, 212.

50. Baldwin, *Economic Statecraft*, 359. See also Patrick Clawson, "Sanctions as Punishment, Enforcement, and Prelude to Further Action," *Ethics & International Affairs* 7 (1993): 17–37; Lori Fisler Damrosch, "The Collective Enforcement of International Norms through Economic Sanctions," *Ethics & International Affairs* 8 (1994): 73–74; and Albert C. Pierce, "Just War Principles and Economic Sanctions," *Ethics & International Affairs* 10 (1996): 99–113.

51. Drew Christiansen and Gerard F. Powers, "Economic Sanctions and the Just-War Doctrine," in *Economic Sanctions*, ed. Cortright and Lopez, 102.

52. See, for example, Pierce, "Just War Principles and Economic Sanctions."

53. Rodman, "Public and Private Sanctions."

54. The principle of double effect provides that civilians may be killed in war but only if

their death is the by-product of the destruction and violence directly intended against military targets.

55. Pierce, "Just War Principles and Economic Sanctions," 100–1.

56. Michael Walzer, *Just and Unjust Wars: A Moral Argument with Historical Illustrations*, 2nd ed. (New York: Basic Books, 1992), 146.

57. Lori Fisler Damrosch, "The Civilian Impact of Economic Sanctions," in *Enforcing Restraint: Collective Intervention in International Conflicts,* ed. Lori Fisler Damrosch (New York: Council on Foreign Relations Press, 1993), 279.

58. Drew Christiansen and Gerard F. Powers, "Sanctions: Unintended Consequences," *The Bulletin of the Atomic Scientists*, November 1993, 43.

59. Michael Walzer, "Justice and Injustice in the Gulf War," in *But Was It Just? Reflections on the Morality of the Persian Gulf War,* ed. David DeCosse (New York: Doubleday, 1992), 3.

60. Christiansen and Powers, "Economic Sanctions and the Just-War Doctrine," 102.

61. William H. Kaempfer, James A. Lehman, and Anton D. Lowenberg, "Divestment, Investment Sanctions, and Disinvestment: An Evaluation of Anti-Apartheid Policy Instruments," *International Organization* 41 (Summer 1987): 461.

62. Jennifer Davis, "Sanctions and Apartheid: The Economic Challenge to Discrimination," in *Economic Sanctions*, ed. Cortright and Lopez, 178.

63. Kenneth A. Rodman, "Public and Private Sanctions against South Africa," *Political Science Quarterly* 109 (Summer 1994): 323.

64. Thomas W. Hazlett, "Did Sanctions Matter?" *New York Times,* July 22, 1991, sec. A, 5.

65. Helen Suzman, "Sanctions Won't End Apartheid," *New York Times*, October 4, 1987, sec. IV, 23.

66. Alan Paton, *Cry, the Beloved Country* (Cape Town: Hans Strydom Publishers, 1987), 7.

67. Federated Chamber of Industries, *The Effect of Sanctions on Unemployment and Production in South Africa* (Pretoria: FCI Information Services, 1986).

68. Neta C. Crawford, "The Humanitarian Consequences of Sanctioning South Africa: A Preliminary Assessment," in *Political Gain and Civilian Pain: Humanitarian Impacts of Economic Sanctions,* ed. Thomas G. Weiss et al. (Lanham, Md.: Rowman & Littlefield, 1997), 77.

69. The Anglo-American Corporation paid about 20 percent less than the value of traded stock, and it did so with undervalued South African currency (rand).

70. Merle Lipton, *Sanctions and South Africa: The Dynamics of Economic Isolation*, Special Report No. 1119 (London: The Economist Intelligence Unit, January 1988), 92.

71. Crawford, "The Humanitarian Consequences of Sanctioning South Africa," 73.

72. Crawford, "Humanitarian Consequences," 77.

73. F. W. de Klerk, "The Bull in the Garden," *Civilization* 5 (April/May 1998): 61.

CHAPTER 10: ETHICS AND GLOBAL SOCIETY

1. Charles R. Beitz, *Political Theory and International Relations* (Princeton, N.J.: Princeton University Press, 1979), 151.

2. Peter Singer, *One World: The Ethics of Globalization* (New Haven, Conn.: Yale University Press, 2002), 13.

3. Alan Dowty, *Closed Borders: The Contemporary Assault on Freedom of Movement* (New Haven, Conn.: Yale University Press, 1987), 226.

4. For a mid-twentieth century application of Lloyd's metaphor, see Garrett Hardin, "The Tragedy of the Commons," *Science*, December 13, 1968, 1243–48.

5. For a discussion of the regulation of the earth's collective goods, see Per Magnus Wijkman, "Managing the Global Commons," *International Organization* 36 (Summer 1982): 511–36.

6. Some major treaties designed to protect the environment include: the Convention on Fishing and Conservation of Living Resources of the High Seas (1958), the Convention on the International Trade in Endangered Species of Wild Flora and Fauna–CITES (1973), the London Convention on the Prevention of Marine Pollution (1972), the Montreal Protocol on Substances that Deplete the Ozone Layer (1987), and the Basel Convention on the Control of Transboundary Movements of Hazardous Wastes and Their Disposal (1989).

7. Scott Barrett, *Environment and Statecraft: The Strategy of Environmental Treaty-Making* (New York; Oxford University Press, 2003), 364.

8. Reforestation and other major vegetation projects are known as carbon "sinks" because such initiatives reduce carbon dioxide in the atmosphere and thereby decrease greenhouse gases.

9. When the Clinton administration first signed the Kyoto Protocol in 1997, it precipitated strong opposition within the U.S. Senate, in part because of the absence of Third World participation. As a result, the Senate overwhelmingly passed a resolution (95 to 0) that required that developing nations accept binding emission targets before it would consider ratification.

10. Japan, for example, was able to reduce its emissions curbs from 6 percent below its 1990 greenhouse gases to 2 percent below by aggressively lobbying for the emissions credits generated by its reforestation programs. See *New York Times*, July 24, 2001, 1 and 7.

11. Quoted in Stephen M. Gardiner, "The Global Warming Tragedy and the Dangerous Illusion of the Kyoto Protocol," *Ethics and International Affairs* 18, no. 1 (2004): 23.

12. Gardiner, "Global Warming Tragedy," 23.

13. Barrett, *Environment and Statecraft*, 389.

14. Gardiner, "Global Warming Tragedy," 36.

15. For a brief summary of the science of climate change, see Donald A. Brown, *American Heat: Ethical Problems with the United States' Response to Global Warming* (Boulder, Colo.: Rowman & Littlefield, 2002), chapter 6, and Barrett, *Environment and Statecraft*, 362–366. For an overview and critique of widely held views about climate change, see Aaron Wildavsky, *But Is It True? A Citizen's Guide to Environmental Health and Safety Issues* (Cambridge, Mass.: Harvard University Press, 1995), chap. 11.

16. For contrasting perspectives on climate change, see, for example, Marvin S. Soroos, *The Endangered Atmosphere: Preserving the Global Commons* (Columbia: University of South Carolina Press, 1997), and Bjorn Lomborg, *The Skeptical Environmentalist* (Cambridge: Cambridge University Press, 2001).

17. For a moral assessment of "emission rights," see Michael J. Sandel, "It's Immoral to Buy the Right to Pollute," *New York Times*, December 15, 1997, sec. A, 15.

18. Sharon Begley, "Too Much Hot Air," *Newsweek*, October 20, 1997, 50.

19. Henry D. Jacoby, Ronald G. Prinn, and Richard Schmalensee, "Kyoto's Unfinished Business," *Foreign Affairs* 77 (July/August 1998): 60.

20. Brian Tucker, "Science Friction: The Politics of Global Warming," *The National Interest*, Fall 1997, 84.

21. Stanley Hoffmann, *Duties beyond Borders: On the Limits and Possibilities of Ethical International Politics* (Syracuse, N.Y.: Syracuse University Press, 1981), 164–65.

22. For a review of contemporary anlyses of international justice from a procedural perspective, see Chris Brown, *International Relations Theory: New Normative Approaches* (New York: Columbia University Press, 1992), 170–88.

23. Terry Nardin, *Law, Morality and the Relations of States* (Princeton, N.J.: Princeton University Press, 1983), 267–68.

24. Stanley Hoffmann, "The Crisis of Liberal Internationalism," *Foreign Policy*, no. 98 (Spring 1995): 160.

25. The domestic analogy is based on the comparison of international society to domestic order. The a priori rights and duties of states are viewed as comparable to the rights and duties of citizens in prepolitical society, that is, the state of nature.

26. Examples of communitarian thinkers include seventeenth-century German international lawyer Samuel Pufendorf, eighteenth-century Swiss jurist Emmerich de Vattel, nineteenth-century British political theorist John Stuart Mill, and contemporary political philosopher Michael Walzer. For a recent normative justification of the existing international system, see Mervyn Frost, *Ethics in International Relations: A Constitutive Theory* (Cambridge: Cambridge University Press, 1996). Frost's "constitutive theory" provides a normative justification for the communitarian perspective.

27. Examples of cosmopolitan thinkers include sixteenth-century Spanish theologian Francisco Suarez, nineteenth-century German philosopher Immanuel Kant, and contemporary political philosopher Henry Shue. One of the most influential expositions of this perspective is Charles Beitz, *Political Theory and International Relations* (Princeton, N.J.: Princeton University Press, 1979).

28. For a comparative assessment of cosmopolitan and communitarian perspectives, see Chris Brown, *International Relations Theory: New Normative Approaches* (New York: Columbia University Press, 1992).

29. Brown, *International Relations Theory*, 110.

30. For a full exposition of this position, see Beitz, *Political Theory and International Relations,* which applies John Rawls's theory of justice to international affairs.

31. Quoted in David Halloran Lumsdaine, *Moral Vision in International Politics: The Foreign Aid Regime, 1949–1989* (Princeton, N.J.: Princeton University Press, 1993), 221–22.

32. Lumsdaine, *Moral Vision in International Politics*, 257.

33. Nick Eberstadt, "Famine, Development and Foreign Aid," *Commentary,* March 1985, 28.

34. Carol C. Adelman, "The Privatization of Foreign Aid," *Foreign Affairs* (November/December 2003): 10–11. See also Devesh Kapur and John McHale, "Migration's New Payoff," *Foreign Policy* (November–December 2003): 49–57.

35. Lumsdaine, *Moral Vision in International Politics*, 3.

36. John Cassidy, "Helping Hands: How Foreign Aid Could Benefit Everybody," *The New Yorker*, March 18, 2002, 63.

37. William Easterly, *The Elusive Quest for Growth: Economists' Adventures and Misadventures in the Tropics* (Cambridge, Mass.: MIT Press, 2002), 42.

38. P. T. Bauer, *Reality and Rhetoric* (Cambridge, Mass.: Harvard University Press, 1984), 38–62. See also P. T. Bauer, *Equality, the Third World, and Economic Delusion* (Cambridge, Mass.: Harvard University Press, 1981).

39. Jack Shepherd, "When Foreign Aid Fails," *The Atlantic Monthly* (April 1985), 43.

40. For a discussion of this point, see Brian R. Opeskin, "The Moral Foundations of Foreign Aid," *World Development* 43 (January 1996): 21–44.

41. Opeskin, "Moral Foundations," 26–30.

42. In his study *Basic Rights*, Henry Shue illustrates the role of the distributive justice idea to the meeting of human needs. Shue argues that people are entitled to fundamental rights, including the right to subsistence, and he justifies this claim on the basis of the notion of distributive justice, not on the basis of the essential worth and dignity of the human person. Henry Shue, *Basic Rights: Subsistence, Affluence, and U.S. Foreign Policy* (Princeton, N.J.: Princeton University Press, 1980).

43. Peter Singer, "Famine, Affluence, and Morality," *Philosophy and Public Affairs* 1 (Spring 1972): 229–43.

44. According to the parable, a traveler was attacked, robbed, and injured severely. Subsequently a priest and a Levite passed by the injured victim but they did not help; only a Samaritan—a member of an outcast group—stops and takes care of the injured traveler. He is brought to safety and given aid to restore his health. See Luke 10:29–37.

45. See Garrett Hardin, *Living within Limits: Ecology, Economics and Population Taboos* (New York: Oxford University Press, 1993), esp. 276–93.

46. See, for example, Joseph H. Carens, "Aliens and Citizens: The Case for Open Borders," *The Review of Politics* 49 (Spring 1987): 251–73; Joseph H. Carens, "Migration and Morality: A Liberal Egalitarian Perspective, in *Free Movement: Ethical Issues in the Transnational Migration of People and of Money,* ed. Brian Barry and Robert E. Goodin (University Park: Pennsylvania State University Press, 1992), 25–47; and Peter Singer and Renata Singer, "The Ethics of Refugee Policy," in *Open Borders? Closed Societies? The Ethical and Political Issues,* ed. Mark Gibney (New York: Greenwood Press, 1988), 111–30.

47. Dowty, *Closed Borders,* 15.

48. For a discussion of the role of the right of emigration in traditional international law, see David C. Hendrickson, "Migration in Law and Ethics: A Realist Perspective," in *Free Movement,* ed. Barry and Goodin, 223–27.

49. The right of return is a delimited claim for admission. The right of return applies mainly to peoples seeking to return to their nation's homeland on the basis of historic ties of prior membership. For a discussion of how this right applies to Palestinian and Jewish people within Israel, see W. Gunther Plaut, *Asylum: A Moral Dilemma* (Westport, Conn.: Praeger, 1995), 82–88.

50. Brian Barry, "The Quest for Consistency: A Skeptical View," in *Free Movement,* ed. Barry and Goodin, 284.

51. Michael Walzer, *Spheres of Justice: A Defense of Pluralism and Equality* (New York: Basic Books, 1983), 62.

52. Walzer, *Spheres of Justice,* 9–10.

53. Myron Weiner, "Ethics, National Sovereignty and the Control of Immigration," *International Migration Review* 30 (Spring 1996): 192.

54. According to the 1951 UN Convention on the Status of Refugees, a refugee is a person "who owing to well-founded fear of being persecuted for reasons of race, religion, nationality, membership of a particular social group or political opinion, is outside the country of his nationality and is unable, or owing to such fear, is unwilling to avail himself of the protection of that country."

55. U.S. Committee on Refugees, "Key Statistics" in *World Refugee Survey, 2003.*

56. For an illuminating account of the international community's responsibility to the growth of refugees in the late twentieth century, see Gil Loescher, *Beyond Charity: International Cooperation and the Global Refugee Crisis* (New York: Oxford University Press, 1993).

57. Louis Henkin, *The Age of Rights* (New York: Columbia University Press, 1990), 48.

58. Myron Weiner, *The Global Migration Crisis: Challenge to States and to Human Rights* (New York: HarperCollins, 1995), 56.

59. For example, Germany's 1993 asylum law permits the government to immediately deport refugees from a country free of persecution. In addition, the law states that any person who travels through a "safe country" can be deemed to have found protection there and thus may be returned to that state.

60. For an analysis of the ethics of immigration policies, see Joseph H. Carens, "Who Should Get In? The Ethics of Immigration Admissions," *Ethics and International Affairs* 17, no. 1 (2003): 95–110.

61. For example, Peter and Renata Singer, following the principle of "equal consideration of

interests," argue for greatly increasing the number of refugees resettled in rich countries. See Peter Singer and Renata Singer, "The Ethics of Refugee Policy," in *Open Borders?* ed. Gibney, 122–28.

62. Weiner, "Ethics, National Sovereignty and the Control of Immigration," 175.

63. U.S. Census Bureau, "The Foreign-Born Population: 2000: Census 2000 Brief," *U.S. Census 2000* (Washington, D.C.: U.S. Department of Commerce, December 2003), 2.

64. U.S. Immigration and Naturalization Service, "Estimates of Unauthorized Immigrant Population Residing in the United States: 1990–2000," 1. See INS website: http://uscis.gov/graphics/publicaffairs/summaries/undocres.htm.

65. For a critique of the continuing mass migration of Hispanics to the United States, see Samuel P. Huntington, "The Hispanic Challenge," *Foreign Policy* (March/April 2004): 30–45.

66. U.S. Commission on Immigration Reform, *U.S. Immigration Policy: Restoring Credibility* (Washington, D.C.: U.S. Government Printing Office, September 1994), 230.

67. With the creation of the U.S. Department of Homeland Security in 2002, the name changed to the Bureau of Citizenship and Immigration Services.

68. Family-sponsored immigration is governed by the four following preferences, listed in priority: (1) unmarried sons and daughters of U.S. citizens, (2) spouses and unmarried sons and daughters of permanent resident aliens, (3) married sons and daughters of U.S. citizens, and (4) brothers and sisters of U.S. citizens who are at least twenty-one years old. Employment-based immigration is governed by five preferences, listed in priority: (1) priority workers, who have demonstrated extraordinary professional abilities; (2) professionals with advanced degrees; (3) skilled workers with baccalaureate degrees and some unskilled workers; (4) special immigrants, such as religious ministers; and (5) investors.

69. Weiner, "Ethics, National Sovereignty and the Control of Immigration," 195.

70. Singer, "The Ethics of Refugee Policy," 116.

71. *New York Times*, June 14, 1996, sec. A, 1, 13.

72. The Mariel boatlift occurred in the spring of 1980 after Fidel Castro announced that anyone wishing to leave Cuba could do so. As a result, some 125,000 Cubans, with the help of more than a thousand Florida boats, migrated to the United States during a two-month period. Because U.S. law would not allow such a large number of immigrants or refugees, the U.S. government classified such persons as "special entrants."

73. To inhibit illegal Cuban migration to the United States and to deter airplane and boat hijackings, U.S. and Cuban officials signed a similar bilateral agreement that called for the repatriation of Cubans seeking unauthorized entry into the United States.

74. This decision was contested in court. Human rights advocates filed a legal suit arguing that the executive decision was unconstitutional because it violated the 1951 Convention on Refugees. A district court affirmed the decision, and a federal appeals court overturned the lower court ruling. The Justice Department immediately filed an appeal with the U.S. Supreme Court. After granting the Bush administration temporary authority to continue forced repatriation, the high court ruled that the original executive order was not unconstitutional.

75. Walzer, *Spheres of Justice*, 18–21.

76. Weiner, "Ethics, National Sovereignty and the Control of Immigration," 179.

CONCLUSION

1. Quoted in Michael W. Doyle, *Ways of War and Peace: Realism, Liberalism, and Socialism* (New York: W.W. Norton, 1997), 383.

2. Stanley Hoffmann, *Duties beyond Borders: On the Limits and Possibilities of Ethical Inter-*

national Politics (Syracuse, N.Y.: Syracuse University Press, 1981), 19.

3. James Turner Johnson, "Just Cause Revisited," in *Close Calls: Intervention, Terrorism, Missile Defense, and "Just War" Today,* ed. Elliot Abrams (Washington, D.C.: Ethics and Public Policy Center, 1998), 38.

4. Drew Christiansen and Gerard F. Powers, "The Duty to Intervene: Ethics and the Varieties of Humanitarian Intervention," in *Close Calls*, ed. Abrams, 183–208.

5. G. Scott Davis, "Interpreting Contemporary Conflicts," in *Religion and Justice in the War over Bosnia*, ed. G. Scott Davis (New York: Routledge, 1996), 4–5. See also Michael Sells, "Religion, History, and Genocide in Bosnia-Herzegovina," in *Religion and Justice in the War over Bosnia*, ed. Davis, 25–28.

6. Michael Walzer, *Just and Unjust Wars: A Moral Argument with Historical Illustrations* (New York: Basic Books, 1977), 19.

Index

Dajani, J. S., 176
Damrosch, Lori Fisler, 190
Dante Alighieri, 54, 106
Daoudi, M. S., 176
Dayton Accord, 2, 21, 23, 136, 226n3
decision-making strategies, 28–44, 223–24
Declaration on Principles of International Law Concerning Friendly Relations and Co-operation Among States, 127
de Klerk, F. W., 71, 193–94
Delian League, 51, 53
democide, 95
Democratic League of Kosovo (LDK), 21
denial strategy, 62–63, 64
deontological thinking, 5, 35–36
Dershowitz, Alan, 164–65
Desert Storm, 146
development aid, 208–12
dirty bomb, 161, 245n39
discrimination norm, 189–90
distributive justice, 86, 205, 210–11, 252n42
Dobrynin, Anatoly, 60
domestic analogy, 11, 206, 252n25
domestic legitimacy, 130–32
domestic society and politics, 11
Dominica, 140
Dominican Republic, 128, 139
Donaldson, Thomas, 16
Donnelly, Jack, 88, 143
double effect, principle of, 188, 249–50n54
Dowty, Alan, 213
Doxey, Margaret, 176
Doyle, Michael, 142, 231n22
Dugard, John, 73
Duvalier, Jean-Claude, 219

Earth Summit, 198, 199
Easterly, William, 210
Eastern Europe, 20, 155, 185
East Germany, 213
economic sanctions: applying just-war norms to, 187–90, 223; effectiveness of, 181–87; ethics of, 174–94; goals and impact of, 3, 175–81; just-sanctions doctrine norms for, 188–90; moral ambiguity of, 187–94; multilateral participation in, 177–78; political and economic success of, 176–78; as

symbols of communication, 182–83
Eisenhower, Dwight D., 183
ElBaradei, Mohamed, 121
Elizabeth I, 167
El Salvador, 66, 155, 184
Elshtain, Jean Bethke, 116
emigration, 179, 212–20, 248n21, 23
empirical rights, 83
ends-based action, 5, 28–35, 46, 223–24
engagement strategy, 62–63
environmental crimes, 16
environmental resources: buying and selling pollution rights, 200, 201–2, 204; climate change in, 202–3, 251n15; ethics of protection of, 198–204; global commons of, 196, 197–204; reliance on nuclear energy, 203, 204; treaties and initiatives for, 198–201, 251n6
Erasmus, 105, 106
ethical positivism, 13–14
ethical reasoning, 7, 9–10, 221–25
ethical strategies, 5, 28–44
ethical traditions, 5, 28, 45–61
ethics: defined, 8, 9–10; features of, 9–10. *See also* international ethics
Ethiopia, 184, 186
ethnic cleansing, 2, 16, 24, 82, 96, 224–25, 229n55
EU Commissioner for the Environment, 201
European Coal and Steel Community (ECSC), 66
European Economic Community (EEC), 66
extra-territoriality, 184, 249n35

Falk, Richard, 106
famine relief, 28, 37–39, 145–48, 211
The Fate of the Earth (Schell), 31
Fay, Michael, 88, 89
Federal Constitution of Yugoslavia, 20, 23
Feher, Michael, 66
female genital mutilation, 82
Final Declaration and Action Program of the World Conference on Human Rights, 93, 237n32
firebreak, 33, 229n13

fishing, international rules of, 9–10
flogging, Singapore practice of, 83, 88–90
force: amoral realism for, 107–9; moral claim of, 4; pacifist approach to, 105–10; political ethics of, 104–25; principled realism of, 109–10
Ford, Gerald, 167
foreign aid: during Cold War era, 36; ethics of, 30, 208–12; humanity thesis argument for, 211; as moral imperative, 210–11
Foreign Assistance Act, 59
foreign intervention, 5, 6, 126–34, *134*, 135–49
foreign policy: application of moral norms to, 16–19, 27; coercive measures of, 174; elements of, 4; human rights and, 94–97; moralism in, 19; moral norms in, 5, 224
forgiveness, 69–70, 75–80
foundationalism, 12–13
France: humanitarian intervention in Rwanda, 99; opposition to war in Iraq, 123; reliance on nuclear energy, 203; war against Algeria, 161, 164, 245n40
Franks, Tommy, 122
Fraser, Donald, 59
freedom fighters, 156, 160
Front de Libération Nationale (FLN), 161, 164
Fukuyama, Francis, 65

gacaca, 99–100, 238n55
Gaddis, John Lewis, 34
Gairy, Eric, 140
Gardiner, Stephen M., 201
Geneva Convention, 172
genocide, 2, 6, 47, 69, 82, 84, 95–97
Gentili, Alberico, 167
Georgia, 144
Germany: asylum policies of, 216, 253–54n59; Bitburg controversy in, 77–80; Kolmeshöhe military cemetery of, 79, 80; Kosovar refugees in, 21, 228n38; Nazi movement in, 78
Gewirth, Alan, 83
Gilpin, Robert, 48
Gladstone, William E., 45–46
Glennon, Michael, 121

property, arbitrary deprivation of, 15
Proposition 187 (California), 3
prudence/practical wisdom, 40–41, 50
psychological warfare, 159
public apologies, 63–64
public opinion, role in foreign affairs, 17–18
purges, 63

Qaddafi, Muammar, 168
Quick Reaction Force, 146

radical cultural relativism, 88
radical universalism, 88
radiological weapons, 161, 245n39
Rambouillet Accord, 21–22, 23, 24, 228n43
Rawls, John, 8, 13
Reagan, Ronald: Bitburg dilemma of, 77–80; economic sanctions against South Africa by, 18, 191, 192; managing flow of Haitian refugees by, 219; military intervention in Grenada, 140, 141; promoting human rights by, 100; Reagan Doctrine of, 118, 152, 154–59, 186, 240n35; sanctions against Cuba by, 184; Strategic Defense Initiative (SDI) program of, 29, 41–43
realism, 5, 46, 48–54, 221
reforestation, 200, 251n8
Refugee Act, 218, 219
refugee populations: asylum policies of, 215–17, 253n59; from Haiti, 137, 138; from Kosovo, 24, 25; moral challenges of, 9, 212–20, 253n54; political and economic refugees, 216; resettlement of, 216–17, 253–54n61; from Rwanda, 97–100, 144
regime change, 119–25, 137, 139
regime offenses, political reconciliation of, 62–81
religion: role in human rights, 84–85, 236n10; role in pacifism, 106, 239n7
religious war, 107, 108–9
remembering, 79
reparation, 63–64
reproductive rights, 91

restitutive justice, 63–64, 210
restorative justice, 68–70, 233n15
retributive justice, 67–68
Rhodesia, 178
Rieff, David, 98
right to development, 91, 237n30
risk-free war, 24–25
Rousseau, Jean Jacques, 54, 57, 106, 205
Rugova, Ibrahim, 21, 22
rule-based action, 5, 28, 35–39, 43–44, 46, 223
rule utilitarianism, 30
Rummel, R. J., 95
Rumsfeld, Donald, 165
Russia: Chechen war in, 22; greenhouse gas emissions from, 201; human rights abuses in, 144; view on conflict in Kosovo, 24, 124
Rwanda, tribal genocide in, 2, 6, 47, 69, 82, 84, 96, 97–100, 144
Rwandan Patriotic Front (RPF), 2, 98, 99

Sábato, Ernesto, 70
Safire, William, 79
Sakharov, Andrei, 60
Saudi Arabia, terrorist attacks in, 118, 169
Schell, Jonathan, 31, 150
Schelling, Thomas, 34
Schlesinger, Arthur, Jr., 19
Scoon, Paul, 140
sectarian pacifism, 106
self-determination: ethics of, 22–23, 131; moral claim of, 4
September 11, 2001, terrorist attacks in, 3–4, 105, 117–25, 151, 217, 226n4
Serbia: ethnic cleansing by, 2, 16, 19, 20–26, 82, 144, 145, 225; sanctions against, 182
shadow warriors, 152
Shi'a Muslims, 122
shows of force, 153
Shue, Henry, 86, 163, 252n27, 42
Shultz, George, 158
Sierra Leone, 144
Simmons, Menno, 106
Singapore, caning in, 83, 88–90
Singer, Peter, 211, 212
Six Day War, 119
slavery, 17, 69, 82, 90
Slovenia, 20

Smith, Adam, 54, 231n22
Smith, Michael, 56
social justice theory, 86
social pluralism, 14–15
social-scientific theory of human rights, 86–87
social values, 15
soft power, 104
Solidarity Movement, 155
Somalia, U.S. humanitarian intervention in, 16, 82, 127, 129, 145–48, 149, 243n42
Somali National Alliance (SNA), 146–47
South Africa: apartheid regime in, 70–75, 191–94, 233–34n19–20; divestment campaign against, 191–94; economic sanctions against, 17–18, 70–71, 175, 177, 180–81, 182, 190–94, 224; multiracial democracy of, 71–75; political reconciliation in, 6, 63, 70–75, 77, 234n24; Promotion of National Unity and Reconciliation Act, 72; truth commission of, 70, 72–75, 234–35n27–34, 40
Soviet Union: American famine relief for, 37–39; Cold War military operations by, 150–51; collapse of rule by, 20; emigration of Soviet Jews from, 213; interventions during the Cold War, 128, 136; missiles in Cuba, 18; nuclear arsenals of, 32; violations of human rights in, 60, 95, 96
Spanish Inquisition, 109
Sparta, 50–54, 107
Special Forces, 152, 170
star wars policy, 41–43
state sovereignty, ethics of intervention and, 127–34, 134, 135–36
St. Kitts-Nevis, 140
St. Lucia, 140
Stoic thought, 84
Strategic Defense Initiative (SDI), 29, 41–43
strategic intervention, 6, 126–27, 139–43
structural pacifism, 106–7
structural realism, 48
Subcommittee on International Organizations, 59
sub-Saharan Africa, 210
substantive justice, 205
Sudan, 96, 144, 169, 176

About the Author

MARK R. AMSTUTZ is professor of political science at Wheaton College (Illinois), where he teaches courses in international relations, U.S. foreign policy, international ethics, and Third World politics. He is the author of numerous articles and books, including *Christian Ethics and U.S. Foreign Policy* (1987), *International Conflict and Cooperation: An Introduction to World Politics*, 2nd ed. (1999), and *The Healing of Nations: The Promise and Limits of Political Forgiveness* (2004).